Educational

Resources

Management

System

74421

by

DR. WILLIAM H. CURTIS, *Project Director*

published by the

RESEARCH

CORPORATION

A Special Report
Prepared by the ASBO Research Staff on
a Planning-Programming-Budgeting-Evaluating System

PUBLISHED BY THE

RESEARCH CORPORATION

OF THE

ASSOCIATION OF SCHOOL BUSINESS OFFICIALS

OFFICE OF THE DIRECTOR OF RESEARCH
2424 WEST LAWRENCE AVENUE
CHICAGO, ILLINOIS 60625
Printed in U. S. A.

All members of ASBO receive a copy of this book
as part of their 1972 membership or subscription. The
interested general public may obtain copies at cost
from the Director of Research at the address above.

Price: $7.95 per copy
plus $0.50 handling charge

Quantity discounts: 1-5 copies, 0%; 6-15 copies, 10%; 16 or more copies, 20%.

Please make checks payable to:

ASSOCIATION OF SCHOOL BUSINESS OFFICIALS

EDITED BY
CHARLES W. FOSTER, ED.D., R.S.B.A.
DIRECTOR OF RESEARCH AND EDITOR

ii

CONTENTS

Author's Abstract 1

Preface 3

Introduction 9

Statement of Procedures 11

Prologue: Expectations 17

I   Overview 25

II   Conceptualization of an Educational Resources Management System 37

III Planning 59

IV Programming 73

V   Budgeting 91

VI Resource Analysis in an Educational Resources Management System 107

VII Evaluating 147

VIII Staff Development 165

IX Federal-State-Local Interfaces 179

X   Implications for the Future 193

Appendix A: The Role of Analysis in PPBS (ERMS) 207

Appendix B: Cost-Effectiveness Application: Milwaukee 241

Appendix C: The Introduction of PPBES Methodology in a Large School District: Dade County Schools 267

Appendix D: Pilot District Case Studies 293

Douglas County Schools: Administrator's In-Service Program 333

Glossary 337

Bibliography 343

Index 355

AUTHORS' ABSTRACT

This project which resulted in the development of an Educational Resources Management System (ERMS) was conducted under the direction of the Research Corporation of the Association of School Business Officials. The primary purpose of the RC/ASBO project was to develop a conceptual design for an integrated system of planning-programming-budgeting and evaluating (PPBES) which is appropriate for local school districts.

In an ERM System emphasis is upon outcomes in terms of a learners progress in contrast to a reliance upon input measures as a means for evaluating the success of the system.

The ERM System report includes a conceptual design and a description of activities which are essential to each of the processes of planning-programming-budgeting and evaluating. The role of analysis as a means of facilitating choices from among alternative programs is described. Other supporting descriptions include staff development needs, the relationship of state and federal educational agencies to the system and some possible implications for the future of an ERM System.

This conceptual design is only the beginning of the application of the PPBES concept to the field of education with much more research and development required.

June 30, 1971

Preface

It is with pleasure, and a considerable amount of pride, that this volume is presented to you on behalf of the school business administrators and the other school business officials throughout the United States and Canada.

The Association of School Business Officials (ASBO) is a management group. It presents this innovative work to the profession of Education — and to the interested general public — from a management viewpoint. A basic purpose of ASBO is to increase the efficiency of its members. Proper application of the ideas and guidelines in this book will increase the effectiveness of educators and of education.

The preparation of this report, to communicate our conceptual design of an educational resources management system to you, required an extensive team effort.

Heading this splendid team was Dr. William H. Curtis, a former superintendent of schools in Manchester, Connecticut and former President of the American Association of School Administrators, who served for three years as Project Director. He is to be commended for the outstanding leadership and excellent executive ability he demonstrated in the planning, organizing, coordinating and operating of this project.

Dr. Curtis was assisted in the Research Corporation of the Association of School Business Officials (RC/ASBO) headquarters by Dr. Donald R. Thomsen, Assistant Project Director; Mrs. Lynn V. Gobush, Technical Writer; and Miss Diana Culbertson, Research Librarian. Also furnishing valuable assistance from the Chicago office were Mrs. Joan Robbins, Secretary to Dr. Curtis, Mrs. Sandra Iwanski, Secretary to Dr. Thomsen, and Mr. Robert J. Plomin, who served as Administrative Assistant during the first two years of the project. During most of the project, Dr. John W. Gott, a former school business manager, and Dr. Donald M. Levine served as part-time members of the staff in the capacity of Research Associates. Both Dr. Gott and Dr. Levine did considerable research on behalf of the project while enrolled as graduate students at Washington State University and Harvard University respectively. Dr. Gott's research was focused upon the conceptual design itself. Dr. Levine's research was directed primarily toward the role of analysis in Planning-Programming-Budgeting Systems (PPBS).

Although the key writers met periodically for the exchange of opinions and coordination of efforts, each writer assumed responsibility for individual sections as follows:

3

Prologue: *Expectations.*

Dr. Harold Spears, Visiting Professor and Educational Consultant, Indiana University, School of Education.

Chapter I: *Overview.*

Dr. William H. Curtis, Project Director; Dr. Robert Gilchrist, Professor of Education, International University, San Diego, California; Dr. Donald M. Levine, Assistant Professor, Ontario Institute for Studies in Education, Toronto, Ontario, Canada; Dr. Donald R. Thomsen, Assistant Project Director.

Chapter II: *Conceptualization of an Educational Resources Management System.*

Dr. John W. Gott, Superintendent of Schools, North Thurston, Washington.

Chapter III: *Planning.*

Dr. James W. Colmey, Deputy Director, CEMREL, Inc., St. Anne, Missouri.

Chapter IV: *Programming.*

Dr. Sam Bliss, Associate Professor, College of Education, Northern Arizona University.

Chapter V: *Budgeting.*

Dr. Creta D. Sabine, Assistant Superintendent of Schools, Paradise Valley School District, Phoenix, Arizona.

Chapter VI: *Resource Analysis in an Educational Resources Management System.*

Miss Sue Haggart, Resource Analysis Department, RAND Corporation, Santa Monica, California.

Chapter VII: *Evaluating.*

Dr. George B. Brain, Dean, College of Education, Washington State University.

Chapter VIII: *Staff Development.*

Dr. Robert Gilchrist, Professor of Education, International University, San Diego, California.

Chapter IX: *Federal-State-Local Interfaces.*

Dr. Donald R. Thomsen, Assistant Project Director.

Chapter X: *Implications for the Future.*

Dr. William H. Curtis, Project Director.

Appendix A: *The Role of Analysis in PPBS (ERM System).*

Dr. Donald M. Levine, Assistant Professor, Ontario Institute for Studies in Education, Toronto, Ontario, Canada.

Appendix B: *Cost/Effectiveness Applications: Milwaukee.*

Mr. Emmett J. Moll, Executive Director, Budget Planning; Dr. William Webb, Assistant Superintendent and selected members of the Milwaukee staff.

Appendix C: *The Introduction of PPBES Methodology in a Large School District: Dade County Schools.*

Mr. Troy Earhart, PPBE Manager and selected members of the Dade County staff.

Appendix D: *Pilot District Case Studies.*

Developed under the direction of district liaison representatives.

Mr. George Wirth, school board member from New Athens, Illinois and a member of the National School Boards Association's Executive Board met intermittently with the Project Team and served in a consultative capacity for the developmental work on planning particularly.

Throughout the project, a Committee of Consultants served most effectively. Members of this Committee included, in addition to Doctors Bliss, Colmey and Sabine (all mentioned earlier), Mr. Sam B. Tidwell, C.P.A., Professor of Accounting, Michigan Technological University, and Mr. Joseph D. Woodley, Director of Administrative Services, Metropolitan Denver Sewage Disposal District I. Mr. Frank Sibley, Director, Fiscal Planning and Control, Board of Education, St. Louis, was a member of this Committee up to the time of his death in 1969.

Late in 1969, a U. S. Office of Education Review Committee recommended that a second "consultative-type" committee be appointed. This recommendation was accepted and the group was organized under the title of "Panel of Experts." The membership of this panel throughout the project included:

Chairman, Dr. Erick Lindman, Professor of Educational Administration, University of California at Los Angeles.

Dr. George B. Brain, Dean, College of Education, Washington State University.

Dr. George Chambers, Assistant Provost, University of Iowa.

Dr. Jack Culbertson, Executive Director, University Council for Educational Administration, Columbus, Ohio.

Dr. Frederick W. Hill, Assistant Superintendent, Hicksville, New York Central School District, and a Past President of ASBO.

Dr. David Novick, a member of the Corporate Research Staff, RAND Corporation, Santa Monica, California.

The Dade County School System was a partner of RC/ASBO in this project. Its responsibility was to develop an operational design for the application of the PPBS concept to education. Also, the outcomes of Dade County's research for the project were made available to the RC/ASBO

Team. Excellent cooperation was given by members of the Dade Team headed by Troy Earhart, as well as by Dr. Edward Whigham, Superintendent, and Mr. Howard MacMillan, Assistant Superintendent.

Seven pilot districts also furnished valuable input for the project. The names of these districts and the person or persons representing each in a liaison capacity are:

Clark County School District, Las Vegas, Nevada.
> Mr. Edward Greer, Associate Superintendent; Mr. Andy Leibl, Director of Financial Services.

Douglas County School District, Castle Rock, Colorado.
> Mr. Lowell Baumunk, Superintendent.

Memphis City Schools, Memphis, Tennessee.
> Mr. Ray Holt, Assistant Superintendent for Business Affairs; Mr. Herbert Wilson, Assistant Superintendent for Planning and Long Range Development.

Milwaukee Public Schools, Milwaukee, Wisconsin.
> Mr. Emmett J. Moll, Executive Director for Budget Planning; Dr. William Webb, Assistant Superintendent.

Montgomery County Public Schools, Rockville, Maryland.
> Dr. William Brennan, Director of PPB; Dr. James Jacobs, Assistant Superintendent for Administrative Services.

Peoria Public Schools, Peoria, Illinois.
> Mr. Dennis Gainey, Assistant Superintendent for Planning and Development; Mr. Roy Ricketts, Assistant Superintendent.

Westport Public Schools, Westport, Connecticut.
> Dr. Joseph Crawford, Assistant Superintendent.

Mr. Dale Scott, the Chairman of the California Advisory Commission on PPBS and Dr. James Waters, the Executive Director of this same commission were most cooperative in sharing information from the California Project on PPBS. The same situation was true in the case of Dr. Chester Kiser, Director of the Western New York PPBS Project and Professor of Educational Administration, State University of New York at Buffalo.

The National Liaison Committee which consisted of members from several administrative and supervisory professional organizations furnished valuable input and feedback. This same committee included a representative from business and industry.

The ASBO Educational Resources Management Research Committee played an extensive and important role in the feedback and dissemination processes. Mr. James S. McAllister, Assistant Superintendent, Phoenix Unified High School District, Phoenix, Arizona; and Dr. LaMar L. Hill, Assistant Superintendent, El Monte Union High School District, El Monte, California, served as Chairman and Vice Chairman respectively. Dr. Hill succeeded Mr. McAllister as Chairman on January 1, 1971. Dr. James Jacobs, Assistant

Superintendent, Montgomery County Public Schools, Rockville, Maryland, succeeded Dr. Hill as Vice Chairman. It is expected that the research, development and dissemination assignments of this very important committee will increase extensively during the next five years.

The liaison officer for the project from the U. S. Office of Education was Dr. Arch Steiner, Research Associate, Applied Research Branch, Division of Elementary and Secondary Education Research. Additional support and guidance was given by Dr. Glenn C. Boerrigter, Chief, Applied Research Branch, Division of Elementary and Secondary Education Research, and Dr. James P. Steffanson, Research Associate, Applied Research Branch, Division of Elementary and Secondary Education Research.

Insofar as possible, it was essential for members of the project staff to maintain a close working relationship with the persons concerned with the revision of U. S. O. E. Handbook II. Excellent cooperation was given by Mr. Allan Lichtenberger, Chief, Educational Data Standards Branch, and by Mr. Joseph Perkins and Mr. James Jefferies of the firm of Peat, Marwick and Mitchell, contractors for the revision of Handbook II.

Obviously a project of this type requires the close cooperation of a large number of persons. It is not possible to include the names of every participant in our list of acknowledgments. However, the officers, members of the Board of Directors of RC/ASBO and I are most grateful for the cooperative efforts of everyone involved and particularly to those persons mentioned in this introductory statement. The Board of Directors of the Research Corporation of ASBO played a major role in this project. It reviewed every budget; received progress reports at intervals; individual members of the Board presided at each regional meeting; and the entire Board carefully read and approved this manuscript before it was submitted to the U. S. Office of Education or to the printer.

It is our hope that this report will provide a series of guidelines whereby staff members of local school districts may design, develop and implement their own resources management systems. *Warning:* Persons using this report as a guide are reminded that it is descriptive, not prescriptive. The persons responsible for this conceptual design were most anxious to keep it flexible so as to avoid placing constraints upon local school districts.

Finally, the designers and developers of the Educational Resources Management System recognize that this system represents only the beginning of a new procedure in support of educational decision-making. Therefore, we encourage and urge persons with expertise in this field to proceed with further research and development, particularly at the local and state levels.

FOR THE RC/ASBO BOARD OF DIRECTORS:

Dr. Charles W. Foster, CAE
Director of Research

Introduction

This report describes a system designed to support educational decision-making. It is called the Educational Resources Management System (ERMS)[1]. PPBS, PPBES, RADS (Resource Allocation Decision System) and ERMS are similar in many respects.

The primary purpose of the RC/ASBO project is to develop a conceptual design for an integrated system of planning-programming-budgeting and evaluating (PPBES) which is appropriate for local school districts. In an ERM System, emphasis is upon outcomes in contrast to relying upon input measures as a means for evaluating the success of the system.

The ERM System has been developed with the knowledge that school district needs exceed the resources normally available to satisfy these needs. Therefore, a system of logical choices is essential for effective administration of a school district. For every identifiable objective of a school district usually there are several means for attaining that objective. School personnel who are capable of assessing the relative merits of two or more plans for resolving a given problem determine which means are to be used. Consideration is given to the constraints of the resources available. The decisions of resource management, therefore, become functions of resources available and anticipated objectives, each with respect to time.

The system is a guide for the development and implementation of a model for the local school district. Educators using the concept of an ERM System are serving as effective change agents. The system itself is an effective vehicle for change.

The testing of the ERM System has been limited to date. Obviously, the application of the PPBES concept to the field of education is a very complex process, especially when it involves human beings and their development. Therefore, it is recognized that this project and others now in preparation represent only the beginning of the developmental process. Much more in the way of research and development is needed and should be encouraged and supported.

The individual components of this System are not new. The techniques of long-range planning to include goal determination, effective resource allocation, analysis of alternatives and evaluation of results have been used for some time in business and industry. In education, also, there has been some

---

[1]Throughout this report there are references to PPBS, PPBES and ERMS (Planning-Programming-Budgeting System; Planning-Programming-Budgeting-Evaluating System; and Educational Resources Management System, respectively). The use of the initials, ERMS, is a replacement for the traditional PPBS and PPBES. The persons who prepared this report felt that references to PPBS and PPBES related too much to business and industry with a focus upon inanimate objects. The opinion of the Team is that a new title is needed to more nearly fit the concerns for humans which are characteristic of *education*. The rationale for the use of the word, education, in the name is obvious. *Resource management* is relevant to the central concept of the system for identifying, allocating and utilizing resources. When all of the components are put together into a logically conceptual scheme it constitutes a system.

planning, program development and evaluating. What is new about an ERM System is the way these components are integrated into a system and the level of sophistication at which they are used.

The system for managing educational resources is not to be misconstrued as a substitute for an accounting system, a budgeting system nor a management information system. Each of these systems contributes to the success of the application of an ERM System, but are prepared to complement the application.

The statement of outcomes for the project includes three major facets:
1. The development of a conceptual design for educational resources management.
2. The preparation of educators for the acceptance of a resource management system change.
3. Testing the effect of the conceptual design.

The material which constitutes the main section of this report describes a conceptual ERM System.

Statement of Procedures

Preliminary work on the project was begun under the direction of an acting project director in June 1968. Initial efforts during the months of June and July included:

1. A review and analysis of the literature related to program budgeting systems.
2. The preparation and distribution of a questionnaire to the ASBO membership. The purpose of the questionnaire was to make a more thorough study of the more promising practices in PPB in education.

In July a list of possible consultants was prepared. The Director of Research for RC/ASBO, the Acting Project Director and the new Research Project Director selected six persons to comprise the Committee of Consultants. The first meeting of this Committee was held in late July 1968 under the direction of the new Research Project Director.

At this first meeting of the Committee long-range plans for the project were outlined. A study of the returns from the questionnaire was made which resulted in the following observations:

1. Although the majority of the school districts surveyed have adopted some form of mechanical procedures, there are still a large number without this advantage.
2. Of those districts indicating some form of mechanized procedure, more than 50% are still using bookkeeping machines.
3. There is a definite trend toward greater use of data processing equipment with better than half of the districts surveyed indicating usage now or in the foreseeable future.
4. Although there was an indication of great interest in the field of PPBES, comparatively few of the respondees (approximately 10%) had had any formal training in it.
5. Further study of the replies and especially those indicating current usage of a PPBE System resulted in a feeling that there is a lack of understanding of the full meaning of PPBES.

Because the results of the first questionnaire were inconclusive, a second more comprehensive questionnaire was prepared. This second questionnaire was sent to the 99 respondees to the initial questionnaire who indicated that they were using a PPBE System.

A study of the replies to the second questionnaire resulted in the conclusion that only 6 of the respondee school districts seemed to have complete plans toward the development and implementation of a PPBE System.

The results of the two questionnaires including supplementary comments and subsequent contacts with certain of the respondees were influential in the development of many of the plans included in the 1969 proposal.

The Committee of Consultants accepted responsibility for assisting in the review of the literature. At the conclusion of this review a bibliography in the field of PPBES was published. Copies of the bibliography were mailed to members of the Association of School Business Officials and the American Association of School Administrators.

During 1968 and the first part of 1969 the Research Project Director was the only full-time professional member of the project staff. As partial fulfillment of contract requirements he established contacts with and visited many of the other projects, school districts and institutions which seemed to have significance for this project.

An early visit was made to the Dade County Public School System for the purpose of establishing a plan for cooperative research and development.

During the fall of 1968 it became apparent to the Director and the Committee of Consultants that the selection of certain pilot school districts in addition to Dade County would be highly desirable. The most important factors influencing this decision were:

1. The need for additional support and review in the research process.
2. The need to secure the knowledge and experience of school districts of various types and sizes in order to secure diversified opinions.
3. The likelihood that the sheer volume of research needed would preclude such being handled by Dade County alone.
4. School districts of various types and sizes located in different parts of the country would be of immeasurable value in the input-feedback and dissemination processes.

Considerable time was spent during the final weeks of the 1968 calendar year in the development of plans for various activities during 1969. Input for this planning resulted from a study of literature, direct contact with related projects, direct contacts with school districts reputed to be knowledgeable in the field of PPBES, and a series of conferences with the Resource Team of the Dade County School System. The Project Director was assisted in the planning process by the Committee of Consultants primarily. Additional input came as a result of a special meeting of the ASBO ERM Research Committee in Memphis in December 1968.

In December 1968 a part-time research associate was added to the professional staff. This staff member was a candidate for a doctoral degree in school administration. Because of his special interest in the field of PPBES it was agreed that his graduate research effort should focus upon a conceptual design for the application of the PPBES concept to local school districts. His research and developmental work on the initial conceptual design for an educational resources management system took place during the first part of 1969. The Research Project Director met with him frequently during that period to render assistance and guidance, especially in the development of schematics. Additional input was given by the Committee of Consultants, the Dade County Team, the liaison representatives of the pilot districts and his own professional colleagues from the region in which he was doing his graduate work. Incidentally, the Research Associate has continued in a consultative capacity throughout the project.

A search of available literature revealed that educational applications of a planning-programming-budgeting system were minimal. Consequently, the initial conceptual design was developed primarily from a transformation of PPB System procedures and concepts utilized by business and industry. Studies of the PPBS application by the Department of Defense were issued as a reference source.

Since the early stages of the project the design logic and design schematics have been under the careful inspection of the Committee of Consultants, the Panel of Experts and authorities in the field of PPB. The consultants included educational and industrial administrative planning authority personalities. The expertise of the Committee included sophistication in systems development. Another research associate who was a candidate for a doctoral degree in education provided additional expertise in systems.

The influence of the RAND Corporation, which is generally credited with the development of the modern PPB System, was included in the design process through the offices of a member of the Panel of Experts. Additional aid in the conceptual design included interactions with personnel of firms which have a primary interest in the development of systems. This interaction is exemplified in the case of the RAND Corporation which entered into a sub-contract with RC/ASBO to furnish a significant study in resource analysis.

Recognized leaders among school administrators and authorities in school finance were included as members of the basic research and writing team.

Additional inputs and design modifications were provided through a series of planned conferences. The elected presiding officer of each state association for superintendents and for school business officials was invited to participate in the review of the initial conceptual design. Other invitees included the chief state school officers, the National Liaison Committee, which includes representatives of educational organizations, and certain other nationally recognized leaders in education. Each participant was invited to critique the design and to offer suggestions for modifications. Subsequent conferences in the series were held in regionally convenient cities to accommodate additional participants suggested by the initial conferees.

A reaction questionnaire systematically assessed the participants reaction to the design.

The conceptual design for the educational resources management system was tested for internal consistency and logic at each of several presentations during the first two years of the project particularly. These presentations were a major part of clinics, seminars and institutes held in various sections of the nation. Participants in these sessions included mostly professors of educational administration, school administrators, school business officials and school board members. During the first year each presentation was made uniformly to preserve the integrity of the design. At each session the oral presentation with visually projected schematics was made for the purposes of revealing the conceptual design and for encouraging discussion. During the early stages of the project, reaction to the educational resources management conceptual design and to the presentation of the design was recorded systematically by a Likert-type scale questionnaire. Copious notes were also taken to reveal patterns of oral reactions to the ERM System with respect to the geographic region of the meeting.

The reaction to the presentation provided an indicator for the thoroughness of the design's consideration of the educational and political constraints imposed upon a school district. The analysis also served as input-feedback to either clarify a confusing concept or to intercept erroneous design elements.

The questionnaire responses were tabulated by the region in which the respondent resided. Data were also tabulated to reflect the position the respondent held in the school district.

The initial stages of the dissemination process were considered as creating an environment for change. The introduction of a system for managing educational resources represents a system change for school districts. Two basic tactics were used to accomplish the mission of creating the environment for change. One procedure was the involvement of the target group in developing the design and a subsequent assumption of responsibility for disseminating the results. The second method included the transmission of knowledge about the design concepts.

Throughout the project the dissemination system continued to include presentations to professional groups such as those mentioned earlier in this statement. Participants were afforded the opportunity to provide inputs to the conceptual design of the ERM System. Participants were enlisted also to inform others of progress being made in system changes. Involvement was continued when these same participants were requested to be responsible for further dissemination of information on a state and regional level. Thus each participant in national and regional conferences as well as clinics, seminars and institutes was requested to make a commitment to involve others by assuming the responsibility of selecting other leaders within his respective association or institution to become informed of the ERM System.

Members of the ASBO Educational Resources Management Research Committee were especially active in both the developmental and dissemination processes. The Board of Directors of ASBO maintained the membership of the ERM Research Committee on a continuing appointment during the life of the project. As members of this Committee became more knowledgeable about the ERM System they were able to render considerable assistance in the dissemination process.

As interest grew in the ERM System it became a topic for clinics of the National Academy for School Executives. During the first Academy clinics on this topic certain members of the Project Team served as professors. During the past year this pattern has continued with the Research Project Director serving as the Director of all the Academy clinics on PPBS and of some on Accountability.

14

Special target groups of the dissemination process during the past year included another pair of conferences for professors of school administration; a two-day seminar for ninety selected school business officials; a two-day seminar for fifty state education department officials; and, a one-day national conference in April 1971. Invited to this national conference were:

1. the chief state school officer of each state,
2. the state presidents of AASA,
3. the state and province presidents of ASBO,
4. the ASBO ERM Research Committee,
5. the past presidents of ASBO,
6. representatives of the U. S. Office of Education,
7. the consultants of the Research Corporation of the ASBO Project,
8. the Panel of Experts,
9. representatives from the Dade County School System,
10. representatives from the pilot districts,
11. the National Liaison Committee, and
12. the ASBO Board of Directors.

The Dade County School System as RC/ASBO's partner in this project was of considerable assistance in the developmental and dissemination processes. Members of the Dade Team furnished a great deal of input as a result of their own experiences in the preparation of an operational design for the application of the PPBES concept. Assistance of a similar nature was furnished by the liaison representatives of the seven pilot districts.

A "writing team" was assembled to prepare the elaboration of the basic conceptual design for the final report. Inasmuch as the report had a potential for being read by educators and interested school patrons, the team members were selected on a basis of writing ability and for a contribution to the intended elaboration. The resultant team included the following personages:

Former Presidents of AASA
Former Director of a Regional Laboratory
Professors of Education
Practicing School Business Managers
Analysts
Former Director of a Major Information System Project
Full-time Project Staff
RAND Corporation Staff

Each chapter of the report was assigned to a member of the writing team for the responsibility of writing.

The designation for the chapter topics and the arrangement of the topics was the product of the project staff with the concurrence of the Panel of Experts and the Committee of Consultants. As the design for the ERM System evolved, the chapter arrangements were referred back to the Panel and to the Committee for additional advice and concurrence.

The writing team met as a group two days each month for approximately ten months. Each meeting was held in a hotel to assure a remoteness from daily office routines. Characteristically, each meeting included the discussion of chapter outlines or preliminary drafts of specific chapters. The interaction among authors was encouraged by oral readings of the drafts. Each member of the team was afforded the opportunity to contribute to the evolving ERM System concept.

Specific assignments were made to writers which were in the form of schedules for writing or concept development and specific areas for additional research.

A working draft of the report was printed and prepared for a presentation to a limited group of invited educational leaders. The final draft was prepared with consideration of the reactions of the groups of participants.

The final report included materials in addition to the elaboration of a conceptual design. These writings are included as appendices to the report.

A research associate was assigned the task of determining and describing the role of analysis in the application of the ERM System. The task was undertaken in conjunction with a doctoral dissertation.

Each pilot district cooperating with the project was assigned a project as a pilot application of a fragment from the conceptual design of the ERM System. Each case was described in the language of the local school district staff. The purpose of the case study was to present an illustration of the possibilities and problems encountered in the application of the system.

As the writing team developed the elaboration of the conceptual design some words and expressions appeared which required a clarification in the definition. These words were singled out as the basis for the glossary. The criteria for the glossary were basically:

1. Include the word if a stipulated definition varies from the usual meaning placed on the word by educators.
2. Do not include the word if the definition in the Handbook series is adequate.
3. Do not "re-write the dictionary."

A bibliography was prepared and distributed early in the project as a means for reviewing the literature in the field and to encourage suggestions from the several members of the Association. Materials developed by the membership of the Association were collected by the Research Library. Additionally, recommendations for library acquisitions were made by the project writing team and staff. These acquisitions were used as reference materials in the elaboration of the conceptual design. The bibliography included as a part of the final report is the result of these efforts.

An assistant project director was added to the staff in September 1969. This addition reduced the administrative burden to the project director and permitted an increase in the professional staff capabilities for research and writing coordination.

Early in 1970, pursuant to the 1970 proposal, a technical writer was added to the staff. This addition to the staff was for the purpose of providing a coordinator for the preparation of the report documents and to manage the technical details of editorial style, format and language usage.

Prologue: Expectations

Yes, time moves on. It has now been about three hundred and fifty years since those inquisitive and daredevilish English families, who were searching for something better in life, sloshed out of their boats onto the rocky shore that was to become a new England for them. And in no time at all they had built cabins, cleared enough land for ready sustenance and made enough candles to enable them to read the Bible in their homes after the long day's work. Recognizing the necessity of community action through cooperation they erected a town meeting place, set up a school committee and in turn a school so that the children could be taught to read the Bible.

Realizing that the entire community reaps the benefit of the public school, not merely those in attendance as pupils, the costs were levied upon all the families who resided in the community. For the next two centuries, the eighteenth and the nineteenth, school enrollments and teaching methods — and consequently school costs — progressed at an insignificant rate considering the two-hundred-year time span and the phenomenal development of the nation from the East coast to the West and from the Canadian to the Mexican border. One can wonder how so much could have been accomplished with so little total national schooling. One can wonder if we are securing full return on the vast school operation today.

The reasons were obvious for the progress of the past century. The westward movement was in progress, with frontiers to be conquered, ambitions to be realized and governmental land to be possessed by those with the spirit to stake out their claims and harness the strength of all members of the family to make the land their servant. Youth did not need to sit in classrooms — there were too many natural demands upon their time. Trees were to be felled, land to be cleared and cultivated, crops to be sown and harvested and stock to be tended. Towns with all their diversified demands for help were springing up to serve the new farming and industrial areas, and inventive genius was not limiting labor in the field or factory.

Woman's work to be done in the homes was as demanding of the girls as the out-of-home work was for the boys. Such courses as home economics, industrial arts and agriculture were not to come into the curriculum until youth could be released from the natural demands of a developing nation to provide them the time to attend such courses. Age had not yet been recognized as the distinction between childhood and adulthood — only the ability to do the job marked the difference. This same distinction between work and school attendance existed in the towns and in the cities as well as on the land.

As late as 1900, as was so strikingly indicated by the sparse attendance in the high schools, formal education beyond the early grades was still relegated to a second-class position, as something to do if the time could be spared—if there were nothing more demanding. Compulsory attendance had not yet found its place in state legislation, opportunities being so prevalent that youth were not yet seen as a threat to adults in the labor market. Secondary education was not yet a necessity, either to protect adult workers or to elevate youth into the economy. It was a luxury, a privilege, for those who had the time to attend and the ability to pass the examinations at the end of the eight-year common school. Those who attended high school for the most part reflected homes not needing youth's contribution to the family economy.

But within our time the school has been yanked down from its quiet academic retreat on the hill, plumped down at the teeming crossroads of society's main thoroughfare where social and economic strife intersect, and given the directive, "Now you do something about all this." This change, from what might be called the professional's school to that of the public's school, has come since World War II. Although the Bible has lost out in the school amid all the rights confusion, the germ of faith of our pioneer forefathers has multiplied and re-multiplied in a progression paralleled only by the public controversy that now attends the school operation. As the administrator now sits down to handle the routine, he cannot escape the noise by closing his window.

The funding of the school from the beginning has been in keeping with the community's expectations. Once the early school building was erected and the benches installed, town by town, the school bill was largely that of the teacher's salary, a salary commensurate with the level of the position — one of a trade and not a profession. And here again, the matter of teaching was so much that of having nothing better to do. The town committee administered and inspected the school, and costs of management came only with the expansion of the district in keeping with the growth of the communities. And not until this present century was well on its way was the concept of instructional improvement to blossom into its variegated garden of supervisors, curriculum planners, and in-service leaders. As costs have gone up so has direct public participation in school operation. The citizen's ever increasing school tax bill has been his license to participate openly and forcefully in public school affairs, to advocate this and that, and to oppose that and this. He frequents the board of education meetings as an active party, remindful of his legacy — the early New England town meeting. And he goes to the polls where he can express himself on the mounting number of school proposals that parallel the mounting demands of the public for school services.

Being nobody's fool, Mr. Citizen recognizes that the growing controversy over education — what to teach, how to teach it, to whom, where and for how long — is in direct proportion of the mounting complexity of his community's existence. For the more trouble he has, the more he turns to the schools to do something about it, and consequently the higher the cost. The greater the sophistication of our automated existence, the smaller the so-called laboring force, and consequently youth is relegated to an ever lengthening period of schooling.

A society whose ancestors first asked little more of their school investment than the ability to read and write and cipher have snowballed their demands into such a bill of particulars that the assignment now runs the gamut, from the three R's to the graduate's adjustment to every aspect of the highly complex social, economic and governmental existence that attends the citizen's day. And naturally, with the breadth of program comes the breadth of controversy. Founded as it is on the hopes and fears of its supporting society, the American public school reacts normally to this pulse beat of its community. It is one organ — a most significant one — in the body politic.

Consequently, it is no surprise that school support, both moral and financial, is influenced by the response of the school program to these public demands. The reaction of the school's management on such social concerns as racial equality, youth's moral behavior, and teacher's bid for attention is revealed at the polls when a school financial proposal is on the ballot.

The more socially sensitive the school administration, the greater the success in providing an educationally sound and reasonable program, and consequently the greater the success in securing the public support that is required. By social sensitivity we mean the awareness of the feelings of all segments of the community and an impression of how much financial support can be expected. It is true that, in a sense, the public is fickle or inconsistent in asking so much of the schools and yet rejecting demands for any financial support. But it is to be remembered that the miscellaneous demands beyond a so-called basic program are promoted by various segments of the community, and the ballots cast are those of the whole. Perhaps most people accept the grades one-through-twelve program as the common school worthy of support, and most would add kindergarten. But various subjects within this sequence arouse controversy. Free adult education has its supporters and its doubters. Summer school raises some questions.

Planning for education, budgeting for carrying out such intentions, and evaluating outcomes is no longer conducted in a closed room nor even within the confines of the professional school family. It is actually done in the public market place, within full view of the citizenry, whose participation in the process and whose reactions to every step are reflected in one way or another. State legislation years ago opened the doors of the board of education meeting which had been closed to the public. At about the same time the superintendent was brought out of his office into the light of the citizen's day. He lost the venerable title of Professor, and has been called many things since.

To say that school revenue and school expenditures have their sole foundation in the basic purposes of the school is such an obvious truth it may seem an oversimplification to repeat it in a study of management such as this document presents. The justification is that, the more sophisticated and elaborate a school district becomes, the more likely the "beep-beep" of the basic intentions will be drowned out by the clatter and confusion that attend the miscellaneous programs of today's public school system. There is a tendency for school superintendents and board members to yell to high heaven or to squeal like a stuck hog if the electorate turns a financial proposal down at the polls. Instead, the reaction should be one of deliberation and reassessment;

reassessment not only of the specific proposition on the ballot but of the entire provision of schooling represented in the budget. The reaction of a voter may be not to the specific issue on the ballot, but to something else he rejects in the school operation. Having only occasionally the opportunity to express himself effectively about what the schools are doing, he expresses himself when he draws the curtain in the voting booth. Astute school superintendents and boards of education analyze the results in such a defeat to ferret out the hidden causes. In a large district, in which votes are recorded by precinct, such a search may reveal a school situation in a particular neighborhood.

In a treatise such as this on planning and budgeting, there is no place for the history of our schools. But there is justification of the search for the factors that throw light upon the situation school districts currently face in determining and financing the programs which are to qualify as public education for the required years of schooling; those that make up the so-called common school, the program society tells its children and youth as necessary for both their future and the community's.

This is not to underestimate the pressure that is placed upon school administration today; rather, it is to recognize that with sounder planning must necessarily come evaluating. Time can buy new positions carrying new promises, but it is still to be determined through evaluation if anything has actually been bought for the pupils served.

To varying degrees school systems are currently subject to distinguishable active areas of concern, some packed with possible controversy and all with uncertainty, in planning, funding and evaluating progress. Among these are: the teachers' rights movement, the civil rights movement and the provision of federally promoted programs. Funding is dependent upon the two uncertainties, that of meeting specific qualifications and that of securing continued funding once the program is inaugurated.

As the study of pedagogy has advanced there has been the accompanying search for ways of distinguishing among youth which would justify separating them from their peers, taking them off the common belt of the production line for special treatment in special programs. In schooling just as in manufacturing, it is realized that the standard unit is most economically produced, and the special or custom product increases the cost noticeably.

Any school administrator can enlarge the list of areas of concern on the basis of typical local experience, including the unpredictability of the local voters and that of the state legislature in facing its financial assignment.

But in spite of all this, school budgeting goes on year after year. Preparation begins in the office of the superintendent and ends at the board of education where the allocation of bucks — or anticipated bucks — receives final approval. Needless to say, in all the confusion, schedules in planning programs and budgeting for them cannot be put off until the brass section has passed. Who knows how long the parade will be?

New ideas carry a price tag. We see boards of education which are badgered face to face, giving in to proposals that bear little more than the faith of their backers as collateral, floated on the idea that there's nothing to be lost in trying. But the school official knows through experience that once something enters the budget the sales tag "experimental" is lost and the term is never entered in the ledger. We may slip up cautiously onto a new proposal, but once it is implemented the odds are overwhelming that it is now permanent.

As the last two decades have shown, there is a growing faith on the part of both the professional and the layman in an extension of the years of school attendance for the individual and an expansion of the program at each year. This extension is at both ends of the school ladder — earlier separation from the home and longer retention once the student has entered the school door. We are experiencing a period in school affairs when the turbulence leads the professionals to grab frantically at one new program after another without clearing the shelves of the old stock that doesn't seem to be moving.

The present period of public education may well go down in history as the problem era, the frenzied drive for help, establishing a significant number of new positions at both the instructional and the administrative levels with no increase in pupil enrollment. For instance, in a large system the staff members, graded by five or six levels of salary, were invariably assigned to a specific area of work which reflected the overall concept of the operation at the time the system was set up. As new ideas, new demands, come along the practice is to provide new personnel in new positions attached in some half sensible relationship to the existing line-and-staff framework rather than realign duties within the present force, recognizing that changing times call for changing emphasis and conseqently changing work loads. Industry cannot afford such luxury, and the failure of school tax measures at the polls is indicating that the public is also doubting if the public schools can do the same.

If there were ever a time that school services demand the close scrutiny of the board and staff, it is today. The proper educational service of a school district calls for continuous planning, financing and evaluating — the three not always coming in the comfortable rhythm that is implied. Budgeting is commonly done on an annual basis, but the irregular spurts of both state and federal funding have conditioned school administrators to the uncertainties and irregularities of an exact plan — or system. Furthermore, planning curriculum and programs is something that defies the exact rhythm implied in annual budgeting. But in any case planning and budgeting seem simpler than evaluating, if we can judge by usual school practice. The invitation to systematize the interaction of evaluating with planning and budgeting more definitely is in the wind. It deserves no quarrel, only more consideration. It stands to reason that in the subjective science of pedagogy we cannot be right every time we add a new program or procedure. But practice shows we are more interested in the wares of the current huckster than in judging those we picked up from the last one who passed.

There exists in the minds of school operators, and rightly so, the question of the applicability of the science of systems to the subjective business of school management — the fear of sacrificing our development of human beings on the altar of business efficiency. To what extent the fear is of something new — the unknown — rather than the fear of a systems approach, only time and trial can tell. The concept of a system is certainly nothing new to American education. In spite of local freedom in determining procedures and local pride in such control, the image exists that the American school is so systematized that a teacher can move readily from one state to another, one school to another, and pick up his new class, be it the fourth grade, eleventh grade American history, or whatever. Without losing a step, a syllable, or the page in the book he is immediately at home, finding quite familiar —

The system of twelve grades, preceded by a kindergarten

The movement of the pupils up this ladder

The system of promotion and failure

The system of a standardized entrance age that leaves the child at home if he misses it by two days

The system of home report cards calling for parent's signature

The system of standardized achievement tests that places half above and half below the grade average

The system of standardized textbooks used nationwide

The system of three reading groups by ability in the primary grades

The system of recitations in the grades above, the question-and-answer approach conducted by the teacher from his desk in front of the room

The system of the school day broken down into periods, the secondary school student moving daily through all of his subjects

The system of bells for the passing of classes

The system of graduation requirements with the uniform halting step the graduates are conditioned to follow as they move down the aisle to the world beyond, to the tune of *Pomp and Circumstance*

The system of extra-curricular activities that carry no graduation credit

The system of athletic eligibility tied into classroom performance

The system of term reports

The system of examinations by grading periods

The system of fire drills

The system of hall passes

The system of counselors

The system of student honors

The system of monthly faculty meetings

The system of withholding the child's reading until first grade

The system of a standardized single salary schedule based on years of training and years of teaching experience

The system of sick leave, sabbatical leave and business leave

The system of negotiations

And so on.

Of course ingenuity can be found within the system, such as the primary teacher who named her three reading groups taxis, trucks and tractors, instead of the usual butterflies, birds and bees.

The American school certainly operates in the security of a *systems ap-*

proach, the school organization as a whole being security-oriented rather than change-oriented. Just one example: the writer successfully inaugurated team teaching in two different high school districts over 30 years ago, but schools are still flirting with the idea as a new theory, afraid to change the single teacher-single subject system that we have been caught with for more than a century.

As for budgeting procedures, every school has a system that it religiously follows annually — good or bad. As for evaluating the various programs that are funded, this is seldom done. Experience shows that anything added to a school program is carried on, emotionally anchored by the additional personnel who have been employed. It immediately becomes a vested interest. The main exceptions are programs that have been funded by the federal government. But in so many cases if support is withdrawn, these are carried forward, the tab being picked up locally, whether or not they have been effectively evaluated. Yes, we move comfortably through a maze the entering student soon learns to run with us. There is a system of planning and preparing the budget in every school district, some simple and some intricate, some hurried and some drawn out. But in any case the procedure followed deserves the term "system."

As school administrators we are currently problem-oriented rather than change-oriented, a condition that has been stimulated by the mounting strife that in recent years has engulfed the schools — strife both from the street and from within the school family itself. Neither the superintendent nor the principal need look for his job: it is brought to his desk daily in packages of controversy, delivered personally by both the laymen and the professional, without realizing this is a gradual modification in the leadership role. But if he stops to size up his position, he may find himself merely a reactor to situations brought by others, change so often being limited to agreements he makes in meeting demands. Compromise is a poor road to school advancement and it becomes an expensive, cheap system to follow.

We tend to lay the blame for ineffective schooling on the lowly taxpayer, thus escaping from the responsibility of fiscal efficiency in providing education. Building a school budget has always had its political overtones, and more so since the negotiating table was accepted as a main feature of the procedure. It remains to be seen how a school district can adopt budgets based on programs with the economic base built into objective evaluation of the programs and at the same time play the political game with the teachers which has gone on since the budget was lugged over to the bargaining table. For instance, to agree to a uniform reduction in class size in order to get the schools open refutes the basic principle of program budgeting — the effective use of management of educational resources through planning, programming, budgeting and evaluating in order to affect future planning.

An industrial enterprise can follow a budgeting system that is geared into program planning and evaluating without dealing with a segment of society such as a school neighborhood or an element of the district demanding a program reflecting a private interest. Effective objective evaluation procedures on the part of school administration represent the road to sound budgeting. In other words, the procedures outlined in this study are not a panacea for ineffective school management. They invite school boards and administrators to take off the blinders that have confused schooling as education, and instead to distinguish between what is effective and that which is ineffective in educating children and youth.

It is to be recognized that boards of education and superintendents are operating today in a period of national desperation, the intensity of the social and economic turmoil that accompanies our advanced state of existence. Amidst the affluence of household gadgetry, instant coffee, and instant transportation, the difficulty of a child in reading seems incongruous. What's wrong with the schools in this period of phenomenal advancement.

Coming loud and clear through the educational halls from coast to coast is the new byword "accountability." As in the case of so many catchwords of the past it has been picked up and geared into our educational jargon overnight. And as with so many of its predecessors it runs the danger not only of lacking practical delineation but that of false application.

It comes in the wake of the byword "change," which in recent years has stood as the directive to the schools, securing so much of its impetus as the password to federal funds. In fact, as school administrators, we face the danger of these two movements crossing paths, thus inviting the false assumption that one can meet his obligation to accountability by merely making changes in his schools.

And change in schools so often means adding something without replacement of practices which have not proven effective, adding personnel rather than replacing personnel. And in this connection, it is so natural to add a director or supervisor of a new program rather than shift the responsibilities to present personnel.

School administration is now faced with the offers of outside entrepreneurs to take over the teaching of reading, mathematics, or even the entire curriculum for a specific fee. Nonprofessionals are also coming into the schools, and consequently into the salary account, as paraprofessionals.

The concern of the study at hand is the effective handling of public funds in the operation of the schools in a professional manner, not in the diversified means of educating the clientele. However, in this spirit of efficiency it is to be pointed out that mere change in itself is not enough.

Perhaps the key word in the discussion that follows is *alternatives* — the different means for attaining the stated objectives of education. So wedded we have been to a common concept of schooling, so difficult it is for us to try alternatives. To what extent are we willing to question the concepts of schooling that we have inherited from the past?

CHAPTER I

Overview

Great strides have been taken in the last four decades leading to a better understanding of the educational process. Advancements in the sciences are truly amazing. A man has been transported to the moon. A human heart has been implanted into another person's body. The computer has become a commonplace tool. However, the same potential of human knowledge has not been applied to the management of education. The plea of Engelhardt and Engelhardt in 1927 still echoes today. This is an unmet challenge for . . . "securing a better educational return for the money made available for education." (Engelhardt & Engelhardt, 1927).

One of the problems of 1923, "the community is unable to distinguish between what it wants more and what it wants less," (Haig as cited in Engelhardt & Engelhardt, 1927) remains before us. *The potential of human resources has not been loosed upon rational choices among viable alternatives.*

This book is addressed to the purpose of developing a means for finding an effective system for managing educational resources. What is proposed is a planning, programming, budgeting, evaluating system which is appropriate to the local school district. Just as the Engelhardts in 1927 had no vision for producing the panacea for all management ills, the system proposed here is not the "black box" either.

The practices of school administration have evolved into a group of systems that follow a pattern. The pattern has been built upon historical decisions which met the issues important in the past. Each decision, therefore, contributed to the formation of a policy. Each person and each agency affected by the policy grew to expect the actions of the other. The systems mentioned in the prologue are only a sampling of the means for administering education which have become convenient to use.

A change in the pattern for administering education is evident as decisions fail to follow the usual pattern. That is, an unprecedented situation which requires a decision never before rendered is a symptom of a change in the pattern. If the pattern changes, old procedures are no longer effective. The feedback to the system is meaningless.

Patterns for planning have been available to school planners for several decades. In recent years particular attention has been paid to school building planning. Architects have been retained as professional planners. In these efforts, the concepts of the educational specification has been developed. Professional designers have been engaged and educators have been relieved of classroom teaching to permit full attention to the needs for which the building is to be designed.

The concept of management of school facilities and attention to the use of resources has developed within a generation. School business administrators, curriculum directors and school facility managers have become accepted staff assignments. More recently, the data processing manager, the systems analyst and technical aids to the instructional process have been introduced into the school management concept.

The school districts of today are under pressure to change. A young generation presses for decisions to situations that school managers have not faced before. The expected interrelationship of what had evolved over a period of many decades is cast aside as youth demands to know the why's of rules and sanctions. The demand for change in a management system is evidenced by the preponderance of decisions, required by a board and the school administration, which are unprecedented. Previous policy is to no avail if the situation requiring a policy has never existed.

Additional symptoms of a need for change are found in the enactments of the legislatures and in The Congress. The legislatures of the several states are beginning to mandate planning systems, evaluations and evidences of accountability in exchange for the appropriations for school support. In one state a bill was introduced in the 1971 session of the legislature requiring that each school district would attain specified levels of average achievement or lose state support. Each "aid" title of The Congress stipulates a form of evaluation.

The media reports overt aggression between citizens and school personnel in establishing goals for education. Taxpayers express the same degree of unrest of almost open hostilities in the defeat of school measures subjected to a plebiscite. Teachers in the negotiative process are reported as being "militant" in expressing demands for personal compensation, benefits and authority.

Change is inevitable as decision-makers face the situations existent within the school districts. Policy cannot be the authority for a decision on a problem that is not recognizable in the policy. Each confrontation, each situation, however, requires a decision. The natural reaction is to fall back to a reinterpretation of a policy. There is a temptation to resist. Eventually each of the reactions will produce a new set of problems. The administration of education will be characterized as a continuation of administration by "crisis."

The "crisis to crisis" situation can continue unless new means are applied to support the decision-making process. "Doing something substantial about the problem is impossible unless we satisfy and obtain the cooperation of many semi-autonomous groups not accustomed to joining up to work together" (Ramo, 1969, p. 7). What is needed is a new arrangement of people working together and people working with things. This arrangement requires an information flow and a management of resources for which no precedent exists The challenge is for a system of untried interconnections.

If an untried system is to be developed it is not possible for the participants in the system to make random choices and still form a "coherently organized and functioning social system" (Parson, 1951, p. 25). New problems

26

create the need for new solutions. The range of soultions extends from the remotely possible to the probable. The impossible of yesteryear is the probable of today.

The possible course of action is modified primarily, by the consequences faced in the event the action is implemented. The consequences fall into the domain of "What price will you pay." The consequence of introducing a fad is the threat of being extravagent. The consequence of initiating a new program is the responsibility for eliminating an old program. The consequence of making a change is the frustration of exploring the unknown. The consequence of a change in a system is the possibility of wasting scarce resources.

Obviously if action is to be taken to alter educational practices, new objectives must be stated. The new objectives represent a change in the system for educational management. Criteria to guide the development of the new system are essential. The criteria may include these generalities:

1. The system for education is to be responsive to the society of which the school is a part.

2. The system for education is to be alert to the changing needs of students in a dynamic society with rapidly changing values.

3. The system cannot ignore the future as though the future is to be the same as today.

4. The system for education is to be developed by making choices among alternatives in the face of limited resources.

5. The system is to provide for an analysis of consequences to illuminate the selection of alternatives.

6. The system for education is to account for the resources used in the light of the public trust for a human mind.

The alteration of educational practices is dependent upon the sanctions which encourage or permit a change. A pattern for action remains rigid so long as the points of interaction with other agencies remain unchanged. A reporting system represents a point of interchange between the two agencies or offices. An unyielding system for collecting and reporting data, therefore, encourages a continuation of traditional practices. The evolving system for recording financial data is typical.

At least two decades ago, school officials were being criticized for the "casual" way in which school funds were accounted. A part of the problem resulted from a lack of standard terminology for data among the states and districts. Without the standardization, the desired comparisons among school districts were difficult. The response to the concern was Handbook II, *Financial Accounting for State and Local School Districts*. Gradually, most of the states adapted the Handbook for use within the state, thus providing a nearly standard chart of accounts for local school district record keeping.

The popular system of budgetary control and financial accounting at the time of the development of Handbook II was a line-item budget. The account classification chart which was developed supported the system by carefully describing functions and objects. The concept of a Planning, Programming, Budgeting, Evaluating System had not been applied to local schools at that time. The chart of accounts established in the 1956 Handbook is adequate for an effective application of a PPB System.

The concept of *standard terminologies* is carried forward to other data and information needs of educational agencies through the several "Handbooks" in a series. Each of the handbooks builds upon terminology of the others so that consistent files of information can be produced for educational facilities, personnel, pupils, finance and programs. Planned revisions for the documents within the series encourage alterations in reporting procedure in response to changes in program plans.

Currently there are several instances of research and development activities using the name of program budgeting as the general descriptor. Many of the activities examined by the personnel of the RC/ASBO project bear a close resemblance to the traditional line-item, function-object system for budgeting and accounting. Many of the attempted transitions from one system to another retain a firm attachment to existing grouping of activities which are called *programs*. Many of the results reported thus far are in the name of budget procedures. Others are reported as innovative cost analysis processes utilizing available computers and other data processing equipment.

Several stages of development occur which have been loosely termed "an application of PPBS." Frequently, the label of involvement has been attached by persons external to the school district undergoing the development. In some instances it is convenient to classify the effort as "PPBS" and thereby avoid lengthy discussions that become inane. Three generalizations are evident.

First, in a possible generalization is the district which has responded to a pressure for immediate action to change. The pressure may stem from a dissatisfaction with people or with "results" in school. Typically, the pressure is applied to the budget process. The result is the development of a program budget which arrays educational costs by existing administrative units. The programs thus defined are the focus for formulating goals and precise objectives. Evaluation designs are either developed at the time of objective formulation or are anticipated as the "next step" in the implementation process.

The process provides an early evidence of change and sustains a maintenance of the *status quo*.

Second, closely related to the first generalization is the school district which has responded to the oft asked question, "How much does it cost?" The resultant is an action limited primarily to the data handling personnel, especially the accounting offices. A cost accounting system emerges with a degree of detail limited only by the imagination of the decision-makers and the management staff for the school district. Cost analysis can be applied in this situation.

The process provides an answer to the question most frequently asked by the individual: "who pays the bill?"

Third, some school districts have started to apply the knowledge developed through assessment designs and the technological tools utilized by planners external to school systems. The general process follows a sequence of activities which include an assessment of needs, a study of available resources, a review of the ability of a school staff to make changes and an analysis of potential benefits to be derived from a specific plan of action. In the application, the goals for education are defined by the community and plans are set in motion to attain those goals.

Typically, the action for the third generalization is slow and methodical with no great concern for immediate results. Rewards are anticipated in isolated areas in an atmosphere of "proving that it can be done."

Obviously, a whole new series of sociological, political and economic issues and problems is being placed at the doorstep of education. The schools are regarded alternately as the "whipping boy" or the panacea. Regardless of the label, the challenge is clear — be relevant, be responsible and be accountable or relinquish the "reins" to others! The call is for mature actions by mature people. Gardner (1964) expresses it as:

> "Every individual, organization or society must mature, but much depends upon how this maturing takes place. A society whose maturing consists simply of acquiring more firmly established ways of doing things is headed for the graveyard — even if it learns to do these things with greater and greater skill. In the ever renewing society that matures is a system or framework within which continuous innovation, renewal and rebirth can occur. . . .

> "Over the centuries the classic question of social reform has been, 'How can we cure this or that specifiable ill?' Now we must ask another kind of a question: 'How can we design a system that will continuously reform (i.e., renew) itself, beginning with present specifiable ills and moving on to ills that we cannot now foresee (p. 5)?' "

Many persons are searching for the cures to ills. Suggested solutions to the concomitant problems likewise abound. The application of PPBS is not the lone means for attaining goals established by the school district. Management by objectives, systems analysis, performance contracting and "voucher" systems have also been promoted as applicable to the problems of education. These are but a few of the plans under study.

The emergent concept as a result of the application of several management tools is the possibility that alternative solutions to problems are available. The alternatives presented implicate the use of analysis to assist in determining which alternative is preferred.

Analysis is vital to the application of any planning-programming-budgeting system.

PPBES concepts represent a great potential for enabling educational leadership to justify management decisions, i.e., to be successfully accountable for the use of educational resources. Moreover, there are certain other contemporary forces which need to be considered such as: the increasing demand for broadening the scope of the educational program; the impact of the negotiative procedure with its greater demands of all types; the thrust of new ideas and new technology; the increasing burdens upon school districts toward solving great social problems; and, the greater competition for the tax dollar. All of these forces suggest the need for a new approach in support of the decision-maker.

Decision-making is not limited to the administrative and supervisory staff members. A distribution of the decision-making responsibilities is influential in the working of a system. The values attached to the power and prestige of the responsibility are significantly associated with the fulfillment of a plan. There has been an increasing demand and acceptance of the fact, teachers must have a stronger voice in the decision-making process. Recent contracts with teacher organizations have included a requirement for an increased involvement of teachers in decision-making. The increased authority relates especially to curriculum development, support services (including pupil personnel services), facility planning, instructional materials selection and procedures for evaluation. This represents a sampling only of the more frequent types of requests. The position of organized teachers, in particular, has been clearly stated: the aim of teachers is to become a part of the mainstream of educational policy making.

A study of the systems described as being like PPBS reveals some common elements of concern. Probably planning and evaluating represent the two most important processes common to the systems. The importance of these processes were affirmed and decribed as "neglected" by educational leaders.

The understanding of human needs, the involvement of people affected by the educational process and the development of a sound environment for learning are accepted as essential in the development of a system for the managment of educational resources. No system, however, is a panacea. The system, when used properly enables a school district to institutionalize planning procedures and to structure school district goals and program objectives through an understanding of human beings and the learning needs of students. The emphasis is upon involving individuals and groups whose focal point of endeavor is upon the *learner.*

Within the last five years, there have been several endeavors by various agencies to develop models for the field of education. Many of these have the planning-programming-budgeting system concept as a foundation. These efforts have been at all levels of governance — local, regional, state and national. Regardless of which system or combination of systems becomes more acceptable, it appears that the educational process in the future will involve more long-range planning and much more concern for an effective allocation of resources. The processes, though simply stated, are complex in nature. The following represent the major steps to be taken.

1. An assessment of the needs.
2. The examination of existing goals.
3. The establishment of a set of priorities.
4. The tentative determination of major programs.
5. The careful analysis of alternatives.
6. A selection of alternatives.

7. The preparation of a program and financial plan.

8. The development of a comprehensive plan for evaluation.

The reference to long-range planning will evoke some controversy because many educators will insist that they have been planning on an extensive basis for some time. In support of their argument they will refer to such areas as the planning of school facilities, long-range population studies, curriculum development, transportation studies, etc. Admittedly, these claims are correct and considerable progress has been made as a result of these studies. However, a survey of the field indicates that the planning process has proceeded on a random basis. In other words, most planning to date usually has been spasmodic and representative of only part of the planning process as described in the Educational Resources Management System.

Years ago when budgets for education were comparatively small and uncomplicated, planning on a random basis was acceptable. Systematic analysis and extensive study of the alternatives were rarely given much consideration. Emphasis was placed primarily upon inputs. In most instances a major share of the resources allocated to education came from local sources. Rarely was there a demand for any comprehensive pattern of how effectively resources were utilized. Local boards of education were entrusted with the responsibility of making certain the schools were run properly. Generally their reports regarding the effectiveness of their respective school systems were acceptable and final.

During the past two decades some major changes in the aforementioned pattern have been taking place. State legislatures have accepted the idea that more resources for education must be allocated at the state level. In the 1960's it became a greater source of funding and must continue if the needs of our children are to be met adequately. Now it appears as though a major share of educational resources will be forthcoming from the state and national levels before 1980. This possibility, along with the fact that education seems likely to become the "largest business" in the 1970's has resulted in a demand on the part of the state legislatures and The Congress for education to adopt a more effective means for allocating and utilizing the resources required.

The United States Office of Education and many state legislatures have suggested that the application of the Planning-Programming-Budgeting System (PPBS) concept to the field of education might serve as the foundation for the design of a better management device for the handling of resources.

This particular project represents tangible evidence of support by the United States Office of Education. Funded under Title IV of the ESEA legislation of 1965, the major thrust of the project is the development of a conceptual design for the application of the Planning-Programming-Budgeting System (PPBS) concept for use by local school districts. The basic processes of the PPB System have been retained by the ERM System even though the name has been changed, for reasons given earlier.

The essential role of the Educational Resources Management System is to provide a framework for the organization of information which will assist a school district's efforts to structure its objectives and evaluate the means to achieve them. The thrust of the Educational Resources Management System is a focus upon the analysis of alternatives. The framework facilitates asking the questions:

1. Where is our educational system?
2. Where does it wish to go?
3. What are the different ways of getting there?

Answering these questions requires an examination of the long-term implications of the alternative programs which the school district may consider — the cost implication, the resource implications, and the achievement implications. These considerations are weighed against each other and each alternative is assessed in this way. In addition, the Educational Resources Management System encourages the local school district to examine the impact of implementing a program on the other programs in the district. Thus, at the very heart of the ERM System is an analytical activity, the aim of which is to help administrators and school district managers to determine the implications of investing in different program options. The set of continuums (Figure 1) is illustrative of the dimensions in content (what to learn), method (how to learn), and organization which deserve consideration. These particular dimensions as stated represent the extremes of educational practices; therefore, it becomes important to indicate the present position of a school district's programs, and to clarify directions for change. Guidelines for decision-making can and should be consistent with knowledge and research on learning.

Who does analysis? How is it done? Does it imply that quantitative processes are to replace intuitive judgment? The analysis of alternatives can be accomplished by an individual or by a team. The number of persons involved will depend upon the complexity, size and resources of a school district. The important point is not the number of people involved in the analytical activity but rather that the activity exists as a focal point for a school district's planning. The analytical activity should allow for the organization and for the examination of information on a regular basis so as to clarify the school district's objectives, and the utility of different ways of achieving them. The level of sophistication which a school district can bring to the analysis of possible alternatives to achieve its objectives is not as important as the adoption of the "analytical" point-of-view. That is, the critical message of the ERM System has more to do with an attitude or approach to a school system's decision-making than with the adoption of a particular program structure, mathematical enrollment model, or use of advanced quantitative techniques.

The message is simple: School district decision-making can be improved by taking a common sense but systematic look at what its resources are; what its direction or goals are; and what costs, resources and effectiveness implications of the alternatives it can consider. There are, of course, issues in the analysis of alternatives which require more research and greater knowledge than is available presently. Yet formalizing the process of critical evaluation in school district planning opens the door to testing the use of more advanced

CONTINUUM

WHERE IS YOUR SCHOOL?

WHICH WAY ARE YOU GOING?

Marking system of A - B - C - D - F.	←	→	Evaluation of growth for each student.
Graded classrooms K thru 12.	←	→	Non-graded continuous progress.
Prescribed curriculum.	←	→	Learners actively participating.
Rote learning, facts and skills.	←	→	Problem solving concept curriculum.
Egg crate classrooms and textbook learning.	←	→	Flexible space and materials.
Standard class size and periods.	←	→	Flexible learning conditions.
One teacher for each class.	←	→	Teams of teachers for learning.
Certificated teachers only.	←	→	Differentiated human and technological resources.
180 school days, uniform hours.	←	→	Year round, open to community.

Figure 1

techniques as they can be applied usefully to the analysis of educational programs. The school administrator already has the tools needed to make a start at structuring the collective knowledge for more effective planning in the school district.

Much of what has been said about the role of analysis in the ERM System may not seem especially new. Quite often administrators ask the staff to assess a program or to produce a report on some aspect of school district activity. The administrator in the 1970's, whether in a large metropolitan district or a small rural community, is a busy man. There is very little time to organize the information which might be useful in determining school district needs and program effectiveness. Much of the activity involves the direction of others and the putting out of "brush fires" with the staff, community and students. The processes of analysis are not new to some administrators, yet analysis in school district life has been marginal.

The ERM Sytem provides an approach to institutionalizing a planning life in school districts so that the organization and analysis of information is done pointedly and regularly. Further, it provides a focus for the interaction of different parts of the system in relation to educational planning. For example, the use of cost estimating relationships will require that the budget personnel participate in the planning process. The identification of resource requirements for a projected program will involve teachers, principals and curriculum specialists in the planning process. The attempt to project the effectiveness of a new program or of an old program will require that there exist among the school district personnel well-developed skills in testing, measurement and evaluation. Thus, because of these analytical activities, the ERM System requires a central location for the interaction of school district personnel who can contribute to the planning process. Often budgeting, program design and evaluation have been accomplished separately. The relationships among cost considerations, program requirements and anticipated effectiveness have often been blurred. Even more vague has been the delineation of the relationships between resources and expected results for alternative programs. Thus, the ERM System provides a framework for tying these considerations together so that an administrator will have better information about the implications of decisions on program alternatives. The final ordering of preferences is left to the administrator. The object of the ERM System is to "wipe the windshield" so that the effective investment decision is somewhat less obscure.

Analysis is used to identify controllable variables and non-controllable environmental factors which affect the relationship of inputs and outputs. A program is an example of a controllable variable. When it does not satisfactorily contribute to the achievement of a goal, it may be modified or replaced with another program. There are also controllable variables such as instructional materials which can be identified and manipulated within programs.

The most critical problem in the development of an ERM System is the training and cultivation of personnel who can do sensible, useful analysis. Sometimes a school district has a person or persons already who can act in an integrative role and have analytical capability which can be used and developed. Often, however, it is necessary to consider new personnel who have a special capacity for analytical work and can be trained in educational applications. Consultants can be used to help develop an analytical capability in a school district, but *the success of an ERM System will depend on the school district's ability to develop an in-house capability.*

Many obstacles stand in the way of a full implementation of an ERM System. The obstacles represent an adherence to traditions — a reluctance to change from the familiar.

Traditionally, there has been a lack of long-range planning. Rarely is there evidence of a long-range commitment of resources for education.

Financial plans are annual budgets rather than multi-year plans. Generally speaking, unless the chief administrator (superintendent) has developed a unique planning approach of his own, the contemporary administrative pattern tends to encourage and sustain a planning procedure of one year in duration. Adjustments to plans are a result of political expediency rather than on the basis of continuing educational requirements.

The credibility of the present system of school management is based upon the acceptance of the integrity of the educators employed by the school district. The extension of community resources to education, as a consequence, is accompanied by safeguards in the form of evaluations and evidences of accountability.

Planning and decision-making in the past have been characterized as being centralized in the "hands of a few top level administrators." Political and social issues impinging upon education are requiring a distribution of the decision-making process.

Members of the project team, during the development of this document, gave thorough consideration to the literature on the subject; to the opinions of persons in the field of education as well as from others. Despite the extensiveness of this effort this conceptual design should be considered as the beginning only of the application of the PPBS concept to the field of education. Much more research and development of the system will be required during the next decade.

The chapters which follow describe the ERM System. The description of the conceptualization of the ERM System is followed by an elaboration of three of the four major processes in the system: planning, programming and budgeting. The supportive role of resource analysis is recognized and is introduced. The fourth process, evaluating, completes the cycle of the concept elaborations.

Subsequent chapters discuss staff development needs, the relationship of state and federal educational agencies to the system as well as some possible implications for the future of an ERM System.

The document is completed with some illustrations of the role of analysis, the application of PPBES in a school district (Dade County) and case reports from some pilot districts in which fragments of a PPB System were applied.

CHAPTER II

Conceptualization of an Educational

Resources Management System

The first chapter of this document has placed the problem in perspective. How can public educational institutions (districts) be managed more effectively? This chapter presents an Educational Resources Management System (ERMS) in conceptual outline as an answer to this question.

An ERM System should be viewed as a basic conceptualization of a planning, programming, budgeting, evaluating system (PPBES) application. The system is designed for the management of educational resources in local school districts. The major processes of an ERM System as presented here are not new to education. The novelty is in: 1) the suggested relationships of these major processes, 2) the implications for the evolution of much greater sophistication in the operation of each of the processes and 3) the possibilities for improving the effective operation of local public education through better decision-making about the use of educational resources.

The Rationale for a System

The reasons for developing a system are inherent in the discussion of the preceding chapter. The guidelines for developing an ERM System are a set of assumptions which are based upon a composite of observations of education and of observations reported for planning, programming, budgeting systems (PPBS) used in industry and in the federal government.

Assumption Number One

The resources available to a school district are less than equal to the demands of that district. There are at least two major inferences emanating from this statement. One is that the school district should use its resources, financial and otherwise, in ways which will take full advantage of their potential benefit. Furthermore, the term "resources" is to be interpreted broadly. Time and human capacities and other factors, as well as money, should be viewed as being resources for a district. The second inference is that the effectiveness with which a school district uses its resources may somehow influence the availability of those resources. This influence could be exerted in two ways. It is possible that the effectiveness of school operation will upon occasion persuade citizens to invest more heavily in the purchase of education, thus making the available financial resources more nearly equal to the demands of the district. It is also possible that over an extended period of time improvements in the operation of the educational enterprise will produce greater returns on the educational investment. These returns could include society being more adequately equipped with knowledge, skills and attitudes. Should this be accomplished to a significant degree, then the total resources of society will have been increased. The fund of resources available for distribution to educational purposes as well as other purposes will be greater.

Assumption Number Two

The school district exists to produce a set of outcomes — to achieve certain objectives expressed as specific changes in characteristics of the learners. The implications of this assumption will be more fully treated in succeeding parts of the chapter and in succeeding chapters. At this point, the stress is upon specificity of purpose. The experience of industry and of the federal government supports the belief that sharp identification of purpose is important to achieving effectiveness of operation. In an ERM System, clear identification of objectives is strongly supported.

Assumption Number Three

Objectives of a school district can be achieved theoretically in a multitude of ways (program plans), some of which are more effective than others. Again this assumption is based upon experience from industry and the federal government. Quite often the easy way to do things is the accustomed way, but the foregoing assumption implies that there is an advantage in considering other possibilities. Accordingly, a major characteristic of an ERM System is its provision for considering alternative ways of achieving objectives. The effectiveness of the design is markedly dependent upon imaginative use of this provision for considering alternatives. Existing practices, procedures and devices must not be retained simply for the sake of tradition. A change in level of funding to accomplish an objective in a traditional matter is *not* the kind of alternative envisioned.

Assumption Number Four

Productivity of a school district can be increased by the organization of learning activities and supporting services into programs specifically directed toward achieving previously defined goals and objectives. The inference is that related activites and services can be handled more productively if they are handled together. This procedure allows maximum opportunity for the elimination of non-productive overlap and duplication of activities and services.

Examples of learning activities are to be found in the illustrative program structure contained in Chapter VI of this book.

Assumption Number Five

Better decisions regarding the selection of program plans and greater benefits from their operation result when the costs thereof are considered on a long-term (multi-year) basis.

For example, a school district may decide possibly to use closed circuit television as part of a plan to achieve an objective in music education. Questions pertinent to long-term projection of cost will illustrate the point.

One might ask, "How soon will the equipment require replacement and will the resources likely be available at that time?" Or, "How much of the cost can be apportioned to other program plans?" And, "Over five years, how will the costs of this plan compare with those of an alternative plan of similar effectiveness?"

Assumption Number Six

Better decisions regarding the selection of program plans and greater benefits from their application result when outcomes are related methodically to objectives. One of the unique characteristics of education is that many of its products are relatively intangible — in fact, are frequently most difficult to quantify. It is often difficult (and will likely continue to be difficult) to evaluate educational outcomes in relation to educational objectives. However, appropriate combinations of quantitative measurements and formally made professional judgments of educational outcomes are possible and acceptable. The information generated by planned evaluation will prove to be very valuable in the management of resources available to the educational district. Consequently, this presentation of an ERM System includes a strong emphasis upon the evaluation of educational outcomes in relation to objectives.

The logic upon which an ERM System is developed is based upon the foregoing assumptions.

The Relationship of the School and Society

In an ERM System, it is emphasized that the local school district is a part of society. The school is viewed as being within society, created by society, serving society and accountable to society for the performance of specific functions. In Figure 1, these relationships are illustrated. Society provides inputs of resources for the educational process. The school exists as an open system within society and is subject to the specific requirements that society may impose. The school uses the input of resources in the educational process and delivers to society outcomes in the form of the growth of learners, e.g., knowledge, skills and attitudes. These outcomes should be those specified in the objectives adopted by the school district.

A question may arise as to what Figure 1 is intended to suggest regarding the philosophic placement of the school within society relative to the future. This question is not appropriate. The focus of an ERM System is upon the effective management of the resources available for the production of specific growth of learners. The utility of an ERM System is neutral to the matter of philosophic placement. Consequently, Figure 1 is flexible to accommodate differing points of view.

It is important that the term "resources" be construed broadly. The resources listed in the schematic are examples only. For example, people, including their time, may well constitute the most important resource available to the school district. Many of the resources which are available potentially

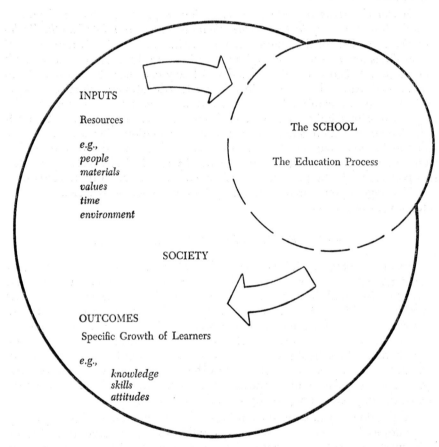

INPUTS

Resources

e.g.,
people
materials
values
time
environment

The SCHOOL

The Education Process

SOCIETY

OUTCOMES

Specific Growth of Learners

e.g.,
    knowledge
    skills
    attitudes

Figure 1. The Relationship of School and Society.

may be neglected or overlooked if there is no careful effort to identify them. It is important to note that the availability of some resources will not be influenced by applications of dollars. There is much potential benefit to be derived from a formal inventory of the resources which can be secured by the school district.

The specific outcomes are identified by the goals and objectives which are chosen for attainment by the school district. As has been suggested previously, these outcomes may vary from one school district to another and may vary also among the various populations or target groups within a single school district.

The Interrelationship of the Major
Processes of an ERM System

The processes of an ERM System are called *planning, programming, budgeting and evaluating.* Figure 2 provides a schematic view of their interrelationship. These processes are thought of as the major processes involved in the effective management of educational resources. The key relationship among these processes is the mutual function of providing support for decision-making. Decision-making is directed toward achieving the best use of available resources to accomplish the greatest attainment of specified educational outcomes.

Decision-making is the central activity of educational resources management. Decision-making in its various phases is supported by the processes of planning, programming, budgeting and evaluating. The information generated in one process must flow to one or more of the other processes. The arrows between the processes in Figure 2 represent this information flow.

Carzo and Yanouzas (1967) have comments on decision-making:

"The decision process may be separated into three phases — the decision itself, transmittal of the decision to action centers for implementation, and the control phase. All three phases involve information flow and/or the transformation of information from one state to another."

In Figure 3, the relationship of the processes is portrayed in still greater depth. Each process requires information. Those persons responsible for a process may receive required information from a number of sources. Information may flow from other processes as previously referred to in Figure 2. Information may also flow from, or be gathered from, sources external to the school. People who are not directly part of the school may represent an external source. Other agencies and institutions within society may be sources. In addition to receiving information from outside the school, each process may be charged with gathering information directly from the operation of educational programs conducted by the school and from other processes within the district.

Figure 3 suggests that information which is gathered or received must be analyzed and reported. Analyzing and reporting information has the purpose of translating data to increase its utility for decision-making.

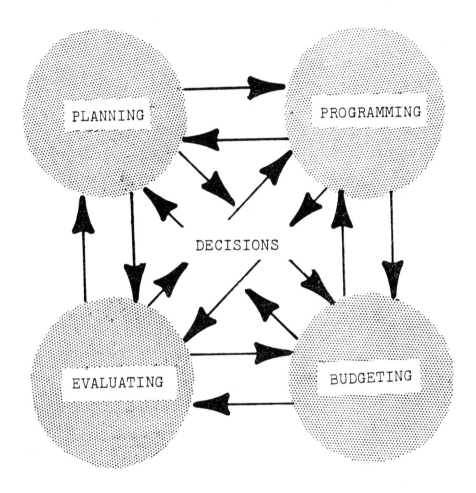

Figure 2. The Major Processes of ERMS

In Figure 4, illustrations are given of information analyses and reports which are pertinent to the responsibilities of each of the major processes of an ERM System. Consider the illustrations of information required by planning. Among these illustrations is information on needs and problems. Figure

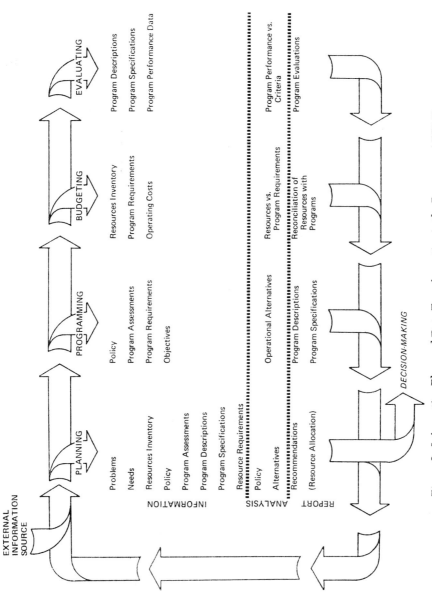

Figure 3. Information Flow and Data Transformation in the Processes of ERMS.

43

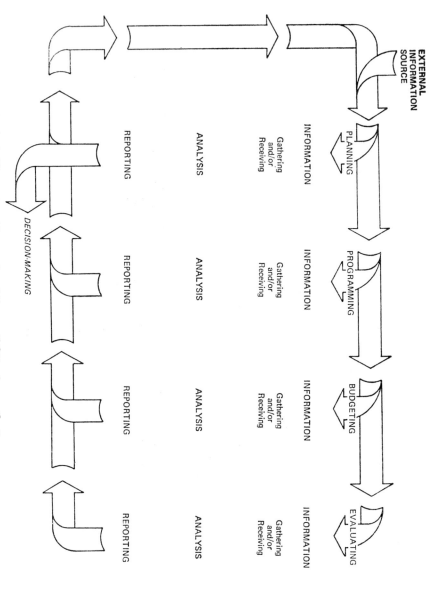

Figure 4. Illustration of Interaction of Responsibilities Among the Processes.

44

4 indicates that information pertaining to needs and problems is obtained partially from external sources and may be construed to include needs and problems of the immediate community at large. Figure 4 further indicates that information pertaining to needs and problems flows from the process of evaluating, suggesting an emphasis upon the needs of students. By analysis of all of the information available to the planning process, reports are generated which guide decisions regarding policy changes.

Information regarding policy changes as effected in planning is shown as flowing to the programming, budgeting and evaluating processes. Policy change information should typically include program identification and general objectives. In the programming process, information of this sort is coupled with information on program performance (program assessments from evaluating) and on program costs and resources (reconcilations provided by budgeting). After analysis of the information is gathered, a typical report of the programming process is the description and specifications for a program. The reporting output of the programming process is shown in Figure 4 as an information requirement of each of the other three processes.

The assertion was previously made that the key relationship among the processes of an ERM System is the mutual function of providing support for decision-making. Decision-making is supported by a careful integration of information flow and information translation within and among the processes of an ERM System.

Planning

Planning is the process of guiding internal change so that the school adapts effectively to the dynamic society of which it is a part. Planning is concerned with developing recommendations of policy changes for the school district. These proposed policy changes will typically identify goals, general objectives and programs to be adopted. The process, however, is more complex than may appear at first glance. The definition implies an appropriate response to the needs of society and it implies a constantly changing situation. In an ERM System, planning requires extensive involvement of lay citizens and representatives of other agencies and institutions as well as the involvement of school faculty and students.

As will be explained more fully in succeeding parts of this chapter and in Chapter III, the procedures leading to the determination of objectives and programs involve:

1. Establishing, organizing and/or modifying task forces for planning.
2. Identifying problems, needs and resources:
   a. As these exist nationally, regionally and locally.
   b. As emerging trends indicate these will exist in the future — nationally, regionally and locally.
3. Identifying and selecting goals — (*The Imperatives in Education* may be cited as a source for national goals.)
   a. Identifying established national and regional goals;

and established and potential local goals.

  b. Developing priorities for relating available resources and identified goals.

  c. Analyzing problems, needs, resources, benefits, etc.

  d. Selecting a set of goals having implications for the school district.

4. Developing tentative general objectives and identifying potential programs for recommendation to the school district.

  a. Developing broad statements of responsibilities for tentative assignment to the school district.

  b. Analyzing potential benefits to be derived from the school district's assumption of these responsibilities.

  c. Screening these broadly stated responsibilities against previously identified problems, needs and goals.

  d. Selecting general objectives and identifying related programs for recommendation to the board of education.

5. Adopting goals, general objectives and programs as the planning policies of the board of education.

  a. Transmitting the recommendations for goals, general objectives and related programs to the board of education for their consideration.

  b. Studying, modifying and/or adopting activities by the board of education.

6. Adjusting for new information (including feedback).

It should be noted that the foregoing procedures correspond closely with the activities which are discussed in later parts of the chapter. Figure 5 illustrates the work of the task force. Much of the emphasis of planning may be upon updating previous planning work. This will involve consideration of new information derived from community and society and feedback from the *in-system* processes of programming, budgeting and evaluating.

Planning is ongoing and adaptive. New information emerges externally from society or internally from within the school system itself. The planning process then produces an adjusted picture of reality for decision-makers to consider. This is not to imply that planning awaits perfection before being used as a basis for action. David Novick (1966) uses the automobile industry to illustrate the relationship of planning, uncertainty and time:

"In the current time period, next year's model or the automobile for Year I is a fixed thing with only a little possibility of change. The article for the year after that, or Year II, is almost a fixed thing because commitments must be made to long lead times, as much as 18 months in advance. Even the automobile for Year III is fairly well developed at this point in time and they are also planning for automobiles for Years IV and V."

This is much the sort of arrangement envisioned in an ERM System. Short-term plans will be less flexible and long-term plans more flexible. Adaptation to emerging changes will normally be made by modifying the

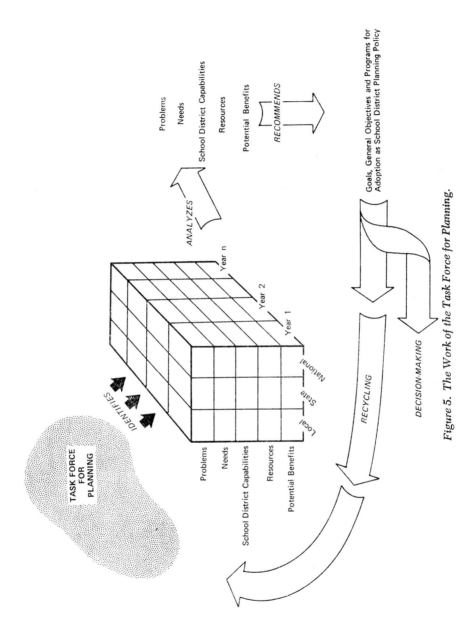

Figure 5. The Work of the Task Force for Planning.

47

long-term plans. The adaptation may typically require three kinds of action:

1. Increasing or decreasing emphasis upon one or more objectives
2. Phasing out one or more objectives
3. Phasing in one or more objectives

Changes in the goals and objectives of a school district will require adjustment in the program plans of the district. It is the purpose of planning to provide the school district with clear guidance toward making internal changes consistent with current and emerging changes in the problems, needs and goals of society.

In the usual meaning of the word, planning is also done within each of the other processes of an ERM System. Also, within usual meanings, some evaluating is done in the planning process. Some evaluating is done in the programming process and some in the budgeting process. Similar statements could be made for each of the other processes. For the purposes of describing an ERM System, however, it is convenient to treat each of the processes as discrete but carefully coordinated and interrelated subsystems of a total educational resources management system. Accordingly, this approach to describing the planning process is followed in treating each of the other processes.

Programming

Programming is the process of developing program plans. The programming process is dependent upon the other processes to generate certain items of vital information. The development of program plans requires identification of goals, objectives and related programs, all of which is accomplished in the planning process. The programming process requires information about costs and the availability of resources which is supplied through the budgeting process. Essential data concerning criteria and designs for evaluation must be supplied by the evaluating process. The programming process accomplishes the development of program plans by utilizing these kinds of information from the other processes together with the best current knowledge of how children learn.

A program plan, when completed, will detail information such as the following:

a. program name
b. program objectives (and sub-objectives as required)
c. target populations
d. content
e. organization
f. procedures (e.g. learning experiences)
g. sequence
h. relationships
i. operating responsibilities
j. required resources
k. performance criteria

l. projected effectiveness

m. time frame

The following is an outline of procedures involved in the programming process:

1. Creating, maintaining and/or altering professional teams for programming.
2. Generating and/or modifying performance objectives.
    a. Translating general objectives into arrays of performance objectives for general use in the district.
    b. Relating performance objectives to target populations and to criteria for evaluating degrees of success or failure in attaining these objectives.
3. Selecting and/or modifying procedures suitable for the objectives.
    a. Developing sets of alternative plans for achieving each objective including learning activities and support services.
    b. Preparing basic evaluation plans.
    c. Defining resources required for each alternative program plan.
    d. Projecting the anticipated effectiveness of each alternative program plan.
    e. Analyzing alternative program plans.
    f. Selecting the most feasible program plans for each general objective (feasible within the constraints of reality.)
4. Communicating with the system.
    a. Organizing program plans into arrangements for most effective management and meaningful reporting.
    b. Communicating data developed in the programming process.
5. Adjusting the new information (including feedback).

Figure 6 depicts generally the work of the programming teams.

Budgeting

Budgeting is the process which includes in addition to final reconciliation of programs and available resources according to established priorities, the preparation of the budget documents, the approval by a board of education, and the execution of the budgetary plans. This administration of the plans is related to the management of, accounting for and reporting use of resources. Explicitly, it is a budgeting function to accomplish final reconciliation among available resources and selected program plans as these have been organized for implementation and operation. But it should be clear that the selection of the best or most feasible program plans will have required this work to be largely accomplished in the programming process. "Most feasible" is thought of as the best possible arrangement within the constraints of reality. Hence, the reality of availability of resources must be initially considered at the point when program plans are being considered on the basis of projected effectiveness. If at a point of final reconciliation, the total requirements exceed total resources, then adjustments must be made. If such

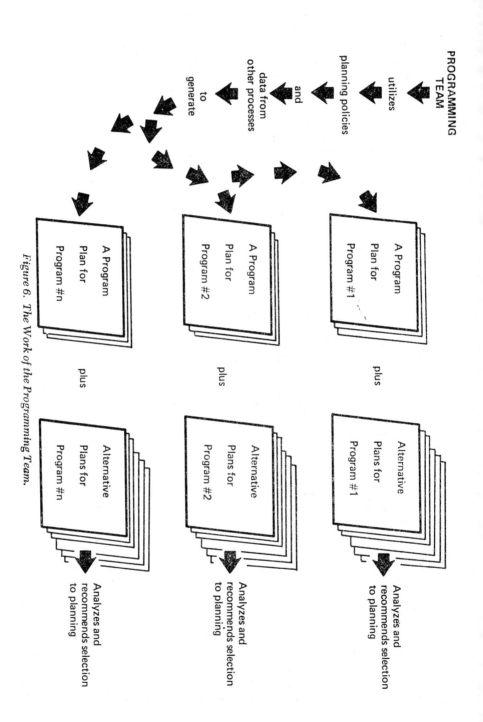

Figure 6. The Work of the Programming Team.

adjustments must be made, they are to be accomplished by persons who have appropriate professional ability in curriculum and instruction. This implies a referral to the programming and possibly the planning process for prior recommendations to be reconsidered by the programming team(s). Again it is emphasized that the program plans employed in education can be feasible only in terms of the reality of available resources. "Most feasible" must be defined in terms of both projected effective and available resources rather than in an ideal or utopian sense.

The budgeting process is characterized by public visibility. Typically, it is through budget documents that a host of data becomes apparent to interested public members and interested staff members.

Budgeting within an ERM System can be characterized as a process which involved procedures such as these:

1. Defining and/or modifying capabilities and organizational relationships required for budgeting in an ERM System.
2. Reconciling program requirements and available resources.
   a. Translating the assembled data into a program budget format.
   b. Reconciling program requirements data and resources availability data on both long-term and short-term bases.
3. Developing budget documents.
   a. Preparing the program budget and supporting documentation.
      1. Multi-year program and financial plan or program budget.
      2. Program memoranda.
      3. Specific analytic studies.
   b. Considering proposed budget documents and appropriate decision-
4. Managing, accounting and reporting use of resources.
      making by the legally constituted external authorities.
   a. Insuring use of resources according to plan.
   b. Accounting.
   c. Progress reporting of program operation.
5. Recycling the budgeting process.

Since a significant aspect of the above characterization of the budgeting process has to do with visibility, it is appropriate that the descriptive units used in documents be as meaningful as possible. The primary emphasis must be upon accomplishment of *objectives* rather than upon the *objects* of expenditure that historically have received major attention. Earlier conceptions of PPBS for education have stressed cost accounting for programs. In an ERM System, there is much greater significance in reflecting costs in relation to *purposes* of programs and their intended *outcomes*. Cost accounting on a program basis is involved, but only in support of clarifying the allocation of resources to achieve the outcomes specified within performance objectives and performance criteria.

Evaluating

Evaluating is the process of assessing the attainment of objectives and the worth of programs. In the basic evaluation plans designed for the examination of educational services, evaluation should compare and contrast performance, both projected and actual, with the requirements that led to the creation of the program plans. In the preceding discussion of the programming process, mention was made of preparing basic evaluation plans for the program plans developed as ways of achieving objectives. It has also been suggested that these program plans will detail the anticipated effectiveness of the various procedures for target groups within a meaningful time frame.

It is important to note that the type of information to be produced from the evaluating process is of vital concern to the planning and programming processes. Information produced by the process of evaluating must be merged with information relating to the utilization of resources to form bases for decision-making regarding both long-term and to some degree short-term planning.

One must assume that in due course that which has been planned, programmed and reflected in approved budget documents will also have been implemented and operated according to program plans. A crucial aspect of an ERM System lies in the question of *how well* the programs have operated.

Are the programs producing the outputs specified in adopted plans?

When the programs are completed for a given group of learners, how well have they worked?

While the basic evaluations referred to above are directed toward ascertaining the facts of production of outcomes, the information generated thereby should serve to suggest appropriate evaluation of that which is an ancillary function. Specifically, the successes and failures and degree thereof that are revealed in evaluation of these functional outcomes compared to objectives should guide the evaluation of ancillary functions such as:

1. educational management, including planning, programming, budgeting, evaluating and decision-making processes;
2. personnel;
3. facilities;
4. supplies and equipment; and,
5. proposed program plans.

The evaluating process within an ERM System includes:

1. Defining, establishing and/or modifying internal and external capabilities and organizational relationships required for evaluating in an ERM System.
2. Accomplishing planned basic evaluation.
   a. Assessing and projecting effectiveness of alternative program plans.
   b. Administering evaluation plans for operating programs and processes.
   c. Communicating evaluation data.
   d. Maintaining records of evaluating activities and procedures.
3. Performing evaluation of ancillary functions.
   a. Analyzing data obtained in basic evaluations.
   b. Developing plans for evaluation of ancillary functions to include:

1. management,
2. personnel,
3. facilities,
4. supplies and equipment and
5. the ERM System.
   c. Administering plans for ancillary functions.
   d. Communicating the added evaluation data.
   e. Analyzing the added evaluation data.
4. Accomplishing appropriate program modifications within the school district.
5. Adjusting established procedures to respond more adequately to new information including feedback.

Placing Responsibilities for the Activities in the Processes of an ERM System

Providing guidelines for assigning responsibilities for carrying out the activities which have been described presents an interesting challenge. This is especially true because of diversity of school district size and associated variations in staffing and operating patterns. Another factor which complicates the preparation of guidelines is the variation existing among state systems of education. However, the potential for the impairment of administration because of a failure to clearly identify placement of responsibility is too great to be ignored.

Tables 1, 2, 3 and 4 are presented as generalized recommendations. The activities listed in each matrix are selected ones. Others could be added by a district in analyzing its own approach to each of the processes. Likewise, the headings constituting groups of personnel are generalized and a district could employ those of its own choosing instead. The trends toward increased use of differentiated staffing arrangements preclude the possibility of preparing a guide that will fit every situation. What each table does is provide a pattern which has some applicability in most school districts. The legends at the bottom of each table provide definitions of the various symbols which are used.

Summary

Chapter II is concerned with the conceptualization of a system for educational resources management. A schematic outline of the relationship of the school to society is presented. In keeping with the assumptions and with the school's relationship to society, the outlines of the major processes within an ERM System are developed. These processes of planning, programming, budgeting and evaluating are decribed basically as they contribute to the central process in management, which is decision-making.

Each of the processes — planning, programming, budgeting and evaluating — is explained in terms of the interrelationships for supporting the flow, analysis and reporting of information. Additionally, by use of tables and diagrams, the attempt is made to conceptualize the appropriate placement of responsibilities for selected activities.

Chapters III, IV, V, and VII develop each of the four major processes in greater depth.

Selected Major Activities in the Planning Process	Board	Superintendent	Task Force (Planning)	Task Force Staff	Resource Personnel	District Professional Staff (Teachers and Administrators)	Citizens	Students
Establishing the task force	D	R_{1-2}						
Specifying the responsibilities of the task force	D	I	D					
Organizing the task force	T		D					
Identifying problems, needs and resources			D	I	I	I	I	I
Identifying goals			D		I	I	I	I
Developing potential general objectives			D	R_2	R_1			
Selecting and recommending goals, general objectives and related programs to the board		C	D	R_1	R_1			
Adopting goals, general objectives and related programs as planning policy	D	R_2				I	I	I
Recycling the planning process	T	D						

Legend:

D   Principal decision-maker   C   Concurs in or approves decisions
R_1 Initiates recommendations   T   Technical responsibility
R_2 Reviews, amends and transmits recommendations   I   Provides relevant information

Table 1. Planning Responsibilities Matrix.

Table 2. Programming Responsibilities Matrix.

Selected Major Activities in the Programming Process	Board	Superintendent	Planning Team(s)	Programming Team(s) Staff	Resource Personnel	District Professional Staff (Teachers and Administrators)
Creating professional team(s) for programming	T	D				R₁
Specifying roles and responsibilities of the programming team(s)		D			I	I
Translating general objectives into appropriate performance objectives			D	R₂	R₁	I
Developing alternative program plans			D	R₁	R₁	I
Allocating resources to program plans		C	D	R₁	I	I
Selecting "best" program plans	T	C	D	R₁	R₁	I
Organizing plans for implementation and operation		C	D	R₂	R	
Communicating accumulated data		C	D			
Recycling the program process	T	D				I

Legend:

D Principal decision-maker   C Concurs in or approves decisions

R₁ Initiates recommendations   T Technical responsibility

R₂ Reviews, amends and transmits recommendations   I Provides relevant information

**Selected Major Activities
in the
Budgeting Process**

Selected Major Activities in the Budgeting Process	External Authority	Board	Superintendent	Professional Administrative Staff	Teaching Staff	Citizens
Defining capabilities and required organizational relationships			D_1	R_1		
Specifying roles and responsibilities for accomplishing budgeting tasks		T	D_1	R_1		
Casting programming data into program budget format			C	D_1		
Reconciling of program requirements and resources availability			T	D_1		I
Making visible the planned use of resources			D_1	R_1		
Preparing the proposed budget documents			T	D_1		
Transmitting proposed budget documents to board of education			D_1	R_1		
Decision-making regarding budget adoption	D^*	D_1	R_1	I	I	D^*
Procuring resources		T	D^*	D_2	D_2	
Applying resources according to plans (initiation of program plans)		T	D_1	D_2	D_2	
Converting resources into outcomes			T	C	D_1	
Accounting and reporting on use of resources			T	D_1		
Recycling the budgeting process		T	D_1	R_{1-2}	R_1	R

Legend:

D^*	Placement of prime responsibility varies from state to state	R_2	Reviews, amends and transmits recommendations
D_1	Principal decision-maker	C	Concurs in or approves of decisions
D_2	Makes subordinate-level decisions	T	Technical responsibility
R_1	Initiates recommendations	I	Provides relevant information

Table 3. Budgeting Responsibilities Matrix.

Selected Major Activities in the Evaluating Process	Board	Superintendent	Professional Administrative Staff	Teaching Staff	Resource Personnel	Students	Noncertificated Staff
Defining required internal and external capabilities and relationships	T	D_1	R_1	R_1	T		
Specifying roles and responsibilities for accomplishing evaluating tasks		D_1	D_2	D_2	I	I	I
Administering basic evaluation plan (prepared in programming process)	T	T	D_1	D_2	R_1	I	I
Developing plans for ancillary evaluation		C	D_1	I	R_1	I	
Approving plans for ancillary evaluation		D_1	D_2	R_1	I		
Administering ancillary evaluation plans		T	D_1	D_2	I	I	I
Analyzing evaluation data		T	D_1	R_1	I		
Communicating evaluation data	T	D_1	D_2	D_2			
Making appropriate modification within the school system	T	D_1	D_2	R_1			R_1
Recycling the evaluating process	T	D_1	D_2	R	R_1		

Legend:
D_1 Principal decision-maker
D_2 Makes subordinate level decisions
R_1 Initiates recommendations
R_2 Reviews, amends and transmits recommendations
C Concurs in or approves of decisions
T Technical responsibility
I Provides relevant information

Table 4. Evaluating Responsibilities Matrix.

REFERENCES

Carzo, Rocco Jr. and Yanouzas, John R. *Formal Organization.* Homewood: Dorsey Press, 1967.

Imperatives in Education. Commission on Imperatives. Washington, D.C.: American Association of School Administrators, 1966.

Novick, David. *Origin and History of Program Budgeting.* No. P-3427. Santa Monica: the RAND Corporation, 1966.

CHAPTER III

Planning

Planning is the continuing process of guiding internal change, so that the school adapts effectively to the dynamic society of which it is a part. As new information emerges (either externally from within society or internally from within the school system) an adjusted picture of reality is described for consideration by decision-makers. Planning is oriented to the relative emphasis upon the modification, creation or elimination of programs required to achieve the long-range goals for the school district.

The planning process in an ERM System provides perspective on what is now being done, what should be done and what is feasible in the light of available resources. This perspective provides a base against which to assess alternative ways to do what should be done. Planning is a deliberate action and not a casual activity.

This chapter is an elaboration upon the concept of planning treated in Chapter II. Conceptualization of an Educational Resources Management System. The concept is also presented graphically in Chapter II, Figures 1, 2, 3 and 4. An ERM System planning process emphasizes the dependence upon an interaction with the programming, budgeting and evaluating processes (Figure 2, Chapter II).

The application of an ERM System provides the school board with a perspective which can be used to enhance the policy-making role of the board as it is anticipated by the community. The analysis emphasized in an ERM System gives the board a framework for developing a planning policy based upon reason and insight for the probable consequences of actions taken by the board.

The planning process is dynamic and continuous. Planning is not begun or terminated at prescribed points in time. Planning is long range, not year-to-year. Decisions are not the termination of the planning process; rather, the process can be the means of providing a picture of consequences over a period of time which assists decision-makers. The remainder of this chapter describes the process and identifies problems likely to be encountered. Establishing an organization for planning is the beginning.

The Task Force for Planning

School officials work with citizens, members of the professional staff, students and other personnel with specialized talents in a variety of organizational patterns which have been developed as planning activities.

The closer decisions are associated with the people affected and the more intimately the people are involved, the more critical the political climate becomes. School activities are a natural part of this climate. Nevertheless, the political pressures generated in this environment do not present insurmountable obstacles to planning. An important responsibility of school administrators is to maintain the delicate balance between the analytical and political for extended periods of time. The various political forces bearing on decision-making can be influenced by the facts illuminated through analysis. Planning, as conceived in an ERM System, strengthens the influence of school officials and makes it possible for them to meet these responsibilities.

Each school district will develop a particular style for establishing a task force for planning and each community within the district will have a unique set of needs. However it is agreed generally that the planning process cannot be isolated from the community nor can the expert advice of specialists be ignored. The day of the superintendent carrying out the school district's planning functions in "executive session" with the board of education is vanishing.

Members of the planning task force are selected for a contribution that can be made to the planning needs of the community. The contribution made by some will be in the form of expertise representative of experience in an activity. The expertise of others will have been attained through education or training. Participants include lay citizens, educators, school business officials as well as instructional personnel and students. Typically, the team is appointed by the board with an intent to achieve a "balance" of persons and personalities representative of the community. There is no one best way to proceed.

School officials will wish to involve a variety of people in the planning process through a task force or through a committee. In the establishment of a planning committee, school officials are guided by these considerations.

1. Consider members which include citizens, school staff and students.
2. Select members capable of making meaningful contributions.
3. Specify the time duration of member appointments.
4. Describe the committee's functions and limits.
5. Prescribe the authority limits of the committee. (Authority should not encroach upon that of the school officials.)
6. Inform members of events which relate to their endeavor and assure that each member receives information beyond the time of his active participation.

Caution should be exercised in avoiding the selection of planning team members who may have a singular point of view. If there is a tendency for all members of the team to agree on basic points at issue, there is little need for a team; otherwise, the planning function may as well be fulfilled by one person who can speak for all persons in the community.

The presentation of information is dependent upon a knowledge base which includes economic, political, social, health, cultural and behavioral information as well as educational. Some of the information needed is supplied by the persons assigned programming, budgeting and evaluating functions.

Some of the expertise needed for planning is supplied by consultants who may be temporarily retained for the specific purpose of guiding the school district. The consultant is especially valuable in the small school district as a means for securing services which the district could not afford otherwise. The consultant is also valuable in the district that could not economically justify an extensive training program. The special training programs which can be undertaken by consultants provide the superintendent and selected members of the staff with an expertise required for planning.

In the larger school district, the trend is toward the employment of full-time personnel with experience in analytical techniques and especially personnel from the fields in which the analysis techniques are dominant. However, whether planning is done by the superintendent and a limited staff or by planning personnel, the process is essentially the same.

Committee members must be properly informed. Inputs from both internal and external sources must be analyzed by specialists familiar with the local school district and translated into terms meaningful to the entire community.

In all instances, it should be clearly understood that the board of education is the legal authority for policy determination, and the superintendent administers these policies.

The relationship of the task force for planning to an Educational Resources Management System can be seen in Figure 5 of Chapter II.

An interrelationship should be maintained between local, state and federal planning activities. National and state planning agencies have a tendency to extend downward to include the local community on a limited basis, but there has been less effort on the part of local communities to extend upward in an effort to find ways of expressing themselves at the state and national level.

A developing trend among school districts, especially in the larger communities, is for the superintendent to assume a role of community leadership. The superintendent is in the position to take the initiative to encourage other agencies within the community to have school personnel assigned to meet with formal and informal groups for the purpose of planning community inter-agency policy. The superintendent can be of increasing value in this role if he develops techniques for the coordination of inter-agency planning. In this way, the school officials can share the responsibility for defining the responsibility that education can assume for certain societal goals and thereby broaden the base of community support for the long-range educational plans for the school district.

Interaction among local, state and federal planning personnel can be accomplished through liaison representatives who participate in various planning activities or maintain contact with the activities. While some local school districts have personnel who work incidentally in the liaison capacity, many districts have personnel who work almost exclusively in this capacity. This type of position will become more popular and necessary in the years ahead with the extension of the complex planning process that is required to produce relevant learning experiences. Some districts may have to be content with written information or maintenance of informal contact with the agencies.

As the relative share of state and federal funds available to local school districts increases, so does the influence of state and federal agencies. This influence creates both opportunities and constraints which must be recognized by local planners. Thus, the local school district's planning policy must be coordinated with state and national needs and resources.

Problems, Needs, Resources

Society's educational problems cannot be resolved exclusively by the local school district. Much of the planning for local school districts is done by State Legislatures which have the incumbent authority for the development of educational programs. Therefore, studies of needs and resources must take into account local, state and national agencies and activities which relate to educational problems. To help solve these problems, most school districts will be seeking additional resources from outside the local community.

The problem of resource allocation in its simplist form is: What resources are to be applied toward which goals in what proportions and with what effect?

A narrow analysis of a problem can unnecessarily reduce the range of tentative solutions. As an example, in an affluent community, children may learn the alphabet and the rudiments of the numbering system in a variety of ways. The parents may have read to the children. The children may travel, watch TV or participate in community activities through which children learn. The need to teach children these things may not exist. In another community, however, a program may be required in the school to meet the need. The more complete identification of the problem reveals that part of the assumed need was met by the application of resources from other community agencies.

Another study might show that fifty percent of the high school graduates did not continue in post high school educational programs, but did find it difficult or impossible to obtain employment. Evaluative reports, perhaps requested as an input to the planning process, would encourage the reordering of objectives and the development and implementation of new programs.

The focus of problem solutions in education is upon the needs of students which are not being adequately met. These needs are economic, sociological, psychological and physical as well as educational needs. Thus attention is placed upon personality development as well as the organic development of the student. The examination of the needs of students by the community cannot be accomplished by groups of planners working in isolation from each other. Planners will find it essential to understand the interrelationship which exists among the different expressions of needs. A decision eventually will have to determine which needs can be fulfilled by the application of resources from within the community and which problems will require resources from beyond the immediate community.

Once the problems are clearly identified and the needs carefully expressed, the educational planners and other representatives of the community cooperate to generate statements of appropriate goals and objectives for consideration by the community. Interaction is encouraged among personnel of the school system as well as with other agencies which may have a responsibility to help meet and serve the needs of students. Cooperative planning and resultant opportunities for interaction lead to an improved delineation of programs designed to satisfy student needs.

The planning task force develops a means for discovering the resources which may be applied to the productive process of education as well as conserving the scarce resources which may be applied. In the light of assumption number one, Chapter II, the planning task force is cognizant of the desire to apply effectively, the resources whether tangible or intangible. The recognition of the resource potential is initially presented in Figure 1, Chapter II. In the diagram the inputs to the school from the community are expressed as resources in the form of people, materials, values, time and environment. The list is not intended to be a complete tabulation of all resources.

Traditionally, labor, land and capital are treated as resources. The more tangible resources of "people", "materials" and "facilities" stated here can be related easily to the traditional list. The less tangible "time", "values" and "environment" are not as easily perceived.

"Resources are those things that have the capacity to contribute to productive processes (productive in the sense of creating economic goals)" (Benson, 1961, p. 26). Thomas (1970, p. 3) extends this concept to include the thesis that "education is produced" and therefore education is the result of a productive process. If this view is accepted time is a resource and so are a set of values and educational programs as well as students. MacKenzie (1971, p. 200), declares that "time is our most critical resource" even though the measurement of the value of time is difficult.

Identifying Goals

Some of the goals for a school district are established before a planning task force has had an opportunity to consider the problems and needs for the district. These goals are implied by tradition or have been accepted without question. A source for goals is frequently a report of a commission[1] for planning or policy which has been established for the study of national or regional problems in education. The commission identifies problems and needs with varying degrees of complexity which lead to goal development. The result of the effort is the publication in which the problems are delineated. Sometimes means for solving the problems are included. Planning in an ERM System utilizes the reports of these commissions but, of necessity, goes beyond the mere listing of desired goals. The statement of general objectives clarifies the meanings of the district goals.

For example, it is inadequate in terms of program development and evaluation to state a goal of "literacy". To give meaning to this goal, it is essential that general objectives be stated precisely and clearly to describe literacy.

The general objectives for evaluating upon the goal of literacy might be stated as:

1. All students will be able to read a newspaper.
2. All students will be able to write.

These objectives are too broad to be considered in the evaluating process without further development. However, they are specific enough to be the basis for suggesting possible programs.

If, in satisfying a goal of literacy it is determined that students learn to read, the programs could include the following activities:

1. Pre-school reading,
2. Reading readiness,
3. Linguistics,
4. Perceptual skill developments and
5. Library experience.

Obviously, in order to relate inputs to outputs, and to develop criteria for measurment or observation, it becomes necessary to describe programs to include the above activities in program plans. This includes the preparation of performance objectives and the description of the activities to be included in the program plan. The developmental cost studies and subsequent evaluation work related to each of these program plans can be accomplished in the programming, budgeting and evaluating processes and will be discussed in detail in the four chapters which follow.

1The AASA Commission on *Imperatives in Education* (1966) is one example of such a commission report which is often used as a source of goals.

Role of Analysis in Planning[2]

Analysis in the planning process concentrates on a logical, systematic means of illuminating information so that experienced personnel may supplement intuitive judgment related to decision-making. Analysis provides insights that are not readily observable. These insights are frequently lost as a result of data voids or in the "mountains" of data that are often collected. It is essential, therefore, that data are presented in an orderly fashion for ease in interpretation.

Analysis provides an opportunity through the systems approach to improve planning in the following ways:

1. Reduce errors of omission typically caused by lack of information or over-sight;
2. Reveal errors of commission typically caused by short-term planning;
3. Provide for the systematic considerations of alternatives; and
4. Allow time for major decision-making.

No attempt will be made in this chapter to describe the many techniques for analyzing the cost and effectiveness in terms of inputs and outputs. Some of the techniques are suggested in Chapter VI. "Resource Analysis in an Educational Resources Management System," and at Appendix A, "The Role of Analysis in PPBS (ERMS)", and Appendix B, "Cost-Effectiveness Application: Milwaukee". The differences in the approaches described are but samples of the techniques that can be used by analysts. Additional information is available through other publications currently available.

If an effort were made to quantify all aspects of goal selection and priority determination, rather than to clarify relevant choices and their probable consequences, much of the effectiveness of educational planning would be lost. This does not, by any means, rule out any of the spectrum of analytical approaches or the use of analysis based upon quantifiable data. It does mean that less rigorous analysis can prevail when relating to the broad, complex characteristics of the development of school district planning policies.

Excellent data, well analyzed and presented is not enough. Judgment provides the creative element in planning. An ERM System provides maximum opportunity for both analysis and intuition to complement each other through the systematic organization of information.

An essential role of an Educational Resources Management System is to provide a framework for the organization of information which will assist a school district's efforts to structure its objectives and evaluate the means to achieve them. A thrust of an ERM System is a focus upon the analysis of alternatives.

The framework for the organization of information forms the basis for planning. Information, esentially, is collected for the purpose of supporting

---

[2]The role of analysis is cited frequently in this document. The "role" is initially stated in Chapter I in general terms which outline some of the activities of the analyst. Detail functions are stated in Chapter VI as an analysis of resources is related. An additional elaboration is included as Appendix A wherein specific techniques are illustrated. The treatment at this point in the document is intended to be timely rather than explicit.

a policy decision or for verifying the affect of a decision. (Obviously, information may be collected for other reasons but ultimately these are the main effects.) Thus the system for data collection follows the pattern for the organization of the staff that uses the data in the decision-making function. The staff organization, logically, reflects the emphasis or priorities given to the programs for education. The normal pattern for the aggregation of data therefore follows the flow of decisions.

As an example, suppose a school district has identified a set of goals and objectives for which programs have been designed as follows:

- Intellectual Skill Development
- Understanding the Environment
- Personal Development
- Exploratory Studies

It should follow that the assignment of the personnel to pursue these objectives is on the basis of idenifying with the objective and the supportive intion of the activities follows the same pattern. The pattern for program action of the activities follow the same pattern. The pattern for program activities is also set for identifying the relative importance of each activity in a priority consideration.

Upon the assumption that the determination of priorities has been on the basis of a careful study of needs, goals and resources available as well as consideration for the capabilities of the school system and the potential benefits, there is agreement that these priorities, once established, shall be honored. Therefore, in giving priorities to educational goals and programs for the local school district, questions to be answered in the planning process include the following:

1. Are the current needs being met effectively?
2. Can local education agencies meet the need more effectively than state or federal education agencies?
3. Can the local school district meet the need more effectively than other local agencies?
4. Are mutual efforts to meet the need by different agencies being coordinated?
5. How will an objective be phased into the school district plan in the years ahead?
6. Can an objective be accomplished and phased out in the years ahead?

An important mission in the planning process is the preparation of recommendations based upon an analysis of choices among programs or program activities. Programmers take on the task of analyzing and proposing program plans. Each program plan should be analyzed as a possible alternative for achieving the specified objectives.

The local community has educational problems which are unique to its locality. It is also true that many of these problems are frequently similar to problems throughout the state and nation. When determining priorities, it is important to consider the impact of state and national problems as well as local problems.

It is the responsibility of the planners to make final recommendations on the priorities of programs for the local school district.

Implications for the School District

The organization of schools has evolved into patterns that are rather predictable. Typically the school district recognizes an elementary school and a secondary school with certain tolerances of grade level designations. Further refinements in the structure reveal middle schools, junior high schools or some similar name to classify the school elements according to the "achievement age" of students. The management of the programs for the school districts is partitioned along the same structural lines. The array of the staff assignments also follows.

In a manner of speaking the typical student is classified by a "grade level" which is probably related to an "achievement age" for the student. Laws and regulations govern the entrance age for students at the earliest point of formal schooling. The pattern for advancement through the school follows a chronological aging of the student, assuming the student succeeds. The pattern for students therefore becomes an advancement from kindergarten through grades one to twelve in equal intervals of time. The apparent objective is to prepare the student for the next "grade".

The next level of structural classification of schools, in the traditions of the past, is a subject matter designation. The emphasis placed upon a subject-matter field is indicated by the assignment of instructional personnel to supervise or guide the teaching of the subject. Additional emphasis is indicated by the reporting system to parents on the progress of the student by subject area. Rules are formulated to support or sanction the emphasis.

A complex information system, to include an accounting system, is developed to support the many demands of the organizations present within the school district. Many of the demands are extended to variations requested by state and federal administrative conditions. The result is a system that inhibits a natural aggregation of data of value to decision-makers.

The implication for the school district is for a means to focus the activities of the entire school district upon a set of goals which are acceptable to the community. The subsequent objectives therefore should likewise reveal the needs of the students of the community and the priorities the school district places upon the means for attaining those objectives. *The basis for the priorities is in terms of desired student outcomes representative of programs designed to attain the objectives.*

Proposing Potential Programs

When an ERM System is introduced, it must be recognized that a "system" already exists in which practicing school officials are working. With this thought in mind, a review of Figures 1 through 5 in Chapter II may be appropriate.

The planning process cannot be isolated from reality. To do so could be an exercise in futility.

The introduction of a new planning process could be a disruptive influence on the normal process of policy development. Planning cannot be considered as a neat set of logical steps, particularly at the goal level. A continuous flow of new information from appropriate sources is essential. The quality of analysis is affected by the kind of information available. The planning process cannot wait a year or two while feasibility studies and new ideas are being investigated. Recommendations and decisions are made continuously and are modified if the results of an interim plan operation suggest such action.

If a purpose of analysis is to organize information in a logical manner, the logic must be clear. Moreover, since a major emphasis in an ERM System is upon the learner, and especially upon learner outcomes, the logic of the organization of information should be supportive of this emphasis. What is needed is a means for displaying the information which reveals the logic of the organization as well as an emphasis upon learner outcomes. The mechanism should be designed to portray the relationship between established educational priorities and educational programs for the school district. The array should be clear-cut and definitive so as to reveal the same message to all who may read it.

An illustration may help. Assume a school district planning team has gone through the process of identifying community goals for the school district. In the process, a student objective is stated that calls for the development of intellectual skills. The nature of the objective suggests this is a focus for a program which would be supported by many different activities and at many different stages of the student's development. If, however, a focus upon the objective is intended, the many activities at the many ages of the student somehow must be interrelated or coordinated. Through an analysis of the objective, it appears there may be three distinct facets to intellectual skills, namely: (1) Communication Skills, (2) Computation Skills and (3) Reasoning Skills. Thus three subprograms can be established which when aggregated become the program of intellectual skill development.

If the three subprograms are arrayed in relation to the major program, it is clear that the major program is composed of subprograms. Each subprogram, by the nature of the name, suggests additional objectives. Any subsequent listing of program elements or activities ascribable to each of the three subprograms reveals a support for the objective. That is, reading as an activity within the school would support the objective of the development of communication skills which in turn, supports the development of intellectual skills. In a similar taxonomic pattern, the place of mathematics in the school curriculum is justified, in this array, as a means for attaining an objective of computational skills development. Subsequently, the objective is for the development of intellectual skills. The introduction of any activity, therefore, is in response to the question: What objective is to be served? An illustrative taxonomy for the Intellectual Skill Development Program follows:

Program	Subprogram	Program Element
		Listening
		Oral
		Reading
		Writing
	Communication Skills	English
		Additional Languages
		Spelling
		Handwriting
		Etc.
INTELLECTUAL SKILLS DEVELOPMENT	Computation Skills	Number Skills
		Mathematics
		Problem Solving
		Etc.
		Deductive
	Reasoning Skills	Inductive
		Problem Solving
		Etc.

What has taken place is the beginning of an array which is called a *program structure.* The array shows a priority for learning outcomes through the organization of program emphases. Some criteria for the development of the structure can be discerned from this brief discussion. For instance, it appears logical to note these:

1. The basis for a program structure is an orientation for goals or objectives.
2. Programs relate to specific student needs.
3. The prime focus is upon a learner outcome.

The emphasis of learner outcomes expressed as desired skills, preferred attitudes and appropriate behaviors should be evident in a program structure.[3]

The program structure for a school district becomes the focus for all of the activities of the school district. It serves as the format for the Program and Financial Plan-the Program Budget. (See Chapters V and VI.)

Each school district is a unique entity that must develop programs suited to the needs of the students of the district. As a consequence, the program structure developed for one school district may not satisfy the plans and objectives for another school district. To fulfill the purposes suggested for the development of an Educational Resources Management Sys-

---

[3]A more complete program structure is included in Chapter VI, "Resource Analysis in An Educational Resources Management System." The program structure which is developed for the school district serves as a guide for the organinzation of the school district.

tem, however, the program structure is an important planning device that reveals the emphasis of the school district upon educational programs.

A screening of the various program potentials through analytical techniques provides answers to questions like the following:

1. What conflicts exist among the school district's competing goals?
2. What information is necessary about competing goals that will make it possible for planners to logically relate to the problems of reordering the school district's priorities?
3. Can each objective be accomplished?
4. Is the accomplishment of the objective worth the cost?
5. What alternatives are suggested?
6. How effectively can the objectives be accomplished?
7. Can the required accomplishments be obtained at a lower cost?

The answers give guidance for the recommendations for the school district.

Assumption number three, Chapter II, states that the objectives of a school district can be attained in a multitude of ways. The question for the school district becomes: Which alternative is to be selected?

Once objectives have been stated and programs have been designated, some means for selection must be devised for determining the courses of action.

At this stage of the planning process, planners may not know what actual programs or resources are needed to provide a solution to the problem. It is necessary to determine first whether current programs are adequate. If they are not, new programs are suggested, developed and tested for feasibility. Early in the feasibility studies, it can be determined whether resources are currently available to the local school district for conducting these programs.

Planners assume the responsibility for the development of the program structure and for tentatively identifying the resources which can be applied to the individual program. The programmers develop and analyze the alternatives which are to be considered for the eventual board decision. Programmers and planners rely upon the staff assigned to budgeting for essential data which supports the program decisions.

Establishing Programs

The planning task force serves as a "clearing house" for the recommendations of the community as well as for the staff member teams which have been designated for programming, budgeting and evaluating functions. In fulfilling this obligation, a program and financial plan is maintained by incorporating the financial and program implications of board decisions. The mission is to show how the resources of the school district are being used in a concerted effort toward accomplishing the goals established for the school district.

In addition to the program budget and its supporting documentation a number of other reports serve to make up the file of information needed for an ERM System. The information is maintained in a manner that provides easy access for all who must use the data. Some of these reports are:

1. School and community surveys,
2. Evaluation reports,
3. Annual budget (traditional format),
4. Staff projection reports,
5. Resources inventories,
6. State statistical reports and guidelines,
7. Regional statistical reports and guidelines,
8. National statistical reports and guidelines,
9. Codified state statutes, and
10. Congressional reports and public laws.

Planning is a continuous process of guiding internal change. In essence, communication is its tool. Analysis is its method. The program budget is its product. Advice is its purpose. The superintendent is its master. The board is its guide. Goals, programs, objectives and program structure are its substance.

The Program and Financial Plan is submitted by the superintendent to the board with his recommendation. The resulting multi-year Program and Financial Plan with its supporting documentation becomes the communicating device between the superintendent and the board, between the superintendent and the public, and from the board and the superintendent to the employees. The board has information through the Program and Financial Plan about the consequences of the decisions made earlier.

Summary

It is most essential for school officials to determine the degree to which existing programs are effective in meeting and solving the previously identified problems and needs. Officials should be prepared to eliminate those programs which are shown to be ineffective in meeting the identified needs. Furthermore, officials have a responsibility to recommend changes in existing programs and the establishment of new programs for potential fulfillment of need requirements.

The aforementioned activities require the generation of information from the programming, budgeting and evaluating processes. The resulting information provides a basis for communicating to the public the problems and needs of the district. Thus, an ERM System is designed to provide a basis for accountability.

School district planning must be on a current and a multi-year basis. More emphasis is needed on medium-range and long-range planning which look farther into the future than one year. Plans should be revised continuously based upon internal information from the programming, budgeting and evaluating processes and information from external agencies.

The ERM System will assist decision-makers: 1) to identify local school district goals on a continuing basis, 2) to determine priorities for these goals, 3) to search and suggest alternative means (programs) for reaching these goals, 4) to relate resources to achievement over extended periods of time; and 5) to evaluate programs to assure the effective allocation of resources.

REFERENCES

Association of School Business Officials. *Annual Volume of Proceedings, Addresses and Research Papers.* Chicago: The Association, 1970.

CHAPTER IV

Programming

Programming, another process in an ERM System, is defined as the process of developing program plans consisting of interrelated learning activities and support services with each plan representing a design for attaining educational objectives. Thus an ERM System development includes the programming process which brings together certain types of educational information essential to the planning, budgeting and evaluating processes.

This chapter is an elaboration of the programming process concepts included in Chapter II. Throughout the chapter, emphasis will be placed upon defining the particular characteristics of programming and describing the interaction of the programming process with the other processes in an ERM System. In a broad sense, educational program information included in the programming process encompasses the following:

1. Objectives,
2. Resource requirements,
3. Procedures for transforming inputs into outputs,
4. Alternative ways of achieving objectives,
5. Anticipated effectiveness resulting from the utilization of resources, and
6. Criteria to be used for program assessment.

The major product of the programming process is referred to as the *program plan.* The program plan is a document through which educational program information is presented concerning student learning activities and support services considered essential to the achievement of the district's objectives. Typically, the program plan will include descriptive information for the program's goals and objectives, services to be rendered and evaluation measures to be taken. Resources, in terms of people and time involved, supplies, equipment and facilities are indicated. The cost of all resources is listed. Moreover, alternative objectives, services, evaluation measures, resources and costs information is presented.

Frequently, in the literature, the term *program memorandum* is used to describe program information. In some instances the program memorandum is used as a planning and communication document for presenting program information prior to the final adoption of the program. However, the term *program plan* seems to be more descriptive and suggests a greater definition of purpose. Therefore the term program plan will be used in this chapter. Information flowing from the other major processes and the decision-making occurring in the planning process are utilized in developing and eventually implementing the district's program plans. Information developed and contained in the program plan becomes an important product input to planning, budgeting and evaluating. This continual exchange of information among the four processes is an essential characteristic of an ERM System.

In the programming process, a program plan will be prepared for each individual educational program deemed necessary to the achievement of the goals of the school district. The data aggregated and displayed in the program plan assists in the analytic process essential to the selection, implementation and evaluation of the school district's programs. The analysis with the subsequent decision regarding the selection of the most acceptable program plans to implement is a function of the planning process. To further illustrate this point, a program plan for the teaching of mathematics may present three alternatives. The development of the most acceptable program plan is a responsibility of the planning process. Perhaps none of the program alternatives is acceptable. It may be necessary to develop additional alternatives through the programming process, which are then presented for further consideration in the planning process. Thus program plans may be described as working documents which are essential to the analytic and decision-making responsibilities inherent in the planning process.

Creating an Organization for Programming

Programming must be a carefully organized process in an ERM System which encompasses all program areas set forth in the program structure of the planning documents. Because of this inclusiveness, programming requires information from all program and service areas in the school district. A school district capacity must be developed for the express purpose of accomplishing the programming process.

One possible way of creating the capacity for developing the programming process is to establish a representative committee or group composed of staff members selected from within the school district. It is suggested in Chapter II that a professional team or teams be formed to work in the programming process. The definition of the membership of the professional team should be broad enough to allow for membership from the instructional and the non-instructional program areas. The professional teams will, of necessity, coordinate their work with the work of the school's task force created for planning.

The creation of the professional teams requires that certain basic questions be resolved by the appropriate school officials. The questions are all related to the subjects of authority, responsibility, priority, resource commitment and control. Some of the questions are:

1. Who among the staff should be involved?
2. How should these staff persons be organized?
3. What resources will be needed to accomplish the work?

4. When should the group begin work and how long should the team work together?
5. Where or at what place in the current activities should the group start work?
6. What is the limit of authority that the teams should be given?
7. Where does the authority come from?
8. Where in the hierarchical organizational structure should the effort be placed?
9. What relationship should the professional team have with the task force of the planning process?

Since there are many different organizational patterns that may be developed for the purpose of handling the programming process, each school district, after careful thought and study of its specific needs, will no doubt establish its own unique organization. Perhaps, school officials should also consider the involvement of representatives from the student body, lay citizens and possibly technical assistance. The extent of student involvement can only be determined in the context of each specific situation. In small districts, one single team of staff members may be responsible for developing the entire ERM System. In the larger districts where duties and responsibilities are highly decentralized, several teams may be formed with each team given individual and specific tasks to perform.

Program Plan Documents

The program plan is a document which describes in detail the related components of each individual program included in the program structure for achieving the goals of the school district. It is conceivable that many program plans will be prepared before all of the desired educational programs in the school district plan are exhausted. The program plan document may include information related to the following:

1. Identifying description such as name and code number;
2. Performance objectives and sub-objectives;
3. Student target populations;
4. Content;
5. Organization;
6. Procedures, e. g., learning experiences, service activity procedures;
7. Sequence of activities;
8. Interprogram relationships;
9. Operating procedures;
10. Resource requirements;
11. Performance criteria;
12. Projected effectiveness;
13. Time factors;
14. Other information deemed appropriate, e. g., recommendations and suggestions for the implementation of the program.

The program plan document is the result of an information interaction which may be characterized as being more horizontal than vertical in nature.

That is, each of the four processes is dependent upon information flowing freely within the entire ERM System. Also, each process is developed in conjunction with all of the other processes. There is no top-down or bottom-up developmental linear procedure implied in the statements regarding program plan development. Program plans do not just suddenly appear; rather they are the result of an integrated information exchange and decision-making in an ERM System.

Much of the information to prepare program plans is obtained from the other three processes. Planning products, such as goals, general objectives, available resources and the suggested programs assist in program plan development. The budgeting process provides information related to the availability of resources and cost data for the program plan resource requirements. The list of resources specifically required to attain each program plan alternative over a period of time is used in the budgeting process for purposes of providing cost information and program budget development. Criteria and procedures for the assessment of each program plan will be provided through the evaluating process.

Formulation of Program Plans

After the basic organizational approach for conducting the programming process has been determined, usually the first activity will be the work of developing tentative program plans. This activity may begin as soon as the planning process has provided information in the form of tentative general objectives and related programs as developed in the school district plan. This planning information provides guidance and direction to the initial work of program plan development.

Specific program plans must be prepared for each of the basic programs included in the district's program structure.

The program structure is one of the products of the planning process. The program plans may be short-range or long-range depending upon the need as defined in the planning documents. Many of the basic programs are continuous and span the length of time set forth in the long-range planning document. However, other special programs may have a limited operational period which is shorter than the period of time established in the long-range school district plan. These particular programs may be classified as short-range type programs.

Another situation which must be dealt with in the programming process is the distinction between the current on-going operations of the district and new programs yet to be implemented.

An ERM System will be implemented in an on-going educational program environment of a school district. School officials will be working within the on-going system except in the rare occasion when a new district is being started. The technique of developing program plans for the current programs and any new program is, for all practical purposes, essentially identical. There are several issues to be encountered in the formulation of program plans. The issues generally relate to such things as:

1. Resource availability,
2. Different resource commitments,
3. A change in objectives,
4. Differing time periods,
5. Improved assessment of programs, and
6. Other similar type transition considerations.

There are also additional issues associated with the process of converting from a currently operating program plan to a new program plan. The issues are unique with each school district. It is very possible that for a period of time the district may be involved in operating old programs which are to be phased out before new programs can be implemented. The current programs in operation may not have been provided for in the school's newly developed program structure. The authority and responsibility of various personnel may be altered and this can cause some difficulties which must be resolved properly. Since it normally takes some time to develop and test new programs and acquire resources, the phasing out of old programs may not be excessively disruptive when implementing an ERM System. As implied in the previous discussion, program plan alternatives are prepared for the various programs as described in the school's program structure. Program plan documents when completel furnish much information essential to the planning, budgeting and evaluating processes. Thus, information needed for the developmental and decision-making activities of the district is made available concerning the educational programs of that district.

Activities associated with the continued development of the selected program plan which occurred in the planning process may be described as progressing through four stages. These four stages and related definitions may be illustrated as follows:

Program Plan Development Stages

Stage		Definition
I	Exploratory Plan	A program plan described to explore the potential of a means for achieving a desired objective.
II	Prototype Plan	A program plan designed to test the accumulated evaluations of exploratory plans.
III	Interim Plan	A tentative program plan designed to test the general advisability of prototype plan evaluations.
IV	Operational Plan	A program plan which is designed to put into practice interim plans which have been evaluated to be effective.

Each stage is evaluated and the resulting information is used to revise or modify program plan development.

Program Plan Objectives

The initial activity in the development of program plans is the definition and listing of performance objectives. The statements concerning goals and general objectives and related programs created in the programming process provide essential information to begin this work.

Performance objectives are prepared for each program. The development of performance objectives might be somewhat easier if the performance objectives are divided into sub-objectives with each lower subdivision becoming more definitive and specifically designed to correlate with the particular levels of activities.

Regardless of the terminology used, it is important to recognize that program plans are more realistically developed when written performance objectives progress from the more broadly defined objectives to the more specifically defined objectives. The extent of specificity depends upon the inherent needs of each program situation and the desires of the school staff working in the programming process development. It is not in the scope of this chapter to develop specific performance objectives, but rather to relate performance objectives to program plan development.

For each general objective, there are usually many performance objectives which could be sought. Realistic planning of performance objectives requires that many be considered and a carefully analyzed selection should be from those which are most urgent and in the greatest demand. The definition and selection of performance objectives is subject to certain restraints as represented by limited resources which are available to carry out such objectives.

Performance objectives should be stated in output terms which indicate desired behavior or activities. With the performance objectives stated in terms of expected outcomes, it becomes possible to develop alternative program approaches and assign resources to them. These alternative approaches may yield differing degrees of learning changes in the target group. Also, it is important to recognize the relationship of performance objectives to the evaluation process. The general purpose of evaluating is to measure the extent or degree of achievement regarding stated performance objectives. In the evaluating process of an ERM System the performance objectives will be used to establish criteria for measuring the achievement of the objectives. Evaluation of programs is discussed in greater detail in Chapter VII, Evaluating.

Some rather difficult problems can be encountered in defining and stating performance objectives in output terms and establishing programs and activities to achieve the defined objectives.

It is relatively easy to state the ideal of performance objectives in terms of output. But it is quite another problem when attempting to apply this ideal to many of the variables encountered in education. Some of the incalculable stems from within the school and much from outside the school. These factors influence the quality and quantity of educational outputs.

One problem is the difficulty of identifying outputs. In the instructional area many quantifiable types of output measures could be used as criteria for measuring the achievement of performance objectives. The following are examples:

1. Number of graduates and/or promotions;
2. Reduction in the number of failures and dropouts, etc.;
3. Number of graduates prepared for post-secondary education;
4. Number of graduates prepared for post-secondary employment;
5. Various salary levels;
6. Participation in various social and civic activities;
7. Achievement levels, skill development, ability measures and interest changes.

Admittedly, there are deficiencies in most of these output measures, but when they are used in combination with other criteria they become useful in measuring output.

The problem of stating performance objectives becomes somewhat easier in most, but not all, support service areas. Determining output measures is relatively straightforward in the area of school operation and maintenance in that typical business and industry measures can be utilized; for example, square footage of floor space cleaned, acreage of ground mowed, area painted. In the management support area, one might measure the number of records and forms processed, reduction of errors, production of manuals and reports, number of interviews and research findings. The important fact to keep in mind is that it becomes possible to develop a program plan with alternative approaches, specify resource requirements and develop evaluative criteria for measuring program performance.

A problem is encountered in defining performance objectives because it is sometimes difficult to ascertain discrete units of input and output. Consequently the effectiveness of a program may not lend itself to quantification in meaningful terms. The situation occurs due to the complexity of overlapping programs and activities which contribute to the attainment of several performance objectives. Resources in this instance are also shared in indefinable proportions.

Perhaps a solution is in the division of the program into smaller, but recognizable subprograms with program plans developed to reflect the division. Each subprogram which is somewhat independent is therefore listed individually. If it is important to display the interaction of these subprograms it may be possible to devise a matrix which appropriately arrays the relationship. An example of the shared inputs-overlapping outputs program is in the area of communication skills. Many persons contribute to the level of communication skill either positively or negatively. The influences and the results cannot be clearly isolated.

Problems may also exist in the student area; for example, students, as target groups, take part in school activities for various reasons. Some students may participate in a woodworking course purely for avocational reasons while others are enrolled for a defined vocational purpose. This particular kind of problem suggests a multi-dimensional approach that allows for classification of learning activities and students if the essential distinctions are to be forthcoming in the analysis and evaluating processes.

Performance objectives play a vital role in an ERM System. They provide the bases for the further preparation of program plans and for evaluating the outcomes of the programs. The variances between the performance objectives and the actual results furnish school staff with information which it would not have available otherwise. This information prompts new insights and decisions which lead to designs for bringing about a continuous improvement in program operation.

Student Target Groups

Program plan development includes the identification of student target groups for whom the programs are designed to effect learning changes. This identification usually occurs in the development of the performance objectives, since the various student target groups often require different types of educational programs.

School districts are committed to provide educational opportunities for all of the students within the district boundaries. However, the school operates in different neighborhood settings which have different philosophies. The kinds of opportunities the school district offers may vary depending upon the special needs of the students.

Generally it is possible to develop classifications of students who are in need of differentiated educational programs. Also, as these special groupings change over a period of time, this movement should reflect changing needs.

This analysis of student needs usually provides a base for developing the different educational programs suitable for each group. Usually the identification will occur during the planning process. Some examples of student groups are:

1. Students enrolled in the basic school program. This group may be classified as the "regular" or "normal" type students. They usually represent the majority of students in the district.
2. Students with a need for a program designed to overcome certain environmental situations or cultural backgrounds. This group usually requires specific types of so-called compensatory programs.
3. Students with mental, physical or emotional exceptionalities.
4. Students with specific vocational or career needs. Usually there are two groups to this category: those preparing for continuing education and those specifically preparing for employment immediately upon graduation from secondary school.

5. Students not normally included as a part of the school population. This group usually includes adults in a continuing education program and others enrolled in activities for self-improvement.

The above listing is only illustrative of potential student target groups. School districts will no doubt have other student target groups for which program plans will be prepared.

In the non-instructional program areas, the identification of student target groups is of lesser importance in the development of program plans. To illustrate, in the management service program area the entire student body may be the student target group whereas in the transportation program plan only those students which the district transports by choice or necessity become the student target group. The major consideration in identifying student target groups is that each of the district's program plans is designed to assist the student in acquiring an education. The identification of student target groups is desirable if the school staff is to engage in meaningful analysis of program effectiveness which is an important concept of an ERM System.

Methodology of the Program Plan

Another information component of the program plan is the procedure which is to be utilized to achieve the program plan objectives. The particular program method depends largely upon the nature of the performance objectives and the learning experience desired. The instructional program will be used as an example. Generally speaking, there are two major considerations for development of the design of an instructional program plan. The first may be characterized as those related to the question concerning *what* is to be accomplished in the plan. In the instructional program area this question relates to what to teach in the schools. This question may also be expressed in terms of what is to be learned and what is worth learning. Basically these questions are dealt with in the written statement of performance objectives.

A second major consideration is concerned with *how* to accomplish the things that have been determined to have sufficient value to be included in the school's program structure. In the instructional area this concern may be expressed in terms of how students can learn best that which is worth learning. Certainly the foregoing is directly related to how learning takes place and how the teacher can direct the learning processes.

Thus, it is first necessary to determine what is to be accomplished, a product of the planning process and expanded upon in greater detail in the programming process. Then secondly, it becomes possible to devise an acceptable methodology for getting what is to be accomplished in the school district. For example, if it is agreed that the training of carpenters is a school responsibility, then it is necessary to define what components of carpentry are to be taught. After the two aforementioned steps have been completed, it is possible to relate to how the potential carpenter can best learn the use of tools, wood, and the procedures for sawing, measuring, etc.

The determination of how to accomplish the desired outcomes in a program plan requires a careful consideration and an appropriate balancing of the various resources available to the district. To illustrate, in the instructional program area much thought must be given to the techniques of instruction, length of time a student is to use materials, supplies and equipment under (or not) the direction of the teaching staff. In the non-instructional area, the how is generally related to developing operating procedures and obtaining the required resources. By varying the resource mix and techniques involved many alternative program plans may be developed. It should be recognized that many program plan decisions will be made as the staff develops program plans for the school district.

Thus, the method for accomplishing the performance objectives of the program plan can be summarized into two major areas:
1. The procedure (what is to be done).
2. Techniques and resource requirements
   (how it is to be done).

In developing the methodology of the program plans, information is created which is essential to the continuance of the programming process development. For example, the method to be used for achieving objectives provides much of the information needed for estimating the resource requirements and the development of alternative approaches in the program plan. In practice, this entire procedure is cyclical in nature and is not accomplished in a linear fashion. That is, it is essential to develop all program elements in conjunction with each other rather than to develop each one separately and distinctly one from the other.

Program Plan Resource Requirements and Alternatives

Projection of resources available to the school district is provided in the planning process. The planning process development continues with the estimation of resources required for each plan and development of an alternative program plan. Included in this activity is the projection of the anticipated effectiveness of each alternative program plan. The information needed for estimating resource requirements is provided through the development of the previous components of the program plans. Resources essential to the conduct of programs include such items as provision for building and floor space, staff, time, students, equipment, appropriate furniture, materials, supplies and other items as determined to be necessary for the achievement of each program plan.

Also, it would be prudent to consider the long-range aspects of program resource commitments in developing alternative program plans. For example, the district may have sufficient resources to operate a specific program plan for the next fiscal year, but a forecast change in enrollment or size of the student target group during the second, third or fourth year may materially alter the resource commitment. Thus, it is essential to consider the multi-year resource commitment of each alternative program plan.

The program plan projections of estimated resource requirements are submitted to the budgeting process where dollar costs, if feasible, are assigned to the resources listed. This cost information is utilized in the programming process for further program plan development. This aspect of the programming process provides much of the information needed in the planning process for making resource allocation decisions and ultimately the selecting of the most appropriate alternative program plans to implement in the school district.

Alternative program plans offer appropriate decision makers in a school district a choice between two or more plans, courses of action or propositions, of which one may be selected. An alternative program plan is another program plan which has certain differences in its various components. Those differences may be quantitative or qualitative or both. An example of a quantitative difference may be the number of students, time or staff required for a program plan. A qualitative difference might be the particular methodology used to teach a certain subject. The basal reading method may be contrasted with the language experience approach. The inherent task in developing alternative program plans is to recast the program specifications to the relevant cost and effectiveness information needed by the decisionmakers of the school district.

The determination of estimated resource requirements in the programming process and the assignment of dollar costs to the estimated resources in the budgeting process clearly illustrates one of the interrelationships existing between these two processes.

Another aspect of developing alternative program plans is the determination of resource utilization as related to cost effectiveness. Program plan resource analysis is concerned with the effective use of the district's available resources in transforming program resource inputs into program outputs. The cost-effectiveness analysis, which is one form of resource analysis, allows the consideration of the anticipated gains in the student target groups in relation to resource costs. The anticipated gains in pupil accomplishments are stated as performance objectives in the program plan.

Resource analysis, basic to an ERM System, requires an understanding of the techniques of analysis — its nature, its elements and its processes. Therefore, if an ERM System is to be implemented in a district, appropriate staff must be able to perform meaningful resource analysis. This skill may not currently exist in some school districts; however, it may be acquired through re-education of the current staff or through the employment of new staff or both. A more definitive discussion of resource analysis is presented in Chapter VI.

Each resource requirement requires the acquisition of certain goods and services through the purchasing process. Supplies, materials, equipment, etc., needed for a program plan represent resource purchases and the expenditure of school district money. Also, staff manhours imply the employment of personnel of various skills and experiences which again require a financial expenditure. This translation problem is shared by both the programming process and budgeting process which illustrates a further interrelationship between these two processes. Basically, the programming process must present information concerning resource requirements that can be translated into dollar costs in the budgeting process. The translation factors will of necessity need to be defined and information presented in accordance with the agreed upon definitions. The estimating of resource requirements in program plan development creates a capability to assess costs of program alternatives in order to utilize the district's resources in the most effective way possible.

Preparation of Evaluative Procedures

Since the evaluating process of an ERM System is discussed in Chapter VII, this presentation will be limited to evaluating as it relates to the development of program plans and the responsibilities of the staff involved with the programming process.

Another component of a program plan is the evaluation procedure essential to determine program effectiveness. Some of the information necessary for the preparation of the evaluating component is provided in the content of the program objectives. These written statements describe what the program plan seeks to accomplish. The evaluating process produces the performance criteria to be used to assess performance and the evaluation instruments and procedures to be included in the program plan.

Performance criteria may be expressed as indicators of output in the program plan. The following examples may be helpful in understanding the use of output indicators in program plans as criteria to be used for assessing performance.

In the instructional area, assume that in a computation skills program, an alternative proposes the performance objective of: Improve the mathematics skill of 9th grade students by four score points during the first semester as determined by a comprehensive mathematics achievement test. The output indicator may then be defined as the test scores of students at the end of the first semester. The achievement criteria (success of the program) would be determined by comparing the student's level of achievement at the beginning of the first semester with the test scores (level of achievement) at the end of the first semester.

In the non-instructional area, assume that the program structure specified a major program as Facilities Services and that Maintenance is a subprogram. Also, assume that the staff, in preparing the program plan for maintenance, establishes the performance objective of: Reduce deterioration of buildings caused by natural elements and normal usage, and maintain a satisfactory interior and exterior appearance. A lower order objective might be: To paint the exterior of each building once every three years. The creation of these objectives allows for the development of several criteria which may be used as output indicators of performance. Some of these indicators might be:

1. Cost of contracted painting services,
2. Cost of school staff painting services,
3. Number of buildings painted each year,
4. Number of comments received from school personnel and others viewing the buildings, and
5. Actual years lapsed between each painting.

This listing is only illustrative, and school staff in preparing an actual maintenance program plan will no doubt be able to create many other output indicators which would be more appropriate.

The development of performance criteria which serve as output criteria for measuring performance may be extended to all other program plans. Performance development in the instructional program plan areas may be somewhat more complicated, but staff in a real district situation should be able to produce many output indicators which can serve quite satisfactorily as criteria for measuring performance.

Generally, in most situations, the staff will prepare the list of output indicators for the program plan and this information is utilized in the evaluating process to identify or create the evaluation instruments and methodology for assessing each program plan.

Communicating Program Plan Information

The information developed by school staff in the form of the program plan may be arrayed and presented in any number of a variety of formats for communication purposes. The special responsibilities of the various school personnel and the ways in which they use information will assist the staff in designing the different types of program reports needed in the district. Operational personnel such as teachers, custodians, clerks and other staff usually need information in the detailed form, whereas managerial personnel such as superintendents, school business administrators, principals, and other supervisory staff generally require information in summary form. Without summary-type formats, it would be very difficult for school personnel to comprehend and intelligently work with the program plans in carrying out their responsibilities.

The program plan detail prepared for operational staff provides information for the various summary-type formats. The school district program structure will also help in the design of the various program formats. Generally, the summarization of program plans will follow the program classification scheme as presented in the program structure. That is, the taxonomy of the program structure is applied and extended in the program plan development. The information in program plans for the program elements can be abstracted for aggregating into subprograms and the subprogram information can be further aggregated into the major programs.

Also, for analytic purposes, the various components of the program plan may be arranged in special and differing formats. One such format might array the program objectives with appropriate indicators of performance on one side of the page and the evaluative instruments and procedures on the other side of the page continuing in this manner until each program objective and the corresponding evaluation procedure has been displayed. Another special arrangement of information included in the program plan might be a simple listing of the program plan title, student target group, planned activity and the anticipated product or outcomes. There are many ways in which program plan information may be arranged for purposes of enhancing the communication of program information to staff in the school district. The key point to recognize is that program plan information should be flexible enough to allow for a rearrangement into formats designed to meet the special information needs of all levels.

The development of a long-range program plan creates a problem in presentation. This problem can be resolved by presenting a program plan in summary form with respect to time with the summary documents. That is, a summary statement is included at each significant point in time, thereby reserving the details for the plan for supporting documents which may be attached.

The communication and reporting of program plan information will require school staff to consider several types of activities such as:

1. The specific design of each document,
2. The identification of the personnel for whom the document is intended,
3. The provision for the completion of the document,
4. The scheduling of the document for distribution, and
5. The final disposition of the document.

Communication of program plan information within the school district enables the appropriate school staff to engage in the analysis of alternatives which leads to the eventual selection of programs to be implemented.

Recycling the Programming Process

Recycling the programming process is, in reality, a re-planning of the activities associated with the development and operation of program plans. This re-planning occurs on a continuous basis during the original development of a program plan and is made possible through the interaction of the programming process with the other three processes in an ERM System. Re-planning also occurs after the program plan is placed into operation.

The purpose of re-planning during the initial development of a program plan is to create the most acceptable program plan possible and to maximize the potential use of the resources of the district. After the program plans are operational, the purpose of re-planning is to improve the plan in order to achieve a higher level of performance and effective use of resources. The re-planning that occurs during the initial development of program plans is possible because of the interchange of information between the four processes in an ERM System, and the analytic techniques employed in the planning process. Information obtained from actual operations and the evaluating process should be analyzed and compared with the information in the plan. Then the appropriate personnel will be able to adjust the operation of the program plan in order to increase the achievement levels of the student target group.

Since the initial development of program plans has been discussed, the remainder of this chapter will focus on re-planning as it relates to the program plan in operation. Once the decision has been made to place a program plan into operation, one of several methods may be employed to implement the program in the school. For example, the program plan may be placed into operation at once throughout the entire school district, or it may be pilot tested in a small segment of the school district and eventually *phased* into the complete district. Another procedure might be to simulate the operation of the program plan before the pilot testing and final implementation throughout the district. The method to be followed in placing a program plan into operation is largely dependent upon the particular set of circumstances existing in the school district. Generally, it is a recommended practice to test the new program plan before placing it into operation in the entire district. Usually the results of the testing provide new information which causes some re-planning on the program plan.

After the program plans are fully operational in the school district, it becomes necessary to monitor the plan through the use of the evaluation procedures previously included in the plan. The evaluation procedures usually will provide for the periodic assessment of progress, and the identification, and analysis of variances. The feedback information obtained from the evaluation procedures usually prompts the re-planning of the program plan in the planning process. Re-planning may follow a variety of courses of action. The time factor may be changed, resources may be increased or decreased, program objectives may be changed, or a combination of any number of changes may be made, all of which are designed to improve the program output. Perhaps the evaluative information may lead to the discontinuance of the program effort.

In re-planning program plan operations it is essential to consider the question of the level of authority and decision making for instituting the recommended changes. Some program changes may be made by the staff in charge of the program plan operation. Generally these are only minor adjustments which involve the immediate program only. However, if the adjustment requires a major change — those which materially alter the district's resources commitments or those which affect other program operations — it may be necessary to refer the decision to the higher levels of authority, e. g., the school board or the staff responsible for the planning process.

School officials receive, over a period of time, much information which reflects the status situation and the future expectations of the school district, regarding program plan operations. The purpose of this information is to enhance the understanding of the program plan and to assist the staff in the judgmental processes. It should be recognized that good information alone does not automatically produce good decisions, since many other kinds of stimuli may motivate the decision-maker. Personal characteristics, e.g., knowledge, training, intuitive judgment and the capacity to influence other persons are some of the factors which influence the output of program plan decisions.

Administrative Review and Operational Control

Administrative review focuses on the complete stream of on-going program activities in the district, whereas operational control focuses on individual tasks or specific transactions as related to program plans. Operational control is a logical, rational, objective process which is usually guided by a clear set of rules and regulations. However, administrative review is a planning process procedure which depends quite heavily upon social, political and economic considerations. The results of administrative review are that it:

1. Signals the need for action,
2. Usually indicates the scope and nature of the action,
3. Communicates the essential information to those who must act,
4. Fixes responsibility for the action, and
5. Establishes techniques for measuring the results of the action but does not in itself enter into the prescribed action.

For a school district to engage in meaningful administrative review, it must:

1. Recognize the need for the review,
2. Create the appropriate organization for conducting the review,
3. Establish channels of communication,
4. Schedule the review activities, and
5. Disseminate outputs of the review activity.

Administrative review and operational control are important activities of an ERM System and play an important role in assuring to all concerned that the program plans, as developed and implemented, are the "best" available under the particular set of circumstances existing for the school district.

Summary

The programming process, as described in this chapter, presents a way of developing educational program plans through which the district can achieve desired goals. A program plan is prepared by the programming staff for the educational programs established in the school district plan. In general there are six basic components in the program plan:

1. Program objectives,
2. Student target groups,
3. Criteria for measuring performance,
4. Resource requirements,
5. Design requirements, and
6. Evaluation procedures.

Information essential to the development of the programming process is required as the result of a continuous interaction with each of the other three processes in an ERM System: planning, budgeting and evaluating. Also, the other three processes depend upon and use the information created in the programming process. Program plan information may be displayed in a variety of formats which can be designed to meet the information needs of the user.

The information developed in the programming process provides essential input for the analysis and decision-making activities of the planning process, budget information for the development of the program budget and basis for program evaluation.

CHAPTER V

Budgeting

Budgeting, in an ERM System, includes a series of activities which provide the decision-makers with resource and cost information essential for planning, programming and evaluating the allocation of resources within the district.

The budgeting activity interacts with the planning, programming and evaluating processes, from the inception of a possible plan to its implementation, modification and/or deletion. The activities include determining available resources, preparing the program budget, program costing and making special studies. Resource requirements are weighed against resource availability.

Through the integration of budgeting with the planning, programming and evaluating processes, a more systematic and rational approach to resource allocation may be made. The emphases in the budgeting process, as well as in the ERM System as a whole, are upon programs and output rather than upon input and items of expenditure. Because of these emphases, there will always be a need to supply information for other decision-making levels in formats which differ from the program budget.

In the implementation of an ERM System, budgeting plays the role of translating the programs developed in the planning and programming processes into their financial implications. The result is called the Program and Financial Plan — the Program Budget. As mentioned in the chapter on planning, the program budget provides the necessary base against which to assess alternative ways of accomplishing the objectives of the programs.

In developing the program budget the resource requirements for each program are identified for a period of years. These are reconciled with available resources so that the decision-maker is presented with a feasible program budget. A technique for reconciling program resource requirements with availability is discussed later in this section.

Three major concerns have been identified for the budgeting process. These are:

1. The reconciliation of program resource requirements and available resources.
2. The development, updating and maintaining of budget documents.
3. The monitoring, accounting and progress reporting of the uses of resources.

Characteristics of the Program Budget

In an ERM System, the program budget includes all of the programs in the district as developed in the planning and programming processes. Each individual program plan will have its own key design and operational characteristics, complete with a full description of the total resources needed to accomplish the objectives of a program plan over a multi-year period. The program plans are aggregated at different levels as supporting documents for the program plan and become summary documentation for the program budget.

The program budget and the supporting documentation are organized with reference to programs, subprograms and program elements designed to accomplish goals and objectives. As an example, a program may be planned to include the development of intellectual skills, with a subprogram for the development of communication skills, of which reading may be a program element. The program budget will indicate the cost of the program elements and the subprograms as well as the cost for the program. The program budget conveys information about the consequences over time of decisions made today. In other words, the program budget shows the cost of continuing to maintain the existing educational programs.

The program budget is developed by the selection of program plans which will accomplish the objectives selected to support the attainment of district goals. The resource requirements and the cost of the activities of each alternative plan are determined. This necessitates that the planning, programming, budgeting and evaluating processes provide an input to the analysis and evaluation of alternatives. An alternative is selected as the most effective plan to accomplish the objective and becomes a part of the program and financial plan of the district. The program and financial plan is another name for the program budget.

Based upon the decisions made, an individual alternative becomes a part of the formal "multi-year program and financial plan." The alternative or individual program plan contains information and details which indicate to the users of each plan the scope and magnitude of that program. Both capital and operating costs are shown, by program, in the program budget.

The use of the multi-year plan does not require a legal commitment to the longer period of time but the planning for a longer time period does necessitate making better current decisions. It encourages examination of future implications of current decisions and also allows systematic investigation of the aggregate cost impacts versus a single year cost of pursuing a particular program.

The long term projection of the program budget assists the decision-makers in relating activities and the resources required to achieve the objectives of the school district over a period of time.

The Reconciliation of Program Resource Requirements and Available Resources

Approved program plans display for each program the specific requirements of facilities, personnel, materials, equipment and the time dimension in accordance with the specifications made in the programming process. However, the requirements for resources must be calculated and reconciled with the inventory of resources.

Resource requirements implies the use of goods or services. (A discussion of resource analysis in ERMS follows this chapter.)

Resource requirements are translated into dollars and are projected on a multi-year financial plan. The costs of the activities applicable to the program over a meaningful time dimension are displayed in the program budget. The cost for individual programs for a specified time, five years perhaps, is a necessary input to evaluating alternatives. This information is of prime importance when related to the total of all programs for each year. When aggregated, the dollars needed as well as the total available resources can be compared with the planned allocation of the resources.

As tentative selections of alternatives, programs and subprograms are made in the planning and programming processes, it is through the budgeting process that program requirements are reconciled with the available resources for both long and short periods of time.

In the reconciliation of program requirements with the available resources, it is essential that information is accessible which describes the available resources. The district maintains an inventory system of available resources. A display in the form of a matrix can be of great help in visualizing the reconciliation of program requirements and available resources by program. This technique is similar to the "crosswalk" technique described later in this chapter. Figures 1, 2, 3 and 4 in this chapter illustrate this technique as a way to organize information about resources. The forms illustrated permit the insertion of data in physical units of the resources as well as monetary units.

Figure 1 illustrates a projection of resource requirements by program.

Figure 2 illustrates a distribution of the resource requirements by program over a period of years.

Figure 3 illustrates a form that can be used for projecting available resources for each of five years.

Figure 4 illustrates a distribution of resources by program for a specific year.

Figure 5 is a conceptual model representing a multi-year projection.

Figure 6 is a projection of the resources of a district in a likely format through a multi-year period.

Figure 7 shows the revenue of a district by program allocation.

Developing Budget Documents

The development of the budget documents involves the translation of program decisions into an appropriate allocation of resources. The needed information can be developed through the use of three types of instruments.

Program Name _____	Year 1	Year 2	Year 3	Year 4	Year 5
PERSONNEL					
Teaching Staff	___	___	___	___	___
Paraprofessional	___	___	___	___	___
Manager	___	___	___	___	___
Other	___	___	___	___	___
MATERIAL					
_____	___	___	___	___	___
_____	___	___	___	___	___
EQUIPMENT					
_____	___	___	___	___	___
_____	___	___	___	___	___
FACILITIES					
_____	___	___	___	___	___
_____	___	___	___	___	___
OTHER					
_____	___	___	___	___	___
(the information is in units of the resource or in dollars)					

Figure 1. Sample Projection of Resource Requirements for a Specific Program.

Requirements for FY___ to FY___					
Program	A	B	C	D	E
PERSONNEL					
Teaching Staff	___	___	___	___	___
Paraprofessional	___	___	___	___	___
Manager	___	___	___	___	___
Other	___	___	___	___	___
MATERIALS	___	___	___	___	___
EQUIPMENT	___	___	___	___	___
FACILITIES	___	___	___	___	___
(the information is in units of the resource or in dollars)					

Figure 2. Distribution of Resource Requirements by Program.

	Year__	Year__	Year__	Year__	Year__
ANTICIPATED STUDENTS					
Pre-School	___	___	___	___	___
Elementary	___	___	___	___	___
Secondary	___	___	___	___	___
Post-Secondary	___	___	___	___	___
PERSONNEL					
Teaching Staff	___	___	___	___	___
Paraprofessional	___	___	___	___	___
Manager	___	___	___	___	___
Other	___	___	___	___	___
MATERIALS					
(identify specifics)	___	___	___	___	___
EQUIPMENT					
(identify specifics)	___	___	___	___	___
FACILITIES					
(summarize)	___	___	___	___	___
REVENUE ANTICIPATION					
Federal	$ ___	$ ___	$ ___	$ ___	$ ___
State	___	___	___	___	___
Private	___	___	___	___	___
Local	___	___	___	___	___
Other	___	___	___	___	___

Figure 3. Sample Form of Projecting Available Resources for Each of Five Years.

YEAR ___ Program	A	B	C	D	E
PERSONNEL					
Teaching Staff	___	___	___	___	___
Paraprofessional	___	___	___	___	___
Manager	___	___	___	___	___
Other	___	___	___	___	___
MATERIALS	___	___	___	___	___
EQUIPMENT	___	___	___	___	___
FACILITIES	___	___	___	___	___
(the information is in units of the resource or in dollars)					

Figure 4. Distribution of Resources by Program.

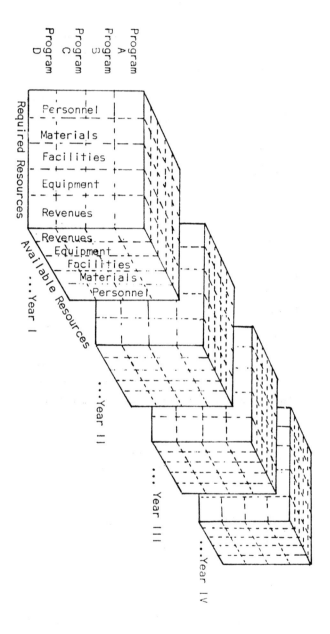

Figure 5. Reconciliation of Required Resources to Available Resources.

96

Source of Revenue	Year 1	Year 2	Year 3	Year 4	Year 5
Local					
Taxes	....	....	....	....	....
Tuition	....	....	....	....	....
Transportation Fees	....	....	....	....	....
Investment Earnings	....	....	....	....	....
Food Services	....	....	....	....	....
Pupil Activities	....	....	....	....	....
Other (specify)	....	....	....	....	....
Intermediate					
Grants-in-aid	....	....	....	....	....
In lieu of Taxes	....	....	....	....	....
Other (specify)	....	....	....	....	....
State					
Grants-in-aid	....	....	....	....	....
Special (specify)	....	....	....	....	....
Other (specify)	....	....	....	....	....
Federal					
Grants-in-aid	....	....	....	....	....
E.S.E.A. 1	....	....	....	....	....
E.S.E.A. II	....	....	....	....	....
E.S.E.A. III	....	....	....	....	....
E.S.E.A. Other	....	....	....	....	....
School Lunch	....	....	....	....	....
Vocational Ed.	....	....	....	....	....
Other (specify)	....	....	....	....	....
Other					
(Identify as Needed)	....	....	....	....	....

*This is a compendium of sources collected from several states.

Figure 6. Projected Available Revenues.

1. Multi-Year Program and Financial Plan or Program Budget.
2. Specific Analytic Studies.
3. Program Memoranda.

These instruments, which are the budget documents, facilitate the collection of data necessary for the presentation of the program budget.

The program budget is a program and financial plan which serves as a pattern for the future operation of the educational programs of the school district. The general pattern is established by the program structure adopted by the school district. One intent for the development of the program budget

97

is the elimination of a need to re-design the operational patterns of educational activities as a result of an annual re-appraisal of available resources.

In a program and financial plan, the pertinent data relating outputs, cost and the financing of each program are presented in tabular form and are extended into the future for several years. The plan reflects the decisions which have been made in the planning and programming processes and shows the future implications of current decisions. The output and costs are shown for each program element, subprogram and program, which are grouped in terms of the program structure and are arranged by fiscal year for each year of the planning period covered by the program and financial plan.

By presenting the future year data, the expected results of programs may be projected, thus permitting a reflection on the future financial requirements which will result from the program budget decisions. The program and financial plan will facilitate a more efficient presentation of information on future operating costs in relation to future enrollment projections and the correlation of this information with the proposed program plans.

PROGRAMS of the DISTRICT

Source of Revenue	Total	Intellectual Skills Development	Understanding the Environment	Personal Development	Exploratory Studies	Preparatory Post-Secondary Education	Preparatory Post-Secondary Employment	Management	Educational Media	Facilities Services	Community Services
Local											
Taxes											
Tuition											
Transportation Fees											
Investment Earnings											
Food Services											
Pupil Activities											
Other (specify)											
Intermediate											
Grants-in-aid											
In Lieu of Taxes											
Other (specify)											
State											
Grants-in-aid											
In Lieu of Taxes											
Special (specify)											
Other (specify)											
Federal											
Grants-in-aid											
E. S. E. A. I											
" II											
" III											
" Other											
School Lunch											
Vocational Ed.											
Other (specify)											
Other											
(Identify as Needed)											

Figure 7. Allocation of Revenues by Program.

The program budget is created by the accumulation of program plans and financial plans which reflect the current decisions of the board. The presentation of the plan includes a description of the means by which resources will be utilized to attain the objectives selected for each program in operation. The detail plans are organized within the program budget according to the hierarchy described by the program structure so that aggregations of objectives follow the aggregations of costs and resource requirements. At each level of aggregation, the data are summarized. The highest level of summary is at the program level. For instance, at the level of a program element the activities and associated costs are reflected in relation to each other. This presentation includes projections for the future for the use of resources, the objectives anticipated and the continuing costs.

The program budget presents a projection of the continuing operation of the programs within a school district. Once the program structure has been determined, the program budget pattern is also determined. The pattern is altered by an action of the board in the form of decisions affecting the operation of programs. Once established, the plan is updated as is necessary.

The program and financial plan is an instrument intended to present the record of the present and future budgetary and outcome consequences of the current year's decisions.

Updating the Budget

The program and financial plan, a summary of all program plans, displays the expenditure consequences for a multi-year period as contrasted with the anticipated available resources. This permits the analytical examination of one program against all others in terms of the impact of each upon the total district resources as well as an attainment of goals and objectives.

The multi-year program and financial plan is reviewed regularly and updated as required. This requires analysis and revision or deletion of the on-going programs as well as the addition of new programs. Budgeting will have the responsibility for developing the review information and presenting it to the planners for necessary program changes and subsequent updating of the program and financial plan.

Within an ERM System, a review of the budget continues throughout the year. Normally a schedule is prepared for a formal review. However, an opportunity is provided for intermittent adjustments based upon the latest program evaluations. It converts the annual routine of budget development into a conscious re-appraisal of both ongoing and new programs relating to the goals and objectives of the program plan. In the interim period, adjustments will be made.

Additionally, an important aspect of an ERM System is the establishment of "thresholds" below which organizational units can alter the program and financial plans without requiring executive approval. Personnel initiative is encouraged and administrative effectiveness is improved. Such "below-threshold" changes are recorded and periodically entered into the financial plan to keep it up-to-date.

As needed in the planning and programming processes, special studies are made indicating the effect of particular specifications on the allocation of resources. For example, the specifications for the instructional design may affect the salary portion of the budget to the degree that approximately 75 percent of the total program budget may be affected. Certain information is essential in the determination of educational specifications as it may directly affect the total resources available.

Specific studies prepared for individual programs, or several programs, provide the analytical background for recommended program changes. In-depth studies will encompass cost analysis activities by which cost and program data are compiled, analyzed and used to project future costs. These studies draw heavily upon the analytical tools of the professional disciplines in attempting to identify, quantitatively to the extent possible, the cost implications of the range of feasible alternatives. Cost analyses do not provide complete answers; they are intended primarily to provide information to decision-makers concerning trade-offs and implications existing among alternatives being considered.

Plans and programs are made on a continuing basis throughout the year as planners review, analyze and modify current programs; new programs are added and/or established programs are deleted to meet changing needs, requirements and constraints. Well-defined program plans are the source of information for the updating of the program budget.

If a particular school or department recommends a new program, the planning, programming, budgeting and evaluating processes are all involved. Ideas flow through the planning, programming, budgeting and evaluating processes by means of the program memorandum which carries complete information on a recommended change, needs to which a program is addressed, the objectives of the program, the required resources, the expected effectiveness and the target population.

The program memorandum is prepared and the issue proceeds through the usual processes of evaluation and debate. Proposed new plans, changes and deletions are reviewed and finally submitted to the decision-makers for action.

Major capital improvement plans are coordinated on a five to ten year basis. These plans are documented in detail and have the approval of the governing board before being incorporated into approved budget documents. In the making of decisions, of course, the acquisition costs for programs are included with the operating requirements; thus, when decisions are made, the total requirements of programs are considered in conjunction with the projections of available resources.

Recommendations on the program alternatives as presented in the program memoranda are the basis for analysis and resultant decisions are reflected in the program plans.

Managing, Accounting and Reporting Use of Resources

In an ERM System, the budgeting process includes the tasks and activities of managing resources. Broadly defined, management assumes responsibility for making resources available in the form required to fulfill program plans. The availability infers a further responsibility for control or management to assure that the resource is applied to the intended program activity. Fulfilling the intent leads to accountability. It should be obvious that a haphazard or capricious system for managing resources is incongruous with the basic tenets of an ERM System.

The account classifications reveal the objectives of information sought and then allow a translation of the operational activities into appropriate accounting records and reports. This implies identifying the available resources and the costs associated with specific program alternatives at the most elemental organizational unit and preserving the cost entity throughout. Accounting provides the means by which expenditures are compiled, analyzed and used to estimate and project future cost. Through accounting, each of the separate cost elements may be identified at any step. Thus decision-makers are furnished information by the accounting department to facilitate future planning and performance reviews.

The size of the district will determine the type of information system necessary. The systems concept as applied to information systems is involved with effective flow of information and the interrelatedness of all components, thus permitting a more comprehensive and efficient system for decision-making. For effective decisions to be made in a school district, it is necessary for information in a usable form to be available continuously regarding student utilization of programs, achievement of students, personnel, inventories of the facilities, buildings and equipment — in short, all information within the school district which is relevant for administrative decision-making. The information must be complete enough for financial accounting, but it must also be readily accessible for program cost implication projections for those persons in a decision-making capacity. In a large district, information relevant to the operation of the district may be readily obtainable by interrogating the computer files. In a district where a computer is not available, this information is available through manually maintained files.

The accounting system provides information to serve as an input to the analytical process which is the foundation for decision-making in an ERM System.

To provide assurance to school officials and the community that resources are being used in accordance with the adopted plans, budget classifications are organized in forms which coincide with the objective-oriented programs.

Distribution of accounting information provides a basis for preparing financial reports which will be of use to personnel at each level of operation. It also promotes the translation of operational data into record-keeping forms and procedures at the point where the information will be utilized most effectively. A schedule of resource utilization makes information readily available so that decision-makers are able to visualize the cost consequences of the current and long-range plans thereby exercising a necessary control for the success of a program. The schedule of resource utilization is in time measures commensurate with the units of the program.

Information needs to be collected and maintained so that a historic picture may be used to estimate future requirements for program projections. It is advisable to include in the reporting the history of the expenditures during the prior one or more years. It is from this information that trends are determined to assist in projecting program costs.

Under an ERM System a district's reporting system may need to be modified greatly, as the primary goal in this area of responsibility is to furnish information on the use of resources to the management areas in a program format and appropriate to the specific level of decision-making. Reports are actually forms of written communication; these reports provide the users with results of recent investigations of both the internal and external environments which impact upon the staff and its operation.

Information showing the availability of resources and expenditures is recorded so that it may be reproduced in a variety of content and format appropriate to the program, subprogram and activity for which it is being reported. Resource information is organized to allow flexibility in reporting. Exception reporting is developed to allow for an increased visibility in needed areas of expenditures.

The various aspects of reporting important to the evaluation of the program are determined during the planning of the program. All guidelines are flexible so that those who are responsible for managing a program may delete or request supplemental reporting as necessary. Legal requirements of reporting are always followed, regardless of the value the report has to decision-making in the management of the program.

In some states the legal requirements may necessitate the translation of the classification system of the program and financial plan into the codes of another chart of accounts as used in a revenue source budget. These translations may be accomplished through the procedure known as a *crosswalk*. A crosswalk is a means for cross referencing budgets from different classification systems. This technique can be used to develop required administrative budgets such as an appropriations budget and a revenue source budget.

The technique of crosswalk makes it possible to translate data which has been prepared in a program budget into the traditional budget format so that the legal requirements may be met. The crosswalk technique may be used to translate information from one classification to another. The crosswalk is also helpful when used in the early stages of implementation of an ERM System since it provides a framework and a link between the old and the new budgeting procedures and documents. Dei Rossi (1969, p. 47-51) discusses the concept of crosswalk illustrating the technique with a tabular array, showing the traditional budget cost categories in rows and programs in columns. Figures 8 and 9 of this chapter illustrate a crosswalk of the

ACCOUNT NUMBER	FINANCIAL ACCOUNTING, HANDBOOK II, U.S.O.E. ACCOUNT	PROGRAMS OF THE DISTRICT											
		INTELLECTUAL SKILLS DEVELOPMENT	UNDERSTANDING THE ENVIRONMENT	PERSONAL DEVELOPMENT	EXPLORATORY STUDIES	PREPARATORY POST-SECONDARY EDUCATION	PREPARATORY POST-SECONDARY EMPLOYMENT	MANAGEMENT	EDUCATIONAL MEDIA	FACILITIES SERVICES	PUPIL SERVICES	COMMUNITY SERVICES	*TOTAL
100	Administration							129					129
200	Instruction	500	75	30	50	420	420	200	30				1,725
300	Health							10			22		32
500	Transportation			5					5		5		15
600	Operation									217			217
700	Maintenance									80			80
800	Fixed Charges	50	8	5	5	42	42	30	3	2	2		189
	SUBTOTAL	550	83	40	55	462	462	369	38	299	29		2,387
900	Food Service										50		50
1000	Community Service											10	10
	TOTAL CURRENT EXPENSE	550	83	40	55	462	462	369	38	299	79	10	2,447
1,200	Capital Outlay	20		5	2	11	25	2	25	10			100
	TOTAL CURRENT EXPENSE AND CAPITAL OUTLAY	570	83	45	57	473	487	371	63	309	79	10	2,547

*(in $ thousands)

Figure 8. Crosswalk of the Appropriation Budget to a Program Budget.

Financial Accounting Handbook II, Revised, U.S.O.E. ACCOUNT	Intellectual Skills Development	Understanding the Environment	Personal Development	Exploratory Studies	Preparatory Post-Secondary Education	Preparatory Post-Secondary Employment	Management	Educational Media	Facilities Services	Pupil Services	Community Services	Total*
100 Instruction	500	50	10	14	413	403	100					1,490
300 Pupil Personnel Services			5									5
400 Instructional Support								40		14		54
420 Instructional Administration	5		15	8		22						50
430 Research Planning Development and Evaluation				9			41					50
510 Board of Education							10					10
520 Data Processing							20					20
530 Facilities Acquisition												
540 Fiscal Services							50					50
550 Food Services										50		50
560 General Administration	20	25	10	10	50	61			10			186
570 General Services	45	8	5	15	5				13	9		100
580 Information Services							50					50
590 Operation and Maintenance									300			300
600 Pupil Transportation							50					50
610 School Administration										15		15
620 Staff Services					1	5	1					7
630 Statistical Services							50					50
710 Community Services											10	10
TOTAL	570	83	45	57	473	487	371	63	309	79	10	2,547

*Figure 9. Crosswalk of the Appropriation Budget to a Program Budget.**

appropriations budget using the chart of accounts of *Financial Handbook II* and *Financial Handbook II, Revised,* respectively. An additional discussion is included in the Memphis Case Study in this document. (See Appendix D.)

Recycling the Budgeting Process

The total budgetary process is a continuous recycling of the above process which systematically provides for the revision and updating of the decisions. Through the system's responsiveness to changing needs, a base is provided for assessing new program plans and program changes. Program analyses and proposals for change may originate at any time in an ERM System. There is no specific date for proposing program changes. Each proposal is considered in the planning and programming processes, and if acceptable, becomes a part of the program plan as soon as feasible.

REFERENCES

Dei, Rossi, J. A. "The program budget and the traditional budget," in S. A. Haggart, et al. Program budgeting for school district planning: concepts and applications. Santa Monica, California: The RAND Corporation, November, 1969.

Lindman, Erick L. Research Needs in School Finance, in *Partnership in School Finance,* Washington, D.C.: Committee on Educational Finance, National Education Association, 1966.

Moll, Emmett J. Brochure of Instructions to Building Principals. Milwaukee Public Schools, Division of Planning and Long-Range Development, March, 1970.

CHAPTER VI

Resource Analysis in an Educational
Resources Management System

The role of resource analysis in an ERM System, described in this book, may be thought of as encompassing those activities by which cost and program data are linked to provide information in the form of resource and cost estimates. Throughout this discussion cost refers to the dollar implications of carrying out an activity. Resources include personnel, land, buildings, equipment, materials, supplies, time and services.

An ERM System is organized around outputs — around the useful thing an educational system does or should accomplish. Resource analysis is very much concerned with the inputs, i. e., resources and their costs, needed to achieve these outputs. This output orientation shapes the way in which data about the inputs are perceived, presented and analyzed.

The role of resource analysis can be stated as follows:

To generate, collect, store and retrieve *data* — financial, program and other — that will assist in relating inputs (resources) to outputs (educational outcome).

To organize and link resource data to the program structure to produce *information* that will aid the decision-maker in analyzing alternative means of attaining his objectives and in formally documenting the resources required for the alternatives chosen by the decision-maker.

To reduce, wherever possible, the unknowns of resource requirements, and, where information explicitly answering decision-makers' questions cannot be provided, to determine the bounds on the range of uncertainty in the future about resource requirements and their cost, i. e., to perform sensitivity analysis.

Basic to both an ERM System and a discussion of resource analysis is the program structure — output oriented by definition. The program structure groups activities by programs according to the activities' contribution toward meeting the broad, but measurable objectives of the programs. As such, the program structure represents an overall conceptual organization of the school system activities. It provides a framework for the planning, programming, evaluation and budgeting aspects of an ERM System and a framework for consideration of certain kinds of objectives, even though they cannot be measured quantitatively.

In addition, the program structure serves as a common point of reference during the discussion of the concepts, the methodology, and the techniques (especially the crosswalk technique) of resource analysis for an ERM System. The intention is not to prescribe a specific program structure; the program structure presented here is only one of many possibilities. It is, however, goal-objective oriented, rather than organization (grade-level) or site (school) oriented. For this reason, in particular, this illustrative program structure provides an excellent base for the discussion of resource analysis in educational planning.

Concepts of Resource Analysis

Intrinsic to an ERM System is the consideration of alternative courses of action, each of which implies an obligation for resources — facilities, personnel, equipment and supplies — over a period of time. Ideally, decisions are based on a full knowledge of the resource implications of the various alternatives. This full knowledge is seldom achieved, however, because estimates deal with future events, and the future is always uncertain. It is important, nonetheless, to project future resource demands and to project them in a systematic and consistent manner so that alternatives can be compared on the same basis. The purpose of this chapter is to suggest guidelines for resource analysis that will help ensure completeness and comparability in the cost projections used in an ERM System.

Since school districts have been recording financial information and preparing annual budgets for a good many years, it can be argued that administrative officials have always been engaged in resource analysis with some degree of success. There are important differences, however, between the program budget and the conventional budget that lead to different concepts of resource analysis. Resource analysis for an ERM System is more comprehensive in one sense and more restrictive in another. Thus, we speak of "total cost," implying that all costs of a given activity are to be included, yet the qualification is added that only *relevant* costs are of interest, i. e., *costs that are relevant to a decision.*

The use of such terms as *total, cradle-to-grave,* and *life-cycle* cost can be misleading, because we do not mean total cost in the accounting sense where all costs, including an allocated share of indirect expenses, must be attributed to a program. Nor do we mean a summation of all costs from the time a program is started until it ends. Since the end cannot be foreseen in most cases or is expected to end in the far distant future, it is generally more precise to speak of the cost over some definite period such as five years. The length of time is not critical, but it must be long enough to show the estimated, however grossly, financial impact of both nonrecurring and recurring resource demands. The terms "nonrecurring," "investment," and "acquisition" cost will be used interchangeably. "Recurring" cost will be used as synonymous with "annual" or "operational" cost.

Cost Concepts

A general definition of acquisition, or nonrecurring, costs would be all costs incurred up to the point where a program or project becomes operational. This would include development, facilities, equipment, supplies, and pre-service training. For example, designing a new curriculum for teaching foreign languages in the elementary school would be a development cost. A pilot program in which the curriculum is tested in selected classrooms, evaluated, and revised would also be considered a development expense. It might then be necessary to train teachers in new instructional techniques, purchase materials and equipment such as tape recorders, and perhaps convert classrooms into language laboratories. The costs thus incurred would be one-time, or nonrecurring, costs and it is sufficient to distinguish them as such rather than divide them into separate broad categories of research and development and initial investment. Since research and development in education has seldom been a major expenditure in the past, it has often been treated as a supporting service. Conceptually, however, the cost of development activities associated with a specific objective should be attributed to that objective. Once an activity is incorporated into the school program the continuing expenditures for salaries and many of the same things — materials, equipment, teacher training — are referred to as operational, or recurring, costs. These normally continue throughout the life of the program activity.

The expression *total* cost is thus defined to mean the sum of the relevant nonrecurring and recurring resource demands that occur over a specified period of time — usually five years. By *relevant* we mean the incremental or additional costs that will be incurred to obtain some specified additional capability. Sunk costs, that is, expenditures made in the past, are not relevant to comparisons involving future resource commitments. The fact that a school facility cost $1 million to build is irrelevant when the problem at hand concerns future outlays to acquire new facilities or to modify existing ones. This does not mean that inheritable assets are excluded from the analysis. If an existing building can be used for a new activity, this will reduce, in effect, the incremental cost of the new activity. The asset value of the existing building is not, however, included in the total cost.

One more qualification of the term "total cost" should be mentioned. Although we say that comparison of alternatives should be based on total cost, there are external (or spillover dollar or nondollar) costs that are difficult to measure and are not borne by the school district itself. Building a new athletic stadium in a residential neighborhood can cause parking problems, noise, traffic congestion, etc. The cost of these is borne by the community and individual citizens, in some instances in the form of reduced land values. These costs are difficult to measure. For many alternatives these costs will be beyond the control of the decision-maker in a quantifiable sense but will be a consideration in the final selection process. However, where it appears that these external costs could be important, they should be recognized in the report of the analysis. A good treatment of these cost concepts can be found in Fisher [1970, pp. 24-63].

The expression "total cost," used in the above discussion, was defined to mean the sum of the relevant acquisition and operating resource demands that are a consequence of the decision at hand and that occur over a specified period of time. Relevant means incremental or additional costs that will be incurred to obtain some specified additional capability. The expression, "total cost," may suggest the arbitrary allocation of all indirect or support costs. It should be clearly understood that this is not the intention. To avoid any possible misunderstanding a digression is in order.

The *Financial Handbook II, Revised* lists seven bases for proration of costs incurred for more than one purpose, provides a table of preferred and alternate methods to be used for proration of various kinds of expenses, and states that the reason for these elaborate procedures is to obtain "accurate management information."

Proration or allocation of support and joint cost is quite simply a financial accounting necessity. It does not improve the accuracy of management information. The planners, in selecting from among alternative courses of action, are concerned with those costs that will be affected if one or another of the alternatives is chosen. However, in accounting for the expenditures of public monies, some programs, Categorical Aid for example, require the identification of the indirect costs from which they benefit. Proration methods bring this identification about, but there is not necessarily anything "accurate" about the resulting distribution of cost, although one method of proration may be more acceptable than another.

The problem for resource analysis in comparing the cost of two alternative programs is that any method of proration yet devised may give an advantage to one alternative and penalize the other even though no actual change in indirect cost would result from the implementation of either program. It is generally possible to conceive of more than one logical rule for proration and different rules will often produce different results for identical programs. For example, for many indirect costs it might be equally logical to prorate either on the basis of number of students or on the number of square feet of classroom space used. Programs that use classroom space on a high density basis will then cost more using the first rule than by using the second — even though the rule used in no way changes total cost or real incremental cost.

Multi-year Cost Analysis

In any but the most simple cases, an attempt should be made to derive the incremental program cost by first developing a total multi-year program cost for continuation of present commitments — a baseline case — and a total cost for a comparable multi-year period for each alternative program to be considered. By a process of subtraction — the baseline case total cost from each of the alternative case total costs — the incremental cost for each alternative, unbiased by the introduction of prorations, can be determined.

110

The program budget displays resource requirements over a period of time, typically, five years instead of one. This does not mean that funds must be obligated for more than one year at a time — single-year funding is in no way incompatible with long-range planning. It does mean that if funds are committed in Year 1 to an objective, the financial impact of this decision can be viewed over a period of years. By forewarning planners of future commitments implicit in current decisions, a program budget reduces the likelihood of unforeseen requirements. The longer budget period makes it necessary to examine the future implications of current decisions — the essence of planning. In this way the budget provides a warning about programs that require little money in their early stage, but in which acquisition or investment will affect significantly the operational cost in ensuing years.

On the other hand, it is unwise to project costs too far into the future. In a practical sense, it should be realized that future resource requirements are projected, and then these requirements are translated into the projected dollar costs. The uncertainty shrouding estimates of resource demands five years ahead can be substantial. Changes of all kinds, including changes in the value of money, make long-range projections suspect. Moreover, since a dollar spent in the current year is worth more than one spent a year or more in the future, the time-value of money should be taken into consideration when the time-horizon is extended more than a few years.. The procedure for doing this is called discounting, and its general impact is to lower the relative effect on total program costs of expenditures that occur in the future. Where two programs have the same cost profile over time, discounting will not affect their relative costs; but where the profiles are different, discounting can change the cost relationship of the alternatives.

Total Program Cost Analysis

Up to this point we have been talking about the resource requirements of individual programs and program elements. There are cases, however, where requirements, derived without considering possible interactions with other program elements, may be overstated. One activity may be phasing down because of a shift in population or a change in educational objectives. This implies that certain inheritable assets, such as instructional materials, equipment, and classrooms, will become available for some new activity. It also implies that experienced teachers will be available, and this may reduce the training or recruiting requirement for the new activity. Whatever assumption is made about the availability of these assets will affect the estimated nonrecurring cost of the new activity. Presumably the estimate will be lower than if the activity had been considered in isolation.

Another example of the need to consider the total program has been suggested above in the discussion of multi-year budgeting — the problem of time-phasing available funds. If two programs with cost profiles similar to the ones sketched in Figure 1 were started in the same year, the peak cost could well be prohibitive in the first year. Postponing the start of one project would smooth out the resource demands, but it might also change the cost, because the availability of inherited assets may be different in the following year. Interactions of this kind can be ascertained only when program elements are examined together rather than in isolation.

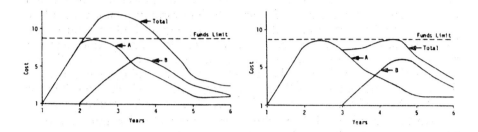

Figure 1. Total program cost profiles.

Accuracy of Estimates

Resource analysis for educational planning in support of an ERM System demands quite a different approach from the procedures of traditional cost accounting. One major difference, already discussed, concerns the need to emphasize the analysis of resource requirements rather than cost. For decision-making purposes, it is necessary to know the impact of a program in terms of resource requirements as well as cost.

Another important difference revolves around the idea of accuracy. In analysis for planning, techniques for translating resource requirements into cost estimates that would be unsatisfactory from a cost accounting point of view might be used. An example is developed in Carpenter and Haggart [1969, p. 15]. An estimate for a teacher might be given as $12,000 per year — without breaking this $12,000 down by the amounts for each regular budget appropriation category, such as instruction, retirement fund, or fringe benefits. This type of breakdown is, of course, required in cost accounting for financial accountability.

The concept of accuracy is tricky. It is not the intent to convey the idea of sloppiness or a disrespect for accuracy, per se. Rather, the purpose is to recognize that most cost measurements are approximations and that estimates often have to be made with incomplete data. Although it is traditional in financial accounting to express cost in dollars to two decimal places, the truth is that because of arbitrary allocations of joint costs and other accounting conventions, the costs are not accurate to that degree. It may be desirable for other reasons, however, such as balancing transactions and accounts, or for determining the amount of cash on hand, to carry the additional decimal places.

For the costing and examination of alternative programs it is not at all necessary to strive for such accuracy. After all, one does not need to know the outside temperature to a tenth of a degree in order to decide whether

112

or not to wear an overcoat. In fact, in deciding among educational alternatives it is often sufficient to know only that one program costs about twice as much as a competing program (without knowing even within a thousand dollars what either of them will actually cost) in order to make the requisite decision.

Very often, the analyst and the planner will find that a rough approximation of cost available today is often more useful than a more accurate figure published a year from now. The cost of owning and operating a school bus includes the purphase price of the bus plus the cost of labor, gasoline, repairs and other operating items less anything that is received when the bus is sold or traded. Thus, the more "accurate" cost cannot be known exactly until after disposal of the bus. Planners, reasonably, cannot wait for this more precise cost and instead should find the estimates available now sufficient for their purposes.

The degree of approximation is especially high in the case of figures used for planning. Such figures are always estimates of what will happen in the future. But it is obviously impossible to be precise about the future; because of this imprecise knowledge, the figures used for planning can be no better (regardless of the time spent or the number of decimals used) than the estimate of what the future holds.

Another aspect of accuracy concerns incomplete data. The planner almost never has exactly the information he would like to have in order to make a decision. In nearly every case, one can think of additional information he would like to have if only it were available. In other cases, page after page of historical cost data are available but only a small fraction of them are relevant to the problem and, perhaps, none of them are quite what is needed to reach a decision.

It is a fact of life that decisons must be made, and often the decision cannot be delayed until all the pertinent information becomes available. This point is also illustrated by the example of the school bus. One does the best he can with what he has and moves on to the next decision. Yet, a decision should not be made if a vital *obtainable* piece of evidence is missing. Deciding whether or not to act on the available evidence is one of the most difficult decisions in the whole planning process. The objective of an ERM System is, obviously, to increase the availability and the quality of the information needed in the educational planning process and to make explicit the areas in which information is lacking.

Where desirable information is not available, the decision-maker acts in uncertainty and in part on explicit or implicit assumptions, whether employing an ERM System or not. Within the field of resource analysis, there are techniques available to the analyst to deal rationally with assumptions and uncertainty. One of these techniques, sensitivity analysis, varies the possible values that might reasonably be associated with an assumption to show the bounds on the possible effects. Thus, where the analyst cannot say precisely what the cost effect of a program or action will be, he can sometimes show the upper and lower limits within the area of uncertainty. Discussions of other techniques for dealing with uncertainty can be found in Mandanski [1968, pp. 81-96] and Fisher [1970, pp. 201-217].

Techniques for Resource Analysis

A recapitulation of the points above makes it clear that there is a considerable difference between the resource analysis required for an ERM System and that required for conventional budgeting and financial accountability. There is the need to look at the resource requirements of alternatives, to include both nonrecurring and recurring costs, and to project the cost of the resource requirements over a multi-year period. Of necessity the emphasis shifts from the necessary accuracy in an accounting sense to comparability. The estimated requirements for each alternative must be based on comparable assumptions, comparable cost element structures, and comparable cost functions. This suggests the need for a wider-ranging set of estimating procedures, i. e., a model, than is typically utilized in preparing a conventional budget. A model, which may or may not be programmed for use on a computer, enables a district to look at wide ranges of alternatives. A model also can help assure that the resource implications of the alternatives have been examined consistently.

Cost Element Structure

The basic requirement for a cost model is a framework in which resource demands can be aggregated to arrive at a total cost. This framework, generally referred to as a cost element structure, is comparable to a list of expenditure accounts, although the number of accounts, or cost elements, is sometimes more limited. The cost element structure, however, is always more readily related to cost-generating activities. The goal is to be comprehensive; it is not to assign all projected costs to an account in a financial accounting system. On the other hand, since much of the cost data used will come from school accounting systems, the existence of a relationship between cost elements and expenditure accounts should be clear.

The outline of expenditure accounts in Figure 2, from *Financial Handbook II* and *Financial Handbook II, Revised,* cannot, however, be construed as a cost element structure. The major accounts are descripters of items or services purchased.

Under *Instruction* the cost items are further broken out as Salaries, Textbooks, School libraries, etc. To the extent that these items meet the criteria below they could be incorporated in a cost element structure to be used in an ERM System context. In general, however, an ERM System requires a more comprehensive structure and different levels of aggregation.

The first requirement is that a cost element structure specify what general categories of resources are needed. The categories should correspond as closely as possible to the needs of decision-making and include all relevant categories. One would not exclude land and buildings, for example, on

	Instruction
	Pupil Personnel Services
	Instructional Media
	Research, Planning, Development
	and Evaluation
	Board of Education
	Data Processing
Administration	Facilities Acquisition and
Instruction	Construction
Attendance & Health Services	Fiscal Services
Pupil Transportation Services	Food Services
Operation of Plant	General Administration
Maintenance of Plant	General Services
Fixed Charges	Information Services
Food Services &	Operation and Maintenance
Student Body Activities	of Plant
Community Services	Pupil Transportation Services
Capital Outlay	School Administration
Debt Service	Staff Services
Outgoing Transfer Series	Statistical Services
	Community Services

Fig. 2a. Financial Handbook II   *Fig. 2b. Financial Handbook II, Revised*

Figure 2. Expenditure accounts

the assumption that they belong in some other part of the budget. Second, the resource categories represented by the cost elements should be relatively important in a quantitative sense. Third, the cost element structure should be no more detailed than required to provide the educational planner with the information needed to compare alternatives. The cost element structure will also include provision for capturing the relevant share of costs actually incurred in other programs. For example, an instructional program element for reading would include not only the direct cost of, say, teachers, but also a share of the educational media services program. The conceptual basis underlying this provision in the cost element structure was discussed earlier in the part on concepts of cost. This implies a structure that is much more aggregated than is customary in the conventional budget.

A summary cost element for two levels is shown in Figure 3 to illustrate some of these considerations. The intent, however, is not to prescribe a cost element structure but merely to show the major cost elements that should be included in such a structure. Level I would be the display-type structure for an ERM System and Level II would be an intermediate structure between Level I and a detailed worksheet level of resource analysis. The content of each element will be explained later.

LEVEL I	LEVEL II

LEVEL I	LEVEL II
Acquisition Cost	*Acquisition Cost*
Program Implementation	Program Implementation
Equipment	Equipment
	Program-related
	Student-related
Materials	Materials
	Program-related
	Student-related
Pre-service Training	Pre-service Training
Facilities (Space)	Facilities (Space)
	Installation
Operational Cost	*Operational Cost*
Staff	Salaries
	Teachers
	Paraprofessionals
	Specialists
	Other
In-service Training	In-service Training
Materials & Supplies	Materials & Supplies
	Program-related
	Student-related
Equipment	Equipment
	Replacement
	Maintenance
Other Support Costs	Facilities O&M
	Contracted Services
	Media Services
	Transportation

Figure 3. Cost element structure.

    This cost element structure is appropriate for all "programs" of the district. The programs will be delineated in an illustrative program structure developed as a basis for the discussion of resource analysis and the use of a crosswalk. Both the program structure and the crosswalk will be discussed shortly.

    It will be noted that greater detail is shown for the quantitatively more important elements such as *Salaries*, which, in the traditional budget format, is shown as about 85 percent of the typical operational school budget. Any cost element may be aggregated or disaggregated according to the focus of a particular analysis. The basic objective is to have a structure that is comprehensive enough to be generally useful and flexible enough to adapt to the immediate planning need.

Estimating Relationships

Once a cost structure is established, the next step is to develop estimating relationships for the various cost elements. Many estimating relationships are simple mathematical statements that a cost or resource is directly proportional to some known characteristic of that resource. The relationship is often direct and obvious, e. g., the cost to build an elementary school is a function of the size of school, and this can be stated in terms of cost per unit area ($20 per square foot), per student ($1500 per student), or per some other dimension. Similarly, there are factors for estimating nondollar resources; a student-teacher ratio is such a factor.

More complex estimating relationships can be derived by curve fitting or regression analysis if the data sample is large enough, but the procedure is the same. First, we postulate a functional relationship between cost (or other resource) and one or more resource-influencing characteristics (number of pupils, number of teachers, area, volume, etc.). Second, we empirically derive the relationship. Third, we test the validity of the results. These procedures are illustrated briefly here. Dei Rossi [1969, pp. 105-114] provides a more complete treatment of the subject.

In order to make a five-year projection of requirements for operations staff, a school district with a steadily increasing enrollment wanted to estimate the annual increase in its operations staff. To develop an estimating relationship it was postulated that the requirements for operations staff are a function of district size and that average daily membership (ADM) is a reliable indicator of the district size. The following data were gathered from 13 school districts:

District	ADM	Operations Staff	District	ADA	Operations Staff
1	11,715	64	8	7,160	31
2	2,825	14	9	5,240	24
3	16,710	103	10	62,755	342
4	10,125	43	11	2,435	14
5	635	10	12	10,700	67
6	28,525	118	13	17,875	82
7	30,375	149			

Fitting a curve to these points by the least-squares method, the following estimating relationship was obtained:

$$\text{Operations Staff} = -2 + .00525\,\text{ADM}.$$

The intercept of the regression line, -2, is the result of straight statistical fitting of the data "points" of the small sample. It is also possible to force the equation, statistically speaking, through a positive intercept. This procedure results in an acceptably valid, and more practical, equation with an intercept of 5. That is, a school district's operations staff might well consist of 5 staff members with added staff based on increases in enrollment. The equation to be used for planning purposes is then as follows:

$$\text{Operations Staff} = 5 + .00503\,\text{ADM}.$$

As a test of the validity of either equation, the data could also be plotted; all the data points fall pretty much along a straight line — a linear relationship. Both the slope of the line and the equation tell us that on the average the requirements for operations staff increase by 5.03 for each 1000 increase in ADM. Thus, in a school district anticipating ADM to increase by 2000 each year, the requirement for operations staff will increase by 10.5.

The quality of resource analysis can be improved by making the development and maintenance of estimating relationships an explicit activity in the management services subprogram. By making the activity explicit, attention will be focused on both the needs and the usefulness of the activity. The source of estimating relationships should be recorded as should the limitations of the relationship and any other relevant information. This recording will be a time-saver when additional program studies are done — the search does not have to start from zero each time a factor is needed. This activity is not new in the operation of a school district but is mentioned here to reinforce the importance of the activity to an effective ERM System.

Resource/Cost Model

Deciding on a cost element structure and developing estimating relationships are two important steps toward developing a cost model, which is a convenient instrument for translating descriptives of alternatives into resource requirements. (Barro [1969, p. 64] describes this process more completely.) This translation is made through the use of estimating relationships for each cost element and of rules for aggregating the requirements calculated with these relationships. The degree to which the translation is successful depends, first, on the variable included in the relationships and, second, on the level of aggregation chosen for the cost structure. The variables included must characterize the major differences among the various alternatives, and the more variables included, the more successfully the model can represent the real world. Similarly, the more detailed the cost element, the more responsive the model will be to program changes. However, the workload occasioned by too much detail is such that separate elements should be shown only for major resource categories or those that reveal information of a particular interest.

Use of a well-defined model insures that all alternatives will be treated consistently. It also makes it possible to use electronic data processing equipment to calculate total cost. Modeling should not, however, be equated with automation. While automation greatly facilitates the calculations, it is not essential and beyond a certain point is not necessarily desirable. Total automation tends to make a model inflexible, and since a model must adapt to changing needs and uses, this is an undesirable characteristic. If available, data processing equipment should be used where it greater facilitates computations, but a fully automated model is not a requirement in many cases.

118

Sensitivity Analysis

One of the advantages of automation is that it simplifies the task of testing the sensitivity of, or the impact on, total program cost to changes in the configuration of the program or in the cost of specific resources. We must accept the idea that a certain amount of uncertainty is inevitable in any action occuring in the future. In a projection of teachers' salaries it may seem reasonable to assume an average increase of five percent per year, but the rate could be lower or higher than that. In a comparison of alternatives the question arises: What would be the effect of assuming a different rate? Sensitivity analysis is the name given to a systematic testing of the key assumptions to see how variations in these assumptions affect total cost.

We can postulate a situation in which two alternatives are being considered. Alternative A calls for a heavy investment in teaching machines, closed-circuit TV, or other audiovisual devices, and a slight reduction in the number of teachers. Alternative B calls for an increase in teachers and no expenditures for special instructional aids. The cost and effectiveness of the two alternatives are estimated to be about the same, so any change in the basic assumptions will shift the balance to favor one of the alternatives. An assumption of higher salaries will favor the capital-intensive alternative. An assumption of lower enrollments implies that under Alternative A a district may have bought more equipment than it can use effectively; Alternative B might allow more flexibility in reducing costs to match lower enrollments. If the results appear especially sensitive to one or more assumptions, more careful scrutiny of the basis for these assumptions is indicated. In any event, sensitivity analysis gives educational planners a quantitative notion of the implications of the uncertainty in projecting costs for long-range planning.

The Program Structure

As was mentioned earlier, the program structure is especially necessary in a discussion of the relationship between the traditional budget and the program budget — the program structure is, in fact, the format of the program budget and the basic framework for the analytical effort of an ERM System. The total program structure is presented in Figure 4 and shows a suggested grouping of current subjects into the illustrative goal-oriented program structure of an ERM System.

The program structure is also presented in a series of figures, arranged in much the same way the program structure would be arranged and used as a part of the documentation of the planning process of an ERM System. The program budget and its supporting documentation is depicted in Figure 5. For example, Figure 6 — along with the number of students enrolled, the sources of revenues and the general objectives of the district — might be the first display in the budget. Figures 7 to 10 would then be displayed along with the additional information. Notice that this manner of presentation provides an increasing amount of detail about the programs of the district. The supporting documentation to the budget would include, of course, or-

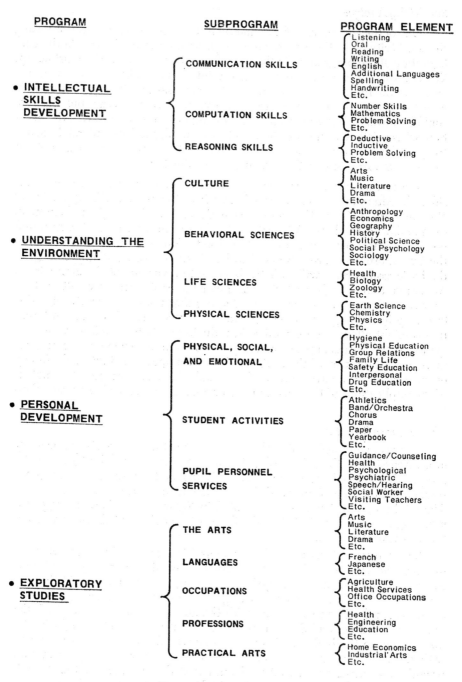

PROGRAM

SUBPROGRAM

PROGRAM ELEMENT

- **INTELLECTUAL SKILLS DEVELOPMENT**

COMMUNICATION SKILLS
- Listening
- Oral
- Reading
- Writing
- English
- Additional Languages
- Spelling
- Handwriting
- Etc.

COMPUTATION SKILLS
- Number Skills
- Mathematics
- Problem Solving
- Etc.

REASONING SKILLS
- Deductive
- Inductive
- Problem Solving
- Etc.

- **UNDERSTANDING THE ENVIRONMENT**

CULTURE
- Arts
- Music
- Literature
- Drama
- Etc.

BEHAVIORAL SCIENCES
- Anthropology
- Economics
- Geography
- History
- Political Science
- Social Psychology
- Sociology
- Etc.

LIFE SCIENCES
- Health
- Biology
- Zoology
- Etc.

PHYSICAL SCIENCES
- Earth Science
- Chemistry
- Physics
- Etc.

- **PERSONAL DEVELOPMENT**

PHYSICAL, SOCIAL, AND EMOTIONAL
- Hygiene
- Physical Education
- Group Relations
- Family Life
- Safety Education
- Interpersonal
- Drug Education
- Etc.

STUDENT ACTIVITIES
- Athletics
- Band/Orchestra
- Chorus
- Drama
- Paper
- Yearbook
- Etc.

PUPIL PERSONNEL SERVICES
- Guidance/Counseling
- Health
- Psychological
- Psychiatric
- Speech/Hearing
- Social Worker
- Visiting Teachers
- Etc.

- **EXPLORATORY STUDIES**

THE ARTS
- Arts
- Music
- Literature
- Drama
- Etc.

LANGUAGES
- French
- Japanese
- Etc.

OCCUPATIONS
- Agriculture
- Health Services
- Office Occupations
- Etc.

PROFESSIONS
- Health
- Engineering
- Education
- Etc.

PRACTICAL ARTS
- Home Economics
- Industrial Arts
- Etc.

Figure 4. Program Structure.

120

PROGRAM	SUBPROGRAM	PROGRAM ELEMENT

PROGRAM   **SUBPROGRAM**   **PROGRAM ELEMENT**

- **PREPARATORY/ POST-SECONDARY EDUCATION**
  { No attempt has been made to present an array of subject matter areas. Implicit in the program structure supporting ERMS is the premise that there is no fixed point at which assignment to the program is made.

- **PREPARATORY/ POST-SECONDARY EMPLOYMENT**
  { No attempt has been made to present an array of subject matter areas. Implicit in the program structure supporting ERMS is the premise that there is no fixed point at which assignment to this program is made.

- **MANAGEMENT**
  - **SUPERINTENDENT**
  - **PLANNING**
    { Research
    Program Development
    Program Analysis
    Program Evaluation
    Facilities Acquisition
    Staff Development
    Coordinated Planning - Other Agencies
  - **PROGRAM COORDINATION**
    { Responsibility Centers
    Federal Programs
    Special Program Coordinator
    In-Service Education
  - **PROGRAM OPERATION**
    { Intellectual Skills Development
    Understanding the Environment
    Personal Development
    Exploratory Studies
    Preparation/Post - Secondary Education
    Preparation/Post - Secondary Employment
    Educational Media
    Facilities Services
    Pupil Services
    Community Services
  - **MANAGEMENT SERVICES**
    { Financial/Fiscal
    Accounting/Budgeting
    Information
    Personnel
    Statistical Reporting
    Resource Control
    Cost Analysis

- **EDUCATIONAL MEDIA SERVICES**
  { LIBRARY
  AUDIO/VISUAL
  COMPUTER-ASSISTED INSTRUCTION
  EDUCATIONAL TELEVISION

- **FACILITIES SERVICES**
  { OPERATION
  MAINTENANCE
  SECURITY
  CENTRAL SERVICES

- **PUPIL SERVICES**
  { FOOD
  TRANSPORTATION

- **COMMUNITY SERVICES**

Figure 4. (Continued). Program Structure.

7L621

121

ganized information about the cost and effectiveness of program elements, or subject level activities, or of different arrangements of the program data by grade level, school, or type of student, depending on the decision needs.

The Crosswalk

There are significant differences between the traditional budget and the program budget, but it is usually possible, conceptually, to translate budget format, and conversely. (Mechanically it is always possible, but the result may not have much meaning.) The translation from the program budget to the traditional budget format is essential when planners are required to state their plans in terms of appropriation budgets or other funding documents.

A "crosswalk" is the expression of the relationship between the program budget and the traditional budget. It is a tabular array, with the columns showing the program budget cost categories and the rows showing the tradi-

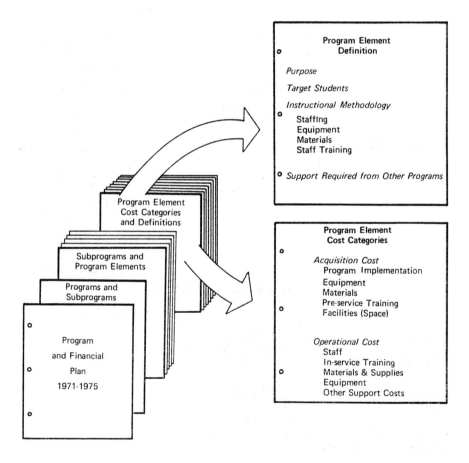

Figure 5. The program budget and supporting documentation.

PROGRAMS	1970-1971-	1971-1972-	1972-1973-	1973-1974-	1974-1975-
Intellectual Skills Development					
Understanding the Environment					
Personal Development					
Exploratory Studies					
Preparatory/Post-Secondary Education					
Preparatory/Post-Secondary Employment					
TOTAL INSTRUCTIONAL					
Management					
Educational Media Services					
Facilities Services					
Pupil Services					
Community Services					
TOTAL PROGRAM					
DISTRICT DATA					
Number of Schools					
Teachers					
Other Staff					
Enrollment					
Elementary					
Junior High Schools					
Senior High Schools					
TOTAL ENROLLMENT					
Sources of Revenue					
Federal					
State					
Local					
TOTAL REVENUE					

Figure 6. Program and Financial Plan (total by program).

PROGRAMS & SUBPROGRAMS	1970	1971	1972	1973	1974

Intellectual Skills Development
  Communication Skills
  Computation Skills
  Reasoning Skills					

Understanding the Environment
  Cultural
  Behavioral Sciences
  Life Sciences
  Physical Sciences					

Personal Development
  Physical, Social, and Emotional
  Student Activities
  Pupil Personnel Services					

Exploratory Studies
  The Arts
  Languages
  Occupations
  Professions
  Practical Arts					

Preparatory/Post-Secondary Education					
Preparatory/Post-Secondary Employment					

Management
  Superintendent
  Planning
  Program Coordination
  Program Operation
  Management Services					

Educational Media Services
  Library
  Audio/Visual
  Other (CAI, ETV)					

Facilities Services
  Operation
  Maintenance
  Security
  Central Services					

Pupil Services
  Food
  Transportation					

Community Services					
TOTAL DISTRICT PROGRAMS					

Figure 7. Program and financial plan (total showing subprograms).

124

INTELLECTUAL SKILLS DEVELOPMENT PROGRAM						
SUBPROGRAMS	Program Cost Phase	Year 1	Year 2	Year 3	Year 4	Year 5
Communication Skills	Acquisition Operation Total					
Computational Skills	Acquisition Operation Total					
Reasoning Skills	Acquisition Operation Total					
Total—Intellectual	Acquisition Operation Total					
STUDENTS		xx	xx	xx	xx	xx
TEACHERS		xx	xx	xx	xx	xx

Figure 8. Program and Financial Plan (Program/Subprogram).

(A program and financial plan would be provided for each of the major programs in the district).

COMPUTATIONAL SKILLS SUBPROGRAM						
PROGRAM ELEMENT	Program Cost Phase	Year 1	Year 2	Year 3	Year 4	Year 5
Number Skills	Acquisition Operation Total					
Mathematics	Acquisition Operation Total					
Problem Solving	Acquisition Operation Total					
Total—Computational Skills	Acquisition Operation Total					
STUDENTS		xx	xx	xx	xx	xx
TEACHERS		xx	xx	xx	xx	xx

Figure 9. Program and Financial Plan (Subprogram/Program Element).

PROGRAM ELEMENT — MATHEMATICS					
COST STRUCTURE	Year 1	Year 2	Year 3	Year 4	Year 5
ACQUISITION COST					
Program Implementation					
Equipment					
Materials					
Pre-service Training					
Facilities (Space)					
ACQUISITION COST					
OPERATIONAL COST					
Salaries					
In-service Training					
Materials & Supplies					
Equipment					
Facilities O & M					
Contracted Services					
Media Services					
Transportation					
Other Program Support					
OPERATIONAL COST					
STUDENTS	xx	xx	xx	xx	xx
TEACHERS	xx	xx	xx	xx	xx

Figure 10. Program and Financial Plan.

Acct. No.	Account	Total	Intellectual Skills Development	Understanding the Environment	Personal Development	Exploratory Studies	Preparatory Post-Secondary Education	Preparatory Post-Secondary Employment	Management	Educational Media	Facilities Service	Pupil Services	Community Services
								PROGRAMS OF THE DISTRICT					
100	Administration	600	----	---	---	---	---	---	600	---	---	---	---
200	Instruction	16,900	3,800	3,400	2,100	2,500	1,000	800	3,000	300	---	---	---
300	Health	300	---	---	250	---	---	---	50	---	---	---	---
500	Transportation	400	---	---	25	---	10	15	---	---	---	350	---
600	Operation	1,800	---	---	---	---	---	---	---	---	1,800	---	---
700	Maintenance	1,000	---	---	---	---	---	---	---	---	1,000	???	---
800	Fixed Charges	1,400	270	240	145	170	70	60	250	20	160	15	---
	SUBTOTAL	22,400	4,070	3,640	2,520	2,670	1,080	875	3,900	320	2,960	365	---
900	Food Service	500	---	---	---	---	---	---	---	---	---	500	---
1,100	Community Service	700	---	---	---	---	---	---	---	---	---	---	700
	Total Current Expense	23,600	4,070	3,640	2,520	2,670	1,080	875	3,900	320	2,960	865	700
1,200	Capital Outlay	900	---	---	125	---	---	300	250	100	50	75	---
	Total Current Expense and Capital Outlay	24,500	4,070	3,640	2,645	2,670	1,080	1,175	4,150	420	3,110	940	700

Figure 11a. Crosswalk example (In $ thousands).

PROGRAMS OF THE DISTRICT

Acct. No.	Account	Total	Intellectual Skills Development	Understanding the Environment	Personal Development	Exploratory Studies	Preparatory Post-Secondary Education	Preparatory Post-Secondary Employment	Management	Educational Media	Facilities Service	Pupil Services	Community Services
100	Instruction	xxx	xxx	xxx	xxx	xxx	xxx	---	xxx	xxx	---	---	---
300	Pupil Personnel Services	xxx	---	---	xxx	---	---	---	xxx	---	---	---	---
410	Instructional Media	xxx	xxx	xxx	xxx	xxx	xxx	xxx	---	xxx	---	---	---
420	Instructional Administration	xxx	---	---	---	---	---	---	xxx	---	---	---	---
430	Research, Planning, Development & Evaluation	xxx	---	---	---	---	---	---	xxx	---	---	---	---
510	Board of Education	xxx	---	---	---	---	---	---	xxx	---	---	---	---
520	Data Processing	xxx	---	---	---	---	---	---	xxx	---	---	---	---
530	Facilities Acquisition & Construction	xxx	xxx	xxx	xxx	xxx	xxx	xxx	xxx	xxx	xxx	xxx	---
540	Fiscal Services	xxx	---	---	---	---	---	---	xxx	---	---	---	---
550	Food Services	xxx	---	---	---	---	---	---	---	---	---	xxx	---
560	General Administration	xxx	---	---	---	---	---	---	xxx	---	---	---	---
570	General Services	xxx	---	---	---	---	---	---	xxx	---	xxx	---	---
580	Information Services	xxx	---	---	---	---	---	---	xxx	---	---	---	---
590	Operation & Maintenance of Plant	xxx	xxx	xxx	xxx	xxx	xxx	xxx	xxx	xxx	xxx	xxx	---
600	Pupil Transportation Services	xxx	---	---	---	---	---	---	---	---	---	xxx	---
610	School Administration	xxx	---	---	---	---	---	---	xxx	---	---	---	---
620	Staff Services	xxx	---	---	---	---	---	---	xxx	---	---	---	---
630	Statistical Services	xxx	---	---	---	---	---	---	xxx	---	---	---	---
700	Community Services	xxx	---	---	---	---	---	---	---	---	---	---	xxx

Figure 11b. Crosswalk example.

tional budget cost categories. The crosswalk translation can be performed at any level of detail decided on by the individual school district. Figures 11a and 11b show an example of a crosswalk, aggregated at a high level using the expenditure accounts of *Handbook II* and *Handbook II, Revised*, respectively. The first three columns show the traditional budget as currently required. The major programs of the illustrative program structure for an ERM System described earlier are shown at the top of the columns.

The crosswalk is a useful communication device between those familiar with the traditional budget and those who must implement an ERM System in a new environment. The crosswalk is also useful when the program categories cut across organizational units such as particular schools. The crosswalk translates the data by program into a school-based organizational structure. Other crosswalks can also be developed depending on the needs.

In using a crosswalk it should be remembered that it is only a partial, although useful, bridge between two systems of thought applicable to the same subject matter — educational resources. A caveat: A fully developed program budget consists of much more than dollar summaries of resources, but only the dollar summaries are considered in the crosswalk.

Another important part of the program budget — the *full description of physical resources by program* — is not translatable into traditional budget format. The immediacy of the traditional budget time frame closes off translation of anything more than a summary of those resources required for current operation. Thus, the existence of a crosswalk covering only the dollar aspect of the program budget is sometimes erroneously viewed as an indication that the traditional budget and program budget are different only in format. The very important differences in data base and analytical approach that arise from the differences in intended use of these two types of budgeting must not become obscured simply because a portion of one budget can be converted to the format of the other.

Methodology for Resource Analysis

The concepts and techniques of resource analysis have been discussed and the major points have been supported by brief examples. This part welds the concepts and techniques into a methodology for resource analysis in an ERM System. Resource analysis is an important component in the analysis of current programs and of alternatives to the current programs. Together with the analysis of effectiveness, resource analysis provides the quantified information for decision-making. It should be remembered, however, that there is another crucial aspect of this decision-making process: It is the consideration of those dimensions of the problem that cannot be quantified. The process of trying to make explicit some of the qualitative considerations inherent in defining the problem and in seeking possible solutions probably contributes more to making a better analysis than amassing and manipulating data. (This process is discussed by Haggart, [1969, pp. 152-159].) With this caveat in mind, we will delineate, using examples, a methodology for the orderly manipulation in order to develop consistent estimates of the resource requirements and of the cost of educational programs.

The methodology has three identifiable activity components: The definition, or description, of the program is the first activity; the estimation of the resources required for the program is next; the output of these components is then followed by the translation of the resource requirements into an estimate of program cost. The explication of these three components will provide the structure for the discussion of the methodology in resource analysis. The relationship of these components is shown in Figure 12.

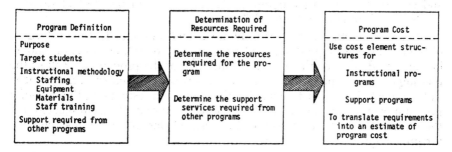

Figure 12. Activity components for resource analysis.

Definition of the Program

The nature of the program is defined so that all the cost-generating activities and their resource requirements can be identified. In the near future, it is more likely that alternatives will be considered at the subprogram or program element level rather than at the program level. (In the following discussion, however, the term "program" rather than "subprogram" or "program element" is used for ease in reading.) Definition of the program includes a description of the way in which resources, such as teachers, equipment, and materials, are combined to achieve an educational program. Additionally, the requirements of the instructional program for services from the support programs is determined. Thus, from these two areas of information (the program resource requirements and the supporting services requirements) an estimate of the total requirements impact of having this program as part of the overall school district program can be calculated.

This is an important function of defining the program. The purpose is to seek the answer to the question: What cost is incurred because this program is selected rather than an alternative program? This is the reason for separately identifying the requirements for the support services. To digress for just a moment — in selecting from among several alternative programs, it is necessary to know the demand each alternative will make on the support programs (such as the Educational Media Services Program) of the district. If one program makes no demand on the Educational Media Services Program and another program does, then this fact adds to the basic information for decision-making purposes. It is also important to know whether or not the program definition of each alternative reveals no impact on support programs. This program of allocation was discussed earlier but is repeated here for emphasis and because it provides the reason for explicitly defining the requirement for services from the support programs.

The definition of the program includes the specification of all the items shown in Figure 13, Program Descriptive Data Requirements. The figure is provided for illustrative purposes and additional data, of course, should be given as necessary to adequately define a program. Notice also that it is specifically tailored to instructional programs. Information of the same general type would be provided as a basis for estimating resource requirements and cost of the support programs. The emphasis on per-student requirements would, of course, be much less.

There is another aspect of program definition — that is, time. Because of the need to develop estimates of program cost over time, an effort should be made to determine the expected time-span of the program as well as the phasing of the resource requirements. This was discussed earlier, of course, but is repeated in order to make another point: In estimating the cost of a program over a period of time, the resource requirements are projected and then translated into an estimate of the cost. Dollars alone are not the basis for projection.

In recent literature, other methods have been used to develop and display program cost for future years. One method calculated a cost per student for, say, the current year and then increased this cost by five percent and multiplied by the expected enrollment to obtain program cost. Another method calculated program cost and then projected a ten percent increase in total cost for each succeeding year. Neither provides the planner with adequate information about the impact of the program or its resource requirements over time. No matter how crude, an effort should be made to project resource requirements, rather than cost alone.

Estimation of Resource Requirements

The project or estimation of resource requirements demands a close look at what the program is to do and what resources are needed. The amount of care and effort spent on defining the program will have a direct effect on the quality of the projection of resource requirements. The data derived from the program definition activity are structured in much the same manner as shown in Figure 13 — with the added dimension of time. This is a very straightforward process. It is an interim step in estimating program cost. In this step, nondollar factors are used (for example, materials per student, equipment per classroom) to develop estimates of some of the resource requirements. The results of the two components of the resource analysis methodology — program definition and the estimation of resource requirements — provide the basis for the estimation of program cost.

Estimation of Program Cost

In an ERM System, the goal is to know with a greater depth of understanding which resources are buying what in terms of educational outcomes

Purpose	State objective
Students Served	Number, SES, grouping (grades, classes), academic achievement, etc.
Staffing	Number/unit measure, such as class, student.
Regular Teachers	program, week, etc.
Special Teachers	
Paraprofessionals	
Equipment	Type and quantity/unit measure, such as program, class, student, etc. Include installation requirements, if applicable.
Materials	Same as Equipment, above. Distinguish between consumable and nonconsumable materials.
Facilities	Additional space required by the configuration of the particular program, classroom, laboratories, mobile classrooms.
In-Service Training	Unit of time, who is involved, cost/per unit of time, number of units.
Support from other programs	This is not a proration of the cost of these programs. It is, instead, the additional support
Management	generated because this specific instructional
Educational Media	program exists. For example, transportation
Facilities Services	for special field trips in support of the in-
Pupil Services	structural program.
Food Service	
Transportation	

Figure 13. Program descriptive data requirements.

and through this knowledge to be able to assess the impact of different ways of using these resources. One part of realizing this goal involves the capability to estimate the resource requirements and the cost. Another centers around setting the criteria of success and measuring the effectiveness of a program or of alternative programs. The concern here is the estimation of program cost. Within an ERM System, alternative programs are considered in the resource and cost context of all other programs in terms of the estimated consequences of having, or not having, a specific educational program.

This is the reason for having an illustrative program structure as a basis of discussion in resource analysis. The program structure groups all the activities of the district, both instructional and supporting, into programs according to their contribution toward meeting the broad objectives of the district. As can be seen, some of the programs are more directly student-related than others. These are the instructional programs. The other programs and their activities support the instructional purpose of the district, some more directly than others. The Management Program will be used to demonstrate the point that, although some programs will demand more of the support programs (and this cost will be considered as part of the program cost), most of the cost of the support programs will remain unchanged regardless of the specific instructional programs within the overall district program.

The Management Program, with its subprograms and program elements, is shown in Figure 14. This program covers a wide range of activities. One is program, or curriculum, development. In some cases, a particular activity of this program element can be identified as contributing to an instructional program element, such as Mathematics. More often, however, the program development effort in this program element is directed toward continuing

MANAGEMENT PROGRAM

SUPERINTENDENT

PLANNING

    Research
    Program Development
    Program Analysis
    Program Evaluation
    Facilities Acquisition
    Staff Development
    Coordinated Planning — Other Agencies

PROGRAM COORDINATION

    Responsibility Centers
    Federal Programs
    Special Program Coordinator
    In-Service Education

PROGRAM OPERATION

    Intellectual Skills Development
    Understanding the Environment
    Personal Development
    Exploratory Studies
    Preparation/Post-Secondary Education
    Preparation/Post-Secondary Employment
    Educational Media
    Facilities Services
    Pupil Services
    Community Services

MANAGEMENT SERVICES

    Financial/Fiscal
    Accounting/Budgeting
    Information
    Personnel
    Statistical Reporting
    Resource Control
    Cost Analysis

Figure 14. Management Program, showing subprograms and program elements.

curriculum improvement. Making an arbitrary allocation of some part of this cost to specific instructional programs does not increase the information available for decision-making.

Another example, more clear-cut, is the Management Services Subprogram. Almost without exception, the cost of this subprogram will remain the same whether the instructional program comprises ten courses of history and three courses of art or whether ten courses of geography are substituted for the ten courses of history. As long as an educational system is of approximately the same size, this cost will be approximately the same.

In still another example, the Educational Media Services Program is separately identified. This is in spite of the fact that its cost could be almost completely allocated, on a usage basis, to specific instructional program elements. The reason for this is slightly different from the rationale for separately identifying the other support programs such as the Management Program. In the forseeable future, the resources required to achieve a significant instructional capability using educational television (ETV) and computer-assisted instruction may be beyond the capacity of an individual school district. It is conceivable, therefore, that several schools could band together and develop a production center for ETV or a central computer facility. Each district would then buy services from these centers according to their instructional needs. Each district's share of the management or operation of the centers would be included in the Educational Media Services Program and each instructional program would be charged on a usage basis.

An ERM System is concerned with increasing the information about the impact of alternative instructional programs in changing the effectiveness of the educational outcome. Allocating management-type, or educational media, costs to these instructional programs does not improve the decision base. Changes in the quality or quantity of resources — or changes in the way in which they are used — and the related change in program cost become the important considerations in decision-making. For effective management of all the resources devoted to education, the support programs themselves should be subjected to analysis. This means that the resource requirements, costs, output indicators, and program descriptive data for these programs should be available in one place in order to facilitate this analysis.

The discussion of program definition, the program structure in Figure 4, and the cost element structure displayed in Figure 3 all provide a hint of what is to follow. The objective is to develop a methodology for arriving, consistently, at the cost of the activities or program elements that are required to produce an educational outcome. Figure 15 depicts the *conceptual basis for the estimation of total program cost as required for decision-making — as opposed to accounting — purposes.*

The key lies in the shaded area. This area represents the cost of instructional support programs that should be considered a part of the total cost of the instructional programs. The boxes are identified as the Cost of Instructional Programs and the Cost of Instructional Support Programs. The cost is the sum of the individual estimates of the cost of all the sub-programs

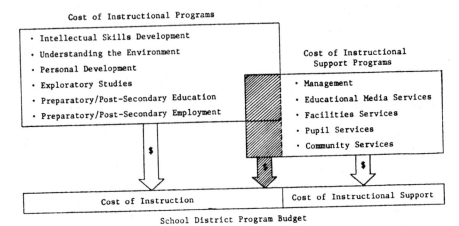

Cost of Instructional Programs

- Intellectual Skills Development
- Understanding the Environment
- Personal Development
- Exploratory Studies
- Preparatory/Post-Secondary Education
- Preparatory/Post-Secondary Employment

Cost of Instructional
Support Programs

- Management
- Educational Media Services
- Facilities Services
- Pupil Services
- Community Services

Cost of Instruction

Cost of Instructional Support

School District Program Budget

Figure 15. Total school district program budget.

and their program elements. This conceptual basis for the estimation of total program cost precludes any necessity to prorate support costs.

The cost estimates are developed using concepts discussed earlier and the cost categories of Figure 16 for the instructional programs and Figure 17 for the non-instructional programs. Notice the attention to student-related cost items in Figure 16, as compared to Figure 17.

The cost categories, or the cost element structure, in these figures were used previously with the promise that the meaning of each would be discussed later. Later is now. The most efficient procedure is to provide a brief statement about the content and special constraints of each category.

Acquisition Cost Categories

Program Implementation — Covers the direct cost of those activities required to implement a specific program on an operational basis. This does not include curriculum development, in general, but may include the cost of preparing materials for the program.

Equipment — Includes the cost of the equipment and furniture necessary to the program. There is a distinction made between the equipment and furniture needed by the program (may be classroom) and used on a scheduled basis by many students and that equipment needed for each student.

Acquisition Cost

    Program Implementation
    Equipment
        Program-related
        Student-related
    Materials
        Program-related
        Student-related
    Pre-service Training
    Facilities (Space)
    Installation

Operational Cost

    Salaries
        Teachers
        Paraprofessionals
        Specialists
        Other
    Materials & Supplies
        Program-related
        Student-related
    Equipment
        Replacement
        Maintenance
    In-Service Training
    Facilities O & M
    Media Services
    Transportation
    Contracted Services

Figure 16. Individual instructional program elements (detailed) cost categories.

Acquisition Cost

    Equipment
    Equipment Installation
    Facilities
    Materials
    In-Service Training

Operational Cost

    Salaries
    Materials
    Supplies
    Equipment
        Replacement
        Maintenance
    Contracted Services
    Facilities O & M
    In-Service Training
    Media Services
    Transportation
    Travel
    Communications
    Other Expenses

Figure 17. District-wide support program-elements (detailed) cost categories.

Materials — Includes the materials needed to begin operation of the educational program. Such items as textbooks, workbooks, initial stocks of paper, scissors, paint and so forth would be included here. The same distinction made between program- and student-related equipment is applied to the Material category.

Pre-Service Training — The training provided to the teachers or other instructional personnel before the start of the program is included in this category.

Installation — The special installation cost of the equipment is included in this category, if it is applicable. In some cases the purchase price of the equipment includes the installation charge.

Operational Cost Categories

Salaries — This includes the salary costs of the staff required by the instructional program. Employee benefits are included in this category rather than in the Fixed Charges account of the traditional budget. The reason: This shows the major personnel-related cost at a glance for analytical convenience.

In-Service Training — The training provided the staff during the course of the program. Training both for maintenance of capability and for improvement is included.

Materials and Supplies — Includes the consumable materials and supplies for the program. Again, separate estimates are given for the program-related and the student-related requirements.

Equipment — The cost to replace the equipment because of normal wear and tear and the cost to maintain the equipment is shown in this category.

Facilities Operation and Maintenance — The cost for the operation and maintenance of additional or special facilities required for the program.

Contracted Services — Special contracted services not provided for in other programs. An example might be the time on a computer or special telephone charges.

Media Services — The charge for direct support of the instructional program by the instructional support program. Provision of audio/visual equipment or services would be covered.

Transportation — This would cover the cost of transportation required for field trips taken as part of the instructional program.

In the discussion of the program definition activity — the initial step in determining resource requirements and estimating cost — the need to distinguish instructional support related to specific instructional programs from other support programs was pointed out. In terms of cost, this translates into an added cost to the support program because of a change in the instructional program. This support is specified by a quantity of output from the programs, such as 50 class hours of computer time, but transportation for 60 students, or a special evaluation of a regular program activity. The cost is then estimated based on the total number of units needed over the time of the program.

The sequence of activities described above results in an estimate of cost for an educational program. More importantly, the estimated cost of one or several programs can be derived in a consistent manner. This consistency is important. It allows for the meaningful comparison of alternative programs when selecting from among alternative programs competing for always scarce resources.

The conceptual model of resource analysis underlying this discussion is developed with a very real constraint in mind. The constraint is that most of the nation's 19,000 school districts do not at this time have an extensive data processing or cost/resource modeling capability. Thus, the methodology is developed to be equally appropriate for school district planners with either extreme of data processing capability — with or without computers and with or without educational management information systems.

Cost-Effectiveness Analysis*

Cost-effectiveness is both a powerful and an often misused technique of analysis. Its misuse stems from its very power, for it gives superficially simple, quantitative "answers" to highly complex problems, of which the sources and repercussions are very poorly understood. So that the results of cost-effectiveness analysis may be used most wisely in educational planning, it is necessary to know how to structure, conduct, and interpret the analysis.

Educational planning is ultimately concerned with achieving a more effective use of educational resources in improving pupil performance. There are several intermediate steps in the realization of this goal. The educational planner must first determine what resources are being used directly to produce specific educational performance or outcomes. From this base of knowledge, the resources required to make changes in various aspects of the educational process may then be estimated. These changes may range all the way from changes in the objectives of education, per se, to changes in instructional methods. This means the planner must be armed with an informational framework about the current system that is as complete as possible and with a methodology for estimating the future consequences of proposed changes.

Cost-effectiveness analysis is a tool that can assist the planner in relating the resources required by an educational program to its effectiveness, often measured by pupil achievement. For the purpose of analysis, schools are viewed as "systems." From this analytical viewpoint, an educational

---

*This material (with minor changes) was first published by The RAND Corporation in March 1970 as p-4327, *Cost-effectiveness Analysis for Educational Planning*, by Margaret B. Carpenter and Sue A. Haggart. It was subsequently published in the November 1970 issue of *Educational Technology*. It is presented here in order to reinforce the discussion of the concepts of resource analysis.

system is perceived as being an arrangement of elements (such as teachers, classrooms and the like) and processes (such as instruction and counseling) that combine to produce student learning. There are factors within the system that influence the relationships between the resources used by the system and the student learning that results; there are also factors external to the system that have impacts on these relationships. Just what these factors are is being widely discussed now and will be for some time to come. It is not intended to explore, directly, the many facets of this question here. (Their consideration is, of course, an integral part of analyzing the educational process.) The purpose is to look at the problems involved with the use of the technique of cost-effectiveness analysis in educational planning.

It was mentioned that cost-effectiveness analysis is concerned with *educational programs*. The term "educational program" can have many meanings, such as the in-service teacher training program. From this point on, the term will be restricted to apply to *a set of activities and resources that, taken together, bring about a specific kind of student learning*. A program must be described in terms of certain basic characteristics — its effectiveness, its dollar cost, its resource requirements, and the way it is carried out.

Cost-effectiveness analysis is, quite frankly, a technique for comparing programs, and may be used:

To help assess the relative worth of several innovative programs with the same educational outcome (such as improvement in reading achievement).

To determine whether a single program is becoming more or less effective as time passes, so that steps may be taken to improve it, if necessary.

To help assess the relative worth of the same program for different student populations (such as those with differing socio-economic backgrounds) or in different school settings.

The goal of the analysis is not to provide the planner with the alternative that maximizes or minimizes specific characteristics; the goal is to provide information that, together with the judgment of the planner, permits a compromise among the characteristics of the alternatives within the various environmental constraints, such as budget level or political atmosphere.

The term "cost-effectiveness" should be broadened to "resource-effectiveness" for reasons that will be made clear later in the discussion. *Resource* will be used in the common way to mean *a source of supply*. The way in which the resource requirements of a program are analyzed is inseparable from the purpose of the analysis — to relate the resources used by the program to program effectiveness. Program cost should include only those resources that can be related directly to program effectiveness.

Problems concerning resource-effectiveness analysis can be broken into two largely parallel sets, one focusing on resource analysis and the other on the analysis of effectiveness. Common problems are those of definition of the misleading nature of single measures, and of the lack of well-developed methodologies for analysis. These two sets of problems will be discussed in turn and then the problems concerning resource-effectiveness analysis itself will be addressed.

Resource-Oriented Problems

In order to be able to choose among alternative programs as applied to different educational situations, the planner must have techniques for comparing and evaluating estimates of the resources required by the programs throughout the time span of interest.

Determining the Resources Required by a Program

In the past, educational institutions have accounted for the cost of doing business primarily for the purpose of financial control. Funds for different purposes have come from different sources and may not be traded from one account to another. Keeping track of these accounts in terms of end-items of expenditure was the major task of the budgeting and accounting activity.

When cost is used for choosing among alternative programs, however, the source of funds is of secondary significance. *Rather, it is necessary to know what each alternative will require in terms of personnel, facilities, equipment, training activities, dollars, and the like, not only at present but throughout the forseeable life of the program.* Few school systems can describe the resources that go into existing programs, let alone estimate what existing programs or alternative programs will require in the future.

This is not, however, an insurmountable problem. It is possible to draw up a set of variables describing the resource requirements of alternative programs that is sufficiently broad to encompass the major variables in each program and that is, at the same time, sufficiently compact to be manageable. This must be undertaken at the outset if cost-effectiveness analysis is to be carried out.

There is a more subtle problem, however, that may not be so easily solved. This is the problem of definition of the "real" resources in education, that is, the resources that actually are the *source of supply* of learning. Many attempts are now being made to identify such resources, and some small progress has been made, viz., teacher verbal ability to have a positive effect on student learning. The amount of time a student participates actively in some learning process may well be another resource, but there seems to be no easy way to measure this at present. The amount of time that a teacher devotes to the subject in the classroom is only a proxy measure. Much work in this area will be necessary before it is possible to identify the real resources in education.

The Misleading Nature of a Single Measure

Resource analysis has a seductive quality engendered by the availability of a single measure, the dollar, by which most resources can be measured. Given this, it is a natural step to add all the dollars to obtain a single indicator of resource requirements — the "cost of the program." Although in some cases such a number might be adequate for resource-effectiveness analysis, in most instances the single measure buries many characteristics of the program of which the planner should be aware before making his choice.

One significant aspect concerns the timing of the expenditures: Are they required in a lump sum, can they be spread over several years, or will they recur as long as the program is in existence? Thus, projections of expenditures over the expected life of the program are required to provide a true picture of dollar needs. A display of the expenditures required over several years contrasts with the usual practice of assessing the cost of a program solely in terms of the initial research, development and implementation costs.

Another significant aspect is that, in general, the resources required are of very different kinds and dollar measures do not reflect these differences adequately for decision-making. For example, a program may require that a certain percentage of the teachers belong to a particular minority group, but these teachers will receive the same salary as any teachers with similar background and experience.

Thus, the cost-effectiveness analysis should always display the major resources required for each year of program life, along with their associated dollar costs, and should particularly note items that may be difficult to obtain (but whose scarcity may not be reflected adequately in their dollar costs). The problem is to identify and estimate the major, crucial, or scarce resources that will be required for full implementation of the program.

The Lack of a Fully Developed Methodology for Resource and Cost Analysis

Some of the methodology required for the analysis of cost within cost-effectiveness analysis has already been developed, although it is not in general use in educational institutions. Much of the methodology can be developed in a rather straightforward fashion simply by using techniques that have been developed elsewhere to identify and cost those resources that contribute directly to a given program. Several pitfalls exist, however, of which the analyst and the planner should be wary.

The objective of cost-effectiveness analysis is to facilitate choice among alternative programs. Therefore, costs that actually will remain fixed regardless of which programs are implemented (within limits) should not be "allocated" to particular programs. For example, a school district with enrollment in a particular size range will require a relatively fixed administrative staff to run it, with concomitant facilities to house and supply the administrative function. If the total cost of central administration were to be allocated to instructional programs, it would have to be done by largely arbitrary rules (except in some special cases where curriculum experts work in specific areas, for example); worse, if such allocations are made, changes in the direct cost of a program will appear to generate corresponding changes in the indirect, or allocated, cost, when, in fact, such changes would not actually follow. The key to realistic cost analysis in these instances is to identify those resources that will not change in response to program

140

changes and to set them aside under *unallocated* functional categories such as *administration* or *student services.* The question of which costs to allocate to which programs is of very real importance and will have to be resolved if cost-effectiveness analysis is to be carried out.

Special problems of resource allocation are also posed by "core" programs, programs that teach two or more subjects within a single session. If student achievement on each subject is measured separately, some decision must be made on how resources and activities within the program are apportioned among the subjects. If, however, a single measure of student achievement encompassing the several subjects has been devised, there is no need to allocate resources within the program.

These problems of resource allocation are most easily, and consistently, handled if a resource/cost model of the district has been developed. The development of a resource/cost model is also an essential step in achieving a workable methodology of analysis for educational planning. This model would comprise a set of mathematical expressions that relate variables describing the district and the programs to estimates of resource requirements and cost. With such a model, the analyst can formulate a description of the district at each future date and simulate the results of conducting each alternative program within the district.

The model must be broad enough so that each of the alternative programs can be fully described by the basic variables and relationships that make up the model. For example, requirements for teachers are usually directly related to projected enrollment, but if a program is largely self-paced, the number of teachers required may be more sensitive to the number of points in the learning sequence at which a teacher's assistance is needed than it is to enrollment.

Often, analysis will suggest that alternative programs be combined or that parts of programs be used in ways in which they were not used before. The model should be able to accommodate such variations as these, also. At the same time, care should be exercised to keep the model to a manageable size. There are so many aspects of school districts and educational programs that it is very easy for the number of variables included in the model to reach astronomical numbers. The only way to avoid this is for a skilled model builder who is well informed on the workings of educational institutions to tailor the model to the questions being addressed.

Effectiveness-Oriented Problems

The effectiveness of a program is a set of measures or indicators that describes the learning that the program has brought about. The impact of the program on such groups as parents, teachers, or the community at large may suggest peripheral benefits and can be used to choose among programs of apparently equal teaching effectiveness, but these benefits are not central to the problems surrounding effectiveness.

Measuring Effectiveness

The problems of defining and measuring the effectiveness of educational programs must be dealt with before the cost-effectiveness of alternatives can be analyzed. A central problem is the selection of valid and reliable instruments to measure the attainment of program goals. In many academic areas, there are tests of student achievement that may be used with some confidence. But if program goals include such objectives as changes in a child's conception of his own self-worth or improvements in the child's relationships with his peers, it may be more difficult to obtain or devise instruments that are valid and reliable; sometimes very expensive techniques such as individual observation or interview by trained psychologists must be used.

Even if acceptable measuring instruments are at hand, care must be taken to assure that they are administered in a consistent fashion; otherwise, the comparability of scores may be in question. This may require, for example, that a single team of testers administer all pre- and post-tests that are to be used as measures of effectiveness.

Finally, in interpreting measurements, the evaluator must decide which scoring mode is appropriate for the program goals. Grade-equivalent scores show the grade level at which the students are performing, but are not appropriate for inferences about the effect of the program on the rates of growth of children who started at different grade levels. For this purpose, percentile scores, which allow comparison of the relative position of students at different time points, are preferable. But the comparison of percentile scores is misleading as a measure of that *amount* of change, although it is useful as a measure of the *direction* of change in relative standing. A more accurate representation of the amount of change would be given by standard scores.

The Inadequacy of a Single Measure

Because of the complexity of the learning process, a full analysis of effectiveness should produce a *set* of measures and indicators, rather than a single measure. These measures and indicators should be monitored for several years in order to determine the effects of specific programs, because temporary spurts in growth may be of little value in the long run.

It is also important to determine the effects of specific programs on student performance in other educational programs, for example, the effect of a reading or mathematics program on those programs that make use of reading and computational skills such as history, science and the like. Although it seems logical to assume that improved performance in reading would carry over into improved performance in most other areas, some programs may encourage more of such carry-overs than others and some could even have negative effects. These considerations are important. In spite of the fact that they add a considerable burden to the task of analysis, parallel longitudinal testing programs in several subjects should be conducted. This is a potentially more valuable approach than just measuring achievement in a single dimension such as reading or mathematics. This means that setting up a research program specifically designed to test hypotheses about the interdependence of student achievement among academic subjects may be required to obtain a full description of the effectiveness of a single program.

As suggested earlier, educational programs may be directed specifically to goals other than improvement of student achievement in such subjects as reading and mathematics. For example, the program may seek to change the attitudes of the parents toward their children's schooling. Objectives such as these are usually thought of as fostering the attainment of the primary objective of student achievement, but the casual relationship may go in both directions. In any event, if the program devotes resources specifically to attain such ends, some means for determining to what extent the ends have been gained should be set up; and experimental design should include similar programs that do not devote resources to attaining such goals. This is particularly important when questions arise concerning whether to apply a successful program as a "package" or to use only those portions of it that seem to have been most conducive to its success.

If it is accepted that a single number for the dollar cost of a program conceals most of the information needed for decision-making, it should be even clearer that no single measure of program effectiveness will tell the whole story about the worth of the program because any program promotes several different kinds of change in the student. Because these changes are different in kind, no single unit exists to make commensurate the various changes attributable to a particular program. Thus, the effectiveness of a program can only be presented as a *set* of measures and indicators. In order to choose among alternative programs, the planner must then judge the relative importance of the various aspects of program effectiveness *as they apply to particular schools*. For example, the teaching of reading may be of primary importance in inner-city schools but may carry much less weight in schools in upper middle class neighborhoods. One of the major tasks is to decide how to rank measures and indicators of effectiveness vis-a-vis schools in various socioeconomic areas.

The Lack of a Methodology for Estimating the Effectiveness of Future Programs

Many aspects of the effectiveness of past and on-going programs can be measured by pre- and post-tests of student achievement. The relationships among test results and educational resources of various kinds can also be inferred by using standard techniques of regression analysis. Unfortunately, such analyses can only describe what has happened in the past and cannot be relied on to predict future program effectiveness if major changes in factors influencing learning (such as the social environment) are likely to take place. In addition, because the "real" resources in education may not yet have been identified, regression analyses may fail to treat the resource-effectiveness relationships that are crucial to the success of the program. Longitudinal studies address just such matters as these. It is to be hoped that such studies will contribute to the future development of program effectiveness models that can be used in educational planning in the same way that resource and cost models can be used today.

The Need for Criteria of Effectiveness

Lacking reliable models that relate educational resources to program effectiveness, it is necessary not only to weigh the relative importance of measures and indicators of different aspects of effectiveness, but to judge what levels of effectiveness are acceptable. If, for example, growth in reading achievement of one month-per-month of schooling is acceptable, is a growth rate of .95 month-per-month unacceptable? What if the latter growth rate is provided by a program that has more evident peripheral benefits than the former? Or what if the latter program reached more students for the same cost?

A rationale for the resolution of issues such as these is an integral part of the analysis; setting criteria, or standards for judging effectiveness, can help to supply this rationale. An important problem is whether different criteria are to be chosen for students with different characteristics, such as socioeconomic background, or whether the same criteria are to be applied to all students. An obvious need is to identify the average achievement of students with different characteristics under current educational programs. Whatever criteria are chosen, however, they should only provide general guidelines to the planner, rather than draw fine lines between the acceptable and the unacceptable. This is because the measures available are subject to error and, at the same time, are only proxies for what we would really like to assess — student learning. And this is why peripheral considerations can often tip the balance of decision between one program and another.

Analysis for Educational Planning

From the foregoing it should be clear that a single number purporting to be a cost-effectiveness ratio must hide more than it reveals about the overall value of an educational program. This is because the requirements of a program for resources are multidimensional and time-variant; the same may be said for indicators of program effectiveness. The educational planner, whether the analysis is aimed at a modest change in the current way of doing business or whether the analysis addresses the question of incorporating a major innovation, must have adequate information — information about the change and about its impact on the resource requirements of other programs and on the effectiveness of other programs. When the planner is considering the implementation of promising innovations in his district, he will need to know, for example, to what extent the success of the innovations depends on the *characteristics of the schools in which they have been used,* particularly the socioeconomic status of the school population. Because of the great variability among school districts and among schools within a given district, it seems unlikely that any innovation can be replicated in a new school without some modification. For example, the new school may already have some of the equipment needed for the program or may have to add more or fewer specialized personnel. Therefore, the resources required to implement the alternative innovations will have to be estimated for the new school. Ideally, this work should be done by collaboration between people familiar with the original programs and the school district personnel. If each district has information readily available about the resource requirements of its programs, it should then be able to estimate the resource requirements of the innovations as alternatives.

In addition, there are characteristics of a school that are related to the effectiveness of an innovation. It is very unlikely that the characteristics of the new school will exactly match those of the school successfully using the innovation. The characteristics of the student populations will differ in some respects; the relationships among the teachers, students, administrators, parents, and community will not be the same; and other educational programs in the schools will also be different. The impacts of these differences on program effectiveness will need to be estimated, through collaboration between people familiar with the original programs and the school district personnel. During the course of this work, a rationale for ranking criteria of effectiveness will be developed that will be tailored to each school in the district.

Because of these problems in comparing programs, the best way to use cost-effectiveness analysis is to construct *equal-cost alternatives,* that is, to adjust the dimensions of each program (such as the number of students enrolled) so that each program will incur approximately the same total cost over some appropriate period of time. In this way, the educational planners will be freed from having to consider cost when choosing among alternatives and can concentrate on the more difficult aspects of effectiveness, the phasing of dollar requirements, and the requirements for scarce resources. Because the use of a single measure of effectiveness (since any program brings about student changes of several kinds that are not commensurable) is less defensible than is the use of dollar cost, the reverse of this procedure — to construct *equal-effectiveness alternatives* — is a dubious approach. Moreover the projection of the estimated cost of a program can be done with a great deal more confidence than can its effectiveness.

In educational planning, one alternative, simply to continue current practice, should be included for baseline data. Although this alternative will usually not incur the same cost as will the innovative programs being compared, it is important to know its projected future cost and effectiveness so that the added resource and cost requirements incurred by the innovative programs can be estimated. Then the *incremental* requirements that are associated with improved effectiveness will be known. (It often turns out that these incremental requirements are small compared with the requirements simply to maintain current practice, even though they might seem large when considered in isolation.) Thus, the first step toward cost-effectiveness analysis must be to estimate the future resource requirements and effectiveness of current programs.

There are many instances in which the future resource requirements of an innovative program are quite uncertain. This may arise because of uncertainties in projected enrollments, for example. In such a situation, it is important to know whether the choice among alternative programs would change if the future were different from some "most likely" case. If one program appears desirable under a wide range of future possibilities, it is obviously a good choice. If not, it is possible that the educational planner will want to choose a program that hedges against future change rather than the one that seems best in the most likely case.

The results of all this work will be estimated measures or indicators of resource requirements, cost and ranked aspects of effectiveness projected over the time period of interest for each program and for alternative futures. The display of these items, along with supporting explanatory test, will provide planners with the information of the resource requirements and effectiveness of alternative innovative programs that they will need for making informed choices. Thus, a carefully designed display and textual presentation is a significant part of the resource-effectiveness analysis. Only in this way can the educational planner guard against the indiscriminate use of a single cost-effectiveness "number" so far removed from its limitations that it is not only useless, but dangerous.

REFERENCES

Barro, S. M. "Modeling resource utilization in a school district," in S. A. Haggart, et al. *Program budgeting for school district planning: concepts and applications.* Santa Monica, California: The RAND Corporation, RM-6116-RC, November, 1969.

Carpenter, M. B., and S. A. Haggart *Analysis of educational programs within a program budgeting system.* Santa Monica, California: The RAND Corporation, P-4195, September, 1969.

Dei Rossi, J. A. "The program budget and the traditional budget," in S. A. Haggart, et al. *Program budgeting for school district planning: concepts and applications.* Santa Monica, California: The RAND Corporation, RM-6116-RC, November, 1969.

Fisher, G. H. *Cost considerations in systems analysis.* New York: American Elsevier Publishing, 1970.

Haggart, S. A. "Considerations in developing a program budgeting system," in S. A. Haggart, et al. *Program budgeting for school district planning: concepts and applications.* Santa Monica, California: The RAND Corporation, RM-6116-RC, November, 1969.

Mandansky, Albert "Uncertainty," in E. S. Quade and W. I. Boucher (eds.) *Systems analysis and policy planning: applications in defense.* Santa Monica, California: The RAND Corporation, R-439-PR (Abridged), June, 1968.

CHAPTER VII

Evaluating

The evaluating process is an essential part of an ERM System. The validity of the evaluating process which was conceptually presented in Chapter II rests directly upon the establishment of effective objectives and upon the development of effective measurements to evaluate the extent to which the objectives are attained. This is a simplified view of the evaluating process, but in essence it is what must occur if the evaluating function is to have any value in an ERM System. A discussion of the role of evaluating and procedures to be utilized in evaluating educational programs and planning activities is found in this chapter. It also discusses the relevance to an ERM System of some of the current evaluation activities which are being utilized by school officials for the improvement of school processes and services.

Evaluating in Educational Resources Management

An Educational Resources Management System holds promise of compelling educators to the earlier accomplishment of an effective breakthrough in the application of evaluating to operational processes. The concern is to evaluate the effectiveness of both total and specific program operations against criteria established for various program objectives. The evaluating process is concerned not only with the measurement of the intermediate and final outcomes of programs, but also with the use of data in the feedback procedures as it relates to the development of the planning and programming processes. Evaluation results are used in the management process as a means of monitoring each inter-related segment of the process. Evaluation plans for use in each of these activities should be included in the design for each program plan.

The management of educational resources should initiate a system which requires all current programs and planning activities to be subjected to a systematic and an analytical process. As ineffective programs are phased out through this process, their replacement with more meaningful qualitative learning processes and services should be subjected to the same procedure — a kind of *phase-in* and *phase-out* operation.

Effective evaluation is dependent upon selecting the correct procedures for evaluating the objectives of a program. Evaluation cannot be treated as an afterthought. Careful planning for evaluation is essential from the initial phase of a program. Too often evaluation has been used to justify what has been done. Evaluation must be built into the management structure of all educational decision-making operations. The overall strategy for developing an effective evaluation plan that will assess the quality aspects of an educational program is to build a mode which will be usable in the future with a minimum of change. At the same time some changes will be desirable in an evolving program. The mode for evaluating must include systematic data collection, research design planning, analysis, feedback, the utilization of the research findings, and dissemination and monitoring of the processes of planning, programming and budgeting.

Evaluation as used in an ERM System context is more than testing. Measurement devices, properly designed and used, permit the collecting, analyzing, and interpreting of vitally-needed data. Evaluation embraces but transcends measurement. To these objective data are applied the judgmental process to make assessments regarding which processes and outcomes are deemed to be of most importance, of greatest worth and of highest priority. These assessments are inescapably somewhat subjective. At the budgetary level, for example, after all program analysis has been completed, feedback received and interpreted, recycling accomplished, old and new performance data analyzed against original or modified objectives — then informed, rational, analytical *decisions* are still to be made about what is best for the reinforcement of learning and the total development of the students.

The Primacy of Objectives

Since evaluation strives to measure the outcomes of a certain method, system or function in relation to stated objectives, it provides a fundamental basis for planning and decision-making. Before evaluation is undertaken, performance objectives need to be established through the planning and programming activities in which a desired outcome is expressed. Objectives, as pointed out previously, should be as specific as possible in terms of the expected end results. With these objectives clearly and precisely set forth, school officials can select the procedures, content, activities and methods from among several alternatives which might be followed to reach the intended destination.

Well defined objectives will allow for the continuous evaluation of the program plan. Continuous evaluation will provide for the adaptation of the program plan to a given situation. Without continuous evaluation it is impossible to introduce feedback into the program, not only to the planners and other administrative officials, but to the teachers as well, all of whom may use this feedback to alter teaching styles and plan revised learning activities. Therefore, objectives established in terms of anticipated behavior and related to the specific conditions and criteria of acceptable performance at various levels encourage continuous evaluating as a planned and integrated process in all programs. Objectives stated in substantive terms permit subsequent evaluation to be meaningful.

148

Characteristics of Evaluation Personnel

Essentially, the concepts and techniques which assist evaluating activities have their roots in philosophy, sociology, anthropology, linguistics, history, economics, and psychology. Persons from these disciplines have frequently contributed to evaluating activities. The contributions have not been in the answers provided but in the perspectives generated. Different viewpoints do not resolve automatically the perplexing problem of planning, programming and budgeting but they do enable school officials to see the situation in a new light or to try a new remedy that otherwise may not have seemed plausible. Evaluating specialists will be needed increasingly to lend proper support and assistance to educational resources management activities. Personnel assigned to evaluating activities must possess the competence to cope with evaluating problems. Above all, personnel assigned to the evaluating function must be able to derive the principles on which to make decisions about educational practices.

Evaluating includes the task of gathering information about the nature and worth of alternative programs in order to improve decisions about the management of those programs.

Evaluating can be viewed as a form of applied research which places special demands upon the methods of inquiry. Evaluating is concerned with finding relevant, immediate answers for decision-making purposes. Evaluation must deal with both personal standards and subjective judgments. Evaluating may be both an individual and a team activity. The need will be for personnel who are facile in using unobtrusive measures for data collection and analysis as well as in more traditional procedures.

Evaluators encourage the use of criteria for assessing program performance by applying the tests of clarity, internal consistency, comprehensiveness, and compatability at each state of the planning, programming and budgeting processes. If criteria are not clearly stated, a restatement of the objectives is to be encouraged.

A job of evaluating is to monitor program operations. Through the educational resources management system pertinent information is collected, analyzed and reported to appropriate staff members responsible for the four processes of an ERM System. Measurement, sampling, report writing, statistical analysis, and technical functions are typical services provided by the evaluating personnel.

Applications of Systems Theory

There have been many technical devices proposed as approaches to evaluation, e.g., operational research, linear and non-linear programming, systems engineering, computerization, simulation, set theory, cybernetics, decision theory, queuing theory, and many diverse forms of model building. None of these is a panacea for evaluation systems.

The essential problem in the consideration of any of these evaluation designs and their application to an ERM System is the limitation imposed by scientific analytical procedures. This procedure operates on hypothetical assumptions which require that an entity be resolved into, and hence reconstituted from, its parts — in both a material and conceptual sense. Any application of these analytical procedures is dependent upon the degree to which the effects of the system can be isolated. It appears, then, that the analysis of education, which exhibits a maximum of interactions and frustrating *nonlinear* relationships, cannot be restricted to such analytical methods.

Evaluation Designs Appropriate to an ERM System

An immediate goal of evaluating is a more effective analysis which leads to a better understanding of the operations of a school system, but the ultimate objective is to make design changes leading to improved operations. The System Development Corporation (Coulson & Cogswell, 1965) combines evaluation with analysis in a series of steps leading toward improvement. The full series involves:

"In the *analysis* phase our objective is to specify the systems structure and operations so that we can identify critical problems — problems that must be given special consideration in any new design. This stage helps us to identify logical errors in the planning, to uncover glaring oversights, and to detect unnecessary overlap in the operations. It is an absolute prerequisite to efficient systems management.

"In the *design* phase, improved designs are formulated. The design recommendation may include improved procedures for handling information, modification in the decision-making procedures, and changes in the role of personnel and in the application of material resources.

"The systems *test* phase is an evaluation of the design recommendations, before implementation. Simulation techniques and field test techniques may be employed. In the case of simulation, the design improvements may be tested in a computer model of the school, or the actual design changes may be tested under laboratory conditions with people playing key roles in the procedures.

"The *implementation* phase of the systems approach is concerned with the installation of the tested design changes. Training personnel is usually of primary interest in the implementation staff."

The analysis and evaluating techniques are not ends in themselves or magic formulas for solving educational problems, but they do offer two advantages over more traditional "common sense" analysis procedures:

". . . First, the formal structure of the flow charts provides a relatively systematic framework for examining interactions among the various components of a complex system. A person who applies systems analysis procedures is less likely to overlook major weaknesses in the communication network or in the decision structure of the system.

"A second advantage is that the school design variables with which a systems analysis is primarily concerned (e. g., communication and decision procedures) are variables that can be manipulated. And this is ultimate purpose of the systems analysis, to identify operations and procedures that can be modified so as to produce a more effective system. The variables that are often examined in conventional analyses, such as the number of square feet of floor space per student or the socio/economic status of students, are much less amenable to direct manipulation." (Coulson & Cogswell, 1964, p.10).

Stufflebeam Model

Stufflebeam (1967) developed the C.I.P.P. (context/input/process/product) strategy for evaluation primarily as a tool in the evaluation of Title III projects. This model appears to have validity also for a systems evaluation as an integral part of a complete ERM System including the planning, programming and budgeting process as well as in the more specific evaluating phase. In brief, the Stufflebeam model stresses four generalized stages of evaluating.

1. *Context Evaluation.* The major objective of this first stage of the C.I.P.P. Model . . . is to define the environment where change is to occur, the environment's unmet needs, and the problems underlying those needs. . . .

2. *Input Evaluation.* Its objective is to list relevant capabilities of the proposing agency, strategies which may be appropriate for meeting program goals, and designs which may be appropriate for achieving objectives associated with each program goal. . . .

3. *Process Evaluation.* Once a planned course of action has been approved and implementation of the plan has begun, Process Evaluation is needed to provide periodic feedback to project administrators and others responsible for continuous control and refinement of plans and procedures. The objective of Process Evaluation is to detect or predict, during the implementation stages, defects in the procedural design or its implementation. . . .

4. *Product Evaluation.* This form of evaluation is used to determine the effectiveness of the project. The objective of Product Evaluation is to relate outcomes to objective and to context and input, i. e., to measure and interpret outcomes. . . .

Churchman Model

Another model selected as relevant to the application of a total ERM System is one proposed by Churchman (1968). This model provides a means of measuring performance of a system in a logical way, which is a goal of any evaluation. Churchman outlines the following basic considerations that must be kept in mind when measuring the performance of any system:

1. The total system objectives and, more specifically, the performance measures of the whole system;

2. The system's environment: the fixed constraints;

3. The resources of the system;

4. The components of the system, their activities, goals and measures of performance; and
5. The management of the system.

To the extent a school district can operate with a clear understanding of its own internal processes, it will almost certainly operate more effectively.

Adaptations and Combinations of Models

With several models and definitions from which to choose, the school official is perhaps placed in the enviable position of being an eclectic — choosing those areas applicable to education and forming a new model. But an eclectic position does not justify a cafeteria approach — just selecting what appeals to one's present whims or appetites. In approaching an evaluating task, it is necessary to select models of evaluation techniques carefully. The process is a rational and logical method of systematically narrowing down the myriad devices available to those which seem the most appropriate for the circumstances.

The model as proposed by Churchman provides a listing of considerations to be kept in mind in the evaluating process. Although there is some similarity between the two models, the Stufflebeam model provides a sound basis for approaching evaluation in an ERM System, with the Churchman and SDC models as checks against overlooking a segment of a program which might provide valuable input to evaluation.

Context evaluation provides for a description of the environment in which the program is to take place. The focus of this description is on the sub systems of the domain to be served, the unmet needs of the domain, and the basic casual factors underlying each of these needs.

Input evaluation describes the capabilities of the school district and identifies available strategies for meeting program objectives and appropriate resources.

Process evaluation requires the evaluator to accept the specific educational program under review as it is actually operating at any given time. The educational program is an operational program, not a carefully controlled experimental design, but one nevertheless capable of being subjected to the most rigorous technical, yet sensitive, scrutiny.

Product evaluation applies multiple criteria appropriate for the objectives of the activity to make rational analyses and interpretations of the outcomes. The product evaluation is a basis for decisions regarding the combination, termination, or refocusing of the educational activities.

Evaluation as Related to Measurement of Student Progress

A significant purpose of the ERM System is to provide more precise knowledge about student progress in alternative educational programs. Student progress is in terms of evaluating the impact of school services and processes on achievement. The measurement of outcomes has taken place

152

in the schools continuously, but oftentimes without a clear articulation of specific objectives designed to improve the quality of education. Measurement usually has not been concerned with the progress of the student toward objectives. Students who have scored above the average are the ones who have been judged as successes in the process of education. A great deal of measurement in the past has been devoid of measures of progress toward objectives. It has focused upon inadequate judgments of quality in education.

Present patterns of measurement are almost exclusively related to achievement in knowledge and skills. The impact is greatest on students whose facility for taking tests is not well honed. The result is that many young people are judged to be "slow learners" when actually their "slowness" may be a matter of reflection on questions and protracted consideration of possible answers. Students who have a skill for dealing with tests generally emerge victorious from the ordeal; those who do not are viewed as poor learners. For these and many other reasons, current patterns of measurement, so widespread in the schools of the United States, have not adequately fulfilled the objective of improving the quality of education.

National Assessment

Rational decisions about the allocation and management of resources in education, as envisioned in an ERM System concept, are greatly facilitated by possession of accurate knowledge of how well students are reaching the educational goals which have been projected. The "National Assessment of Educational Progress," now administered by the Educational Commission of the States, is the nation's most ambitious program for measuring student advancement toward goals. Launched in 1964, this program includes both clearly-stated objectives and appropriate instruments for assessing student progress toward these objectives. Specific performance objectives for ten subject areas have been developed by outstanding scholars and teachers. These objectives were formulated on the basis of three major criteria: (1) considered important by scholars; (2) accepted as an educational task by the school; and, (3) considered desirable as school processes and services by thoughtful lay citizens.

Instruments based upon these objectives have been designed to assess student progress. In response to questions as to why new instruments for assessing student progress had to be developed, National Assessment officials note that:

> "Current tests in use in the schools have not been constructed to provide a means for assessing educational progress with children. They have been constructed to obtain an average score in the classroom, grade, or school and to identify individual differences in performance. For instance, one-third of all children in a large metropolitan area recently tested by a well-known achievement test made zero scores. This does not mean that one-third of the city's children learned *nothing;* it means that the tests had no exercises appropriate for measuring what those children *had* learned." (Womer, 1970, p. 4).

The National Assessment Program is intended to provide an index of learning progress in such areas as reading, mathematics, social studies, vocational education, literature, art, and music. Clearly this national program will have a powerful impact on the entire educational process throughout the United States. Undoubtedly it will serve as a basis for discussion and articulation of educational objectives and for developing reliable procedures to measure student advancement toward those objectives. These objectives can be categorized within the context of some of the broader goals for education and related to the educational programs and services provided by local school districts to accomplish these goals. But it must be kept clearly in mind that the National Assessment Program is concerned with goals and performance — a central focus of an Educational Resources Management System — and not directly with evaluating school services and processes.

Other National and State Approaches

Not only is assessment of student progress toward goals integral to the design and operation of an ERM System, but other kinds of data about the educational system are also necessary if educational resources are to be effectively managed. There are currently several major projects which are concerned with the goals-objectives-school services-processes sequence.

The Colorado Department of Education has announced procedures to define educational goals, and to seek information on how some students are advancing with respect to goals. The Department has developed pilot programs in specific academic areas in 31 school districts involving 62,000 students in grades 3, 6, 9 and 12 to explore more effectively ways for increasing student achievement. California and Michigan have embarked upon similar programs.

The Pennsylvania Educational Quality Assessment is perhaps one of the more ambitious statewide programs for translating educational goals into educational policy. A publication of this project presents data which relate the elements and services relevant to student performance to each of ten enumerated goals. The findings regarding achievement in one area are related to findings in other goal dimensions. The Pennsylvania report is significant as one pioneering attempt of a state to articulate goals for education and to launch an extensive program designed to see what kind of variables affect student progress toward goals.

There are other approaches to more effective measurement which may also provide some insights. The Bureau of School Programs Evaluation in the New York State Department of Education has developed sets of performance indicators to appraise school effectiveness and to point the way for improvement in school processes and services. Performance indicators are considered as a set of modules which relate important variables to the objectives of the schools. Student achievement, non-cognitive functioning and social functioning are three aspects of student performance to be measured by the New York State study.

In Florida the Commissioner of Education has been charged by the Florida Legislature to develop a state educational assessment program. The Florida assessment program is intended to serve both the public and the profession to provide each school district with relevant data to school board members, administrators and the public with which they may appraise educational progress more readily.

The Cleveland-based "Yardstick Program" employs "yardsticks" or various instruments to appraise student advance with respect to school services and processes. This project has a "growth gauge" for school districts to use in measuring progress of students in relation to social and economic backgrounds as well as intelligence. This procedure presumes to measure the contribution of a school district to pupil performance. Data also relate educational costs to student performance.

The efforts now underway in evaluating school programs and services are major ones. They represent a positive and constructive response to the need for a better means of identifying measures of school quality. Perhaps the ultimate goals of these efforts will be the development of a model or set of models for predicting measures of productivity of the educational process which can be applied with considerable precision to educational resources management. But until that time arrives, school officials must proceed with the tools and techniques currently available to them. Criteria and procedures have evolved which are extremely useful to the educational resources management processes.

Criteria and Procedures

Criteria and procedures for evaluating programs and planning activities are established for these purposes: (1) to provide those involved in planning and programming with data to determine how feasible the programs may be, (2) how effective they may or may not be in fulfilling these objecttives, (3) to identify specific weaknesses, (4) limitations of programs as a basis for possible revision and (5) to provide citizens of the school community with information to show the qualitative results of learning activities.

In carrying out these procedures, evaluating has two functions:
1. To provide technical support to those engaged in planning and programming.
2. To serve as a semi-independent assessment unit for the school district.

The obligation to provide dependable data for intended audiences to judge the quality of an effort can best be fulfilled when the evaluating personnel assume the primary responsibility for measuring the effectiveness of learning procedures. Therefore, an evaluation plan is developed for each program plan and documentation of the plan and changes in the evaluating plan are recorded in a monitoring file. It is reasonable to expect that a local school district would want to establish a resource file of the evaluating reports completed by its own staff as well as evaluating reports from other school districts which could be relevant to the local situation. With a local data bank, a school district will have the opportunity to review periodically the data, compare selective criteria and make adjustments on a gradual rather than a crisis basis. When these data are reviewed, (including where applicable a comparison of norms — national, state or local) it will be possible to spot strengths and weaknesses in the educational program. These data are useful in identifying trends in supporting more effective operation within the school district and for the purpose of showing the relevancy of programs to the changing demands of society. With the development of a local data bank, the articulation and network usage and retrieval system can become an indispensable source of information for planning, programming, budgeting and evaluating purposes.

Evaluation and the Evolution of a Program Plan

For most of the program plans under development there is an evolutionary pattern of activities and events. The pattern of activities and events will vary from district to district to some extent because of differences in program objectives and the kinds of resources utilized in planning and development.

One of the concerns of evaluation in relation to program activities is the establishment of the cost of an ongoing activity or existing program as related to its accomplishments. School officials are concerned with achieving an optimal relationship between costs and benefits in both existing and new programs, either in terms of obtaining the desired level of accomplishment at least cost, or a maximum level of accomplishment within fixed cost limits. Thus an exceedingly important factor in the evaluation of any program is the cost of achieving its objectives, including the relative costs of various levels of achievement and the comparative costs of alternative programs having somewhat parallel results. Costs must be measured not only in terms of dollars but also in terms of:

The time required for implementation and effective operation;

The requirements for additional skilled manpower as compared to availability;

The impact upon present manpower in terms of additional training, changed work load and structured roles;

Costs in terms of capital outlays for facilities;

Remodeling (or obsolescence) of present equipment and facilities;

Operations and maintenance costs after initial investment has been made.

Costs typically are obtainable from the records of the administrator responsible for a particular program. In practice, however, cost data are seldom available in usable form. Where a program is part of the school system's larger operation, the portion of cost attributable to it may not be broken out, and seldom can cost and program features be matched other than by estimates. Special effort is thus justified to arrange for the collection of meaning-

Program Plan Developmental Status	Type of Evaluation	Definition of Evaluation	Major Emphasis	Minor Emphasis
I. Exploratory Units	Exploratory Tests -Discard -Recycle -Retain	A tryout of parts of the unit with a limited number of potential users under controlled conditions	Ascertainment of Feasibility	
II. Prototype of Program Plan	Pilot Test -Discard -Recycle -Retain	An intensive tryout of the program plan with a limited number of potential users under controlled condition.	Collection of Revision Data	Replicability
III. Interim Program Plan -Test -Release	Field Test -Discard -Recycle -Retain	A systematic testing of the program plan with a rigorously selected sample from the target group in a realistic setting	Collection of Attainment Data	Revision Data
IV. Operational Program Plan -Discard -Release	Operational Test	A test of the effectiveness of the completely self-sufficient program with evaluation limited to data collection and analysis.	Collection of Evidence that Program Plan is effective	Revision Data

Figure 1. Types of Evaluation and Program Plan Studies.

157

ful cost data, and models for determining the cost data needed for cost benefit comparisons may be developed.

For purposes of evaluation, each of the program plan development stages identified in Chapter IV is seen as demanding different emphases and techniques. Specifically, evaluation within the *exploratory* stage focuses primarily upon the question of feasibility. Evaluation within the *prototype* stage focuses primarily upon the collection of revision data. Evaluation within the interim stage focuses primarily upon the attainment of objectives. Evaluation of the *operation* plan focuses primarily upon evidence that the plan works (see Figure 1).

A needs assessment or a sequential series of them would be a preparatory first step to establish base line data embodying an inventory of current programs, resources, and needs related to stated and specific educational objectives. On the basis of such an inventory and evaluation of existing programs, additional program development activities would typically progress through the four stages discussed in Chapter IV.

The relationship of the program plan, its development status and type of evaluation is summarized in the following schematic where four types of evaluation, their definitions and their relationships of the "various levels" of program plan development are detailed.

It may be possible to find standardized measurements to evaluate existing or newly developed program plans, but more than likely the measurements will have to be developed. The evaluating design should clearly show:

(a) methods of evaluation,
(b) times and uses of evaluation,
(c) auditing procedures,
(d) objective-subjective data,
(e) sampling techniques as necessary,
(f) an estimate of the output differential anticipated, and
(g) a cost-effectiveness ratio, if desired.

The flow of activities and procedures in the evaluating process is shown in Figure 2.

Contents of an Evaluation Plan

The heart of an evaluative effort is an adequate plan. An adequate evaluation plan is derived as the program plan is developed. It is arrived at jointly by those responsible for evaluating and appropriate representatives from the planning and programming teams. A completely evolved plan would fully address all the following essential topics:

1. A brief historical review of the program plan under development.
2. A description of the instructional system including:
   a. Specification of the contents of the activity which is sufficient to enable citizens or school board members to know what the program plan does or contains.

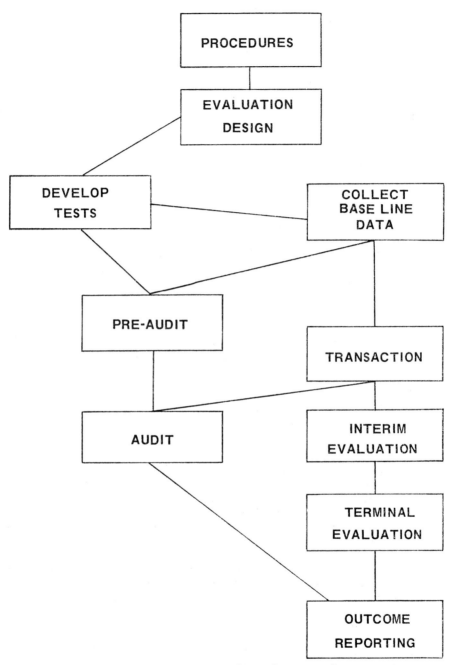

Figure 2. *Flow of Activities and Procedures in Evaluating.*

b. Description of the intended student population including information about the educational levels, cultural backgrounds, age and other characteristics and skills which influence the students' attainment of objectives established for the program plan.

c. Description of procedures and conditions for administering the program plan and criterion tests.

3. A list of the performance objectives which the student will be capable of performing after experiencing the program.

4. Details of the exploratory test including description of:
   a. Materials
   b. Conditions
   c. Procedures
   d. Subjects
   e. Questions to be considered

5. Details of pilot testing:
   a. Specification of questions to be answered and data to be gathered during the test of prototype materials.
   b. Specification of the design, the conditions, and the procedures to be employed in collecting data during the pilot testing phase.
   c. Specification of the sampling procedures to be employed during this phase (the sample, sampling procedure, and criteria in selecting individuals or sites for tests).
   d. Identification of the data collection instruments to be employed or the specifications for selecting or creating such instruments.
   e. Specification of a plan for reducing, analyzing, and reporting data to be collected.

6. Details of field testing
   a. Specification of questions to be answered and data to be gathered during a testing phase to benefit the program team and the intended user (this information may be the basis of the technical report).
   b. Specification of the experimental design, the conditions, and the procedures to be employed in collecting data during the field testing phase.
   c. Specification of sampling procedures to be employed (the sample, sampling procedure, and criteria to be used in selecting individuals or sites for tests of the prototype program plan must be described fully).
   d. Identification of the data collection instruments to be employed or the specifications for selecting or creating such instruments.
   e. Specification of a plan for reducing, analyzing and reporting the data to be collected (the intended recipient of the data should be specified).

7. The details of a field testing must fully explore in rigorous manner all aspects of the target population's performance of the objectives

with recognition and recording of environmental constraints on the use of the program plan.

8. A listing of related items such as plans for implementing the program, reports of current tests of the program by other schools or agencies, etc.

Evaluating Responsibilities

Responsibility for executing the various aspects of the evaluation plan should be affixed. The division of responsibility for carrying out various aspects of evaluating may be as follows:

1. Development of a plan for evaluation should be the joint responsibility of those engaged in the evaluating, planning, programming, and budgeting processes.

2. Within the framework of the plan for evaluating, the programming team should have primary responsibility for conducting and reporting evaluative tests during the early developmental phases. They may, if they choose, satisfy this responsibility through use of support provided by the evaluating team. Each evaluative test of the materials will result in the production of a test report. Depending on the needs of a particular program plan development phase, the test report may vary from a two or three paragraph memo to a fully developed technical report.

3. When the programming team feels that a given version of a program plan is viable (i. e., objective evaluation indicates it will meet the claims made for it), then the primary responsibility for evaluating shifts to those assigned evaluating responsibilities. Typically, the program plan will be considered in interim form at this point. The shift of primary responsibility allows the semi-independent aspect of evaluation to offer assurance the program plan meets specific performance objectives. This activity is termed "operational testing" and follows the established plan for evaluation. Revision data as necessary are made explicit and presented in usable form to the planning and programming team. Outcome reporting typically is made available to the superintendent for both internal and external communication.

Monitoring System

A monitoring system is necessary to document implementation of the evaluating plan. The system utilized for monitoring evaluation endeavors requires the maintenance and periodic inspection of a set of prescribed records. Thus, the evaluative status of any given activity should be readily apparent to school officials by scanning appropriate records. The collection of evidence of effective monitoring should be the primary responsibility of evaluating. However, the records for any activity should be a joint product of the effort of the planning, programming, and evaluating processes.

Briefly, the monitoring system will deal with the following kinds of questions:

1. Is there an acceptable plan for the evaluation?
2. Have the evaluating materials been prepared? (e. g., test, scoring, systems, methods of analyzing data, examiners' manuals, forms clearances)
3. Have major instruments been produced where production is not accomplished by the planner or programmer? (i. e., tests printed, materials purchased)
4. Have the evaluating instruments been administered?
5. Has the aspect or component to be tested been specified? (if an entire system is tested as a unit, this must be specified)
6. Have reports which deal specifically with questions on performance objectives been prepared?

Evaluating and Value Judgments

An evaluation designed to assist the decision-maker necessarily involves a large element of human judgment. An important quality of this approach to evaluation is common sense. A measure of common sense in the systematic analysis of educational problems is simplicity. One fundamental problem in the management of educational resources has been the lack of valid, reliable, agreed upon, and quantifiable measures for educational output. The ability of school officials to characterize adequately educational outcomes has meant that attempts at measuring educational quality have concentrated on cost, choosing a minimum cost system that appears to reach some narrow set of objectives.

Obviously, the problem of defining educational objectives and the subsequent measurement of educational outcomes is a task of considerable magnitude. In applying the techniques of an Educational Resources Management System, there may be a tendency to reduce the measurement of educational outcomes to a minimum. However, the narrowing of measures will not result in any clear-cut answers.

Far more emphasis upon experimentation and evaluation will have to accompany the systems application to education. If measurement techniques can be developed which characterize educational outcomes adequately, then the application of analysis and the evaluation process can hold great promise for the improvement of educational practices.

When observations at the end of learning sequence are used to determine how successful some educational activity has been, the interpretation necessarily must embody value judgments. Thus the results may be viewed positively by one educator and negatively by another. Consequently, the measurement design, if it is to be effective for evaluating purposes, must include separate measures responsive to the local value system. Thus, the task in evaluating is to develop objectives which satisfy the user of the results and at the same time make them sufficiently specific so as to render the results reliable.

Educators will continue to find ways for utilizing modern technical developments more effectively in the evaluating process for the purpose of helping to attain the objectives established for the schools. As changes are introduced in the educational system or in the social setting in which the learner participates, the need for carefully developed evaluation plans will be greatly increased. A systems-based approach to such evaluation is linked with a total educational resources management design. This approach is supported through sound value judgments by competent processors.

Rationale

Pressure is mounting for school administrators to justify the educational programs they administer. Increasing costs of education, restrictions on the resources available for education, and demands for more relevant education are among the factors placing new kinds of processes upon public school districts. At the heart of these pressures is a need for more and better information about the cost, the effectiveness, and the products of education. Current evaluation efforts are not adequate to produce these kinds of information with sufficient precision.

The emerging evaluating process is sensitive to the nuances of the educational process. It is specific enough to relate to the problems of day-to-day operations. It is broad enough to encompass the many influences impinging upon the educational system and the learner. In addition, meaningful evaluating relates all important aspects of the educational enterprise. Studying only students, school processes, or the forces of society as isolated factors provides an incomplete, or perhaps worse, a warped picture of what the educational system is doing.

Finally, evaluating provides the basis for action. Describing and comparing programs are important and necessary, but acting on the best available information should be the culmination of any evaluating activity. The evaluating techniques suggested here are manageable; they comply with the criteria and procedures included in the evaluation models; and they provide for a logical evaluation of a school's objectives.

REFERENCES

Churchman, C. West. *The Systems Approach.* New York: Dell Publishing Co., 1968.
Coulson, John E. and Cogswell, John R. "Systems Analysis in Education." Paper presented at the Conference on the Development and Use of Data Banks for Educational Research, Boston, December 4, 1964.
Stufflebeam, Daniel. "The Use and Abuse of Evaluation in Title III." *Theory and Practice.* June, 1967.
Womer, Frank B. *National Assessment Objectives.* "Education Commission of the United States." Denver: 1970.

CHAPTER VIII

Staff Development

Man as a thinker has turned his energies to the understanding of human development and how man learns. This human potential and the consequent knowledge base which can shape the development of a school system have been subdued by tradition and by force of habit.

The environment for learning created by the American culture based upon the aspirations of a free people has provided a boundless opportunity for the development of an outstanding system for education. This environmental potential also remains virtually untapped.

A third potential is the system of values. The American democratic tradition emphasizes values which include participation. Americans place a high value upon involvement.

A fourth potential poses the possibility of interrelating the elements of the human potential, the environmental potential and the value-system potential into a system utilizing modern management tools of the technological system potential. The methodology of analysis and the management of resources are some of the techniques yet to be applied (in an effective manner) to the education process. The introduction of an ERM System can well be a needed breakthrough in capitalizing upon the potential represented by the technological systems.

The development of a staff to meet the challenge of a system for aiding in the decision-making process for the management of educational resources is the subject of this chapter.

In the sections which follow, particular attention is focused upon the point at which learning takes place. The role of the teacher is not necessarily considered in the traditional sense as one who imparts information, administers tests and distributes grades. Learning may occur with the aid of anyone who assumes the responsibility for the development of knowledge, attitudes and skills — the overall growth and learning of the student. The teacher, therefore, encompasses a different set of attributes. The importance of the role of other school personnel emerges as a contributor to learning — at the point of interaction between the teacher and student. These other personnel include the principal, bus driver, the secretary, and the custodian. The teacher is a facilitator who will include students, parents, and laymen as a means for attaining objectives.

What can a school district do to assist the individual teacher in providing relevant learning experiences for students? An ERM System can help the district to answer this question. Curriculum development and in-service education can and should become an integral part of planning, programming, budgeting and evaluating. Through participation in the decision-making process and through learning new skills and developing new insights as needed, the full potential of the staff can be realized. An ERM System makes the provision for staff, laymen, and students to participate in a joint venture. Efforts then become more cohesive. Learning becomes more significant for students.

Staff Involvement

An ERM System will succeed to the extent that creative, imaginative administrators involve *all* persons affected — boards of education, teachers, students, and laymen. Taking advantage of the potential of an ERM System is a challenge to today's educational leadership.

Earlier chapters include a discussion of the concepts and activities appropriate for each of the four processes: planning, programming, budgeting, and evaluating. These chapters emphasize that decisions affecting learning should be made the basis of insights gained through the interactions of the four processes in the system.

In the discussion which follows, a key aspect of each process is selected to emphasize the importance of staff involvement and understanding. Specific suggestions and examples are given for ways in which staff can be involved.

The importance of the assessment of needs is an essential part of determining goals and cannot be over-emphasized. A superficial process of assembling pre-conceived goals of staff, students and citizens does little to improve planning. People, however, can — and do — sharpen their perceptions by re-examining their thinking through the challenge of interaction with others. In the process new information is gathered and utilized. It is naïve to assume that consensus can be reached in all aspects of the curriculum through the process of interaction. However, goal classification and determination is a developmental and cooperative process wherein there is a continuing re-examination of new data. The consensus gained represents the best possible direction for the district at a particular time.

Determining school district goals is probably one of the most difficult missions involving teachers, students and citizens. The importance of this involvement is emphasized in the conceptual design for an ERM System. A method for involving people is through the use of the *task force* as described in the chapter on planning. It is important to limit the size of the task force to enhance meaningful discussion. Surely a task force for developing school district goals should be small enough that it can be a discussion group. Its best work, however, will result from a maximum utilization of efforts made by representative *sub-groups* from each school-community in the district. Interaction between the task force and the sub-groups is, therefore, desirable.

The task force is comprised of citizens who are representative of sub-groups. Each member is selected for a capability of contributing to the mission of the task force. Through oral and written communication the task force and sub-groups have the opportunity to understand the varying points of view of those involved in the decision-making process. Consideration should be given to the possibility of each sub-group taking part in the selection of the task force members. Citizens, staff, and students are included in the representative groups.

As the task force prepares a report to the superintendent and board of education, a continuing flow of communication is maintained with the sub-groups. People who have an opportunity to be involved from the very outset are more likely to understand and use the results.

General goals have long been considered as something to be talked about, and furthermore assumed to be influential to teaching practice simply because they are written, adopted, and distributed. If the goals which are developed through an ERM System are to be functional, that is, to provide direction for implementation, then goal planning *must* involve the people who are affected. Goals emerge from the examination of the critical issues of living and learning *now*. These issues affect the individual, the family, the sub-community, the community, the nation, and the world.

Many school districts are actively engaged in developing goals as a part of a *systems approach* in which interrelationships with curriculum, budget, and evaluation are recognized. For example, in the Folsom-Cordova Unified School District, Cordova, California, representative groups knowledgeable in a particular area of need produced a brochure to communicate the developed goals, objectives, assessment criteria, and program elements.

Regional educational laboratories are another source of help available to school district planners. As an example, the Northwest Regional Educational Laboratory is actively engaged in a mission to formalize the community planning procedures that establish a closer relationship among agencies of the community and educational planners.

Objectives are developed which are consistent with goals established for the district. The goals are in response to student needs. Consequently, objectives for an individual school take into account the particular needs of its students. The resultant flexibility within the total district encourages a sensitivity to characteristics of the sub-communities within the school districts which is crucial.

Stating objectives in performance terms is central to the success of an ERM System. The implementation of an ERM System may appear mechanistic if the teacher is not directly involved in writing objectives. Peck's plea for personalized education is an appropriate guide (1970, p. 9).

> "Since the teacher is helped to identify highly specific goals for the child, and since she participates in systematic observation of the effects of her tactics, she can diversify her tactics and become more flexibly responsive to the child's reactions in a very specific, well-aimed manner. This is quite the opposite of unguided eclecticism or vague 'flexibility.'"

The most potent properties of the emphasis suggested by Peck are:

1. It takes place in the classroom.
2. Student responses follow immediately.
3. Feedback to the teacher is instantaneous.
4. Cause and effect from consultant to teacher to student are traceable.
5. Objective-behaviors are not limited to test-performance measures.

The unimaginative may develop performance objectives which pertain only to a lower level cognitive domain. Tremendous effort must be expended to find ways — observation, judgment, anecdotal reports, and new evaluative instruments — to write performance objectives in the higher levels of the cognitive, effective, and psychomotor domain.

Some of the justification for the existence of a system lies in the nature of the interaction arrangements of the components found in the system. The benefits derived by the interaction of personnel in the role of planning and for those engaged in evaluating are a result of an expansion of the range of expectations for each group. The range of objectives stated in the planning process encourages the group engaged in the evaluating process to suggest means for measuring the attainment of the objectives. Conversely, as evaluators are able to measure more properties, the planners are led to explicate more objectives. Inability to measure the attainment of an objective discourages the statement of the objective if the system is to be dependent upon objective attainment. Considering objectives and evaluating measures in isolation of each other appears to be an unwise practice.

Not all objectives can be measured with the same degree of facility. In Shaplin's opinion:

> "The more important the objectives, the more difficult it is to measure the achievement of them. It is easiest to measure immediate recall of information or the development of manipulative skills, more difficult to measure changes in attitudes and underlying values, perhaps most difficult to measure the basic process of learning capacity to think, the process of inquiry" (1965, p. 38).

However, the teacher has a greater concern for placing a value on the observation of a consequence of an activity rather than a measure of activity. Thus the teacher is interested in the measure of "changes in attitudes and underlying values."

The role of the teacher in the process of attaining objectives includes the development of some indicators of the properties of learning from which inferences may be drawn. The measuring devices (tests, scales, etc.) developed for use within the classroom are sufficient to infer that learning has taken place provided the measures form a part of a coherently organized and functioning system and not just a random or capricious instrument of the individual teacher (Parsons, et al., 1951, p. 25).

Developing the Staff

New awareness of the skill and insight necessary for planning, programming, budgeting, and evaluating come into sharp focus as objectives are developed in relation to goals. Curriculum development and budgeting are closely interrelated, as are the functions of planning and evaluation. The determined needs of in-service education and the utilization of a process which allows cooperative efforts toward meaningful staff development merge in the functional strengths of an ERM System.

In the discussion which follows new functions and new roles will be considered.

Teachers, in planning sound learning environments for students, are increasingly assuming the roles of facilitators, stimulators and professional guides for learning. In these new roles teachers become more adept as planners, programmers, and evaluators. To provide leadership and service to teachers, principals, school business administrators, and other management personnel should develop expertise in areas not usually given a priority in the past.

Glenys Unruh, in describing the staff development program in the University City, Missouri schools highlights the characteristics of a sound staff development program. It is interesting to note the close resemblance of the activities to the four processes in an ERM System.

> "It is our goal to provide a learning environment for the in-service education of teachers that is much like the environment we believe is desirable in working with students: utilization of group dynamics, a wide range of media, involvement in real problems, skillful use of supportive services and resources, and a research orientation. In-service education activities are planned to meet current objectives, meet the needs of individual teachers, and meet the concerns of groups of teachers. Feedback forms the basis of in-service planning; knowledge of the students, analysis by the teacher of his own feelings and skills, and procedures are devised to assist us in searching for better practices and content. We are beginning to build in a system in which the participants identify their needs, state specific objectives, outline alternate procedures, and plan an evaluation which leads to revision of the process."

The learning environment created for the teacher encourages the teacher to provide a similar environment for the students. A support for innovative practices extends naturally from the program coordinator-teacher relationship to the teacher-student relationship. The resultant implication for the teacher is to accept a new role and a challenge to fulfill a changing function.

The acceptance of a new functional role leads to an expanding concept of the resources available for education and the manner in which the resource can be utilized. Planning and resource utilization originates with the student as a focus. Plans for the identification, value or procurement of the resource grow from this foundation. Student participation in discovering, identifying and utilizing resources is highly important if individual and independent learning is a goal.

Schools can extend the learning environment into the community and also bring the human and material resources of the community into the school. The school utilizes business, industry and all other community institutions for realistic laboratory experiences within the school. Obviously, the school must establish screening devices to avoid being exploited.

An example serves to illustrate the possibility of utilizing resources beyond the school building. In San Diego County, California, the Community Educational Resources Organization (consisting of individuals and corporations in science, industry, military and communications) produces educational materials for students with particular emphasis in the topics of space and oceanography. In addition to utilizing community resources, the use of technology and paraprofessionals enhances the advantage of differentiated staff assignments. This allows a professionally trained teacher to establish priorities for meeting the needs of students.

Educators are continuing to seek ways in which learning can become more personalized — a means by which each student is well known by at least one member of the staff. Many schools throughout the country are experimenting with innovations to give teachers more time to work with students to determine individual needs.

In their publication, *Instruction 1969*, the Denver, Colorado School District discusses possibilities for the use of several promising resources. These are illustrative:

1. Balaret Center for Environmental Studies (Denver's most unusual classroom) located in outlying Denver, consists of 700 acres of mountain terrain including forests, hills, spring-fed streams, meadows, and ponds.

2. A computer which is housed in a trailer is moved from school to school every two weeks. This is in cooperation with the University of Colorado Department of Civil Engineering and nine other school systems under two National Science Foundation grants.

3. An elementary school program called Project Columbine extends the use of audio visual materials and equipment in a manner similar to a lending library. Equipment and materials may be taken home to study and share with the family.

Continuous learning suggests the desirability that the student utilize both home and community resources in learning. This is perhaps the best guarantee that throughout his life he will make better use of the rich resources surrounding him. Advancement in communication, particularly television, and transportation provide more and more people with an increased range of experiences. The implication is that school experiences should be correspondingly modified. Goodlad predicts that by the year 2000, "School, as we now know it, will have been replaced by a diffused learning environment involving home, parks, public buildings, museums, and an array of guidance and programming centers." (Goodlad, 1968, p. 22).

Overall co-ordination of an ERM System will be *least* effective in a traditional line-and-staff organization in which those directly responsible to the superintendent perform functions individually without relating decisions to those of colleagues. Teamwork is essential. An assessment of the responsibilities and roles of top level administrators merits consideration. Superintendents may need to re-examine their priorities in terms of values, use of time, and how best to relate to people.

Perhaps the most significant forward thrust a school district can provide its staff development program would be the priorities which the superintendent and his leadership staff establish for their own development. The American Association of School Administrators through its National Academy for School Executives is providing seminars which are most helpful in this regard. The Association for Supervision and Curriculum Development has two Publications, *Personalized Supervision* and *Toward Professional Maturity*, both designed for those who support the teacher in providing for better learning.

There are several agencies available to local school districts offering assistance in developing the skills essential to the successful implementation of an ERM System. The agencies include both profit and non-profit organizations. Some of these are funded by federal grants such as ESEA support to the regional laboratories. Others include the national curriculum projects and institutions of higher learning. Several commercial enterprises have gained facility which also can be of assistance.

An understanding and an awareness of changing roles and functions are important, but in the final analysis *people* make programs effective. An ERM System is a vehicle for people to develop skills and insights through participation as planners, programmers, budgeters, and evaluators.

If teachers are to develop their fullest potentialities, teacher training institutions must become partners with the school systems in staff development programs. It is encouraging to note that the National Science Foundation (NSF) provides funds for teacher education institutions and school systems to work together on in-service education. An indication of a trend is found in the elementary teacher training model developed at Florida State University. Sowards (1969, pp. 24-25) reports:

A three-phased program, consisting of an underclass phase, a pre-service phase, and an in-service phase was designed to develop the following behaviors:

1. The teacher will plan for instruction by formulating behavioral objectives.
2. The teacher will select and organize contents.
3. The teacher will employ appropriate strategies.

4. The teacher will evaluate instructional outcomes in terms of be-behavioral changes.
5. The teacher will demonstrate the competence and willingness to accept professional responsibilities and to serve as a professional leader.

It should be recognized that there is undoubtedly much undeveloped talent within the staff of the school district. Many opportunities are available providing teachers and administrators with the new skills necessary for a successful ERM System. New insights result from the acquisition of new skills. In some instances, the recruitment of new personnel with expertise in particular areas is necessary. Consultants may temporarily serve specialized roles when a clear need exists. The training of a staff with skills essential for defining performance criteria consistent with objectives and consideration of alternative programs is an example of a task for which consultants may be employed.

Staff development for an ERM System will be most effective if tailored to individual needs. The school districts of Cherry Creek, Colorado and Mesa, Arizona have found that in addition to orientation sessions, the assignment of new employees to teaching teams utilizes some of the leadership talent available within the school district. This is made possible by the differentiated staffing designs developed at each school center.

The Wisconsin Research and Development Center for Cognitive Learning has delineated three types of research and development activities which can be effectively implemented in multi-unit schools. First, there is "staff" research to identify, implement, and carefully evaluate promising materials and procedures. A second type is "development-based" research in which the school develops and continuously refines instructional materials or procedures. A third type is "basic" research which has many variants including controlled experimental and short-term descriptive research.

In answering the question, "How can the entire teaching staff of a school district be given the opportunity to learn to use a new teaching tenchinque?", personnel of the Spokane, Washington, School District, in cooperation with the Northwest Regional Educational Laboratory, developed a training model for preparing the staff in the use of planned teaching techniques. The model takes advantage of:

1. Direct administrative personnel previously trained to use the "Higher Level Thinking Abilities" teaching strategy, and
2. A district owned television station.

The model is pictured on the next page. Many school districts and teacher education institutions are developing plans for an innovative continuing teacher education program. The teaching staff of James Elementary School, Kansas City, Missouri, was enrolled in a graduate program at the University of Missouri in Kansas for one year. The purpose of the project was to develop a faculty capable of creating an innovative exemplary school. The study pro-

SPOKANE INSERVICE TRAINING MODEL

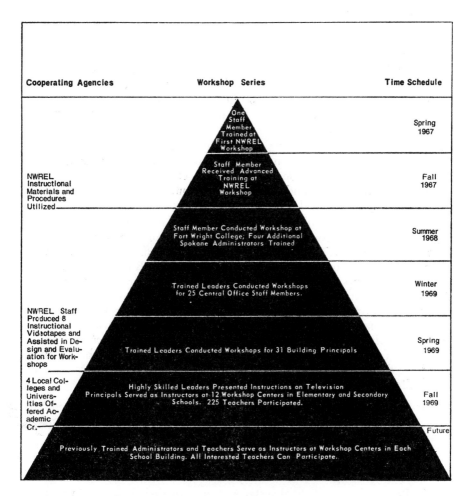

Cooperating Agencies	Workshop Series	Time Schedule
	One Staff Member Trained at First NWREL Workshop	Spring 1967
NWREL Instructional Materials and Procedures Utilized	Staff Member Received Advanced Training at NWREL Workshop	Fall 1967
	Staff Member Conducted Workshop at Fort Wright College; Four Additional Spokane Administrators Trained	Summer 1968
	Trained Leaders Conducted Workshops for 25 Central Office Staff Members.	Winter 1969
NWREL Staff Produced 8 Instructional Videotapes and Assisted in Design and Evaluation for Workshops	Trained Leaders Conducted Workshops for 31 Building Principals	Spring 1969
4 Local Colleges and Universities Offered Academic Cr.	Highly Skilled Leaders Presented Instructions on Television Principals Served as Instructors at 12 Workshop Centers in Elementary and Secondary Schools. 225 Teachers Participated.	Fall 1969
	Previously Trained Administrators and Teachers Serve as Instructors at Workshop Centers in Each School Building. All Interested Teachers Can Participate.	Future

Spokane inservice training model.

173

gram included opportunities for the teachers to acquire knowledge in subject fields and for planning an individualized learning environment at the James School. The study program was a part of the rationale used to assist the faculty in creating the environment for:

1. a non-graded program at all levels and curriculum areas,
2. a multi-media, multi-dimensional approach for education,
3. continuous progress through learning areas,
4. and a balance of emphasis on the intellectual and affective aspects of growth and development.

If an ERM System is to be implemented successfully, the school district must provide the conditions which encourage the acceptance of change in the utilization of time, materials, and facilities. Many good ideas have little chance of success simply because too little is done to provide conditions for success. Time for staff development can often be arranged through a realistic appraisal of activities.

Many educators are finding that teachers have more time for planning and program development by using paraprofessionals, and by taking advantage of the new technology such as television, computer assisted instruction, learning laboratories, and audio visual equipment. Consequently, as students mature, individualized and independent learning is enhanced.

School districts should seriously re-examine sabbatical leave, summer employment, and released-time policies to provide more time for participation in program planning. The importance of providing sufficient time for teacher planning cannot be overstated. In implementing an ERM System, emphasis is given to the importance of the continuous involvement of teachers. Educators who are not directly involved in teaching can often rearrange time priorities, but individual teachers need help in arranging time if they are to be involved in planning. Administrators and boards must resist pressures to develop *excellent plans on paper* which have *little or no effect on learning.* More time for teachers can be found in a number of ways. School districts could use these means for releasing the teacher from the direct teacher-student obligation:

1. As a part of the regular school day: Team teaching, differentiated staff assignments, and independent learning programs can provide for teacher planning time.
2. A special segment of time provided on a weekly basis: This is possible by shortening the student's day on a scheduled basis.
3. Released time: School systems often provide substitutes to permit a small group of teachers to work intensively on a project.
4. Summer employment: This is often accomplished through individual summer contracts. In an increasing number of school districts teachers are employed on a full year basis.

174

There are schools which are employing one or more of the above approaches in finding time for teachers to work on staff development projects. At the UCLA Elementary School, students attend school for six weeks and then are dismissed for one week while teachers plan. In Newton, Massachusetts, students are dismissed at noon on Tuesdays and Thursdays. In the Normandy School in Montgomery County, Maryland, students are dismissed at noon one day each week.

The Princeton, New Jersey, schools have adopted a Wednesday program. Constance Vieland, co-ordinator of staff development programs for Princeton, states in a letter:

"The Wednesday Program is a released time program initially funded by E.S.E.A. Title III, which is conducted every Wednesday from 1:30 to 3:30. Students are dismissed at 1:00. The Wednesday Program is planned and implemented by an elected group of staff members. In addition to instructional and administrative staff, program participants include non-instructional staff and interested members of the community. We have occasional "Home Group" meetings where participant attendance is required. Home group consists of some fifteen participants representing a cross section of the school. A particular group might include teachers from throughout the district, a secretary or custodian, a principal, a community person, etc. Issues related to the purposes and the evaluation of the program are discussed in these groups."

Up to 10 percent of the current expenditures of many private enterprises is attributed to research and development. The American people can expect school districts to invest more in research and development than has been the case in the past. It has been indicated that the average school district's research and development expenditure is less than one percent.

The Dallas, Texas, School System has initiated a "Penny for Innovation" budget. Dallas Superintendent Estes says: "This means that one penny of the new tax rate is designated for locally initiated innovative projects."

A test of the effectiveness of the staff development program is, of course, the degree to which utilization of an ERM System facilitates the strengthening of the educational program. There must be a carefully planned evaluation not only of the staff development program itself, but also of the impact of the program on the quality of learning. As a systems approach, an ERM System provides for program choices to be made intelligently in relation to a promise of enabling students to attain previously determined performance objectives. Evaluation is an integral part of the process. Leadership from outside the system can be utilized for consultation in evaluations of staff development programs.

Promising Practices

Brief resumes of some approaches of a school district and of a university will illustrate the promising practices which are now underway in staff development.

In 1953, prior to a huge population growth, the school board and administration of the Fountain Valley Elementary School District of Fountain Valley, California, developed a master plan for education. In 1953, there were 250 students being taught in one school. District enrollment for 1969 was 10,000 students.

The central question in Fountain Valley is, "How can we provide individually prescribed learning experiences for children?" The educational program in addition to the design of the school is an attempt to solve this question. The district is non-graded to allow children to progress at their own pace. The greatest effort has been made to match students with the necessary materials, equipment, concepts, and people in order to provide an individualized program. Prime requirements for this process are pupil placement, academic diagnosis, prescriptions, and continuous evaluation. Evaluation and placement of pupils is made by the teacher, with involvement of the child. If further testing is required, a psychologist is available. After diagnosis, self-directed learning takes the place of teacher-centered instruction.

The building program in the district was developed with the individual student in mind. The schools are so designed that a learning center or media center is surrounded by six or eight classrooms. The learning center is staffed with a coordinating teacher, a teacher aide, and a parent aide. Other personnel in speech, music and psychology provide assistance as needed. Projectors, recorders, and other equipment are used for experiments and demonstrations and are available for all. When the task within the learning center is completed, the child returns to his regular class where his report is written or discussed.

The differentiated staffing used in Fountain Valley provides a building, educational leader (principal), coordinating teacher (one for each learning center), and teachers. Two or more levels of paraprofessionals and more than 1,000 parent volunteers complete the staff.

A four-week pre-employment seminar is held during the summer for all new teachers. The program begins with an introduction to a non-graded, flexible schedule philosophy and an acquaintance with the curriculum and classroom activities. It then moves to instruction in the use of equipment and teaching aids.

The inclusion of Fountain Valley as a California PPBS pilot school has stimulated even greater community participation than in the past. Needs assessment questionnaires provide for community involvement. Parent questionnaires and surveys are used to improve and modify the educational program where community concerns become evident. More than fifteen meetings preceded the beginning of the use of PPBS in one school.

Fountain Valley uses a modified teaching day. On one day a week students are dismissed at 1:00 p.m. From 1 to 4 p.m., teachers meet for cooperative planning.

A "test bank" which will accomodate the scope and sequence of reading skills on a continuum has been developed by the district. Fountain Valley has entered into contract with a company to market this test. Present plans are to re-invest the royalties in curriculum development. This will increase the research and development budget.

The School of Education at Indiana University is an example of a higher education system joining forces with the public schools in the area to provide improved teacher education and coordinated leadership services. From the university School of Education a joint faculty, administration, and student commission has been organized to serve as a central policy board. It is composed of: two administrators, two faculty members, two members from the policy council, two graduate students, five faculty members from the Division of Curriculum and Instruction, and three faculty members from the Division of Human Behavior.

This commission in turn established task forces whose responsibilities include assessment of the present program, program alteration, and component modification or substitution. Task Force "A" deals with short-range goals, while Task Force "B" deals with long-range goals. The organization is further broken down into study groups which the task forces were empowered to establish. These study groups design new program elements which are turned over to the project team for implementation.

The project teams in themselves are further divided into units to provide clinical, resource, instructional, and development services within their own units on the basic level of operation.

Within the project team, the instructional unit is the group that actually operates within the classroom of the public school. It is composed of four regular teachers (professional personnel), four student teachers (semi-professional) and four undergraduate teacher trainers (paraprofessionals). One member of the team is identified as Instructional Team Leader. This is a key role in that the ITL coordinates policy making, managing, program planning, and training within the basic instructional group as it operates in the school.

The purpose of the progrom is twofold: to provide training for pre-service teachers and to provide in-service training to enable teachers to become more skilled and insightful. Through these teams, they also hope to provide a way to develop innovative programs and systematic program changes.

Evaluation of the program is handled by a third task force called Task Force "C", which is guided by priorities established by the commission. The philosophy is that evaluation should be a means of supplying information to the decision-making group.

An important aspect of the program is the Professional Center. Its function is to identify relevant materials and techniques. It also works with the development unit to devise solutions to problems, to assist in the field trial of proposed solutions and to assist Indiana University staff in training teachers.

Summary

Citizens, students, and educators are more eager than ever to help determine the future of their schools. Many educators, as well as laymen, believe that even though there are many unsolved problems and discouraging happenings, America may be entering a new era in which all concerned groups will learn to work together more effectively to improve education.

With the pressing needs of education and the vast numbers of dedicated people willing to assist, the emergence of an ERM System is most timely. School districts with a strong staff development program will find an ERM System approach will facilitate and strengthen the staff efforts. School systems which do not have a strong staff development program will find an ERM System to be a rewarding approach to a fuller utilization of the most important education resource available — the staff.

With staff development necessary for an effective implementation of an ERM System and with an ERM System so promising in its potential for strengthening staff development, the alert superintendent and board will do well to capitalize on this harmonic relationship.

The Educational Resources Management System provides a tool to help consider each part of the school system as it relates to the total context of the school district. The success or failure of the educational system is within the control of the people who make up the system. The organizational plan for utilizing people may well be the most important asset. The education of the staff and the development of the curriculum can not be left to chance.

Understanding human needs, involving people affected by the school district, and developing a sound environment for learning are recognizable and important considerations in an ERM System. The system, however, is not a panacea for all educational problems. An ERM System is a planning aid which when properly used can enable a school district to base its goals upon understanding humans and the learning needs of students. Emphasis is upon the importance of involvement with a focus on the learner. An application of an ERM System enables laymen and educators to recognize that a relevant curriculum (a good environment for learning) is the central purpose of the school system.

The potential of scientific management has remained virtually untapped in education. The implication for scientific management or a systematic approach to decision-making is probably inevitable. But the continuing commitment of the teacher is even more essential. The quality of teaching is perhaps the most important factor in the success of the learning process.

REFERENCES

Peck, Robert. *Personalized Education. Administration Report No. 21.* The Research and Development Center for Teacher Education. Austin, University of Texas, 1970.
Shaplin, Judson T. "Practice in Teaching." *Harvard Educational Review,* Breakthrough to Better Teaching. 1965: Reprinted from Vol. 31, No. 1, Winter, 1961.
Parsons, Talcott and Shils, Edward A. (eds.) *Toward a General Theory of Action.* New York: Harper and Row, 1951.
Goodlad, John I. *Planning and Organizing for Teaching.* Project on the Instructional Program for the Public Schools. Washington, D.C., National Education Association, 1963.
Elementary Teacher Training Models: Nine Program Models. U. S. Office of Education, OE-58033. Washington, D.C.: Government Printing Office, 1969.

CHAPTER IX

Federal-State-Local Interfaces

The subtle differences anticipated in the application of the conceptual design for an Educational Resources Management System at the federal level of governance and at the state level of governance as contrasted with the local education agency is the subject of this chapter.

This chapter includes an analysis of some interrelationships between the Federal Educational Agency and the State Educational Agency. Of special concern for the analysis is the manner in which the interrelationships have affected the operation of the local school district. The analysis is upon three general dimensions which, for the sake of simplicity may be termed: (1) level of authority as characterized by the federal, state, or local governance of schools; (2) the responsibility for education as expressed through a program management role; and, (3) the process functions as suggested in an Educational Resources Management System. It is suggested that the organization of the local school district and its mode of operation reflects the patterns established by federal and state educational agencies. The emerging trends which are the resultant of federal-state-local interactions can and shall influence the acceptance of a system for educational resources management of the local school agency.

The Process Functions

The process functions specified in the conceptual design for an Educational Resources Management System are the four previously described as planning, programming, budgeting, and evaluating. The application of an Educational Resources Management System is appropriate for substantive matters in education as well as in ministerial matters. The application of an ERM System is modified to accommodate the educational system at each level of governance. Each agency characteristically manifests a set of values, *modus operandi*, and political factors.

The three levels of governance provide for the complete, public-supported school for the individual student. Each level has a varying degree of responsibility, authority, and power to act for the benefit of the student. Until the last decade the Congress has acted primarily within the authority of the commonweal to assume a responsibility for the school child. The power of the Congress has been exercised demonstrably on the categorical selection of educational activities and services — in the vernacular, "picking and choosing."

It appears that the typical state legislature has relegated the responsibility for school operations to a local education agency. The responsibility is accompanied with an authority for limited taxation for the operation of schools. The exercise of the responsibility is subject to frequent review by either the state authority or the local educational patronage. The responsibility for the fulfillment of the educational obligation, therefore, rests with a local education agency. It is the local school board that must protect the interests of the state, the local citizenry, and the students of the school. The same board exercises only restricted powers, but in some manner must approve of the curriculum and of all proposals, locally, to maintain a complete system of operation.

The needed changes implied by implementation of an Educational Resources Management System must be imposed upon an existing system. The current system for education has evolved over many years without a drastic change. A change in a system is possible. Recent moves to encourage the use of a planning, programming, budgeting system among state and federal governmental units is in evidence. By 1970, in thirteen states an action of the legislature or of the governor had moved the state toward the adoption of a PPB system within the state. Five additional states reported a program of PPB was underway. A total of 29 states had either initiated a PPB system or had specific dates determined for the initiation of a PPB system for the state (Bliss, 1971).

Federal Agency Planning

The history of education does not record educational planning as a formalized process. In fact, former HEW Secretary Gardner described the situation as related more to accident:

> "We Americans have a great and honored tradition of stumbling into the future . . . We are just beginning to formulate goals in an orderly way, to evaluate means of achieving these goals, to appraise the effectiveness of present problems, and to estimate costs and strategies for getting where we want to be." (Elam & Swanson, 1969).

The adoption of the Constitution of the United States ushered in an era of persistent distrust of a centralized control of education. The confederation of states was created in a community of self-determination with unity for all states for the purpose of protection from foreign enemies. The Revolution was fought for the distinct purpose of bringing governmental control into the hands of constituents close to the seat of government. Government close-at-hand is government that is responsive to the immediate needs of its people — local government permits a close check.

The fear of a "national design" or a "state plan" has deterred Americans from planning in an "orderly way." Americans have systematically avoided the development of any planned social action which could be branded as "the plan." Several federal *ad hoc* advisory committees established at various times between 1929 and 1967 have levied criticism at the Federal Government for its involvement in education. Summaries of the comments (Quattlebaum, 1968) include these failings:

• The Federal Government has never established a comprehensive policy or program for its educational activities, but has initiated policies of far-reaching effect as mere incidents of some particular attempt to induce an immediate and particular efficiency;

• that these policies are inconsistent and sometimes conflicting;

• that the Federal Government has engaged in overlapping and independent promotions of curriculums in highly specialized fields while neglecting the general curricular needs of the country.

The committees' criticisms may have been inappropriately assumed to be aimed at the U. S. Office of Education. The USOE, or its predecessors, was not created to address the conditions implied above. The Act of March 2, 1867, which established the agency, provided that the primary purpose of the Office was to collect information in the form of statistics and facts which would show the progress of education. The intent included an obligation to diffuse the information as a guide to the establishment and maintenance of efficient schools (Quattlebaum, 1968). Almost a half century later the Commissioner of Education re-affirmed the original enactment in a statement of guiding principles for the Bureau of Education in 1914. Two additional duties were cited as basic responsibilities of the Bureau. The Commissioner viewed the Bureau as being in a position to "give, upon request, expert opinion and advice" for the promotion of education. The second duty was to serve as a point of contact between the United States and other nations in matters of education. (W. T. Harris as Commissioner in the 1890's established a reputation for interchanges with foreign educational systems.)

The need of a planning procedure for fulfilling the ministerial responsibility of the Federal Educational Agency is necessarily related to management efficiency. Consequently, elaborate plans can be anticipated from the Agency relating to forms design, reporting procedures, and schedules. The inferences from this analysis of the ministerial responsibilities at the federal level of operation are seemingly characterized as a development of interpersonal relations that guide the functions of one or more agencies toward an objective typically expressed as a given calendar date. A priority has been placed upon avoiding a duplication of effort and untenable delays among federal and state agencies. Cooperation among individuals in several agencies is sought as a consequence.

Planning for the substantive matters at the federal level is related to the Administration and to the Congress. The time span related to a particular Congress and a particular Administration, therefore, is characterized by intermediate-range goals. Time is "lost" with a change in Administration in the anticipation of new strategies for education. Unfortunately, some time may be dissipated while searching for a means to discredit previously established legislation. Obviously, this was not a program before substantial federal financial aid was provided directly for local school needs.

Secrecy and surprise are some of the tactics used by a party-oriented administration to thwart opposition to a particular plan of action. A member of a Presidential Task Force reported the problem of party secrecy at the Phi Delta Kappa Symposium: *Educational Planning in the United States.* The task force report provided the basis from which the Elementary and Secondary Education Act emerged. The informant stated:

> At this point something occurred that I think is deplorable in a democracy, though it seemed to work for a while. This is, the Task Force report was never published, but was treated as a classified document. . . . Counsel may have been given of this type: "Don't alert your probable opponents; keep under cover until legislation is ready and then push it through before opposition can organize." (Elam & Swanson, 1969)

Typically, the short exposure to the "plan" creates a problem of haste for the implementation. The personnel of the USOE must prepare in haste for the operation of the legislation. Subsequently each applicant for the benefits of the law must act in haste or lose the intended appropriation.

State Agency Planning

The development of the planning function in the State Educational Agency cannot be discreetly isolated from the discussion of the development of plans in the Federal Educational Agency. The two Agency approaches are parallel. The historical development of the two Agencies generally follows the same pattern with one influencing the other. Significant changes in the one Agency created a needed accommodation within the other Agency. As needs emerged from State Agency problem definitions, the Federal Agency responded.

The role of the Federal Government as the "protector" of the states and for the "commonweal" has persisted for many generations. It has been with skepticism on the part of many that Federal financial aid to schools has been accepted. The debate on the Federal authority rose to a climax when the implementation of Title III (PL 89-10), Elementary and Secondary Education Act, "by-passed" State Educational Agencies. Title IV of the same act caused a lesser concern in the creation of the regional laboratories. Title III proposed a modest sum of money to encourage innovations and experimental projects of national significance. It is assumed the proponents of the measure feared State Educational Agency bureaucracy would thwart experimental endeavors. The major concern was for the plight of the metropolitan areas. The rural-orientation of the typical state legislature is usually cited as the cause of this concern.

The resultant of the debate over state vs. federal control for the management of federal monies is the re-emphasis upon the "state plans" concept for distribution and control of Federal aid. The "state plan" became a widely used term with the advent of NDEA, 1958. The expression was used to describe the proposal submitted by the State for the utilization of the NDEA within the state. The practice has been in use for many years with a degree of success, but remains an object of criticism for some. The state plan frequently includes value structures and traditions established within the state. The plans tend to restrict the range of potential solutions to existing problems, thus continuing the binds of conformity.

Some conflict continues between the Federal and State Agency point-of-view in the matter of "categorical aid." Complete planning by the State Agency is truncated by the nature of federal categorical aid, which, seemingly, is always "supplementary" program support and "cannot be used to supplant" operating programs. Thus it is that a small appropriation upon the part of Congress controls a huge expenditure of program effort. The state is viewed as derelict in its responsibility if it does not seek all money due the state from the federal sources. The pressure on the state is to artifically create the "need" within the state to be eligible for the grant. In spite of the possible criticism, as Hitt expressed it:

> "The federal funds, probably the smallest amount in the program, may be said to have had the greatest impact because these funds provided the stimulation, the incentive for the program." (Mimeo memo to USOE)

He probably could have added, "Federal funds provided some risk money."

Gradually the fear of the "planned society" so prevalent in the heritage of America is being dispelled and a new interpretation of planning for education is emerging. The State Educational Agency has avoided the use of the word "planning" as much as the Federal Educational Agency has. An analysis of the professional personnel employed by the states reflects a changing attitude in the use of the expression.

Programming

Programming is described as the process of developing program plans for attaining an educational objective. The descriptions presented and the potential ramifications explicated are sufficiently complete for supporting the conceptual design of an Educational Resources Management System. The expression, "programming," however, conveys variations in definition at each level of governance. Confusion is added by the popular use of the word in contexts peculiar to fields other than PPBS. The confusion is enhanced, especially, by the literature of fields such as data processing (computer applications). In this context data processing as performed by computer through an information system is considered to be an extension of planning, programming, budgeting systems.

The program context of the federal government is usually established through the several "titles" of a comprehensive act by the Congress. The program is described by the act. The federal support of educational activities has been primarily through programs of categorical aid. The rationale of the financial assistance from the acts of Congress was based upon societal goals. The appropriation for improvement of science education, as an example, was justified in the interests of programs for National Defense (NDEA).

An analysis of federal acts in support of education reveals the federal intent for the legislation is the alleviation of burdens or problems for particular students. Categories of students are described as the target populations. The groups include students residing in "low-income communities," students who are "educationally deprived," the children of "migrant agricultural workers," and similar target groups. Apparently, federal support has evolved from a support of a need of society in general terms to the needs of specific children. This involvement may be illustrated by programs which emerged with the Smith-Hughes Acts in support of agriculture as a vocation to an emphasis upon meeting the vocational needs of students who reside in a rural community.

The development of programs as a result of the Congressional Act is characterized by the assemblage of ministerial functions related to services and activities to expeditiously distribute monies for specified student population groups. The federal support system, to a large degree, is a "delivery system" designed to distribute federal appropriations to state and local agencies. The State and Local Educational Agencies translate the appropriations into substantive educational programs. The majority of the program activities from the federal level involve interactions with the State Educational Agencies. Program goals are stated as ministerial, resources distribution goals to the virtual exclusion of substantive educational goals. The pattern of personnel employment practices reflects the agency emphasis. The State Educational Agency seemingly replicates the organization of the Federal Educational Agency.

The state faces a circumstance that divides the staff between the administration of federal programs and the preparation for state-supported programs. Dual functions are indicated within each set of program tasks. Substantive-oriented personnel are employed to execute the mission of leadership for both federal and state program efforts. Managerially-oriented personnel are required, similarly, to perform a dual role. Role conflicts emerge. The influence of program personnel assignments at the federal level has been obvious at the state agency level. The appointment of a "Title I Program Officer" in the United States Office of Education prompted the state agency to appoint a "Title I Officer" and this was further proliferated into the Local Educational Agency.

The pattern for program structures within the states has been quite haphazard. The prestigious position of the USOE in the administration of the early categorical-aid legislation influenced state and local agency personnel to use the words "program" and "project" before any apparent effort was made to clearly define the concept. *Handbook II* appeared in print before any special significance was placed upon the use of the word "program" and the revision of the handbook was too late to alter the course of events. "Program" as a concept has many meanings for many persons. The importance of a stabilized meaning for the word "program" appeared in the deliberations of the Joint Task Force of the USOE and the Council of Chief State School Officers (Belmont project). Trismen, engaged with the development of the Project Descriptor Instrument, met an impasse and noted in a memo:

> "The problem of defining a project/program activity (hereafter called simply a 'project') is basic to the construction of a project descriptor instrument. Until requested to do otherwise, project directors are likely to think of a project as that collection of people, goods and services for which they made application, and received funds." (October 29, 1969, memo to D. Antonopolis)

The problem was again faced with an *ad hoc* committee developing the *Consolidated Program Information Report*. As subsidiary data instruments were being prepared it was discovered that different states have defined "program" and "project" in conflicting terms. The Trismen memo criteria were insufficient to rectify the problem. The committee proffered the following definitions:

> ". . . a 'program' is taken to mean a grouping of one or more projects which have been designed to meet the specified needs of a pupil population group. The 'program' may be funded from more than one source of money and is considered to be a continuous process.
> "The concept of a 'project' is more restricted than the definition for a program. The project is a combination of services and activities which are designed for satisfying the needs of a specific pupil population group. The duration of a project is usually specified in advance by means of a project application procedure. Funds are designated for the project for a specific length of time. Each project is funded by a single source of funds."

Proposal writing was not invented by the USOE with the advent of Public Law 89-10, but the process became familiar to school personnel at all levels of administration soon after the enactment. States were called upon to submit state plans for implementing the "Titled Programs." In so doing, precedence was established for the above definitions. Local Educational Agencies submitted "projects" to implement the legislation. States compiled the projects into the "State Program for the Implementation of P.L. 89-10, Title *n*." The Federal Educational Agency likewise compiled all of the programs from the states to report on the programs for the entire implementation of the congressional intent.

The state is the most acceptable administrator of domestic programs for education and other social programs for the commonwealth. It is politically expedient to support the virtues of local control. However, the states have found it increasingly necessary to use federal tax sources through federal legislation to finance locally important programs. The programs thus created are of national importance, but are designed to relieve local conditions of poverty, transportation, educational deficiencies, and many others. Thus the more localized administration should be in a better position to apply program resources in concert with local resources. Many of the financial aid programs provided by the Congress in the past have been supplementary to local resources and not designed to supplant the local resources. One looming exception is the P. L. 874 which has had a justification that alludes to aid-in-lieu-of-taxes.

Many of the federal legislative acts which support domestic programs include matching funds on the part of the state. The incentive of federal dollars creates a change in the balance of authority between the federal and the state governance. Demands are placed upon state or local funds to support the federal matching programs which, in turn, produces a situation of inordinate control by the federal authority over state programs. The ecology of governance is altered. The ultimate result is an increased clamor, locally, by a decentralization move which proposes a shift of the burden of decision-making to the state authority.

Budgeting

The Executive Branch of the Federal Government prepares a budget which is the estimate of money needed to implement the acts of Congress. The budget is the Administration's support plan. Trade-offs are basically made among the departments of the Executive Branch before being presented to Congress. Subsequent trade-offs in the process of reconciling resources to program plans are a result of congressional conference procedures within Congress or the veto-threat-of-veto confrontations between Congress and the President. In either event, the trade-offs are not necessarily upon crucial educational issues. The Federal Government is far removed from the teacher-student confrontation with no significant precedence for assuming a financial responsibility for the education of students. The federal support is categorical aid, primarily.

The pursuit of the federal sources of financial support to local schools has been with the attitude of a request for a "gift." The pattern of application quite frequently has been in the light of support for a "pet project" that could not be financed with "local taxes." For the school district that has used the federal aid with the "gift" attitude, the federal funds can be eliminated without a deleterious effect upon the local school population. This situation further removes the Federal Educational Agency from a direct responsibility for general education.

The typical state constitution and school code provide for a state system of education. The implication is for a state responsibility for the school system. The state, in most instances, delegates the authority and the ultimate responsibility for the operation of the schools to the local agency. Thus, the final reconciliation of resources with programs (balancing the budget) is solely a local problem. The Local Educational Agency is required to follow the dictates of the state legislature for providing specified education programs. The Local Educational Agency is required to follow the dictates of the state legislature for providing specified education programs. The Local Educational Agency, in many states, must also await the action of the legislature for determining the status of the state appropriation for education. It is evident, even in the so-called "foundation-program states," that the amount of the appropriation is related to the economic condition of the State. As a result, the state appropriation and the local tax support are blended to produce the money for the "regular" program of studies. Far too frequently, this means a minimum program support. Any special program of services and activities goes wanting or other sources of revenue are sought. A typical "other source" is any available "categorical aid" appropriation whether at the Federal or State Educational Agency level.

The state may mandate certain educational offerings but the state relegates budget-balancing to the Local Educational Agency. The Local Educational Agency has only the local populace to provide the matching of resources to educational programs. Traditionally, local financial support for schools has been subjected to a plebiscite in one form or another. Characteristically, the issues of tax support for the operation of schools and for capital expenditures for schools have been influenced by issues foreign to the quality-of-education issue. Disappointment with the status of the economy, a general tax rate or unrelated tax increase, personality differences with school officials or dissatisfaction with the progress of an individual pupil may all contribute to an "anti-school" vote. The election always, so it seems, favors the opposition-to-school vote. The policy board submits a plan for approval or rejection. The election does not permit the selection among alternatives, except to determine a level of financial support in some states.

The implementation of an Educational Resources Management System does not "automatically" alter the restrictive laws of the State. Eventually, a full implementation of a system for educational resources management at the state and local levels of governance could obviate the need for the "overly protective" laws. The conceptual design for educational resources management as presented, herein, anticipates an interactive planning-programming function. It is during this time that several alternatives will have been considered, accepted, rejected, or modified prior to the time of the resource allocation-reconciliation determination. The openness with which these interactive functions transpire is designed to enhance the acceptance of a proposal which may be subjected to popular vote. The process leads to the restoration of a confidence in the public agency.

Evaluating

The Congress has increasingly insisted upon an evaluation of programs for education which have received federal financial support. An interest in a system for planning, programming, and budgeting as officially required by the Federal Government in 1965 has prompted inquiries by the Congress. Generally, each educational support appropriation includes a required evaluation. The concern is for information that will aid Congress in determining if further support is desirable. Apparently, however, the Congress is not particularly interested in an evaluation performed by the U. S.

Office of Education. Hopefully, the task of evaluation can be shifted to the State Educational Agencies.

The information expected by the members of Congress is for more than one purpose. A specific concern is for the "delivery system." The problems in the delivery system stem from the time lapse between the authorization of money for a program and actual service to pupils. This time lapse includes: (1) time devoted to proposal writing and the subsequent acceptance of the proposal; (2) time required to recruit staff or to apply resources to the program operation; and, (3) the period of inactivity caused by the indecision of a delayed funding by the Federal Government. The evaluative feedback to the Congress is intended to aid in the decisions which could alleviate these problem conditions.

A second concern of the Congress is for the manner in which an act of the Congress had provided for the intended pay-off of social services. The information sought is evidence that a target group of students received service commensurate with the level of the resource appropriation.

A new emphasis has been placed upon accountability in American education. The public has grown accustomed to fiduciary accountability through a system of audits. The concept is extended beyond accountability for dollars into a concern for a public trust for the human mind. The evaluation anticipated at the three levels of governance is within the context of the emerging expectations of educational accountability.

The Congress is mandating an evaluation for each activity which is supported by federal appropriations. The U. S. Office is not expected to perform the evaluation. The evaluation performance falls to the State Educational Agency. The State, as a result, is being pressured to proceed rapidly to develop evaluation techniques in response to the Congress, the Legislature, and the Local Educational Agency as well as to the general citizenry. The challenge is formidable.

The techniques of planning, programming, budgeting, evaluating systems appear promising for providing a tool to improve political decision-making. A degree of uniqueness is essential for each area of governmental operations. Certain basics in the management process permeate the entire range of systems. The conceptual design for an Educational Resources Management System anticipates the development of unique system implementations. The design, therefore, proposes a scenario for a system of PPB. The agency completes the system which will be responsive to the needs of the agency. The scenario is the guide for the development of the system. The several units of government must remain free to adapt these general principles to the unique situations faced within the capabilities and resources available.

What has been described as a conceptual design for an Educational Resources Management System appropriate for local schools is also appropriate in an application for a State Educational Agency. Some variations in the implementation plan are needed to fit the special needs of State

Agency operations. *The application is two-fold in nature. One application is for internal agency operation and the other is the function served by the agency in a purveyor-leader relationship between the Legislature and Local Educational Agencies.*

Interfaces

The State and Local Educational Agencies maintain an interface of a communications link with the local district as an operator of schools and the state as a purveyor or distributor of resources for education. The State has the additional role of leadership in the development of the state system for education. In this latter role, the chief state school officer and his staff typically testify for legislation related to the state system for education.

The introduction of a system in support of the decision-making process as an ERM System will alter the existing relationship between the State and Local Educational Agencies. An early manifestation of the change will be a need for information in a new manner. The case for education will be presented in a changed way which must include additional evidence of systematic planning, an analysis of alternatives, and an emphasis upon the evaluative aspects of the proposed programs. The State Educational Agency will need to present an image of accountability.

Organizational theory currently in vogue (Hills, 1968) suggests that a change in the behavior of an organization is affected through an interactive system. Change occurs as a result of a change in a manner in which a person of one organization communicates with a person from another organization. Change does not occur, as readily, by changes in individuals within an organization. The rationale for the hypothesis is built upon the assumption that school behavior is regulated by complementary and institutionaling expectations. Experience reveals that responses of individuals within an organization are predictable. Each organization tends to develop a pattern of response. The pattern becomes quite evident to individuals or to agencies accustomed to interacting with the organization. Obviously, there are limitations to the expectancies but the frequency of unprecedented problems is one measure of an organization undergoing change (Gideon, 1970). Therefore, it follows that if a system to support a decision-making process is to be implemented, the necessary changes in the behavior of the complementary agencies will have to focus upon the points at which the two agencies interact. The Educational Resources Management System is designed to support a decision process and represents a change in the manner in which planning, programming, budgeting, and evaluating affect decision-making.

Any change in the planning procedures of a local school district will be dependent partially upon a corresponding or complementary change in the state agency. *The implementation of an ERM System within the State Educational Agency without considering a corresponding application for the local school distirct would be perilous. Conversely, the implementation of an ERM System locally would be fruitless without appropriate changes in the state sanctions supporting the local school district.*

189

Earlier in this chapter a question was implied that concerned the level of government most suited for decision-making for the benefit of education. Goldhammer (1968, p.74) alludes to the same question and has discussed the concern aptly with this:

"There is considerable evidence indicating that the entire matter of what is meant by local responsibility and control needs to be reconsidered. One approach may be to attempt to determine, in light of prospective developments, what kinds of educational decisions can best and most meaningfully be made at the individual school level, at the level of the local school system, at the state level and at the national level — and what kind of organization will facilitate this decision making process. Perhaps the traditional organization and procedures will no longer suffice."

The earlier chapters in this document include a case for operational decisions for education, placing the responsibility with the Local Educational Agency. The procedures for developing a system to support the decision-makers have been outlined carefully. This chapter points to a need for considering the Federal and State Educational Agencies in the system implementation.

It should be quite obvious that the Federal Educational Agency is not in a position to make operational decisions for education. The federal interest in education is far removed from the specifics of the teacher-student confrontation. The state position in the operation of schools is not as clearly delineated.

There is no line relationship from the U. S. Office of Education to the State Department of Education. There is no line relationship from the U. S. Congress to the State Legislature. Each of these agencies, however, is influenced by its counterpart organization. The local school district, meanwhile, is subject to the state's jurisdiction and is in a quasi-line relationship to the state. Each agency is also responsible for the several processes enumerated in an ERM System, namely: planning, programming, budgeting, and evaluating. The decisions most appropriate at each level can not be discerned clearly but an analysis can shed some light upon where responsibility could exist.

The federal role in planning for education appears to remain in the domain of a material concern with student target population orientations. Consequent decisions, therefore, treat issues of problems facing students and legislation tends to provide support for categories of student target populations. Subsequent evaluating processes, encouraged at the federal level of authority, emerge as assessments of educational conditions and as indicators of need. The tendency also focuses upon a means of attributing results to specific and measurable inputs.

A support for the federal position is the potential for a perspective of educational need that overcomes a regional bias or a localized system of values.

The state is in an advantageous position to analyze alternatives proposed for the educational system of the state. The broad perspective of the state government permits an overview of societal goals that can lead to the trade-offs among alternative state program plans beyond the scope of the public school system. This vista includes higher education, local schools, and technical schools as well as other institutions or activities within the state which may affect education. The state, therefore, can effect decisions concerning public emphasis for the welfare of the citizens of the state and thereby establish a system of priorities.

From the analysis of the potential leadership position for the State Educational Agency, a role for the office of the Chief State School Officer becomes evident. With the leadership of the Chief State School Officer, the societal goals of the state can be translated into a plan of action reflecting the emphasis desired by the State. The plan for education thus supported becomes an integral part of the state system for education. The State Educational Agency moves into a more prominent position in an evaluation process that emphasizes the maintenance of quality for education.

The emergent emphases indicated above are not intended to describe all of the leadership roles traditionally maintained by the State Educational Agency. The description, rather, highlights some of the roles that appear to be essential to the development of a system that supports a decision-making process. Other roles which remain prominent include research, the distribution of money and the several consultative roles essential to the state system for education.

REFERENCES

Bliss, Sam W. *The Extent and Utilization of Management Information Systems and Planning Programming Budgeting Systems in State Educational Agencies.* Denver: Improving State Leadership in Education, 1971.

Elam, Stanley and Swanson, Gordon I., eds. *Educational Planning in the United States.* Itasca, Illinois: F. E. Peacock Publishers, 1969.

Gideon, Victor. *Transition Management.* Boston: Systems Management Corporation, 1970.

Goldhammer, Keith. "Local Provisions for Education: The Organization and Operation of School Systems and Schools" in Morphet, Edgar L. and Jesser, David L. *Emerging Designs for Education.* New York: Citation Press, 1968.

Hills, R. Jean. *Toward a Science of Organization.* Eugene: Center for the Advanced Study of Educational Administration, University of Oregon, 1968.

Hitt, J. Warren. *State Management of Federal Program Funds.* Austin: Texas Education Agency, 1969.

Quattlebaum, Charles A. *Federal Educational Policies, Programs and Proposals.* U. S. 90th Congress, 2nd Session, House Committee of Education and Labor, Washington, D.C.: Government Printing Office, 1968. (3 volumes).

Trismen, Donald. "Rationale for method of defining project in the draft Project Descriptor Instrument." Memorandum to D. Antonoplos, October 29, 1969.

CHAPTER X

Implications for the Future

The Need for Further Study and Development

Although much progress has been made during the past three years toward adapting the PPBES concept to education, most persons who are knowledgeable in the field agree that the lack of expertise will preclude early acceptance of the concept on a large scale. It appears as though inadequacy of skills and techniques and a general lack of understanding of the processes of design, development, and implementation represent major problem areas.

Gott in a recent study (1970) substantiated this point: "Overall, the educators sampled view inadequacy of skills, techniques, and understandings as the top ranking problem area attending adoption of ERMD" (ERM System). When a comparison is drawn between these inadequacies and the lack of publications which document clearly the practical application of the total concept, it becomes increasingly clear that much "hard-nosed" research and development lies ahead.

Even with the advent of this document along with certain others, e.g., The California Project, The Western New York Title III Project and the fine efforts of certain individual school districts, the published results tend to emphasize a guideline approach; or in the case of state or local designs, to reflect a pattern which is somewhat provincial in nature.

The aforementioned statement in no way should be construed to cast negative reflections upon individual state, regional, and local efforts. On the contrary, these efforts are to be supported and the leaders of such are to be recognized and commended.

The ERM System developed by the Research Corporation of the Association of School Business Officials is conceptual in nature. Purposely, it is meant to offer guidelines to local administrators, board members, school business administrators, teachers, and interested and involved lay citizens. These persons are not very sophisticated in the systems approach. It follows, therefore, that most of these people will require more training and experience in the application of practical techniques.

Gott's study reveals that a consensus of educators favors a joint responsibility for providing in-service education to utilize an ERM System or a similar form of PPBES. The study suggests that the responsibility should be shared by local school districts, state universities, and state departments of education, with the state departments, hopefully, accepting the prime responsibility for leadership. Furthermore, the study shows that the least desirable option is for school systems to act alone in providing in-service education.

The implication that state departments of education should accept responsibility for leadership brings to mind the apparent need for the immediate strengthening of these state education agencies. Knezevich (1969, p. 170), in a recent publication, offers the following:

"The state education agency acting through the state board, the chief state school officer, and the state education department, has a most important role in public education. It is imperative that individual state governments, as well as federal government, exert every effort to enhance the leadership capabilities and strength of state education agencies. Unfortunately, in most states the potential of the state department of education has gone largely unrealized, due in large measure to the inadequacy of resources allocated to the department. The state agency has been the most inadequately supported of the three echelons of education, even though no echelon has ever been granted all the funds desired. The lack of sufficient resources has made it impossible, in many cases, to employ a staff large enough and of sufficient quality to fulfill the leadership mandates of state education departments.

"Fortunately there are exceptions to this generalization, and they demonstrate what can be done if adequate resources are forthcoming. For example, in New York, a special study was made of the role of the state education agency in promoting change, and in Florida and California electronic data processing for school systems has been developed.

"It will be extremely difficult, if not impossible, to develop an excellent public-school system without greatly improved state departments of education. Better organizational structure, with appointment rather than election of the state superintendent, and the creation of a nonpartisan state board of education are needed to translate sufficient resources and flexible personnel policies into imaginative programs. State education agencies have traditionally played a significant role in influencing legislative action on educational policies. This role needs to be strengthened to enhance the leadership image of state education agencies. In addition, state planning and evaluation systems must also be strengthened."

Because of the massiveness of this overall effort, even the aforementioned agencies do not appear to have the resources to do the total job. Therefore, it seems only natural that the professional organizations must begin immediately to accept additional responsibility for further research and development.

ASBO, through its initiative and leadership in this particular project, has set a desirable example. The membership of the Association through various media has made it clear that it is desirous of having the organization expand the Association's leadership role in the future.

The American Association of School Administrators through its National Academy for School Executives has conducted successful clinics in PPBES, Futures Planning, and the systems approach. The continuation and expansion of these programs seems assured.

Both ASBO and AASA have recognized that much of their future growth and influence lies in the strengthening of their respective state organizations. Already some of these units have begun in-service education programs of their own.

The National Education Association, the American Federation of Teachers, the National Association of Secondary School Principals, the National Association of Elementary School Principals and the Association for Supervision and Curriculum Development represent organizations which must accept further responsibility for leadership if the philosophy of broader involvement in the decision-making process is to be realized.

As further support for increased responsibility on the part of the professional organizations, reference is made to the 1970 meeting of the Phi Delta Kappa Advisory Panel on Commissions. This Commission recommended five project areas which it felt should be given high priority in the organization and procedures for future PDK Commissions. One of the five was — "Educational Planning for a Changing Society ('The Development of Priorities and Strategies for Educational Planning in a Changing Society')."

In the opening statement of this chapter reference was made to the general lack of understanding of the design, developmental and implementation processes. Gott's study is supported by the feedback from the various conferences, clinics, seminars, and institutes held as part of this project. The results indicate clearly the need for further study, not only of the overall concept, but several segments of it as well. For example, long-range planning and the evaluative process are given particular emphasis. In long-range planning there seems to be a lack of skills in the preparation of goals and objectives, in the process of establishing priorities and in the process of resource analysis. The evaluative process has always been troublesome in the field of education. In this particular design evaluation is considered in its broadest sense, not only as it relates to objective and subjective measurement of the degree of attainment of the various goals and objectives but also to evaluation of such ancillary items as teaching staff, management, facilities, materials, supplies and equipment, and finally — of an ERM System itself.

The aforementioned examples automatically seem to suggest the potential of many new projects (national and state, particularly) which would have objectives toward refinement and further development of the various components and other segments of this ERM System.

The Future Governance of Education

Inasmuch as public education has been, is, and is likely to remain a state function basically, it seems important first to review briefly the present balance between local, state, and federal support and control. In the past 25 years there has been a notable increase in state support programs and in the past decade a similar move has been made by the federal government. The fact remains that the constituency at the local level jealously guards its right to make the fundamental decisions regarding the educational programs of the local school districts. However, in some states, state support has exceeded the 50 percent mark. The growing emphasis toward equalization of educational opportunity, the rapid rise in educational costs, the demand for extensive expansion of educational services and the unequal distribution of our resources, all seem to portend an even greater percentage increase in state and federal support.

With this shift in degree of support, it is only natural to ask the basic question of whether this shift will mean increased state and federal controls. There is a strong feeling on the part of some persons that the states must assume much more responsibility, not only financial, but policy-wise as well. The possible implication of increased state and federal controls immediately raises the question as to the value of an Educational Resources Management System such as this one. Critics are quick to point out that much time and money will be spent on a system which will appear impressive but will have no impact upon bringing about desirable change at the local level. Supporters, on the other hand, emphasize the fact that the state and the federal governments cannot possibly be totally sensitive to all of the needs and problems at the local level. Consequently, a great deal of input (very likely the most) must still come from the local constituency, regardless of additional support from outside a district.

These statements support continued involvement at the local level but at the same time recognize the great need for local districts to shed forever their isolationism and work cooperatively and constructively for better services for the learner.

Lindman[1] has said: "ERMS-PPBES is usually thought of as a local management tool. However, in education we need to be greatly concerned with all three levels of government."

Since its inception public education has had its severe critics. However, in the past few years this criticism has grown, both in severity and in volume. It has become increasingly clear that there are many persons in this country who, for various reasons, are encouraging more competition from the private sector. Regardless of the motives behind this apparent trend, public education has been placed in a defensive position of considerable magnitude. The implied failure has carried with it a strong indictment of the management of education at all levels. This criticism of management, along with a much greater allocation of resources to education, has caused our constituency to call for a much more adequate accounting of our stewardship. No longer will the professional administrator be given jurisdiction of more resources without the demonstration of a set of carefully

---

1RC-ASBO Panel of Experts Meeting, June, 1970.

planned priority programs, developed from a clear set of goals and objectives and subject to effective evaluation procedures.

A study of the field of education indicates there is no carefully planned approach being used by educators for developing a system in support of decision-making, although some administrators have been using segments of the "Management by Objectives" process for sometime. The private sector is suggesting that the world of education could effectively apply some of the business-industrial management techniques to education. The proposed application of the PPBS concept represents a concrete example and one which shows considerable promise. However, a word or two of caution appears to be appropriate at this point. It must be remembered that the world of business and industry is dealing primarily with inanimate objects (products) and their basic objective is profit making. Measurement is relatively simple compared to the complexity of evaluation as a result of dealing with human beings and the educational process.

The proposed application of the PPBS concept to education has resulted in the formation and expansion of many management consulting organizations offering services in this particular field. Whereas there is and will continue to be a great need for consultative services (and such should be encouraged), there is reason to believe that not too much expertise has been developed in the application of this concept to education.

It is recommended that school districts planning to enter into a contract with an individual or an organization for consultative services carefully research the competencies of the consulting firm first. Furthermore, a contract should spell out very carefully the services to be rendered, particularly as they relate to the programming, planning, and evaluating processes. To date, there has been some evidence of consultative services being rendered to school districts under the guise of the PPBES, but which have turned out to be limited to a program accounting procedure primarily. Such practice usually leaves the local district staff to cope with the most difficult processes, namely, basic planning, programming, and evaluating.

There is a comparatively new management idea developing. Basically, this idea proposes the replacement of top professional educator-administrators with management specialists from the field of business and industry. This movement carries with it numerous implications for the future of the management of education. There is the deep concern for the possibility of management specialists directing our educational systems without having had any previous training and experience with the learning process. This idea may well force an evaluation and overhaul in the basic preparation of our administrators so that many of the managerial techniques of business and industry, heretofore spurned or ignored by educators, may be re-evaluated and applied wherever feasible.

All of the aforementioned changes and applications of new techniques suggest the need for an increase in the level of knowledge of the learning process by the board of education members at both the state and local levels. Whereas in-service education in the past has been emphasized for members of the professional staff primarily, it appears now as though an increasing amount of training has become a priority for effective service as a board member.

Recent meetings of the National School Boards Association have reflected a trend toward much stronger support of continuous training for board members. A similar trend has been noted in the programs of state associations of boards of education. A review of these programs reveals a strong emphasis upon such items as long-range planning, resource management, and accountability. The inclusion of these items reflects the timeliness of the project to develop a conceptualization of an ERM System.

Earlier in this chapter and in Chapter IX considerable stress was placed upon the great need for state departments of education to provide a much greater degree of leadership if these newer concepts of management are to be applied successfully at state, regional, and local levels. Those state departments which have, traditionally, confined their efforts to statistics gathering and dissemination will find need for re-organizing, re-training, and establishing long-range plans for many expanded services. Those state departments which have developed a creditable consultative program probably will not face as much re-organization. However, re-training and re-examination of long-range goals and objectives are essential. Finally, those state departments which have followed a somewhat autocratic policy will find it necessary to modify such if the idea of resource management is going to be applied at the local level on the basis of local needs and problems. Regardless of how a state department may be classified, each must accept greater responsibility for influencing creative and more effective educational legislation, if an educational resources management system is to be developed and implemented effectively.

Need for Change in the Preparation of Educators

Experience during the development of this project has shown that the successful application of a concept of this nature in an individual school district is dependent to a great extent upon the understanding of and support given to it by the superintendent of schools. Immediately the question arises: Must the superintendent be a highly qualified specialist in order to ensure proper and successful usage of the concept? We think not. It is our opinion that the superintendent must be well grounded in the fundamentals of planning, programming, budgeting, and evaluating in order to give proper leadership to the team which will be deeply involved in making the system work effectively. A second question arises: Are school administrators now trained in the aforementioned fundamentals? The answer appears to be "to some extent" but admittedly in a much too superficial manner to have a satisfactory understanding of the systems approach and how it may be applied to the field of education.

For example, most school administrators will insist that they have always done a certain amount of basic planning for educational programming and periodically there has been a certain amount of evaluating. However, most of them will admit, quite frankly, that they have not begun to do a thorough job. In some instances failure to do so has been due to such factors as lack of adequate assistance or lack of time due to the necessity of operating under great pressures and essentially just moving "from crisis to crisis." However, in most instances, a limited comprehension of the concept and all of its supportive techniques has been the major deterrent to satisfactory implementation at the school district level.

Earlier in this document reference was made to the fact that much effort has been expended in the name of "program budgeting" and "program accounting" but comparatively little in the true PPBE concept. Too often there has been an interpretation that the concept is built around the budgeting process primarily. Even now, despite a wide dissemination of information during the past three years it would appear as though a majority of educators have failed to realize that the student is the focal point in the system. Developing programs for students is fundamental. Thus persons who must assume prime positions of leadership are the curriculum specialists. It is doubtful that curriculum specialists have had much training in the systems approach. The same observation could be made for those persons classified under middle management. These managers will have considerable responsibility in program planning as well as in the evaluating process.

Our next comments are directed toward the school business administrator who up to now has been considered by most as the person with the primary responsibility for the design, development, and implementation of the PPBES concept in an individual school district. Frequently in the past, and through no fault of his own, he has been called upon to make decisions regarding curriculum. The responsibility for making these decisions has come either because of default on the part of others or because of political expediency. This condition is beginning to change rapidly. With this change has come the much stronger requisite that the training of the business administrator of the future must be much broader in scope. For example, he should learn a great deal more about the total systems approach. Even though he probably will not be making a large number of individual decisions regarding the curriculum, he should serve as an important member of the professional team.

The Educational Resources Management System as outlined in the earlier chapters calls for the broad involvement of members of the professional staff at all levels. Because so much of the System has been developed around the learner and his progress it follows naturally that classroom teachers have a significant contribution to make as members of the professional team. Proper application of this concept would appear to offer an effective means of releasing the creative energies of the teaching staff.

At this point it seems important to call attention to certain recent developments in the teacher negotiations process. A review of some of the more recent contracts between boards of education and teacher organizations reveal the inclusion of agreements which call for greater involvement of teachers in the decision-making process. If this involvement is to represent something more than simple acquiesence to an idea, then certain activities and changes in attitudes must take place. Board members and administrators must recognize and accept the fact that much more expertise in basic planning, programming, budgeting, and evaluating will be required on the part of the teachers. Acquiring this expertise will require time and money. Boards of education and administrators should be willing to support financially this essential continuous professional development. Teachers on the other hand must be willing to devote time and effort toward achieving these special competencies. Later in this chapter more will be said about the time factor and financial support for professional development.

There has been no specific recommendation as to where the day to day responsibility should rest in a school system which has decided to design, develop, and implement an Educational Resources Management System. Furthermore, it is not the intent of this document to outline in minute detail the qualifications of the person who assumes such responsibility. The wide variation in the characteristics of the 19,000-plus school districts in this country preclude the advisability of such a procedure. However, it seems desirable at this point to offer certain reminders as to the special competencies to be considered when selecting a person to head the program. Obviously not all of these competencies will be found in one person.

Knezevich (1969) declares that:

"The operational behaviors, or administrative activities, consistent with the systems approach are:

1. Clear delineation of long- and short-range objectives capable of being translated into operationally meaningful activities and subsequent evaluation.
2. Recognition of the dynamic nature of goals and sensing when new ones have emerged or when a reordering of priorities among existing objectives is imperative.
3. Recognition of change as normal in viable organizations operating within an environment in ferment and creation of methods to facilitate prudent change.
4. Generation of alternative means of utilizing resources to obtain objectives.
5. Creation of models to study part or all of the system.
6. Utilization of quantitatively oriented tools and procedures in analysis of systems.
7. Dedication of a high priority in the time schedule of top-echelon administrators to planning and programming activities.
8. Employment of interdisciplinary teams of specialists in problem analysis, new systems design, operations evaluation, and the like.
9. Consideration of cooperation of the ever-growing number of educational specialists within the system as a matter of high-echelon concern.

10. Implementation of sophisticated, objective, and scientifically oriented procedures in decision making."

The above list incorporates all of the major features of an Educational Resources Management System with the possible exception of a school district's inventory of needs and problems prior to delineation of its long-range goals and objectives.

Knowledge of techniques such as PERT (Program Evaluation Review Technique), CPM (Critical Path Method) the development of MIS (Management Information Systems) and EDP (Educational Data Processing) seems to be essential on the part of the person directing the program. Other items to be added to the list might include CAI (Computer Assisted Instruction), IPI (Individually Prescribed Instruction) and such other aspects of technology as may apply to the field of education.

To find many persons who are well trained in the field of education and who are also knowledgeable in the areas outlined above is an impossible task at this time. Again, extensive re-training as well as change in the basic training of persons is implied especially for those who will become more deeply involved in the decision-making process at various levels.

During the past few years there has been a rapid diminution in unilateral decision-making and the growth of group dynamics. How decisions are to be made, by whom, at work level, and to what extent must be a determination of those concerned with policy making at the local school district level. The ERM System suggests a broad and truly representative task force for initial basic planning. Furthermore, it identifies clearly the necessity and potential of student involvement. Also, it suggests that a number of staff professionals should have extensive responsibilities at various levels. All of which, in summary, supports the need for re-examination of the decision-making process, of the power structure, and the many forces tending to bring about change.

The dissemination process was an important part of this project. The major share of this process was beamed toward selected groups of educators. The groups included local school superintendents, school business administrators, university professors, state department of education staff members, and representatives of teacher organizations. Members of the project team maintained a record of comments by participants at these meetings. These commentaries supported Gott's findings (Gott, 1970).

Gott reported:

"Statements which, according to the criterion used in the study, are accepted as likely to pertain when a school system adopts ERMD (ERM System) or a similar form of PPBES are listed below.

1. "Direct support and personal involvement of the superintendent will be essential for success of the undertaking.

2. "The superintendent will find it necessary to spend more time in the planning process than at the present time.

3. "Personnel chiefly oriented toward curriculum design will exert influence on allocation of resources to a degree that is greater than at the present time.
4. "Boards of education will be vitally involved in approving statements of priorities.
5. "Boards of education will be vitally involved in approving board objectives recommended for adoption as school system responsibilities.
6. "The [school] system will need to develop increased capacity to accomplish research of a practical operational nature.
7. "The skills that will have to be upgraded include those necessary to accomplish: planning; decision-making; formulation of educational objectives; development of alternate programs for achieving objectives; coordinated collection and treatment of diverse data for use in the budgeting process; and evaluating achievement of educational objectives . . .

In addition to the aforementioned requirements, the participants indicated that the following statements would be likely to pertain when a school district adopts some form of an ERM System:

1. The emphasis upon evaluation will result in strong pressure for greater attention to the learning problems of special groups.
2. The use of an ERM System may suggest allocation of resources internally — in ways distinctly different from traditional patterns.
3. A better description of the desired changes in students as a result of teaching leads to the discovery of more effective teaching methods.
4. Legislators would respond with better financial support for schools if evidence of accomplishment were provided for them.
5. An ERM System provides for methodically relating production (outputs) to objectives.
6. An ERM System supports projection of costs of programs over extended periods of time.
7. Use of an ERM System will produce increased precision in identifying objectives for which a school district is responsible.
8. An ERM System provides an increased emphasis upon relating activities and services to specific objectives.
9. Use of an ERM System will provide a school district with improved capability to identify, allocate, and use available resources.
10. Decisions presently made by central office administration will be made increasingly in cooperation with principals and teachers.
11. Educators will become more proficient at organizing community involvement in selection of broad educational objectives.
12. Evaluation in an ERM System will result in increased use of available devices for objective determination of educational output.

A synopsis of both the formal and informal feedback from the aforementioned conferences placed *planning* at the top of the list, both from the standpoint of its importance to the total systems approach as well as being the area in which the greatest number of benefits from the adoption of an ERM System are likely to be grouped.

Overall, the participants view the inadequacy of skills, techniques, and understanding as the top ranking problem areas attending adoption of the ERM System. Secondary problem areas were problems of negative attitudes and problems of operation and implementation, i.e., coordinating, organizing, communicating, and broadening involvement.

Informal discussions with representatives of many institutions of higher learning have left the impression that training for the application of the PPBES concept to the field of education is inadequate. Gradually, colleges of education are beginning to coordinate efforts with other divisions of the universities so as to present the strongest possible training team for this complex undertaking. Many of the professors responsible for training or retraining administrators at all levels are frank to admit that they are in need of a considerable amount of updating in their own training so as to secure mastery of the overall concept.

Of the educational organizations, probably the greatest support (both financial and moral) will be required from the associations for boards of education. If the extensive in-service programs heretofore envisioned are to become a reality, then they will succeed only when boards of education broaden the scope of support well beyond current practice. An objective review of the type and extent of additional knowledge needed and time required for the design, development, and implementation of an ERM System would convince any fair-minded board member that broad and effective staff involvement must be viewed in a new light.

Professional negotiations and collective bargaining are bound to carry strong implications for a school district about to become deeply involved in the application of an ERM System. The negotiators for the teachers with their growing sophistication will insist upon an expansion of contracts which will call for released time blocks (both short and long), extra pay for extra work, and extended contracts. Associated with these items will come requests for full reimbursement for "out of pocket" expenses in conjunction with specialized training requirements.

The trend toward extended contracts, e.g., an extra month's work in the summer, is growing in popularity at a promising rate. Both administrators and teachers seem to favor this idea, especially in relation to curriculum revision and development. Board members and the public in many instances seem to be accepting this pattern also. Experience has shown that work by teachers at a time when they are free of classroom assignments is far more creative and productive.

Even though we can expect more support for better in-service education at the local level the fact remains that the greater potential lies at the state level and beyond. One of the most recent promising sources can be found in EPDA (Education Profession Development Act). It would appear quite feasible to encourage an agency such as the one administering EPDA to accept a prime role of leadership and support. However, EPDA faces the problem of adequate funding and as yet this agency has not been given an opportunity to realize its full potential primarily because of limited appropriations.

Summary

Throughout this document stress has been placed upon long-range planning and the development of programs which meet the needs of the learner and which are beamed toward helping to solve the problems of a school district. Great importance has been attached to the preparation of a *goal-oriented* program structure. In the process of designing the ERM System one of the basic questions raised was: Should the goal structure determine the program structure or — should the program structure determine the goal structure? The designers of the ERM System have taken the position that *the goal structure must serve as the foundation for the program structure.*

The goal-oriented program structure reflects the results of a careful look at the problems and needs of a school district in relation to resources available, the school system's capabilities, and benefits to be obtained. It reflects the results of a thorough analysis of the alternatives and the determination of priorities for the establishment of programs.

A review of many program structures throughout the country reveals that they appear to have been built around such patterns as school system organization, grade level structures, or subject matter-curricular combinations. Too often, program structures with these types of foundations represent the status quo. In many instances the programs in the structure are not based upon a careful analysis of the needs and problems of the individual students of the school district.

A second basic question relates to the evaluating process: Should we emphasize the quality of our product or the quality of our educational process? The designers of the ERM System believe that *it is important to be concerned with the quality of the product and the process.*

Because the original use of the PPBS concept comes from business and industry and the profit motive is of prime concern, it is only natural that evaluation of the product is the focal point. Education, however, deals with human beings and not inanimate objects. The process by which the best results are achieved by one learner will not apply necessarily to the next or to the next. Experience has shown that the educational services offered must be many and varied. The evaluation of the quality of these many educational services cannot be neglected simply because of outside pressures which seek the evaluation of the learner's progress only.

Education in the past few decades has accepted a greater number of responsibilities, part of which may be considered the responsibility of other agencies. When the responsibility has been on a shared basis, there has been a tendency to hold education accountable primarily. A word of caution is to remind educators that other agencies have responsibilities for the learner also and must accept a fair share of responsibility for the outcomes.

A third basic question, and probably the most natural one, is: Have not educators been following many phases of this system for a long time? — So what is new? The answer is — *yes. Educators have been doing some planning* from whence has come some new programs and a revision of others. And there has been some evaluating. But, the fact remains that educators have not started a systematic study with: 1) a careful look at the needs and problems of their districts; 2) an inventory of available resources; 3) the establishment of broad goals and general objectives; 4) reaching agreement on priorities; 5) the consideration and analysis of alternative program strategies; 6) the establishment of programs according to plan; 7) the procurement and allocation of resources according to plan; 8) the preparation of the budget format; 9) the evaluation of the total effort; and 10) finally recycling and revision as seems necessary and/or desirable.

One final basic question: Have the programs of the past and the present always truly been relevant to the basic needs of the learner? What assurance is there that they will be more relevant in the future? An honest appraisal usually results in an answer in the negative. *Therefore, it is essential to recognize the growing demand from the constituency to utilize, at the earliest moment, a new approach to educational management.* The guidelines as presented in the ERM System offer one approach. Other applications of the PPBES concept are currently in the process of being developed. It will be up to the local district to utilize the system which best suits its needs.

One final observation: The ERM System or some variation of it appears to be a device which, when used properly, can be most effective in improving the decision-making process. Abuse of this system by persons with selfish motives can bring results which will be most detrimental to the very persons it is designed to serve — the learners. It is incumbent, therefore, upon the educational leadership at all levels, local, state, and federal, to accept immediately the major responsibility for the development and implementation of this device so as to provide sound assurance that the focal point of the educational effort will be the learner and that his best interests will remain as the number one objective.

REFERENCES

Gott, John Walker. *A Study of Selected Factors Related to the Development and Dissemination of a Planning, Programming, Budgeting, Evaluating System for Public Education.* (Ed.D. dissertation, Washington State University, Department of Education) Pullman, Washington: 1970.

Knezevich, Stephan J. *Administration of Public Education.* New York: Harper and Row, 1969.

APPENDIX A

The Role of Analysis in PPBS (ERMS) *

This paper focuses on the analytical portions of the Planning-Programming-Budgeting cycle. Problems of measurements, the use of cost-effectiveness techniques, the use of multiple criteria evaluation, and the applicability of these considerations to questions encountered in education are discussed. The paper considers the role of analysis as a functional part of PPBS.

1.1 Problems of Measurement

In previous chapters we have discussed the implementation of program budgeting and its potential role in decision-making. The program structure and budget allows us — at least in theory — to ask *why* we are doing something, *what* we are doing, and *how much* it is costing us. Although the elements of objective determination, program description, and cost modeling present problems in any system and whereas these difficulties may be more intense in education, with time and experience they would become significantly more manageable. However, serious and not so readily dismissed objections to the application of PPB to education are encountered in the analytic (the "how well") portion of the cycle. Schick (1969, pp. 821-2, 830-2) contends that the structural formality of systems is incompatible with the "opportunistic" nature of analysis and, as such, PPB is "anti-analytic."[1] In a like manner, Wildavsky (1969, pp. 837, 853) argues that analysis is an art form and should not be incorporated into the routine of a budgetary system; he also criticizes PPB for the premium it supposedly puts on "mindless quantification for its own sake." Hartley (1968, pp. 240-2) and Quade (1966, pp. 8, 24) stress our poor understanding of how to measure objective attainment and the difficulty of quantifying social, and especially educational objectives, benefits and criteria for effectiveness. Whereas this last, the most damaging of the criticisms, may restrict initially the reliability of analytic results, there is considerable room for improvement within even this limitation. We shall see presently that none of these objections need be crippling; even the most troublesome may be satisfactorily resolved with careful and innovative use of analysis in PPB.

* "The Role of Analysis in PPBS" is found in Chapter IV of "The Utility of PPBS for Urban School Systems" by Donald M. Levine (Unpublished Dissertation, Harvard University, Cambridge, Massachusetts, 1971). This work develops further the approach to resource allocation described by Dr. Levine in his paper, "Structuring Program Analysis for Educational Research," (P-4565, the RAND Corporation, Santa Monica, California, March, 1971). This work was funded, in part, by a grant from the Research Corporation of the Association of School Business Officials.

[1] Note, however, that Schick has recently mollified his stand considerably and in fact has written papers favoring implementation of PPB. See Allen Schick, "Multipurpose Budget Systems" in Harley H. Hinrichs and Graeme M. Taylor (eds.), *Program Budgeting and Benefit-Cost Analysis*, (Pacific Palisades, California: Goodyear Publishing Co., Inc., 1969). pp. 358-372.

The selection of objectives appropriate to the system presents major problems, but it can be argued that the objectives are usually quite easily formulated at higher levels. The goals of education elude direct quantification precisely because widest agreement is achieved when they are stated broadly in philosophical terms. Indeed, even many of the sub-objectives will be agreed on: in "to develop fundamental intellectual skills," (S. M. Barro, 1969, p. 33) we would find that "develop language and communication skills" and "to develop quantitative and reasoning skills" have a role in education in nearly any literate society. One could go even further with confidence in saying that "to learn reading and writing" and "to learn mathematics" would fall respectively under these sub-categories. Question arises, however, with respect to the "how," the "how much," and the "when" of these quantities.

Such broad objectives as "to develop fundamental intellectual skills," however, are not very useful as bases of performance evaluation; they must be translated into behavioral approximations. Normally, this is accomplished indirectly: the problem is divided into sub-problems for which we can express objectives in more operational terms, and the ensemble of these sub-objectives is taken as representative of the original objective(s).

There are genuine problems in objective formulation at the lower levels, however, in that the sum of the sub-objectives may not be an accurate representation of the higher objectives (Morris, 1967, pp. II-7 to II-11; Hitch & McKean, 1967, pp. 128-131, 161). At the lower level, objectives cease to be independent determinants of the activities designed to satisfy them; they become shaped by limitations of the present state of knowledge about the educational process and by what is "reasonable" to expect from existing programs. As greater structural detail is introduced, the original objectives — the ones that the combination of programs of lower objectives seeks to attain — may be increasingly distorted. In addition, optimization with respect to one sub-objective may have adverse effects on others that will serve to diminish the overall achievement. Across-the-board optimization of sub-objectives may not be a satisfactory approach to solution of the total problem. These are the problems of distortion and sub-optimization (so-called) encountered generally in systems analysis (Morris, 1967; Hitch & McKean, 1967, pp. 400-402).

A major role of PPB is to aid in selection among alternatives.[2] "Evaluating alternatives is both the *why* and the *how* of program budgeting for educational planning" (Carpenter & Haggart, 1969, p. 1). Given a set of objectives, we wish to choose the program alternative which best satisfies the objectives with due attention to cost constraints. Cost or resource requirements are developed, effectiveness analysis is performed, and the most efficient plan within cost constraints or performance requirements is selected. This is the realm of cost-effectiveness analysis: the development —

---

[2] "(In) program budgeting . . . the name of the game is Alternatives. This is what distinguishes it from the most prior efforts." (David Novick, "Program Budgeting, Its Origin, Present Status and Future," in *Report of the First National Conference on PPBES in Education* (Chicago: The Research Corporation of the Association of School Business Officials, June 10, 1969), p. 26.

in quantitative or qualitative terms — of the relationship between the resource inputs and the outputs for a given program. But in order to do meaningful cost-effectiveness analysis, criteria for evaluation must be developed that in some way measure the effectiveness of a program in terms of its outputs.

Once objectives have been stated, the selection of criteria which accurately reflect how well an alternative attains stated objectives can be very troublesome. As an example, let us consider a program for which one objective is "to enhance creativity." In order to compare the effects of different programs, we seek some measure of creativity. Given this task, does the most accurate indicator arise from an I.Q. test, an analysis of word associations, or an ink blot test? Or is the truest reflection some weighted combination of the three? What better standards can we use? Creativity is probably the most difficult quantity that we would ever want to measure. In many instances the problem of criteria selection is largely definitional. Such nebulous terms as "creativity" are not terribly useful constructs and we must specify more of what we mean by the word if we hope to measure creativity adequately.

In formulating our understanding of the concept, we could first visualize some of the manifestations of creativity and incorporate them by generalization into a definition. Criteria will be implicit in our definition, but they may not be easy to apply. Using the definition to the extent possible, we might isolate a large class of people of different "creativities." From statistics describing members of these groups we might deduce relationships between the more readily observable measures and our first critria for measurement of creativity. If these relationships correlate the original criteria and the new measures very well, the new measures may suffice as representative indicators of creativity. Ideally, we would utilize indicators such that, by their measurement, a scale of system effectiveness is obtained. That is, without further interpretation, these measures correspond directly to different levels of objective attainment. Such measures, however, are rarely available.

Of course, these measures, (e.g., of creativity) must be developed with care and accuracy, but system and definitional uncertainties must not be neglected; too often quantification is equated with precision and accuracy. While quantification may on the surface facilitate analysis, (Quade, 1966, pp 11-14) unless we can specify in equally quantitative terms the uncertainty of the system, any analysis of system data will produce results of questionable validity.

"The need to use proximate rather than ultimate tests opens the door to the selection of incorrect criteria. But the door is really swung wide open . . . by another fact of life . . . the fact that problems of choice must be broken down into component pieces or sub-problems" (Hitch & McKean, 1967, p. 161). Complex problems frequently elude direct quantitative and qualitative criteria and, as such, require fragmentation into sub-problems. The best criteria for each of the sub-problems may be inconsistent with or fail to represent the best criteria for the entire problem if the relation between the higher and lower level objectives is poorly understood. The total problem is rarely the sum of the sub-problems — these are usually interdependent: while "fundamental intellectual skills" may subdivide readily into "language and communication skills" and "quantitative and reasoning skills," they are not independent. Conditions which optimize one element may affect others adversely. As the analyst examines more sub-systems, each of which may demand its own criteria, the chances for selecting inappropriate criteria increase, and system analyses may become suspect.[3]

Complex problems usually involve more than one objective, and the analysis of systems with multiple objectives generally requires multiple criteria.[4] Even for problems with a single objective, several criteria may be necessary. Some criteria (because of the nature of the objectives) may be quantitative while others remain qualitative. Even when restricting ourselves to qualitative or quantitative measures, the former frequently differ in type and the latter in units.[5] The problems of multiple criteria evaluation will be examined in detail in Section 1.2.

Up to this point we have alluded to the problems of objective formulation, the role of cost-effectiveness analysis in program design and selection, and some of the general difficulties inherent in discovering and utilizing criteria which adequately measure goal attainment. Let us return momentarily to the interrelationships of elements of a PPB system before addressing ourselves specifically to issues more central to the analytical portion of the Planning-Programming-Budgeting cycle.

Within the program structure, objectives are the justification for *an* expenditure of resources; they are the *raison d'etre* of a program. It must be understood, however, that objectives are not intrinsic to a program; a program functions quite independently of the objectives. Simply attributing the genesis of a program to a certain set of goals does not bias its function in favor of achieving those objectives any more than if the program was

---

3These are essentially the same problems of distortion and sub-optimization that we introduced above, discussed in terms of the criteria instead of the objectives.

4There are exceptions to this rule, however, in that program administrators are occasionally satisfied with a single, broad measure as indicator of the combined effectiveness of the program activities. An example is cited: the Office of Public Health Service of HEW uses the average number of days a person is in good health as a measure of the effectiveness of all of their diverse programs. (M. B. Carpenter and M. L. Rapp, "VI. The Analysis of Effectiveness" in *Program Budgeting for School District Planning: Concepts and Applications*, Memorandum #RM-6116-RC, The Rand Corporation, Santa Monica, November, 1969, p. 138.) Such an overall parameter for education might be average lifetime income among matriculants of a given socio-economic level. Unfortunately, it requires fifty years to collect such data. Some would argue that this would not be a satisfactory measure in any case: even if means were available capable of effectively predicting lifetime performance from the first five years following matriculation, few educators consciously orient their programs towards maximizing earning power. The objection, in effect, is that we are not measuring performance with respect to the expressed goals of the educational programs, that a single measure cannot purport to adequately represent the complex and frequently dynamic state of the number and relative importance of objectives . . . we wish to avoid such measures precisely because of the type of averaging effects that tend to strip meaning from our results. Such a measure would be of no strategic value; it could tell us nothing that would be helpful in resource allocation or new program implementation. We will return to some of these issues, in particular that of the possibility of obtaining an optimum distribution of resources among program elements, in Section 1.2: Multiple Criteria-Evaluation.

5This can happen even in cost-benefit analysis where cost and benefits are both measured in dollars. When expenditures and receipts occur over different time periods, they are in effect incommensurate quantities, and the analyst must apply discount rates to gain commensurability. ("The prime difference [between cost-effectiveness and cost-benefit analysis] lies in a major attempt on the part of cost-benefit analysts to reduce all benefits to the dollar figure, commensurate to the resource input required" [Morris, 3, pp. 1-6]).

originally established under wholly different auspices.[6] This functional independence of programs and objectives makes it necessary to utilize measures of effectiveness in judging the relative worths of competing alternate programs.

The program may be viewed as a "black box" that, once organized, performs operations on the input functions, e.g., students as described by factors of intelligence, socio-economic level, race, age, beginning achievement level, etc., such that the output functions generated preserve some of the original factors while changing others. Other influences remaining constant, we attribute these changes to effects of the program. The criteria, in effect, seek out these changes and map them into an effectiveness scheme where the value of the changes is judged against what we set out to accomplish. This judgment is tempered by the cost or resource requirements of the program. By establishing a continuum of such effectiveness-cost positions, we could in theory select the most effective program for a given cost or the least expensive program for a given effectiveness.[7]

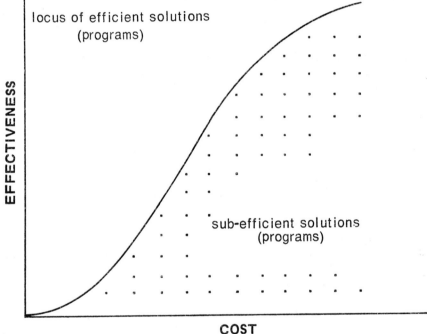

Figure 1.

6Note also Hitch and McKean, p. 159. "But while good intentions are sometimes reputed to be excellent paving materials, in themselves they do not pave the way to preferred action."

7One point should be stressed here: within the framework of cost-effectiveness analysis "optimal" solutions are rare. We have "efficient" solutions which yield the greatest output for a given resource input or the smallest resource input to produce a given output, but unconstrained global minima or maxima implied by the term "optimization" are neither generally available nor sought. This is true even when dealing in industrial cost-benefit analyses: dogma dictates that resources be invested until the shadow price drops to unity, but increasing cost-risk factors very often become the final determinants of preferred action.

We will now examine the roles of criteria and performance measures in the development of cost-effectiveness analysis. In distinguishing these terms and their relations to effectiveness, we will concurrently introduce some of the philosophy and justification of this versus other related systems of analysis.

The frequent confusion of systems jargon by non- analysts is not entirely due to their lay status; analysts themselves are in frequent disagreement. "Criterion" is used quite differently by separate writers in the literature, but, in fact, the concensus seems to present us with a term that assigns to systems analysis an impossible task. Carpenter and Rapp (1969, p. 142) go to the dictionary: "a standard of judging." But just what is being judged is not clear at the outset; is it the *selection* among alternatives or the relative ranking of effectiveness? One infers from such phrases in text as "criteria for success" and "criteria for effectiveness" that the latter is to be understood. Hatry (1969, p. 98), in effect uses the same definition, but is more explicit, defining criteria as "measures of effectiveness." Quade (1966, p. 8), however, calls a criterion "a rule or standard by which to rank the alternatives in order of desirability . . . a means for weighing cost against effectiveness." Effectiveness and cost are taken for granted and the criterion combines these quantities into a single figure by which the alternatives achieve their final ranking. Carpenter and Haggart (1969, #P-4195, p. 3) regard criteria as rules by which one selects one alternative over another — essentially in agreement with Quade — and coin something called "effectiveness measures" by which the contribution of each alternative to meeting the objective is determined. The "effectiveness measure" appears to assume the role of the criterion as cited by Carpenter and Rapp. Morris (1967, pp. II-3 to II-4), possibly reflecting his own confusion over the literature, first states that a criterion "is a measure of how well we achieve the objective . . . used because we do not know how to measure the objective in and of itself"; later he qualifies the initial statement: "While I have not stated it as such, a criterion implies a ratio of desired output to required resource input." He covers himself on both sides of the issue, but proceeds to neglect the cost element of the definition and implicitly adopts the "ranking of effectiveness" use of "criterion" in his own development. Hitch and McKean (1967, pp. 159-160) agree with Quade in labelling criteria as "tests of preferredness," but they admit the use of "partial criteria": selected effects "relevant to the comparison of alternative actions."

The different conceptions of "criterion" are highlighted by the dichotomy presented in the question following the dictionary "standard of judging": "selection among alternatives" and "ranking of effectiveness." The first use of "criterion" is a standard for judging the merit of a program in terms of both its cost and effectiveness, whereas the second is a standard for evaluating effectiveness alone. Quade, Hitch and McKean use "criterion" in the strict sense of providing a rationale for the final ordering of alternatives in terms of relative "preferredness." Criteria for "ranking of effectiveness" as used by

Carpenter and Rapp and Hatry would fall under the category of "partial criteria" in Hitch and McKean's scheme since the cost element is lacking and we are assessing only one portion of the entire problem.

Hitch and McKean (1967, p. 160) observe that "there are times when the term 'criterion' appears to be a misnomer." It is then that they proceed to introduce the concept of the "partial criterion" in deference to the reality that "analysis can unravel only *some* of the consequences of alternative actions." The principle difficulty of the "selection among alternatives" or "test of preferredness" usage of "criterion" lies in the implicit maximization of net benefits. In cost-benefit analysis it may be possible to achieve this by maximizing the present value difference of the discounted stream of revenue and the discounted stream of costs. Consistent with the theory of the firm, inputs are increased until the shadow price equals unity. The characteristic feature of cost-benefit analysis is just this commensurability (after discounting) of input and output measures; all costs and benefits are measured in terms of their dollar value. In such situations it may be meaningful to stipulate selection of the program yielding the greatest net benefit — this is a criterion according to the strict sense of the word.

It is only in special instances, however, that the "test of preferredness" criterion can be utilized profitably. To measure net benefits we must have a means of insuring commensurability among all of the factors to enter consideration. This is accomplished relatively simply in systems to which we might apply cost-benefit analysis, but such transformations seem inconceivable in the context of most other systems; this is particularly true of problems that we encounter in education. Commensurability of inputs and outputs is a relative rarity: often inputs are measured in dollars and outputs in behavioral terms. Even if methods were available to achieve commensurability among these items, it would be a mistake to combine the inputs and outputs into a final rating measure since this would tend to obscure the high degree of certainty associated with the cost figures without enhancing that of the output measures. Any ranking of alternatives under these circumstances would not be very meaningful.

In practice, the analyst rarely goes beyond obtaining separate figures for cost and effectiveness of alternatives (Feeney, 1955, pp. 69-82); the decision-maker normally supplies his own criterion for making the final selection. This sort of decision-making is difficult to systematize as it usually relies on a highly intuitive grasp that is simultaneously cognizant of the background and intended future of a problem. The decision-maker is usually content to apply his personal and hence largely implicit criterion at this point, and, beyond helping to sharpen the decision-maker's intuition, the analyst is well-advised to avoid this last step. The work of the analyst is complete when the decision-maker is at ease with the problem.

By presenting two measures — cost and effectiveness — we obviate the necessity of entering the highly qualitative area of the final judgment. The role of the systems analyst has ethical limitations as well: the final decision should be made by the decision-maker, not the analyst. We derive another

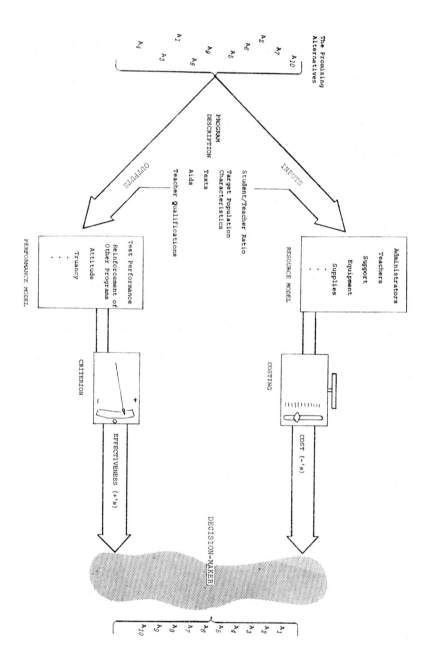

Figure 2. The Structure of Cost-Effectiveness Analysis.

214

advantage from our definition: the dichotomy of costs and benefits is explicity recognized and contrasted within the framework of the program. Not only is it possible to say, "We pay X and we get Y," but our evaluation has produced the estimate, Y, that is a judgment of how effective the program has been in achieving our stated objectives. And thus cost-effectiveness analysis is introduced (see Figure 2).[8]

The result of this discussion is that the concept of criterion as introduced by Quade (1966, p. 8), Hitch and McKean (1967, p. 160) is so limited in its applicability that we cannot use it advantageously. Hitch and McKean (1967, p. 196) underestimate the difficulty of their definition when they state that "on occasion" analysis may be unable to separate out *all* of the consequences of any action; indeed, "analysis can *never* treat all the considerations that may be relevant" (Quade, 1966, p. 23). Even the rather simple-minded example they supply[9] is subject to this criterion. Rather than retain some ultimate ideal called "criterion" and apologize for reality by introducing such artificial terms as "partial criterion" or "'proximate' criterion," we will find it useful to define "criterion" as an operational construct to be precisely "a measure of effectiveness." If we find it necessary, we shall not hesitate to refer to a "criterion (a standard of judging) for the final ranking of alternatives," but in general it shall be understood that "criterion" in the systems sense shall mean "a measure of effectiveness." In this way, we also will be able to entertain meaningfully the consideration of the widely used term of "multiple criteria analysis."

"One of the common problems in dealing with criteria is mistaking performance measures for criteria, or in some cases even objectives" (Morris, 1967, p. II-11). The most straight-forward resolution arises from contrasting "effectiveness" and "performance"; "measures of effectiveness" (criteria) and "performance measures" are distinguished as a simple consequence.

Effectiveness is a scale of the level of goal attainment; it is the degree to which a program succeeds in fulfilling the objectives that justify the program's existence. Performance, however, is a scale of the *effects* of a program, and, despite its positive connotations, "performance" in this usage is strictly descriptive. The *performance* of a system is judged against the *objectives*, and evaluation yields the *effectiveness*. Performance is a vector quantity determined by the magnitude assumed by the program on different "effect" axes; effectiveness, these effect axes are weighted according to their relative importance to arrive at a single value that characterizes how well objectives have been met. The unidimensionality of effectiveness now

---

[8]Contrast with the diagram in Quade, p. 9.

[9]Hitch and McKean, p. 159. Later (pp. 160-164), they introduce the term "'prosimate' criterion." This is to mean that we still attempt to achieve final ranking via application of a "test of preferredness," but we recognize that no test is perfect and that the criterion we use is only 'proximate.' Since, of all the tests we use in analysis of the data, this final test is necessarily the most suspect, our solution instead is to present the decision-maker with the two very *meaningful* measures of "cost" and "effectiveness." The arguments we have cited for a cost-effectiveness system of analysis militate strongly against this excessively structured conception of systems of analysis, regardless of any admission to the effect that any criterion is always going to be, at best, only 'proximate.' The implicity passive role of the decision-maker in Hitch and McKean's definition of "criterion" is probably its most serious liability. Moreover, by dissolving the artificial distinction of "criterion," "partial criterion," and "'proximate' criterion," we have managed to condense with no loss of utility, three terms into one.

permits us to rank our alternative programs in terms of objective achievement. (Ranking among higher-dimensional quantities is not meaningful without prior scalar assignment.)

The evaluation of performance is motivated primarily by our need to assess the effectiveness of a program in achieving objectives, and in this sense this description is only a means to an end. Inasmuch as performance cannot be measured in and of itself (in that no clearly appropriate units or scales of "performance" exist), we must utilize *measures of performance* to represent in operational or behavioral terms selected effects of a program; within statistical limits, the values of performance measures are assumed to represent the axes of a program's performance description. The selection of these axes is somewhat arbitrary in number and type, but we should beware that the description represents adequately those effects which, by their inclusion, would be expected to alter the assessment of effectiveness. However, the need for the performance description to conform to the requirements of the criterion for effectiveness can constrain us to reformulate the performance description for identical systems operating under different sets of objectives. To complicate further, this relative freedom to define the "effect" axes by whatever our performance measures measure can mean that the form of the description can be highly personalized and may vary from investigator to investigator with equal validity; reproducibility of effectiveness assignments therefore may be difficult. But these problems are generally applicable only when it is necessary to reconcile the results of independent studies. For the moment, our concern is to select an array of performance measures that permit a satisfactory yet wieldy representation of the performance of the system.[10]

We have delayed introducing a more operational definition of "criterion," because a correct understanding of the relationship of "measure of effectiveness" to "effectiveness" necessarily involves the concept of performance. The relationship between "performance measure" and "performance" is essentially straightforward; such is not the case, however, with "criteria" and "effectiveness."

Consider a program alternative for the improvement of reading skills among third-graders. Pre- and post-tests are administered, and, by the differences, measures of system performance are gained.[11] In the same way that we "test" the system for performance, we will "test" performance for effectiveness. The plane of evaluation has shifted. No longer are we examining the program with a view to describing its effects; our present concern is to judge

10The design of performance indicators is a problem only indirectly related to our own. For our purposes, tests need only to provide values for the effect axes in such a way that the performance vector obtained is an adequate representation of the effectiveness of a program. Where multiple objectives are encountered, we should like to group performance measures by objectives so that no measure relates to two independent objectives. For example, given the objectives of "improving reading skills" and "improving mathematical skills," we would administer tests (performance indicators) that recognize and preserve the independence of these objectives. It must be remembered that the values assumed by performance measures (derived from the results of the performance indicators) are the connections between what is occurring and what should be occurring and that the relationship of performance measures to objectives is as important as their relationship to reality. To the extent that it is possible, performance measures (and, hence, performance indicators) should be shaped by the objectives.

11Note that this use of performance puts the onus of student achievement on the teaching program.

the value of these effects against the objectives that we originally sought to attain by installation of the program. This is the role of the criterion: it is a "test of effectiveness" (as opposed to "preferredness" in Hitch & McKean, 1967, p. 159), a rule by which we measure the effectiveness of a program in terms of its performance characteristics.

The criterion is an interpretation of the objectives that assigns the weights that each performance measure (performance is typically a function of several variables) should receive in contributing to the overall goal achievement. But the criterion is more than a simple combination rule to be followed in assigning effectiveness to a set of performance measures; it is usually variable in addition. Under the so-called "law of diminishing returns," as a desideratum becomes more available, each additional increment in its availability becomes less desirable. In some cases even monotonicity cannot be assured.[12] Our criterion must account for such non-linearities when they assume significant dimensions. In summary, then, the criterion is an expression of the objectives that:

1. recognize
   a. the relative importance of different performance characters in contributing to the overall effectiveness of a program, and
   b. how the weighting changes as a function of the magnitude assumed by each performance measure (the projection of the performance vector on each of the "effect" axes); and
2. utilize this knowledge in transforming the performance of a system into a final valuation of effectiveness.[13]

Let us consider an example in detail. An examination consisting of three parts — vocabulary, speed comprehension, and grammar — is administered to assess how "effectively" a person reads. This might be the basis for

---

[12]As in Morris' preference for sugar in coffee and the use of arsenic as a beneficial health medicine. (Morris, p. II-41).

[13]By translating into mathematical terms the conceptual relationship between performance, criteria and effectiveness is quite simply demonstrated. Performance is an n-dimensional vector, $\overline{P}$, which is composed by performance measures, $p_1, p_2, p_3, \ldots, p_n$. The criterion is a lxn matrix, $\overline{\overline{C}}$, with coefficients, $c_1, c_2, c_3, \ldots, c_n$. The coefficients, c_j, are weighting factors for the values assumed by the performance measures, p_j, in producing contributions to the overall effectiveness of the program, E(more properly, EI, where I is a one-dimensional identity vector.)
That is,

$$\overline{\overline{C}} \ \overline{P} = E \ \overline{I} = E$$

,where

$\overline{\overline{C}}$ criterion matrix
$\overline{P}$ performance matrix
$\overline{I}$ identity vector ($=1$)
E   effectiveness scalar

$$\left| c_1 \ c_2 \ c_3 \ \cdot \ \cdot \ \right| \begin{pmatrix} p_1 \\ p_2 \\ p_3 \\ \cdot \\ \cdot \\ \cdot \end{pmatrix}$$

$$= c_1 p_1 + c_2 p_2 + c_3 p_3 + \cdots$$

$$= E \ \overline{I} = E$$

217

selecting among applicants to a limited enrollment reading course. The person's performance is described by scores on the separate parts[14] of the reading examination. Our task is to transform these scores into a measure of effectiveness by which we can rank "alternatives" (people taking the examination) in terms of the need for help.

Mr. A, who performed in the sixtieth percentile on both vocabulary and speed comprehension but only in the twenty-fifth percentile on grammar, might be advised that he does not need the program. Mr. B, who performed in the sixtieth percentile on grammar and vocabulary and in the fortieth percentile on speed comprehension, might on the other hand be allowed to enroll. Mr. A's average (48) is lower than that of Mr. B (53), yet only for Mr. B was enrollment recommended. If speed comprehension were two and one half times and vocabulary half again as important as grammar, we would observe that the ordering is reversed: Mr. A's weighted average is 52, Mr. B's is 50. This evaluative scheme would be our criterion.[15]

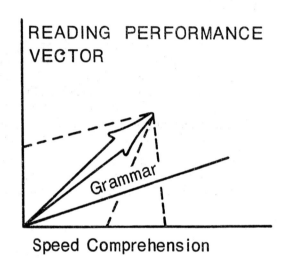

READING PERFORMANCE VECTOR

VOCABULARY

Grammar

Speed Comprehension

---

[14]Each of these parts would be a performance indicator in the context of this example. The actual test scores would be the values assumed by the performance indicators, which, in turn, would be translated into performance levels to be assumed by each of the performance measures. In mathematical terms the values finally associated with the performance measures would correspond to the projection of the reading performance vector onto the separate "effect" axes of vocabulary, speed comprehension, and grammar.

[15]The criterion relates performance to effectiveness. Consequently, we assume here that performance is adequately measured in terms of test population percentile scores. This is at least reasonable (a) if percentiles provide a sufficiently smooth gradation of performance levels and the relation of percentile to performance is familiar to the people utilizing the percentiles for decision-making, or (b) if, for some reason, we wish to isolate all and only those alternatives that represent a certain elite portion of the population on which the percentile scale is founded. Indeed, it is not the SAT score of 750 *per se* on an SAT that impresses an admissions officer, but the fact that less than one percent of the students nationally and less than four percent of the applicants to his college score as high. Let us focus on points (a) and (b).

(a) A gradation of vocabulary size represented by percentiles composed from a test population of equal numbers of lexicographers and first-graders would be unsatisfactory: there would be a discontinuity of several thousand words at the fiftieth percentile. (See graph on next page.) This would be inadequate for the testing of any population, whether of (i) lexicographers, (ii) first-graders, or (iii) anyone else: the worst lexicographer will have a vocabulary that rates him greater than the fiftieth percentile, the first-grader with the largest vocabulary will be at best fiftieth percentile, and the majority of all other people's vocabularies would fall in the tiny region (on the percentile scale) between. By deducting 50 from the percentile scores of the lexicographers and multiplying by two, however, a legitimate percentile

Above[16] we contrasted criterion with performance measure: "In the same way that we 'test' the system for performance, we will 'test' performance for effectiveness. The plane of evaluation has shifted." The components of performance are separately tested for their contributions to the reading effectiveness. In effect, we are finding effectiveness measures for each of the factors, which in turn are combined in some way to arrive at an overall effectiveness figure; the total criterion will be a function of the component sub-criteria. While the total problem becomes clearer by separating out the sub-problems or factors, we encountered difficulties closely analogous to those of sub-optimization.[17]

We will assume that adequate indicators of performance are available[18] and now establish performance versus effectiveness relationships for the per-

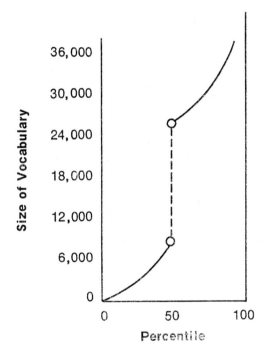

(Footnote 15 continued)
    test scale for lexicographers could be obtained. (This is equivalent to re-ordering the original lexicographer test scores and forming a new percentile scale.)
    (b) A college might seek to establish itself as a first-rate school by composing its student body to an elite whose performance on national examinations was above a certain level; they might accept exclusively those applicants who scored ninety-fifth percentile or better on the College Board Examinations, regardless the size of the first few graduating classes. In effect a school does this when it has a policy of accepting all students with SAT averages of better than 700 without further review or of offering early admission to such students.

16See p. 216.

17See p. 210.

18See note, p. 216. For an example of a discussion of methodological difficulties encountered in designing performance indicators, see also Irving Lorge and Jeanne Chall, "Estimating the Size of Vocabularies of Children and Adults: An Analysis of Methodological Issues," *The Journal of Experimental Education,* 32, 2, Winter, 1963, pp. 147-157.

formance measures. For simplicity, we will consider only vocabulary of the performance measures for the moment. Of course, it is not the value or effectiveness[19] of the test score but the effectiveness of the vocabulary *indicated* by the test score that we seek to assess. Because of the relationship between test score and vocabulary, however, a measure of the effectiveness contribution from this particular performance measure can theoretically be obtained from the test score directly.[20] But the appropriate order must not be neglected in utilizing this shortcut: we must make a prior investigation of the relations of test score to vocabulary *and* vocabulary to effectiveness. (See Figure 3).

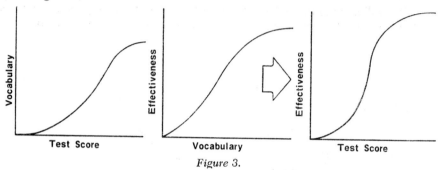

Figure 3.

It is probable that the first thousand words of a person's vocabulary are the most important, and each subsequent thousand-word addition is less significant than the previous. Indeed, there exist words so esoteric that no practical value whatever is derived from knowing them. We are not attempting to establish the limits of a person's vocabulary. In the end we want only an indication of the potential "worth" of the vocabulary in the context of the need for communication skills. It would be possible to administer an examination that distinguishes among people with very large vocabularies, but, because of the generally diminishing value of each increment in vocabulary size, we reach a point above which all vocabularies are of nearly equal value. It would be pointless to utilize a test that did serve to distinguish among people with excessively (in terms of our needs) large vocabularies, since discrimination at this point is of no aid in the framework of decision-making; if effectiveness is not altered, distinction is of no interest.[21]

19One or the other of these terms would be more appropriate, depending on the context, but "value" and "effectiveness" are essentially equivalent. For economy of vocabulary, we will use "effectiveness" uniformly.

20Vocabulary $= g$ (Test score)
 "Effectiveness" $= f$ (Vocabulary) $= f$ (g (Test score))
 let $h = f$ g, the
 $= h$ (Test score)

21See note, p. 218. The difference between the score of 600 and 750 will be significant for the college (A) that rejects a reasonable proportion of people with the lower score, but the difference is non-existent for the college (B) that accepts nearly all applicants with scores of 600 on their college board examinations. While the admissions officer of the latter school may be much more impressed by the score of 750 than that of 600, knowledge of this difference has no effect on the decision process in spite of great variation in other variables relating to the applicant's desirability. The scores are equally *effective* in securing admission, and the difference, in the analytic sense, is therefore uninteresting. The relationship between performance and effectiveness — the criterion — is different for each of the two colleges as is evident by the proportion of acceptances (a reasonable measure of effectiveness here) secured by each score for the two colleges.

220

While the first thousand words of a person's vocabulary may be more important than the second thousand, the first hundred may not be as useful as the second hundred; the curve describing the relation between effectiveness and vocabulary size may resemble Figure 4b more closely than Figure 4a. We may decide that a vocabulary is of no value if it is less than three hundred, a thousand, or two thousand words and consequently assign disproportionately little value to small vocabularies. The shape of the curve will vary as a function of the vocabulary type we are estimating — literary, technical, philosophic — as well as the level of proficiency required to meet the demands of a given field.

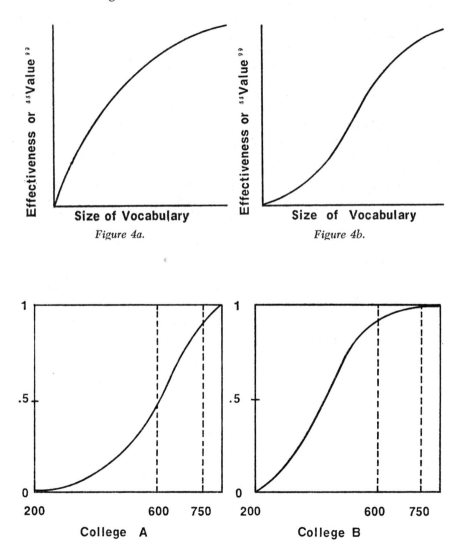

Figure 4a.

Figure 4b.

The criterion is at once the most personal and the most critical aspect of analysis. It embraces the essential elements of the objectives and indicates their relative importance under all conditions. Because of the subjective nature of our feeling for "value" and "effectiveness," it is difficult to specify with precision the relation between performance and effectiveness. Nevertheless, the importance of the role of the criterion militates for making explicit our criterion for effectiveness; our assumptions and methods must be displayed if our results are to be acceptable to any but ourselves. Beyond making our results more comprehensible for others, systematic development of all steps of the analysis will help us to be consistent and it will increase our own confidence in the conclusions.

By this, it might be said that since criteria are highly personal or subjective, then, by their nature, criteria are unquantifiable or even unspecifiable, and any sort of system analysis is foredoomed to unreliable results. But in general the requirement is only that we make explicit what is already known. To this end modern psychological measurement theory can be helpful: many very qualitative judgment schema can be modeled quite adequately by a variety of subjective scaling procedures (Coombs, Dawes, Tversky, 1970, pp. 7-100; Thurstone, 1959).

Frequently, when national objectives are involved, the judgment of a single "expert" may not be satisfactory, but by making this scale explicit, specialists can discuss in much more precise terms the bases of their judgment schema. This discussion in turn could lead to refinement of objectives and the revealing of hidden assumptions. In the vocabulary criterion problem, for example, this entire scaling and evaluative procedure could be seen to be quite productive.

Let us assume that we have established the relationship of performance indicators to performance and of performance to effectiveness for each of the performance measures. In the case of speed comprehension and grammar, performance is not so easily quantified as with vocabulary. What we said before[22] about seeking the effectiveness of the performance *indicated* by the test score still applies, but our description of performance is more in terms of the degree of advancement or type of knowledge necessary to answer correctly each of the questions. A criterion is developed to indicate the relative importance of each of these levels of implied proficiency or performance. Our performance could be a listing of the skills indicated, a percentile ranking, or other possible descriptions; though less desirable, the test designer might retain mentally the performance indicated and intuitively skip to the assignment of effectiveness measures to each *test* performance level. Rather than attempt to develop an appropriate set of descriptions for these more qualitative performance measures, we will not present performance descriptions for speed comprehension and grammar (See Table 1.), but in practice it is wise to be explicit at this step.

---

[22]See p. 220.

Table 1

Performance measure	Test Score	Performance	Effectiveness
Vocabulary	97 - 100	15,000 + (words)	excellent
	90 - 96	14,000 +	very good
	78 - 89	12,500 +	good
	60 - 77	10,000 +	fair
	41 - 59	9,000 +	poor
	below 40	below 9,000	very poor
Speed Comprehension	89 - 100		excellent
	81 - 88		very good
	67 - 80		good
	56 - 66		fair
	38 - 55		poor
	below 38		very poor
Grammar	93 - 100		excellent
	84 - 92		very good
	76 - 83		good
	53 - 75		fair
	30 - 52		poor
	below 30		very poor

Many who are critical of the use of systematized analysis might well accept our progress in analysis so far, they might be content with our qualitative effectiveness assignments, satisfied that nothing but intuitive judgments could utilize them profitably. Regardless whether we use intuitive or systematized or quantitative judgment, however, we insist that something must be known about how much better is "very good" than "good," for example, versus the difference between "good" and "fair." This is especially important when the decision or planning analyst is different from the one or ones who did the test design and preliminary analysis. We achieve the higher-ordered metric scaling (the ordering of all combinations of interpoint distances) of the designer-analyst's conception of the effectiveness values of "excellent," "good," etc., and utilize this to help us understand the effectiveness assignments (Siegel, 1956, pp. 207-216). By numerical assignment of scale positions we record in simple terms our new understanding of the meaning of the effectiveness assignments. We have introduced numbers at one of the most subjective steps of analysis, and our observer reacts. He contends that we are assigning numbers to something incommensurate with quantification and that, moreover, no systematic attempt to assess uncertainty is made. Our response to the first point is to say that, indeed, if we no more than specify "good" and "bad," we are quantifying as we have agreed to divide the objects under consideration into two classes. All quantification *is* classification, and in fact we frequently associate ranges of uncertainty with our measurements to delimit the class to which our object belongs. Consequently, much of "qualitative" judgment is simply a degree of "quantitative."

If the original assessment of values of effectiveness is acceptable, then, surely, our excursion into subjective modeling technology is justified. "Excellent," "good" and "fair" are illy defined quantifications while this scaling is achieved quite readily. Clearly, it is to our advantage as analysts and decision makers to capitalize on every opportunity to substitute the explicit for the implicit, the quantitative for the qualitative, the precise for the vague, provided that the trade-off this requires is not too costly in other areas. The negative part of the trade-off we face here is the possible neglect of uncertainty in the scale construction, which leads us to point number two.

We are not dealing with a statistical sample, so indicators of uncertainty (standard deviation, for example) are not readily available. Firstly, though, our need for effectiveness values is only to supply a ranking of desirable programs (applicants, here) and we do not need to claim great accuracy. Secondly, by the nature of the scaling procedure (the ordering of all interpoint distances), the uncertainty of the model is limited to a reasonably small and estimable range. Moreover, our confidence in the validity of this scale would grow with application and refinement. While the model does not account for uncertainty in the mind of the test analyst, he can specify appropriate ranges for the final value assignments.

This, like other analytic systems,[23] insists on consistency among the rankings — something that the critic's alternative (decision without analysis) does not accomplish. In effect, this is "forcing the analyst to make explicit what elements of a situation he is taking into consideration and . . . imposing on him the discipline of clarifying the concepts he is using" (Helmer, 1965, p. 7). While we may have added the uncertainty of a model to the personal uncertainty of the analyst, have we suffered by the trade-off? Unlikely. We have transformed into manageable and more universally grasped forms such terms as "excellent" and "good" while we have been careful to avoid gross neglect of the uncertainty reflected in these terms. Indeed, by examining the analyst's subjective value scheme, his personal uncertainty may even be reduced through increased understanding of his judgment basis. In all, we claim a refinement over the original valuation system.

So, for the "qualitative" effectiveness terms we establish corresponding scale positions. For example:[24] Utilizing this scheme, Mr. A's and Mr. B's score evaluations would be as follows:

---

[23]See the so-called Dynamic Dialogue evaluative technique, Morris, pp. II-73 to II-90.

[24]This scale could be constructed from the following interval ranking:

$$AF > AE > BF > BE > AD > CF > CE > BD > AC > CD > DF > DE > AB > BC > EF$$

This interval ranking is achieved via an exhaustive set of paired-comparisons. To guide us in assigning numbers to scale positions we stipulate that the smallest interpoint distance be 1.0 and the largest 3.0. The decision-maker is present at every step of the process to check that the implications of his paired-comparison selections and his maximum and minimum interpoint distance specifications do not violate

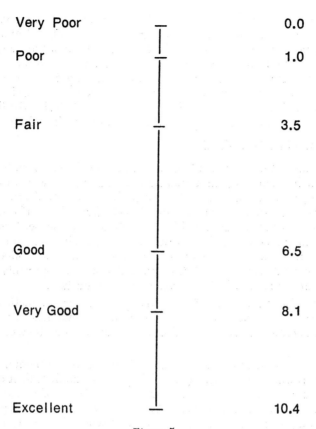

Very Poor	—	0.0
Poor	—	1.0
Fair	—	3.5
Good	—	6.5
Very Good	—	8.1
Excellent	—	10.4

Figure 5.

Table 2

		Percentile Score	Effectiveness description	Effectiveness scale position
Mr. A	Voc	60	fair	3.5
	SC	60	fair	3.5
	Gr	25	very poor	0.0
Mr. B	Voc	60	fair	3.5
	SC	40	poor	1.0
	Gr	60	fair	3.5

outrageously his intuitive conception of the scale. Of course, if the decision-maker's intuition were defined sharply enough, he might be capable of establishing directly an effectiveness scale. In any case, however, the higher-ordered metric scaling provides a good consistency check. See Siegel, 1956, pp. 207-216.

Of course, this system could be refined further quite simply. For each range of test score within a qualitative effectiveness level, "+" and "−" levels might be established to distinguish the top and bottom of the range from the middle. We would than have eighteen rather than six divisions of the effectiveness scale and our ability to discriminate among test scores would be sufficiently dense to distinguish in terms of effectiveness each of the test scores, but in this we are limited by both the statistical reliability of any examination and our uncertainty about the validity of the effectiveness scale.

1.2 Multiple Criteria Evaluation

This done, let us now turn to consideration of the criterion for effectiveness by which we are to gain a final ranking among applicants to our remedial reading program. Each of the sub-problems involved criteria of their own for determination of effectiveness levels from the performance measures.[25] As the total criterion will be a function of the sub-criteria, we must here enter the domain of multiple criteria analysis. The general problem can be rephrased: How do we combine measures of sub-system effectiveness in a manner that reflects how well the assorted system components coordinate to achieve the ends for which the system was established?

As *coordinate* implies, very frequently there are interactions between our sub-system elements. Neglect of these interdependencies can permit inaccuracies to enter otherwise sound analyses, and as such they command our attention.

If we assume that test achievement is uniquely a function of a single specified performance measure (vocabulary, for example), then quite naturally for higher scores we would associate greater levels of performance with that performance measure. If each of two performance measures plays a large role within a given examination,[26] however, it would be hazardous to assign values to either, much less both, of the performance measures. There would be no basis for distributing among the different measures the performance indicated by the test achievement and for this reason it would be a poor examination.[27]

Of course it would be a difficult methodological task to design a test for which achievement is a function of a single, isolable performance measure, but this should be the direction of our efforts. The problem is comparable to knowing the magnitude of a multi-dimensional vector and attempting to distribute among the axes the projection of the vector. To fail to recognize an important factor in our test could sabotage the value of our results: we might believe ourselves to be measuring one thing when altogether something else is being measured as well. Primarily because test scores, by their nature,

---

25The units of the performance measures are actually arbitrary. It is not necessary to transform performance levels into special units before the eventual transformation into effectiveness levels as it is possible to integrate this function into the criterion. To construct the criterion we already have the task of assessing the relative merits of the performance measures, however, and to add this would needlessly complicate analysis even further. Consequently, sub-analyses are performed to gain this commensurability and a preliminary understanding of the elements of the performance description.

26That is, if an examination contained questions testing vocabulary and knowledge of grammar.

27See comments on the use of combined indicators, note, p. 210.

are scalars, and because we seek to assign values to a vector quantity, it is important that each test (performance indicator) relate to no more than a single axis of the performance description. The value assumed by a single performance measure, on the other hand, might very well be compiled from the results of several tests.

The role of interdependencies is just as important at the next level — among performance measures — though the problem is slightly different. With indicators of performance (test scores) we made every attempt to eliminate independent factors from single indices. Now, however, when combining these indices to gain a measure of effectiveness, we find that their independence expedites the analytical effort. But the problem here is not simply the reverse of the previous. With performance indicators a theoretical impasse is encountered when independent factors are involved. With performance measures, on the other hand, independence is preferable but interdependencies do not cripple our ability to construct a criterion for effectiveness; the problem is to make these interdependencies explicit.

Independence essentially means that variation with respect to one performance measure does not affect the contribution that another makes in the assessment of effectiveness.[28] If performance measures are interdependent, then we are not only required (a) to assign weights that each performance measure is to receive in achieving the effectiveness assignment, but also (b) to determine how this weighting scheme should adjust itself for different levels of achievement with respect to each of the performance measures. As the interdependency decreases, the need to perform the latter analysis vanishes.

This makes sense. If A and B, as before, are performance measures and if B satisfies a need 40% as effectively as A, then surely exceptionally high performance with respect to B would decrease the urgency of achievment with respect to A. Installation of playground facilities for physical education, for example, may serve as sufficient attitudinal stimulus for pupils that investment in the form of new teachers to decrease the size of classes might reasonably be delayed. Presumably, the state of the student-teacher ratio would become correspondingly less important, and this would be reflected in the criterion for effectiveness encompassing these programs. This is need interdependency. If A and B are independent, then performance on B does not affect the weight that A should receive; the needs they serve are disjunct.

If the dependencies are more direct, that is, if altering system A affects the performance of system B, investigation of the interactions can be more complex. This is functional interdependency. We might consider the effect of a school's health program on its overall performance in interscholastic athletics. In many instances this type of interdependency is not of much consequence. When comparing distinct programs, whatever the interdependency of their components, it is the outputs that we examine for evalu-

---

28See note, p. 217. Independence of performance measures p_1 and p_2 would mean that neither is c_2 a function of p_1 nor is c_1 a function of p_2.

ation of effectiveness. In planning, however, this type of interdependency is important since the variables we encounter are continuous or many-valued, and data are largely matter for speculation. We should not overlook the broader consequences of localized actions if those consequences figure in the assessment of effectiveness. Nor should we neglect the conflicts inherent in the problem if our model is to be of much predictive value. It should be realized for example that it is not possible both to reduce the student-teacher ratio and to increase teacher salaries within a fixed budget.

It is possible for either, both or neither of these interdependencies to be observed. We can have need interdependencies such that the weighting of performances in our criterion change. We can have functional interdependencies such that the performance of one system is contingent or dependent on the performance of another. This latter type of non-independence, however, is primarily of planning interest and does not affect our criterion as such.[29]

Returning to the example of the previous section, we see that we have only to determine need interdependencies and that the more complex functional interdependencies — those that relate the contributions of grammar to speed comprehension and vocabulary — are not essential in making a selection of applicants. Of course, our task is somewhat reduced, but there still exists the considerable problem of associating different levels of performance on each of the performance measures with the higher objective "to assess reading ability."

Utilizing our lower-level criteria, we established crude effectiveness values for each of the performance measures independent of the content of the total problem. Without prior assessment of the values indicated by the test scores, the problem would have been more awkward.

> The analyst appears to be driven to larger and larger systems . . . But while larger systems analyses may make his criterion problem (or one aspect of it [commensurability of lower- and higher-level criteria]) more manageable, they become more cumbersome and more aggregative. At some point in the process . . . he must accept

---

[29]Let us return momentarily to the example of the footnote on page 217. The two kinds of independence are easily illustrated. Recall that the criterion is the weighting scheme for the transformation of performance (measures) into effectiveness, where $c_1p_1 + c_2p_2 + \cdots + c_np_n$ is the effectiveness. There are essentially two ways of altering the sum of the c_ip_i: change the c_i (as in need interdependence) or change the p_i (as in functional interdependence.)

(a) Need interdependence. If systems A and B are need interdependent, this is reflected in the criterion. The weighting factor for the first system, c_1, would be a function of p_2 as well as p_1. Similarly would c_2 be a function of p_1; that is, $c_1 (p_1; p_2, \ldots)$ and $c_2 (p_2; p_1, \ldots)$.

If A and B are need independent, then neither is c_1 a function of p_2 nor is c_2 a function of p_1.

(b) Functional interdependence. Functional interdependence of systems A and B implies that p_1 is a function of p_2 and vice versa; that is, $p_1 (p_2, \ldots)$ and $p_2 (p_1, \ldots)$. Functional interdependence does not affect the criterion.

It is clear that dependencies in (a) will always be interdependent, that is, if c_1 is a function of p_2, c_2 will be a function of p_1. It is not so apparent, however, that the same will apply in (b). It might be said that one system depends absolutely on the performance of another while the latter system can function quite satisfactorily independent of the state of the first. The logic is deceptive; to cite a level of performance of system A may determine that of system B, but, conversely, citing a performance level for system B constrains system A to perform to a particular level. It may seem more appropriate to label one variable "controlling" and another "dependent," but our point of reference is in fact arbitrary.

a limited context and a less-than-perfect . . . criterion, try to keep aware, in a general and qualitative way, of its shortcomings and biases, treat effects outside his system crudely, and get on with the inevitable job of sub-optimizing (Hitch & McKean, 1967, p. 131).

In the spirit of sub-optimization we have proceeded thus far. It is possible that a person be sufficiently knowledgeable of the content and import of each of the examinations within the context of "reading" to construct a criterion capable of transforming the score into a final ranking among applicants. However, smaller problems are more easily considered than more comprehensive ones, and where interactions are inconsequential or quantifiable, we should capitalize on opportunities to do sub-analysis. Moreover, in transforming the scores into effectiveness measures for the sub-problems,[30] we have made the units of the performance measures commensurable, thereby facilitating subsequent analysis.[31]

Prior to this, our analysis entailed consideration of single quantities; in vocabulary we assessed the results of a single test to estimate the vocabulary size and this, in turn, was judged in terms of its value in the context of the needs for vocabulary. This was adequate for illustration of the term "criterion," but in most systems we eventually have to face the problem of judging the comparative worth of different parts of a given system.

There are essentially two bases for comparison in criteria analysis:

(a) If two measures relate to disjunct needs, we must compare the urgency of each of these needs.

(b) If two measures relate to the same need, we must compare how well these measures satisfy that need.

In our example we have only to consider (b) as our need is simply to evaluate the effectiveness with which a person reads in terms of vocabulary, speed comprehension, and grammar (to select the "best" reading course). Thus, the extent to which performance along each of these measures indicates facility with reading and the extent to which these measures are involved in the reading process are the basis for our criterion. In the context of elementary school instruction, however, where "to understand reading" and "to understand mathematics" are quite disjunct, we must judge the relative importance of these needs in designing our program or in testing the effectiveness of alternative programs. In the same way, however, we could have viewed our performance measures alternatively as representative of disjunct needs ((a) above) and, within the context of the higher level need "to increase reading ability," we compare the urgency of each of the sub-needs in establishing our criterion.[32]

---

[30]See p. 224.

[31]See note, p. 226.

[32]If we start with (a), of course, it then is necessary to move to (b) and compare how well each of the performance measures satisfies the needs to which they respectively relate.

The two bases for analysis are essentially the same but applicable to different levels within the analytical structure. The reason for this, where the assignment of levels is itself arbitrary, is that in fact we often wish to speak of two levels simultaneously, and for purposes of reference it is helpful to have available slightly different but parallel terminologies. The language of more aggregate problems parallels that of smaller ones as we often find that the sub-problem of one context may be the major problem of another. Indeed, the vector space analogy carries at all levels of systems analysis. We have viewed the use of scalars (test scores) to assign values to the "effect" axes (performance measures) which comprise the description of the performance vector. The criterion then maps the performance vector into an effectiveness scale. But the process can continue: effectiveness measures of sub-problems can be taken to be equivalents of either performance indicators or performance measures for the subsuming problem and higher level criteria are developed to combine these measures into measures of effectiveness at the next level. (See Figure 6.) The analysis of interdependencies associated with multiple criteria evaluation is generally required as we move higher in the analytical structure and the outputs of sub-problems come together under higher objectives. Collective analysis potentially could be needed at any level of the system.

Let us complete the example. Our first weighting scheme is 1.5: 2.5: 1.0 for vocabulary, speed comprehension, and grammar, respectively. If we apply this criterion to the converted performance description of our applicants, we have a basis for ranking. Clearly, by this criterion, Mr. B is in greater need of the remedial reading program than Mr. A, whereas no such ranking is apparent from the original scores.

Table 3

		Original test scores	Lower level effectiveness assignments	Criterion weighting values	Higher level effectiveness assignments
Mr. A	Voc	60	3.5	1.5	
	SC	60	3.5	2.5	14.0
	Gr	25	0.0	1.0	
Mr. B	Voc	60	3.5	1.5	
	SC	40	1.0	2.5	11.3
	Gr	60	3.5	1.0	

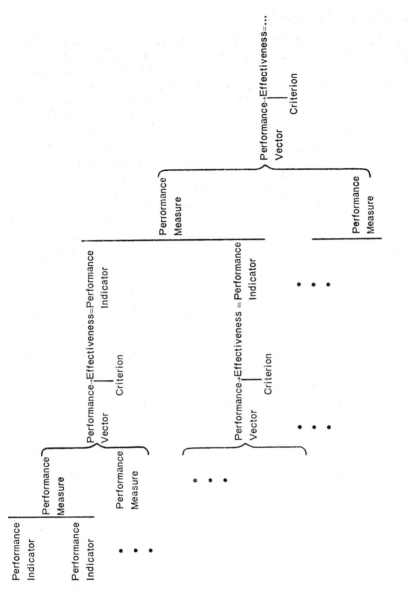

Figure 6. The Structure of Multiple Criteria Analysis.

Because of the conceptual simplicity of need interdependency, little is to be gained from extending our example to illustrate it. To this point we have seen the similarity of the analytic problem at different levels within the structure of analysis. When the criterion must consider more than a single performance measure in assigning an effectiveness value, however, the analysis can be complicated by need interdependencies. Functional interdependencies are important in the context of planning.

231

1.3 Effectiveness Curve Analysis

The discussion of analysis so far has outlined the approach to selection among a finite number of alternative programs on the basis of effectiveness. Measures of output quantities are available or readily predictable. But what of the need to design programs in the first place? How are we to anticipate the effectiveness of a particular program? How do we discover "efficient" solutions to our problems; that is, the most effective solution at a fixed cost or the least expensive solution to attain a given effectiveness?[33]

Cost-effectiveness curves are the ultimate refinement in this analytical system. Where alternative policies take the form of continuous or many-valued variables, however, it becomes theoretically possible to associate cost and effectiveness values with the different levels of performance. For example, how effective are different student-teacher ratios in terms of their effect on achievement? This would correspond to one performance-effectiveness curve, but, again, how would the shape of this curve change as a function of need interdependencies with other variables? This task might initially seem overwhelming, but a good first approximation can often be made by neglecting these interdependencies.

We shall embark on a brief discussion of effectiveness curve analysis more from the standpoint of understanding the scope of cost-effectiveness analysis as we have introduced it for educational needs than as a system subject to ready application. Rigorous development of these techniques requires a more exact knowledge of the criteria and interdependencies than is presently available in education.

Consider functions f, the criterion for effectiveness, and g, the cost constant. From these a new function, F, is derived:

$$F(x_1, \ldots, x_n) = f(x_1, \ldots, x_n) - \lambda g(x_1, \ldots, x_n)$$

where 'λ' is the so-called Lagrangian multiplier and the x_i are the system components. Under conditional optimization all variables but one are fixed at minimum levels of performance and the performance of the remaining variables is maximized within the cost constant.

We take $\dfrac{\partial F}{\partial x} = 0$ and solve for x_r to get the optimal solution under the cost constant. But this provides no guarantee that the combination of system parameters so obtained will be the efficient solution for that total cost level. In this system, our criterion simultaneously evaluates all system components. We differentiate with respect to all of the x_i plus an additional variable,:

$$\frac{\partial F}{\partial x_1} = \ldots = \frac{\partial F}{\partial x_n} = \frac{\partial F}{\partial \lambda} = 0.$$

---

[33] That is, how do we construct Figure 1?

232

The equations are solved simultaneously, eliminating 'λ' to get the variable values which correspond to the optimal system performance for a given cost level.

As presented, the theory appears very straightforward. However, if certain convexity properties are not observed, the critical points of the curve may be "saddle points" which are neither maxima nor minima; local optima may be encountered when global optima are sought.[34] We will not dwell on methodologies for circumventing these mathematical problems, as our purpose at this point is only to illustrate the conceptual basis for this analytic approach rather than to attempt application in its purest form; moreover, the state of educational criteria developed are sufficiently low-level that prospects for actual use of such quantitative analysis are dim in the foreseeable future.

A highly developed economic theory like inventory control can use this book method with a fair degree of security (Feeney, 1955, pp. 69-82). The relation of inventory parameters which minimize cost is explicitly given for the lot size of a particular inventory item. Whereas this is only a two-dimensional problem, the method is distinguished from the conditional optimization approach: the contraints on the system are explicitly stated in the form of equations and a curve is generated presenting efficient outcomes for different cost ratios. It is then the decision-maker's task to select the most appropriate cost ratio for his company.

Nevertheless, the system is adaptable to the more complex, qualitative problems. Ideally, we would work with equations to describe the graphs, but these may be non-existent or too hard to find. To use the Lagrange optimization, we have to make assumptions about continuity and differentiability. but graphical analysis has been developed to perform the differentiation and thereby avoid such problems. In addition, the progress of analysis is more easily monitored by the analyst and decision-maker.

If we can accurately plot effectiveness (E) and system cost (C) against the sub-system performance characteristics (A), we can attempt to find efficient resource allocations. The graphs that we must make comprise (Figure 7):

(1) Effectiveness versus performance
(2) Cost versus performance
(3) Incremental effectiveness versus performance
(4) Incremental cost versus performance
(5) Incremental effectiveness/incremental cost versus performance.

Graphs (3) and (4) follow from (1) and (2), respectively, by measuring and plotting the slopes of the curve tangents (dE/dA and dC/dA, respectively) against the performance characteristic. Graph (5) follows from (3)

---

[34] IBM 7090 SHARE subprogram PKNLP locates global optima of a non-linear function of several variables with continuous partial derivatives subject to a set of linear constraints. If the objective function is convex, the optima are global; otherwise a local optima are obtained dependent on the selected feasible start. The algorithm is suggested in G. Zoutendijk, *Methods of Feasible Directions: A study of Linear and Non-Linear Programming*, (Elsevier Publishing Company, Princeton, 1960), pp. 78-79.

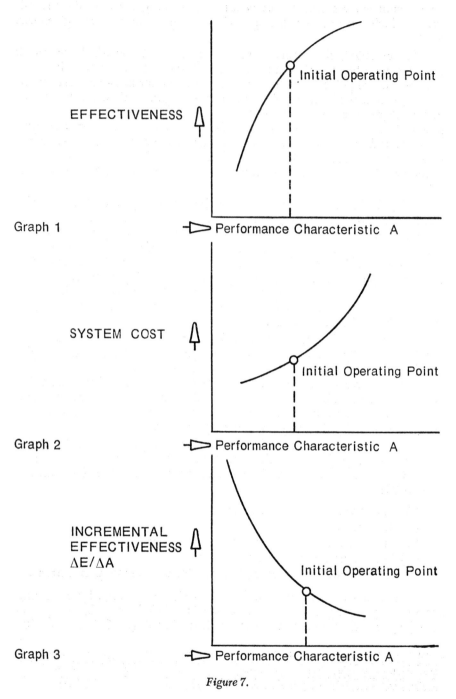

Figure 7.

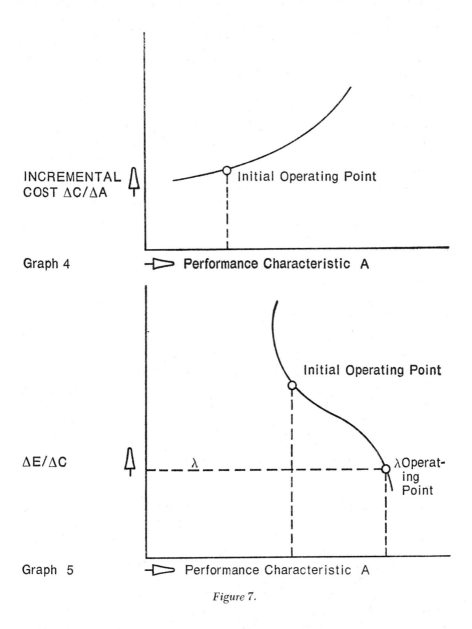

INCREMENTAL
COST ΔC/ΔA

Initial Operating Point

Graph 4   Performance Characteristic A

Initial Operating Point

ΔE/ΔC

λ

λOperating Point

Graph 5   Performance Characteristic A

Figure 7.

and (4) as the quotient of the two slope plots for any given performance position; in effect, $dE/dA \div dC/dA = dE/dC$ versus A. 'λ' is any particular dE/dC ratio and generally specifies uniquely a performance and resource level for the sub-system element. Clearly, any analysis hinges on the development of the first two curves. The graphs must be constructed carefully, for any subsequent operations utilizing the effectiveness and cost models will compound the error of the initial data.[35]

A methodology for achieving efficacious distribution of resources among system components has been described:

> . . . assuming the other variables to be fixed at the initial operating points, the analyst will perturb one of the performance variables to note its effect on system costs and effectiveness levels. Conceptually, all variables will be perturbed until equal marginal gains are determined for all performance characteristics and the analyst then has allocated the resources most efficiently (Morris, 1967, p. II-63).

This is repeated for many marginal gain positions. Performance levels are selected so that "λ", dE/dC ratio is the same for all performance measures. By applying "λ" values uniformly to the performance measures, optimal resource allocation levels are guaranteed for the operating level employed.

An efficiency curve (Figure 1) is developed (defining efficient solutions) to guide policy decisions. For the chosen effectiveness level the decision-maker knows that the system is at lowest cost, and, conversely, at peak effectiveness for a fixed cost at the stage we must decide which operating level best suits his need.

By implementation of this type of analysis, cost and effectiveness models are developed for different performance characteristics or sub-system elements, and the planning ideal best combining these elements is determined. However, only by independent determination of the possibly efficient solutions for each of many different sets of components to comprise the system can the best set be isolated. While we may not be able to discover the *best* possible design for a system — no analytical scheme pretends to provide that — by this methodology we can at least find *better* systems, or the best system within our basic design.

We are no longer evaluating a small number of alternative programs to satisfy a particular set of objectives; instead, we are reviewing a potentially infinite number of combinations of policy alternatives. The criterion yields a measure of effectiveness, but it relates the outputs of a program to objective attainment and does not tell us any information about the input control variables that are required for planning purposes. Consequently, it now becomes necessary to understand the relationship of inputs (in terms of operational characteristics rather than cost requirements) to outputs and the role of functional interdependencies as introduced in Section 1.2. These interrelations must be stated explicitly to delimit the feasible solutions at

---

[35]Graphs 7 - (3) through 7 - (5) are faithfully produced from the base data by using computers to supply continuous function approximations to date points, to supply derivatives, and to produce graphical representations.

specific cost levels. In this way, modeling becomes important in the planning context of cost-effectiveness analysis. While it may not be precisely concerned with the evaluation of effectiveness, performance modeling is frequently a very major analytic task.

In Section 1.1, we related the performance indicator (test score) to performance and the performance to effectiveness. From these relationships we were able to gain measures of effectiveness directly from the test scores. Similarly, through the performance model, we here relate our decision variables — the student-teacher ratio, for example — to the results of performance indicators, which in turn are related to the effectiveness through performance evaluation. In this way we are able to evaluate the effectiveness of different policy decisions. Strictly speaking, then, while it would be possible to construct cost and effectiveness curves for the different performance measures, they are *output* quantities and such graphs would only be of passing interest. To apply our iterative procedure for determining best policies and resource allocations, the performance characteristics, A, should be input decision variables.

Unfortunately, however, education is even a long way from using this more qualitative Lagrangian approach to planning. In general, the input-output processes in education are too poorly understood to be modeled adequately; a great many variables need to be standardized before casual relationships can fairly be deduced.

> . . . a model is necessarily an abstract idealization of the problem, and approximations and simplifying assumptions generally are required if the model is to be tractable. Therefore, care must be taken to insure that the model remains a valid representation of the problem. The proper criterion for judging the validity of a model is whether or not it predicts the relative effects on the alternative courses of action with sufficient accuracy to permit a sound decision (Hillier & Lieberman, 1968, p. 15).

The model and the criterion are independent, but if the output data supplied by the model are incorrect, the criterion will supply a correspondingly inaccurate picture of the effectiveness of the hypothetical program. Since good models for education appear unlikely in the near future, we will not dwell on modeling procedures as such. However, the lack of such models need not deter us from the application of systematized decision-making. The primary role of theoretical models is to supply us with data about non-existent programs, but if we would select the best from the existing programs, we should still have made great progress.

> (a) Theoretical models are possible where the relationships linking resource input to performance are well understood — as in missile systems. In education, these processes are so uncertain that it is difficult to draw inferences from available data due to the great number of variables contributing to the output.

237

(b) Theoretical models are necessary where anticipated costs are so high that *a priori* assessment of effectiveness is necessary to gain acceptance; actual data for performance evaluation are unavailable and must be anticipated from our understanding of the program processes — again, as in missile systems. In education, many different "programs" are now available; methods for measuring and assessing performance are currently what we lack. Moreover, innovative programs are not so expensive that funding for implementation on a pilot project basis cannot be secured if reasonable expectation for success can be demonstrated.

Theoretical models are based on limited data; outputs of programs are only anticipated. To construct such models, the relation of inputs to outputs must be readily traceable. At this point we are unable to do this, but our efforts should be directed towards achieving more precise understanding of these relationships. PPB seems an appropriate framework for that investigation.

1.5 Postscript on Analysis

The approach to this point has been to stress explicitness and to neglect *unquantifiables.* In part, this is motivated by the need to clarify the range of quantities which can be stated in explicit terms: it is much broader than is generally thought. Our reduction of the underlying judgment scheme of the decision-maker to more explicit terms is an example.

Those compelled to work with analytical problems and the concomitant difficulties of objective formulation, performance measurement, and criteria development lose respect for excessively structured forms of analysis. Reckless quantification tends to discredit generally systems analysis as applied to social concerns; the loss is to society.

A point to be remembered in the midst of these dire warnings of inconsistent and irrelevant criteria, is in fact that we are generally dealing with problems of resource allocation among competing requirements. In the resource allocation process, the resources will be allocated each year, with or without analysis. The purpose of programs such as Cost/Effectiveness, is that through this process, subject to error though it may be, we can make better decisions than before. Nowhere is this process better exemplified than in the formulation of criteria which, while not perfect, enables the decision-maker to supplement intuitive judgment with quantitative analysis (Morris, 1967, pp. I-19 to I-20).

We have introduced mathematical models — some as bases for illustrating abstruse ideas and others for explanation of the theoretical foundation of analysis — but we have also been careful to balance these concepts with concrete parallels in the context of education. Certainly, we do allow room for "intuitive" judgment, but it is important that in so doing we do not limit ourselves unnecessarily; data, when quantified, become clearer and analysis is thereby facilitated.

Systems analysis should be looked upon not as the antithesis of judgment but as the framework which permits the judgment of experts in numerous subfields to be utilized — to yield results which transcend any individual judgment. This is its aim and opportunity (Hitch & Quade, 1964, p. 23).

REFERENCES

Barro, S. M., Haggart, S. A., Carpenter, M. B., Dei Rossi, J. A. & Rapp, N. L. *Program Budgeting for School District Planning: Concepts and Applications.* (RAND, #RM-6116-RC) Santa Monica Authors, 1969.

Carpenter, M. B. & Haggart, S. A. *Analysis of Educational Programs within a Program Budgeting System.* (RAND, #P-4195), Santa Monica: Authors, 1969.

Coombs, Clyde H., Dawes, Robyn M., & Tversky, Amos. *Mathematical Psychology: An Elementary Introduction.* Englewood Cliffs, N.J.: Prentice-Hall, 1970.

Feeney, George J. "A Basis for Strategic Decisions on Inventory Control Operations." *Management Science,* 1955, 69-82.

Hartley, Harry J. *Educational Planning, Programming, Budgeting: A Systems Approach.* Englewood Cliffs, N.J.: Prentice-Hall, 1968.

Hatry, Harry P. "Criteria for Evaluation in Planning State and Local Programs." In Harley H. Hinrichs & Graeme M. Taylor (Eds.), *Pogram Budgeting and Benefit-Cost Analysis.* Pacific Palisades, California: Goodyear, 1969.

Helmer, Olaf. *Social Technology.* (RAND, #P-3063), Santa Monica: Author, 1965.

Hillier, Frederich S. & Lieberman, Gerald J., *Introduction to Operations Research.* San Francisco: Holden-Day, 1968.

Hitch, Charles J. & McKean, Roland N. *The Economics of Defense in the Nuclear Age.* New York: Atheneum, 1967.

Hitch, Charles J. "Analysis for Air Force Decisions," in E. S. Quade (ed.) *Analysis for Military Decisions,* (RAND #R-387-PR), Santa Monica: Author, 1964.

Joyce, Bruce R. *Alternative Models of Elementary Education.* Waltham, Mass.: Blaisdell Publishing, 1969.

Morris, Lee R. "Cost-Effectiveness — The Current State of the Art." Unpublished doctoral dissertation, Harvard, 1967.

Quade, E. S. *Systems Analysis Techniques for Planning-Programming-Budgeting.* (RAND EP-3322) Santa Monica: Author, 1966.

Schick, Allen. "Systems for Analysis: PPB and its Alternatives." *The Analysis and Evaluation of Public Expenditures: The PPB System.* Washington, D.C.: United States Government Printing Office, 1969. III.

Siegel, S. A. "Method for Obtaining an Ordered Metric Scaling." *Psychometrika,* 1956, 21, 207-216.

Thurstone, L. L. *The Measurement of Values.* Chicago: University of Chicago Press, 1959.

Wildavsky, Aaron. "Rescuing Policy Analysis from PPB." *The Analysis and Evaluation of Public Expenditures: The PPB System.* Washington, D.C.: United States Government Printing Office, 1969, III.

Appendix B

Cost/Effectiveness Application: Milwaukee

Introduction

The initial attempt to develop and test a cost/effectiveness model resulted in a change in the original conceptual framework as well as the application as it was originally designed. In light of these experiences, a more appropriate and more applicable model has been designed. This report presents the description of the original model, the attempted application, and the revised model based on the experiences of the initial effort.

Statement of the Problem

A problem facing an educational decision maker is that of having to choose among alternatives which have not been quantified and have not been sufficiently defined or identified. The problem is usually characterized by the definition of goal and processes in terms which fail to communicate the specific information needed to discriminate among alternatives. An input to a partial solution of the problem is the definition of goals in terms of specific and measurable objectives and the definition of processes in terms of tasks which consume human and material resources.

A basic element of the approach to the decision-making process, via cost/effectiveness analysis, centers on several assumptions. The decision maker has identified a need and the satisfaction of the need has been given a high priority, thus the decision-maker has completed his choice of the kind of objective to pursue. In addition to the choice of objective, the decision has determined a level of performance or an expectation for quality. At this point the decision-maker must choose a solution which may be either successful or unsuccessful. If the solution is unsuccessful he must find another solution. He may not conclude that because the solution is unsuccessful he must eliminate the project and thus the objective. The decision-maker must ultimately choose between processes as opposed to projects

If a school has identified a need (such as higher student achievement) and initiated a process to resolve that need (a special reading program) which failed, the decision maker must avoid eliminating the project in such a way as to eliminate the objective and thus ignore the need. Rather than ask the question of whether the project succeeded or failed, he must identify the components of the project which were most successful and also those components which were least successful. In the act of discriminating between levels of success, he must also consider the costs of the components. These conditions of the decision-making processes form the need on which the conceptualization of the cost/effectiveness model must be based.

The operational structure of an educational system, however, is necessarily ill-suited to a classical application of a cost/effectiveness design. The application of a cost/effectiveness analysis tool pre-supposes control over the operation of a program. As has usually been the case, control, such as defined in a classical control/experimental research design, is seldom evident in school operations. For example, experimentation with a new method of teaching, a new textbook, or new equipment would be introduced to a sample of students from a defined population. The use of the textbook would be controlled and most intervening variables, such as class size, facilities, the teacher, etc., would also be variables controlled and accounted for. The achievement scores of the experimental group of students would then be compared with the achievement scores of a sample of students drawn at random from the same population, but who were not exposed to the innovation being tested. All variables in both samples would be controlled.

Uncontrolled variables present in a given operational situation greatly hinder a researcher's ability to generalize from findings. This situation necessitates the development of a cost/effectiveness model which, rather than operate on the assumption of control, is designed to account for the lack of control. The model must be set somewhere between the goal of describing an existing structure which is buried under a facade of confusion and the goal of accounting for the lack of structure. The model must be both a descriptive tool by which to compare alternative processes to accomplish similar objectives and a manipulative tool by which needed future directions can be identified for decision-making. As previously mentioned, the cost/effectiveness model, as originally conceived, was considered a descriptive tool which did not interfere with nor manipulate project or program operations. The application of the model was to provide for a comparison of project processes as opposed to projects. In this sense the comparisons were between processes which were common to more than one project as opposed to the comparison of two projects.

Conceptual Framework

In its initial conceptualization, the cost/effectiveness model was more descriptive in nature than manipulative. The results of the experimental application, however, demonstrated rather graphically that a greater degree of emphasis needed to be placed on a manipulative technique if a reliable analysis was to be produced.

Statement of Purpose

The model, as initially conceived and tested, was to be as unobtrusive as possible. The purpose of the cost/effectiveness tool was (1) to identify and define the processes used to attain a common objective or objectives, (2) to determine the relative effectiveness of those processes, and (3) to compare the cost/effectiveness relationships among the processes.

The immediate needs, which the management tool was to satisfy, were the following:

1. Provide for a systematic identification of program components (i.e., inputs, processes, and outputs) which allow for the identification of relationships among program components, both within and among programs;
2. Identify the objectives which were perceived to be the most important to the school program and identify the processes which were perceived to provide the greatest contribution to the attainment of the objectives which are perceived to be most important;
3. Determine sequence of activities which constituted the processes of the project;
4. Establish a means for determining utility/cost ratios for projects and programs of the school system; and,
5. Establish means for determining cost/effectiveness ratios for project processes of the school system.

Definition of Terms

The conceptualization of the cost/effectiveness model is based on the definition of several terms.

A *process* is defined as a task or series of tasks executed within a defined period of time, consuming human and material resources, and leading to the attainment of an objective or objectives.

Cost is defined as the amount of resources in monetary units expended in a process.

The *general application cost* is defined as a monetary unit of resource expenditure adjusting common cost elements to a common amount for a general application of a process or processes.

Utility is defined as the degree to which a process is perceived to contribute to the attainment of an objective or objectives.

Utility/Cost is defined as a decision-making value based on the relationship between the cost of a process and its utility value.

Effectiveness is defined as the degree to which objectives are attained.

Cost/Effectiveness is defined as a decision-making value based on the relationship between the cost of a process and its effectiveness value.

Application of the Concept

Prior to the presentation of data relating to the application of the cost/effectiveness conceptualization, it is necessary to review the operational structure to which the conceptualization was applied. At present, the Milwaukee Public Schools are funding several auxiliary projects designed to improve the ongoing programs of individual schools. These programs cover many subject matter areas and many phases of the school operation. A large group of the projects, however, are centered on the area of reading. In order to accommodate the immediate need of testing the conceptualization, it was decided to choose reading projects and thus obtain large numbers of schools from which to select those for the application.

It must also be noted that the improvement projects operating in the schools are designed to meet individual school needs and are not designed for an experimental research study. The application was clearly defined as a case study with an immediate goal of testing the mechanics of the approach in order to determine if the approach could be applied on a wider and more meaningful basis (an exploratory plan as described in the chapter on Programming).

For the purpose of the test run, two reading projects were selected to be included in the study. The projects were selected because: (1) they were located in the same geographical area, (2) the make-up of their student populations were similar, (3) they shared similar objectives, and (4) processes were common to both projects.

In the conceptualization it was intended to identify the most important objectives and then to identify the processes which were perceived as making the greatest contribution to the attainment of those objectives. To obtain these perceptions a jury of experts was asked to rank the objectives and the processes of the two projects. It must be noted that the comparison was between processes and not projects or schools. The rationale for this comparison was that the decision-maker seeks a solution to the problem that Project A was designed to solve, but if he compared projects and determined Project A to be a failure, he may well have eliminated part of the solution when he rejected the project. By comparing processes, he may select those components which appeared to be most successful and may elect to discard those components which appear to be least successful. This additional flexibility allows for a greater degree of discrimination within projects.

Procedures

The first component of the research design was centered on developing a utility/cost ratio which was based on the perceived importance of project objectives and processes. The steps involved in completing this component were as follows:

1. Selection of a panel of judges for the initiation of a jury approach to the rank-ordering of objectives and processes.
2. Ranking of objectives by the jury members in terms of their immediate importance (i.e., importance of their attainment at the end of one academic year).
3. Ranking of processes by the jury members in terms of the contribution of the processes to the attainment of each objective (i.e., for five objectives a list of processes would be ranked-ordered five times).
4. The conversion of ranking to weighted decimal scores.
5. Determination of a utility value for each process based on the weighted decimal scores.
6. Estimation of process costs.

7. Determination of utility/cost ratios (i.e., the weighted decimal scores of the processes multiplied by the inverse value of the objective rank).

The second component of the research design dealt with the cost/effectiveness ratio. In order to ascertain the effectiveness of the processes used for the subject of this study, three measures were considered:

1. Grade equivalent change (absolute value) as measured on standardized test (*California Reading Achievement*);
2. The difference between the actual grade equivalent change and the expected grade equivalent change (as pre-determined by project personnel); and,
3. Change in student attitude (absolute value) toward reading (Milwaukee Public Schools developed the instrument, twenty items, $n = .96$).

In a control (experimental) situation, samples drawn from a common population would be used to test two processes (Treatment A vs. Treatment B) with a strong effort made to control all intervening variables. In the present conceptualization, a universe of activities directed at the achievement of similar goals was operating at many school sites. These activities involved varied populations and incorporated similar and, in some cases, identical objectives, all of which were stated in specific performance terms.

Identification of Objectives and Processes

Prior to authorization of the projects, several meetings were held with project personnel reviewing each project proposal. As an outcome of these meetings, the following statements of objectives were determined to be common to each of their operations:

1. To produce a higher rate of achievement in reading applicable to the total student body, as stated in a series of specific performance objectives.
2. To produce a higher rate of achievement in reading applicable to a special segment of the student body defined by a particular ability level, as stated in a specific performance objective.
3. To increase the knowledge of the total teaching staff concerning the teaching of reading.
4. To improve the attitude of students toward reading, as stated in a specific performance objective.
5. To improve the actual teaching of reading in all classrooms of the school.

The performance levels, however, were not included in the list of objectives used for rank-ordering by the jury of experts so as to avoid a comparison of performance levels rather than a comparison of objectives.

Project personnel also worked with the research in the identification of processes. After identifying processes in broad terms, the project personnel were asked to define them in terms of tasks which consume resources. Schedules of staff members and listings of materials purchased were converted to cost figures in accordance with the procedures outlined in the section of this paper entitled, "Methods of Cost Analysis." The identified processes were as follows:

1. Resource center teacher visits each teacher's classroom for an average of forty-five minutes a week for the purpose of providing support of reading instruction.
2. Teaching aides work individual classrooms with teachers in the preparation of materials used during the reading period of the class day.
3. Teaching aides tutor individual students in the reading center (one to three students).
4. Teaching aides work wtih small groups of students (five to ten students).
5. Reading resource teachers tutor students (one to three students).
6. Reading resource teacher works with small group of students (ten to fifteen students).
7. Reading resource teacher conducts in-service sessions for the total staff.
8. Administrator of the school (principal) conducts in-service sessions for the total staff.
9. Students participate in self-directed studies utilizing new materials such as reading kits.
10. Teaching aides organize and catalog reading materials for use by the teacher and for use by the reading resource teacher.
11. Reading resource teacher works with individual teachers (one to three) in the preparation and use of materials.

Rank-Ordering Objectives and Processes

A jury of experts was selected consisting of the following members:

Reading Resource Teachers	2
(one from each participating school)	
Principals	2
(one from each school)	
Reading Specialist	1
(from the central administration of the school system)	

The make-up of the jury was based on the need for a cross section representation of the professional personnel of the school system. Because the projects developed out of the local school, the local school professional most directly associated with the subject matter area of the project participated on the jury (reading resource teacher). The school administrator is the project coordinator and was also placed on the jury. The reading specialist is a central office administrator who acts as an expert for the school system in the subject matter area and thus was included on the jury.

In order that the procedures for ranking objectives and processes be understood more clearly, the steps involved are presented in terms of formulas accompanied by narrative descriptions.

Each jury member was asked to rank each of the objectives in terms of importance.

The formula is developed as follows:

Let R = a ranker (a jury member)

Let q = the number of rankers (the number of jury members)

Let O = any objective (O_1 would be Objective 1 or O_A would be Objective A)

Let m = the number of objectives (O_m would be the last objective)

Let S = the score or rank assigned to any objective

Following these symbols, the rank assigned to Objective *1* by Ranker *1* is symbolized by $S_{R_1 O_1}$; likewise, the rank assigned to Objective *4* by Ranker *2* is symbolized by $S_{R_2 O_4}$. The score or rank assigned to the last objective by the last ranker is symbolized by $S_{R_q O_m}$.

To calculate the mean rank of an objective, one sums the ranks assigned to the objective by the rankers and divides by the number of rankers. The formula is:

$$\sum_{i=1}^{q} S_{R_i O_1} \Big/ q = \text{Mean Rank}$$

This is done in the same way for all objectives until a mean rank has been determined for each objective. The objectives are then re-ordered according to mean ranks (i.e., MR_1, MR_2, . . . MR_m where MR_1 is the objective with the highest mean rank and MR_q is the objective with the lowest mean rank).

The mean rank value associated with each objective for the purpose of this re-ordering procedure is now dropped from use. In its place, each objective is given a weighted value equal to the inverse of its place value in the reordering. Thus, an objective ranked first in the reordering is given the weight of q. The objective ranked second in the re-ordering is given the weighted value of q-*1*. Finally the objective ranked q in the re-ordering is given the weight of *1*. If, as in the case of this application, there are five objectives ($q=5$), the objective ranked first would receive the weighted value (wo_1) of five. The objective ranked second (wo_2) in the re-ordering would receive the weighted value of four ($q=1$). The weighted value of the objective ranked last in the re-ordering (wo_q) would receive the weighted value of one ($q-4$).

The five objectives included in this application along with the ranks and the weighted scores are:

RANK		WEIGHTED SCORE
1	To improve the actual teaching of reading in all classrooms of the school.	5
2	To increase the knowledge of the total teaching staff concerning the teaching of reading.	4
3	To produce a higher rate of achievement in reading applicable to the total student body, as stated in a series of specific performance objectives.	3
4	To produce a higher rate of achievement in reading applicable to the special segment of the student body defined by a particular ability level, as stated in a specific performance objective.	2
5	To improve the attitude of students toward reading, as stated in a specific performance objective.	1

The next step is to have each jury member rank-order the processes in terms of a perceived contribution to the attainment of each objective; that is, each jury member rank-orders the list of processes once for each objective. For five objectives ($m=5$) each jury member rank-orders the processes five times. In order to facilitate the weighting of processes, the jury members are asked to rank the processes by assigning a value to each process equal to the inverse value of its rank. If under objective *1* a jury member ranks a process first out of a list of ten processes ($n=10$), the score assigned to that process is ten. The score assigned to the second process is nine. In all cases the score assigned to a process ranked first is m or the total number of processes. A process ranked second receives a score of m-*1*, a process ranked third receives a score of m-2, – a last ranked process receives a score of *1*.

Let P equal any process, then $S_{R_1 P_1 O_1}$ is the score or rank of Process *1*

in terms of Objective *1* by Ranker *1*; $S_{R_1 P_2 O_1}$ is the score or rank of Process

2 in terms of Objective *1* by Ranker *1*. Each ranker performs the following tasks:

In terms of Objective 1, Ranker i places the processes in the desired order and assigns the appropriate score:

$$S_{R_i P_1 O_1} \qquad S_{R_i P_2 O_1} \qquad S_{R_i P_3 O_1} \qquad \cdots \, S_{R_i P_n O_1}$$

In terms of Objective 2, Ranker i places the processes in the desired order and assigns the appropriate score:

$$S_{R_i P_1 O_2} \qquad S_{R_i P_2 O_2} \qquad S_{R_i P_3 O_2} \qquad \cdots \, S_{R_i P_n O_2}$$

This process is continued by Ranker i until the last process has been ranked under the last objective $(S_{R_q P_n O_m})$.

Since all processes are ranked in terms of all objectives by all rankers, then the total for Process 1 on Objective 1 is found by summing the scores assigned to Process 1 under Objective 1 by all rankers. Therefore, the total score for Process 1 on Objective 1 is:

$$\sum_{i=1}^{q} S_{R_i P_1 O_1}$$

The proportion of contribution that Process 1 makes toward the attainment of Objective 1. as perceived by the rankers, is the total score of a process under a specific objective divided by the sum of the total scores of all processes under that objective. The formula is:

$$\sum_{i=1}^{q} S_{R_i P_1 O_1} \Bigg/ \sum_{i=1}^{q} \sum_{j=1}^{n} S_{R_i P_j O_1}$$

If there are five rankers $(q=5)$ and ten processes $(n=10)$, then the denominator of the above equation is

$$\sum_{i=1}^{q} \sum_{j=1}^{n} S_{R_i P_j O_1} \; = \; 5[10+9+8 \ldots +3+2+1] = 275.$$

The proportion of contribution for each process is a decimal score calculated to two places. In order to work with whole numbers, the decimal score is multiplied by 100 and the decimal value is eliminated.

In order to calculate the utility value of a process (U_{P_O}) in terms of the attainment of all objectives, the weighted value of the objectives (WO) is taken into account. The procedure is to multiply the proportion of contribution of each process

$$100 \left[\sum_{i=1}^{q} S_{R P O_{i 1 1}} \Bigg/ \sum_{i=1}^{q} \sum_{j=1}^{n} S_{R P O_{i j 1}} \right] \text{ by the}$$

weighted value of the objective under which the proportion of contribution is recorded:

$$\left[100 \right] \left[\sum_{2}^{q} S_{R P O_{i 1 1}} \Bigg/ \sum_{i=1}^{q} \sum_{j=1}^{q} S_{R P O_{i j 1}} \right] \left[WO_{1} \right]$$

WO. This calculation is continued for processes under all objectives. The last step in determining the utility value is to sum these weighted proportions of contribution (proportion of contribution multiplied by the weight of the objective).

The utility value $(U_p) =$

$$\sum_{k=1}^{m} 100 \left[\sum_{i=1}^{q} S_{R P O_{i j k}} \Bigg/ \sum_{i=1}^{q} \sum_{j=1}^{n} S_{R P O_{i j k}} \right] \left[WO_{k} \right]$$

For an example of the calculation of a utility value for a process, consider an application consisting of five objectives and ten processes.

Step 1   The objectives are ranked by each of five judges and the five ranks for each objective are summed.

Step 2   The objectives are re-ordered in accordance with the total of the ranks assigned and are given the inverse value of the place in the re-ordering (i.e., the objective re-ordered in the first position is given the weighted value of five and the objective re-ordered in the last position is given the value of 1).

Step 3   Under the objective in the first position of the re-ordering, the ten processes are rank-ordered by each of the five rankers by assigning the value of ten to the most important process, a value of nine to the second most important process, etc. This same ranking of the processes is also done under each of the other objectives by each of the rankers.

Step 4   All of the ranks assigned to a process under an objective are summed.

Step 5   Under the highest rank objective there are ten processes each having a score equal to the sum of the ranks assigned to that process under that objective by each of the five rankers.

Step 6   One now sums the scores of each of the ten processes under the objective. This sum equals the number of rankers (five) times the sum of the number of ranks possible (ten ranks for ten processes or $(10+9+8 \ldots +3+2+1) = 5\ (55)$ or 275).

Step 7   Calculate the proportion of contribution by dividing the score of each process by the sum of the possible ranks (275). If the score of the highest rank process is 55 the value of its proportion of contribution is $55/275$ or $.20$. This procedure is repeated for each process for each of the objectives.

Step 8   In order to work with whole numbers, multiply the proportion of contribution by 100 (i.e., $.20 = 20$).

Step 9   Multiply the proportion of contribution of each process for each objective by the weighted value of the objective. The process with a proportion of contribution score equal to 20 under the highest ranked objective (with five objectives in the application) is multiplied by five and equals 100. The value of 100 is called the weighted proportions of contribution. Each process now has five such values, one for each objective.

Step 10 Sum the weighted proportions of contributions of each process.

The Present Application

Given the ranking of objectives for this application, as presented on page 248, the jury members were asked to rank-order the processes (see page 246 for the listing of processes) in accordance with the procedures described above. A graphic presentation of the order of the processes after they were ranked and the ranks were summed is presented (Steps 3, 4, and 5) in Illustration A. The higher rank processes for the higher rank objectives appear in the upper left of the matrix and the lower rank processes for the lower rank objectives appear in the lower right of the matrix (see Illustration A).

The following processes were consistently ranked important:

A. Resource center teacher visits each teacher's classroom for an average of forty-five minutes a week for the purpose of providing support of reading instruction.

G. Reading resource teacher conducts in-service sessions for the total staff.

K. Reading resource teacher works with individual teachers (one to three) in the preparation and use of materials.

The following processes were consistently ranked of little importance:

C. Teaching aides tutor individual students in the reading center (one to three students).

H. Administrator of the school (principal) conducts in-service sessions for the total staff.

J. Teaching aides organize and catalog reading materials for use by the teacher and for use by the reading resource teacher.

ILLUSTRATION A

Objectives*	O_5	O_3	O_1	O_2	O_4
Process Rank	1	2	3	4	5
1	A	G	A	K	E
2	K	K	G	F	I
3	G	A	K	G	F
4	B	J	B	I	K
5	I	H	I	A	A
6	D	B	F	E	G
7	E	E	D	B	C
8	J	I	H	D	D
9	C	F	J	J	H
10	F	C	C	C	J
11	H	D	E	H	B

*Objectives are in rank order, as determined in Step 1.

The completion of Steps 6 and 7 in the application provided a decimal score for each process under each objective which is its proportion of contribution to the attainment of the objective. These decimal scores are presented in Illustration B. In completing Step 8, each of the decimal scores are converted to a whole number, e.g., Process K under Objective E changes from .15 to 15.

In Steps 9 and 10, each of the scores of the processes is multiplied by the weighted value of the objective. Thus, each of the process values under the highest rank objective, Objective O, is multiplied by five (i.e., value of Process A is .15 x 100 x 5 or 75); to calculate the utility value of each process to all objectives, the weighted process scores are summed (Step 10). Thus, the utility value is the sum of the weighted scores (see Illustration C).

ILLUSTRATION

	B Proportion of Contribution of Processes, by Objective						C Weighted Values of Process Contribution, by Objective					
OBJECTIVE PROCESS	O_5	O_3	O_1	O_2	O_4	WEIGHT	O_5 5	O_3 4	O_1 3	O_2 2	O_4 1	*
A	.15	.13	.16	.10	.10		75	52	48	20	10	205
B	.11	.08	.11	.08	.03		55	32	33	16	3	139
C	.06	.05	.04	.04	.09		30	20	12	8	9	79
D	.08	.04	.06	.08	.08		40	16	18	16	8	98
E	.08	.08	.03	.09	.13		40	32	9	18	13	112
F	.05	.06	.10	.13	.12		25	24	30	26	12	117
G	.13	.15	.15	.11	.10		65	60	45	22	10	202
H	.02	.09	.05	.04	.06		10	36	15	8	6	75
I	.09	.07	.11	.11	.13		45	28	33	22	13	141
J	.08	.10	.05	.08	.05		40	40	15	16	5	116
K	.15	.15	.14	.14	.11		75	60	42	28	11	216

*Sum of weights or
utility value

Overview and Limitations

Each of the steps in the calculations of the utility values for the processes provides the decision-maker with more precise information on which to allocate resources; more information is added to the decision-making base.

To illustrate: *After the objectives* are ranked (Step 1) the most important objectives and the least important objectives are revealed. The decision-maker does not yet know which is the most important process. *After the processes* are ranked, the decision maker knows which are the important processes and in terms of the important objectives (Illustration A). If, however it is assumed that all objectives are of some importance, the decision-maker needs information on the general contribution of the processes to the attainment of all objectives. The calculation of the utility values based upon the ranked values of the objectives and of the processes (Steps 9 and 10) introduces this information.

There are several limitations of this approach. The ordinal scaling provided by ranking allows only for the statement that a process ranked first and given a value of five is more important than a process ranked second and given the value of four. The ranking does not allow for the determination of how much more important one objective or process was than another.

In addition to the limitations of an ordinal scale, the variable on which the rankings are based is the combined perceptions of professional staff. The validity of this approach is based on the assumptions that:

1. a professional's perception of what is most important and what is least important actually reflect a real value of importance
2. the combined perceptions of two professionals are better than the perception of one and that the validity of perception as a variable increases with the increase in the number of professionals included in the process.

The next step is to introduce process cost.

Calculating Utility/Cost Values

The utility/cost values of the processes are obtained by dividing the utility values by the per-pupil cost for the process (General Application Cost). See page 259, "Methods of Cost Analysis." The following is a presentation of each process, actual cost, general application cost, and per-pupil cost for general application and the value of the utility/cost ratio.

By including the costs in the analysis of the processes, the list of priorities presented to the decision maker is somewhat different from the list generated by the rank-ordering alone. The high rank order of processes is A, K, B, and J. The low rank order of processes is E, D, C, and F. Processes I, H, and G ranked in the middle of the distribution with utility/cost scores closer to those of the lower rank processes.

With this procedure, the processes with the high utility/cost values are A, K, B, and J. These processes consist of *the reading resource teacher working with the individual teacher, either in the classroom or outside of the classroom, on the use of materials and the improvement of reading instruction and the employment of teacher-aides, both in the classroom and in the reading center, for the purpose of preparing and cataloging reading materials.* The cost of this process in general application is $3,338.00. The estimated cost of this process, as operated in the schools, is $2,193.00.

Processes I, H, and G are ranked in the middle on the utility/cost value scale. These three processes consist of *the in-service sessions conducted by either the reading resource teacher or the school administrator and the self-directed studies by students utilizing materials such as reading kits, tape recorders, etc.* If the processes had been deleted from a general application, the cost deducted would have been $3,470.00. Because the processes do not consume additional resources in the schools, a deletion of the processes would not save an out-of-pocket expenditure. The deletion of the processes from the actual operation would have, however, allowed for the re-allocation of $3,470.00 worth of goods and services, already available in the school, to those segments of the project which have higher utility/cost values.

The processes with the low utility/cost values are E, D, C, and F. These processes all refer to the utilization of the reading resource teacher and the teacher-aides in teaching students in groups of one to three and in groups of ten to fifteen. These processes are perceived as having the large costs and little value in terms of the attainment of the five objectives. The magnitude of the total actual cost of these processes is large because of the limited number of units of application present in the actual school situation.

By introducing the monetary element into the setting of priorities through a utility/cost ratio, the choices presented to the decision-maker are based upon (1) the perceived value of the objectives, (2) the perceived value of the processes in terms of a contribution to the attainment of the objectives and (3) the value of the processes in terms of cost. The remaining element of the decision-maker's information base is the effectiveness which is the value of the processes in terms of achieving objectives.

Relationship of Cost to Effectiveness

In order to determine the effectiveness of each process without a controlled experimental design, an intermediate variable is used. The perceptions of the jury of experts for the importance of objectives and the contributions made by processes to objectives is used for this purpose. The utility scores for processes generated from the rankings serve as the weighted values for the proportioning of effectiveness scores (Illustration C).

The data reported here are based on an interim measure of progress. The schools included in the application represent a small grouping for which conclusions for general applications of effectiveness measures are tentative. The actual data on the achievement of objectives are presented for the purpose of illustration and explanation only. For the purpose of analysis, the application has been conducted as if the projects had been completed. The project is to be completed subsequent to the publication date.

Defining Effectiveness

In consideration of the *effectiveness* aspect of the cost/effectiveness analysis, the present investigation gives rise to many more questions than answers. The first question to be answered centers on the definition of effectiveness. When the term is defined in relation to one objective, the definition is not too difficult. Effectiveness, in this instance, consists of the degree to which the objective is attained. When more than one objective and more than one process are considered, the definition becomes complex. In considering the method to be used for this application, the most basic approach possible is used.

When a decision-maker is presented with data on the achievement of several objectives, a first consideration is given to the value of each objective and a second consideration is the degree to which each objective is attained.

To calculate composite effectiveness scores for a process or project, it is necessary to obtain a common unit which allows for the summation of units of achievement gain with units of attitude gain. The idea is to combine battleships and apples into *Bapples*. In the procedure for computing a composite score, rank scores for objectives are used to determine a weighting of process scores. By using the ranks of the objectives, an ordinal relationship between the measures is obtained, thus giving some indication of the value

255

of effectiveness as compared to another. When a composite effectiveness score for a process is calculated, the rankings weight the individual effectiveness values utilizing the ordinal values of the rank-ordering in so doing. In essence, the *Bapple* is what the decision-maker calls *effectiveness* which was made up to five parts achievement and three parts attitude or some such ratio. The present application incorporates an attempt to quantify a procedure presently used by decision-makers when judging the effectiveness of a process or project. The conclusion is that the quantification used for this application is at least as good as the present means for determining overall project effectiveness.

Measures of Effectiveness

The students at the intermediate levels of two schools provided the test sample for this application. The three measures included in the effectiveness score were applied to these students. The purpose of the analysis was to compare processes and not projects or schools. The schools included in the application were selected on the basis of the similar characteristics so as to avoid the complications presented by intervening variables peculiar to two different locations. It is recognized that in a general application the assumption of identical populations and situations cannot be made but must be accounted for. The next section addresses itself to this difficulty. For the purpose of conducting the initial application, the students from the two schools were treated as if they were from one population.

The data related to student change are:

$\overline{X}_{At}$	Attitude Gain	2.06
$\overline{X}_{Ac}$	Achievement Gain (in grade equivalent)	0.66
$\overline{X}_{C} - \overline{X}_{E}$ D	Difference between the expected and the actual X Achievement Gain	0.02
	Overall Effectiveness Value	2.74

The effectiveness value for each process is determined by multiplying the overall effectiveness score (2.74) by the proportion of contribution of each process, thus allocating a portion of the total effect to each of the component parts.

TABLE I

a. Utility/Cost Ratio
b. Utility Value
c. Per-Pupil Cost
d. General Application Cost
e. Actual Cost

PROCESS	e	d	c	b	a
A. Resource center teacher visits each teacher's classroom for the purpose of providing support of reading instruction	$ 699	$ 845	$ 5.63	205	36.41
B. Teaching aides work in individual classrooms with teachers in the preparation of materials	771	843	5.62	139	24.73
C. Teaching aides tutor individual students in the reading center	788	228	38.00	79	2.08
D. Teaching aides work with small groups of students	781	552	55.00	98	1.78
E. Reading resource teachers tutor students	4,377	482	161.00	112	.70
F. Reading resource teacher works with small groups of students	2,439	728	49.00	117	2.39
G. Reading resource teacher conducts in-service sessions for the total staff	Not Used	3,170	21.00	202	9.62
H. Administrator of the school conducts in-service sessions for the total staff	Not Used	3,170	21.00	75	3.57
I. Students participate in self-directed studies utilizing new materials such as reading kits	Not Used	300	50.00	141	2.82
J. Teaching aides organize and catalog reading materials	723	816	5.00	116	23.20
K. Reading resource teacher works with individual teachers in the preparation and use of materials	Not Used	825	6.00	216	36.00

257

The proportion of contribution for each process is equal to the utility value of each process divided by the sum of all utility values for all processes (Illustration D).

ILLUSTRATION

D Proportion of Contribution to Effectiveness			E Distribution of Effectiveness to Process	
PROCESS	UTILITY	PROPORTION OF CONTRIBUTION	PROCESS	EFFECTIVENESS VALUE
K	212	.15	K	.41
A	205	.15	A	.41
G	192	.14	G	.38
B	169	.12	B	.33
I	141	.10	I	.27
F	117	.08	F	.22
J	116	.08	J	.22
E	112	.08	E	.22
H	75	.05	H	.14
C	75	.05	C	.14

The effectiveness value for each process is determined by multiplying the overall effectiveness score (2.74) by the proportion of contribution of each process, thus allocating a portion of the total effect to each of the component parts (Illustration E).

The distribution of the effectiveness values to each of the processes generated a ranking of processes which was identical to the ranking based on utility values. The addition of the effectiveness variable to decision-making did not contribute to the decision-maker's ability to discriminate between processes. It did, however, allow the decision-maker to view the utility values of processes in terms of measured outcomes. When the effectiveness value of the process is paired with the cost of the process, the decision-maker has some idea of how much of the total effectiveness is gained or lost with the addition or deletion of a process or processes. The paired cost and effectiveness values for each of the processes were as follows:

PROCESS	COST TO EFFECTIVENESS
K	$ 6.00/.41
A	$ 5.63/.41
G	$ 21.00/.38
B	$ 5.62/.33
I	$ 50.00/.27
F	$ 49.00/.22
J	$ 5.00/.22
E	$161.00/.22
H	$ 21.00/.14
C	$ 38.00/.14

Each of the cost/effectiveness ratios is a comparison of a per-pupil cost to a per-pupil effect or change. After the per-pupil effect is divided by the per-pupil cost, the decision maker is given an estimate of how much gain can be associated with a dollar of investment in each process.

For processes J, K, B, and A the gain ranges from .04 to .07 for each dollar invested. For processes I, F, and H the appropriate gain is .01 for each dollar invested and process G is expected to yield a gain of .02. Two of the processes, E and C, would require an investment greater than one dollar per-pupil in order to register a gain of .01 or larger.

The introduction of the measures of effectiveness into the determination of process importance completes the initial application. The product of the application is a list of priorities for processes based on the following variables:

1. the perceived importance of the objectives,
2. the perceived contribution of processes to the attainment of the objectives,
3. the utility value of the processes based on the perceived contribution to attaining the objectives,
4. the costs of the processes, and
5. the effectiveness of the processes.

Implications for the Future

The Milwaukee approach to the conceptualization and application of the cost/effectiveness design manifests limitations for which improvements are needed before implementing a broad application.

The conceptualization of a procedure for a second tryout proposes the use of a *Q-Sort* technique for rating the objectives and for the processes. With the *Q-Sort* it is feasible to remove the limitation of ordinal ranks and to add a dimension of quantitative importance.

The proposed procedure will identify a student target population group. With the stratification of students and processes, it will be possible to assess effectiveness on a more definitive basis.

(The test-project had not been completed at the publication date.)

PROCEDURE SUPPLEMENT

Methods of Cost Analysis

In the determination of cost figures for the resources of particular processes two figures were computed, an *Actual Cost* figure and a *General Application Cost* figure. The Actual Cost reflected the amount actually expended for the operation of the project. The General Application Cost was a standardized figure, adjusting common cost elements to a common amount for comparative purposes among similar projects.

Actual Cost Figure

To identify Actual Costs, all expenses incurred to carry out a designated process were specified as the total, actual expenditure for that process, according to the criterion explained below. No attempt was made to adjust costs to the available resources at the various locations, (see the following explanation of the use of a zero-base). In other words, what was expended on a process for any reason whatsoever was specified as the Actual Cost figure for that particular process and location, in the time designated, and with all particular cost characteristics included.

General Application Cost Figure

The General Application Cost Figure as indicated above was developed to facilitate decision making among alternative processes by adjusting all resources to a *zero-base* and standardizing common cost elements. Decision makers, then, could utilize the cost/effectiveness data developed from the General Application Cost figure with an assurance that only costs that were unique to a process would account for differences in the costs.

Standardizing Common Cost Elements — To standardize common cost elements, all identical resources posted to a process were charged at the same amount. Salaries, for instance, were computed from a mean salary for the specified personnel classification. To do otherwise would skew the cost/effectiveness ratios, as it would be misleading to say that process "X" has a better cost/effectiveness ratio than process "Y" when in reality the reason for its lower cost is that the teacher involved in process "X" is lower on the salary scale than the teacher in process "Y," assuming the effectiveness quotient remains constant.

Use of a Zero-Base — Varying inventories of supplies and equipment in different locations were accounted for by the employment of a zero-base method. To do this, any resource utilized in a process was charged to that process whether the cost item was in inventory or not. If school "X" already had a piece of equipment and school "Y" did not, school "Y's" Actual Costs would necessarily be higher. However, the General Application Cost figures of the two would be the same, as the processes in both school "X" and school "Y" would be charged the same amount for the use of identical pieces of equipment.

Cost Accounts

Costs for the two figures were attributed to the object accounts of:
1. salaries and fringe benefits,
2. supplies and materials,
3. services, including consultant fees, duplication, etc.,
4. other expenses, including evaluation costs,
5. equipment, and
6. facility modifications.

Salaries

To determine personnel costs and salaries, estimates were submitted by the personnel specifying their time spent in carrying out a particular process. These estimates were then pro-rated to the total time spent on all processes and to the salaries of the personnel involved in a process.

Example: Teacher "T"   — 10 hours spent on process "A" @ $10.00/hour

Paraprofessional-Aide "P"   — 15 hours spent on process "A" @ $2.50/hour

Personnel Cost for Process "A" = (10 × $10.00) + (15 × $ 2.50) = $137.50

Supplies and Materials, Services, and Other Expenses

Supplies and materials, services, and other costs were based upon the type and amount employed for a particular process. In addition, these costs were attributed to the process where they were consumed, to the teaching situation, not to the time or occasion of their preparation. If a teacher were to use a set of overlays, the cost for these overlays would be attributed to the teacher's use of them in the classroom with the students, not to the preparation of them.

Equipment

Equipment costs were charged at full value for each item, not depreciated, on the premise that if a resource was allocated for a specific process at a designated time, that piece of equipment was consumed. In order for another process or location to use an identical piece of equipment, the purchase of a new piece would have been required at full purchase cost.

Facilities

Facility costs included only those costs that were required to carry out the processes to meet identified objectives. For instance, if a process necessitated that a study carrel be built into a room and if that carrel was used only for that process, its purchase and installation was charged to the process. Modifications directed toward attainment of an identified objective, but that required no additional resource allocation, were charged to that objective with the modification itself being considered the process. An example of this would be if the objective were to increase student self-perception to some degree and the only thing done was to repaint a room, install carpeting, and buy new furniture, the process would be *the repainting, installing, and buying.* Modifications not necessarily identifiable to any process or objective were omitted.

DATA SUPPLEMENT

*Cost Data**

Process A Resource center teacher visits each teacher's classroom for an average of thirty minutes a week for the purpose of providing support of reading instruction.

	ACTUAL COST	GENERAL APPLICATION COST
Salaries	$696.00	$785.00
Equipment		
Materials		
Other Expenses	3.00	60.00
Total	$699.00	$845.00

Unit Cost which equals one classroom
Indirect Costs — Expenditures for ongoing reading programs

Process B Teaching aides work in individual classrooms with teachers in the preparation of materials used during the reading period of the class day.

	ACTUAL COST	GENERAL APPLICATION COST
Salaries	$771.00	$755.00
Equipment		88.00
Materials		
Other Expenses		
Total	$771.00	$843.00

Unit Cost which equals one classroom
Indirect Costs — Attributed to classroom expenditures

Process C Teaching aides tutor individual students in the reading center (one to three students).

	ACTUAL COST	GENERAL APPLICATION COST
Salaries	$667.00	$ 55.00
Equipment		120.00
Materials	119.00	41.00
Other Expenses	2.00	12.00
Total	$788.00	$228.00

Unit Cost which equals a group of six students for one-half hour per day

*Only those data which affect the derived *Actual Cost* and *General Application Cost* are reported in the tables which follow.

Process D Teaching aides work with small groups of students (five to ten students).

	ACTUAL COST	GENERAL APPLICATION COST
Salaries	$778.00	$264.00
Equipment		200.00
Materials		68.00
Other Expenses	3.00	20.00
Total	$781.00	$552.00

Unit Cost which equals a group of ten students for one-half hour per day.

Process E Reading resource teachers tutor students (one to three students).

	ACTUAL COST	GENERAL APPLICATION COST
Salaries	$4,329.00	$396.00
Equipment		60.00
Materials		20.00
Other Expenses	48.00	6.00
Total	$4,377.00	$482.00

Unit Cost which equals a group of three students for one hour per day

Process F Reading resource teacher works with small groups (ten to fifteen students).

	ACTUAL COST	GENERAL APPLICATION COST
Salaries	$2,437.00	$294.00
Equipment		300.00
Materials		101.00
Other Expenses	2.00	30.00
Total	$2,439.00	$725.00

Unit Cost which equals a group of fifteen students for one hour per day

Process G Reading resource teacher conducts in-service sessions for the total staff.

	ACTUAL COST	GENERAL APPLICATION COST
Salaries		$2,970.00
Equipment		200.00
Materials		
Other Expenses		
Total	Not Utilized	$3,170.00

Unit Cost which equals reading resource teacher and fifteen staff members (cost per teacher for one semester $211.00 — cost per pupil 30/classroom $7.00)

Process H Administrator of the school (principal) conducts in-service sessions for the total staff.

	ACTUAL COST	GENERAL APPLICATION COST
Salaries		$2,970.00
Equipment		200.00
Materials		
Total	Not Utilized	$3,170.00

Unit Cost which equals reading resource teacher and fifteen staff members (cost per teacher for one semester $211.00 — cost per pupil 30/classroom $7.00)

Process I Students participate in self-directed studies utilizing new materials such as reading kits.

	ACTUAL COST	GENERAL APPLICATION COST
Salaries		$785.00
Equipment		varies
Materials		varies
Other Expenses		2.00
Total	Not Utilized	$787.00

Unit Cost which equals one student for one hour per day

Process J   Teaching aides organize and catalog reading materials for use by the teacher and for use by the reading resource teacher.

	ACTUAL COST	GENERAL APPLICATION COST
Salaries	$723.00	$728.00
Equipment		88.00
Materials		
Other Expenses		
Total	$723.00	$816.00

Unit Cost which equals service to one class for three hours per week of five classes for fifteen hours per week

Process K   Reading resource teacher works with individual teachers (one to three) in the preparation and use of materials.

	ACTUAL COST	GENERAL APPLICATION COST
Salaries		$825.00
Equipment		
Materials		
Other Expenses		
Total	Not Utilized	$825.00

Unit Cost which equals a group of three teachers for one class period per day

265

Appendix C

THE INTRODUCTION OF PPBES METHODOLOGY
IN A LARGE SCHOOL DISTRICT: DADE COUNTY SCHOOLS

I. INTRODUCTION

During fiscal year 1970-71 program planning and budgeting procedures were implemented in the Dade County Public Schools. The 1971-72 fiscal year budget, operational plans and summary plans were prepared using those procedures which are now established as an integral part of the management practices of the school system. Planned developments for 1971-72 include efforts to install program accounting and program evaluation techniques. The framework for these developments has been established.

The school system provided educational programs for approximately 240,000 children (sixth largest in the nation) with a total budget of $250,000,000 in 1970-71. Over the past few years a responsibility center concept of administration has evolved with the predominant responsibility center types being schools, district offices,* and systemwide support centers.

II. PROJECT CHRONOLOGY

It is somewhat difficult to identify precisely those management needs which were not being met by existing management information or practices and which led to the decision to explore the utility of PPBES. The following is presented as a chronology of those events which seemed to have direct relevance to the establishment of a PPBES project staff charged with the responsibility of designing an operational PPBE System for Dade County Schools. Subsequent events considered significant in the development are also included.

Spring, 1964: as part of the preparation of the 1964-65 budget, a system of cost center budgeting was inaugurated.

1964-65: the cost center budgeting concept was further developed and continued; initial steps were taken to begin accounting for expenditures on a cost center basis (instructional materials only).

---

*The school system is decentralized administratively into six geographic areas, each administered by a district superintendent responsible to the county superintendent who in turn is responsible to the School Board.

Fall, 1965: Congress passed PL 89-10. The school system secured a series of grants under the legislation and established financial processing techniques which in essence was a program budgeting/accounting system for federally contracted programs.

1965-66: the Superintendent of Schools and various administrators began a series of discussions relative to the need for more effective management techniques including the possible utility of program budgeting. Initial steps were taken during the spring and summer of 1966 to prepare a formal proposal for program budgeting to submit for federal funding.

September, 1966: a management consulting firm was employed to design an improved financial reporting system.

October, 1966: a comprehensive program budget research proposal was transmitted to the U. S. Office of Education with a request for federal funding. This proposal was not funded.

Fall, 1966: various school system administrators began making contacts with agencies and individuals across the nation who were active or interested in program budgeting. These included extensive contacts with the Department of Management in the School of Business Administration at the University of Miami.

February 16, 17, 1967: the Government Research Council of the Dade County Chamber of Commerce sponsored for the School Board and school system administrators a conference on tools for effective management. Numerous references to program budgeting were made at this conference.

September 13, 1967: the Dade County Board of Public Instruction and the Research Corporation of the Association of School Business Officials, as cooperating agencies, transmitted a proposal to USOE for a research grant to design a Program Planning, Budgeting, Evaluating System. This proposal was funded.

September 12, 1968: The first staff member (project director) of the PPBES project was employed.

September - December, 1968: a resource committee was formed to work with the project director in establishing general directions for PPBES development. Toward this end this committee held lengthy meetings on a half dozen occasions between September 26, 1968 and December 3, 1968. The committee was composed of the following administrators:

Superintendent of Schools
Assistant Superintendent for Administrative Services
Associate Superintendent for Instruction
Assistant Superintendent for Finance
District Superintendent — Northeast District
Director of Special Programs
Director of Data Processing
Director of Program Budgeting

Administrative Assistant to the District Superintendent —
Vocational District
Coordinator of In-Service Education

February, 1969: the first program structure was developed.

July 1, 1969: the PPBES project staff that eventually developed the system design and was responsible for the initial implementation was formed.

January, 1970: based on an analysis of the first program structure and reactions received from administrators and teachers, the second program structure was developed.

February, 1970: with the second program structure as the framework and using manual crosswalk procedures, a *Tentative Program Budget for Fiscal Year 1969-70* was produced.

July, 1970: additional analyses resulted in a revised program structure.

August, 1970: Program Budget for Fiscal Year 1970-71, the first official program budget for Dade County Public Schools, was published.

December, 1970: the PPBES project staff was administratively located in the Division of Finance as an operational office.

III. DETERMINATION OF A STARTING POINT

Initial efforts of the project staff were based on the answers to three questions. (1) What information was available about PPBES in general and specifically about the application of PPBES methodology to educational institutions? (2) What were the current scope and administrative location of planning, budgeting, and evaluating activities? (3) What types of PPBES activities and documents were potentially useful in the management of a large school district?

Some literature had become available relating governmental attempts to install program budgeting. There was paucity of information, however, concerning the applicability of PPBES to management practices in school districts and very few school districts had attempted or even considered PPBES as a management tool. The Research Corporation of the Association of School Business Officials was concurrently developing a conceptual model for PPBES that would be appropriate for school districts. Unfortunately, this model was under development and therefore not available at that time.

Early in 1969 a survey was conducted which identified all documents being used for planning, budgeting, and evaluating purposes in the school system. This survey clearly indicated that a wide diversity of techniques and documentation was currently employed by various administrators.

It was determined that potentially useful activities in existing governmental applications of PPBES were, simply stated, program planning, program budgeting, program evaluation, program analysis. Resulting documentation was found in program plans, program memoranda, program budgets and issue papers. This is, of course, an adequate reference to those activities and documents. The point to be emphasized is that in PPBES those activities are integrated and those documents are interrelated; and that in PPBES, the *program* is the integrating unit for those activities and documents.

Potential PPBES activities and documents were compared with existing planning, budgeting, and evaluating activities and documents. As a result, areas of need which could be served by PPBES were identified. "Evolution" was the dominating characteristic of this approach in that it entailed (1) the identification of existing activities/documents, (2) the design of desirable activites/documents, and (3) working to move from the existing activities/documents to desired ones.

IV. STRATEGIES FOR DEVELOPMENT

Certain overriding principles dictated adoption (planned or accidental) of those strategies employed in developmental efforts. These were (1) the PPBE System was to be an evolving one, initially from existing practices and subsequently in refinement stages, (2) tasks selected in the developmental sequence were to be carefully chosen so that they could be readily achieved, so that implications for immediate change in the organization would be minimized, and so that the imposition on persons and/or the organization would be minimal, and (3) that requests for persons in the organization to exhibit certain behaviors (e.g., writing objectives) would not be made until a reasonable probability existed that those persons possessed those behaviors. This latter principle required that the PPBES staff provide numerous orientation/in-service training sessions. Accordingly, the staff undertook certain kinds of pilot activities and sought certain types of pilot products. These were:

— Pilot activities and documents which did not differ substantially from existing activities and documents

— Pilot products which capitalized on the advantage of current activities and documents but offered those benefits of PPBE methodology which could be accrued in the start-up phase.

— Pilot products which offered minimal risk of failure and maximal benefits (e.g., applying evaluation first to administrative and industrial type operations instead of first to instruction)

— Pilot products which had usefulness in themselves and contributed to an evolutionary implementation of the system.

Relative to the involvement of other personnel the following guidelines were adopted:

— To maximally involve other line and staff personnel in the system development with the PPBES staff providing the structures, guidelines, and format for such development.

— To involve other line and staff personnel only after adequate training/orientation had been provided.

V. THE KEY ROLE OF THE PROGRAM STRUCTURE

Although the resource committee was unsuccessful in its attempt to produce a program structure, the direction was set for initial PPBES development, i.e., the first task was to establish a program structure which would provide the framework for future development. The project staff proceeded from this point in attempting to define a logical system for classifying the diverse activities of the school district.

The inductive approach was adopted in an attempt to classify existing activities in a program structure. The rationale for this approach was based on the following assumptions:

— The activities of the past and present do have relevance to the mission of an educational organization.

— The inductive approach affords a reasonable probability for successful implementation of PPBES.

— The implementation of PPBES (possibly most innovations) should be evolutionary in nature.

— The collection of information pertaining to and the assessment of existing programs are beneficial.

However, the danger of being committed to the status quo was inherent in the inductive approach. It was recognized that the PPBES design *must* include the capability to accommodate change when the need for that change was well documented.

The rationale for the first program structure was developed by the PPBES program staff. Division of Instruction* personnel used that structure to produce a manual of Dade County Public Schools Programs and initiated various planning activities based on that structure. The utility of program structure oriented "thinking" was substantiated. The weakness of this structure was primarily one of communication. Although the structure could accommodate the different levels of activities, i.e., elementary, junior high, senior high, that fact was not readily communicated. Although the structure could lead to greater detail in the support programs, such detail was not provided. Additionally, a concept based

---

*The Division of Instruction is comprised of instructional support personnel, e.g., teachers on special assignment and subject area specialists, who have responsibilities for curriculum planning, staff development, educational media, pupil personnel services, and program evaluation.

on and presented with "formal logic" was somewhat alien to school system personnel.

Accordingly, the project staff revised the program structure. The logic and the concomitant definitions were refined with the result that the structure was transformed into a "benefit oriented" model of the school system which included two program areas — Instruction and Administration/Planning.

Formal presentations of this structure were made to groups of personnel which included representatives of each administrative office, instructional personnel such as teachers and subject area consultants, principals, and executive level administrators.

Certain revisions were made in the structure based on interactions at those presentations. The structure then provided the framework for producing a program budget for fiscal year 1969-70 using manual crosswalk procedures. As a result of the formal presentations of the structure and using the structure in pilot activities, conclusions were drawn which indicated the need for further "revisions" in the structure. These were (1) the structure presented an unnatural dichotomy between instructional and support activities, (2) the structure was too much a reflection of responsibility centers and did not adequately portray programs as they crossed organizational lines and (3) the structure did not yield the capacity for analyzing the school system's activities from a perspective of major educational objectives or priority thrusts.

The program structure that finally evolved and was used in the first phase implementation of the system has two dimensions — a program dimension and a responsibility center dimension. Present activities of the organization are readily communicated, using this structure, in terms quite familiar to organization personnel; classification of activities conducted through various offices but having common objectives can be accommodated. This structure provided the framework for the preparation of plans and budget requests for the 1971-72 fiscal year. The principal thrusts of those activities were program planning and program budgeting at responsibility centers; this was accomplished using three appropriation channels — basic, new, and supplemental.

— Basic budget requests accompany plans to continue the ongoing program activities.
— New budget requests accompany plans for an increase in the basic and become part of the basic if granted.
— Supplemental budget requests accompany plans for "project-like" activities and when granted are for one year only.

The program structure assumed a key role as it provided the starting point in the PPBES development and formed the framework for that development and subsequent implementation. Representing a model of the educational organization, the development of the structure necessarily involved persons who were to *use* the structure.

272

VI. THE COMMITMENT TO CHANGE

A major danger in employing the inductive approach to developing the program structure is that of becoming "locked in on the status quo," i.e., the structure reflects current activities and cannot be changed. The Dade County Schools does indeed have a commitment to change and the PPBE System design includes two powerful vehicles to accommodate change — the Special Programs category and the supplemental appropriation channel. Special Programs include programs designed to meet the needs of particular target populations, i.e., Exceptional Child Program; programs designed to deal with contemporary problems, e.g., Drug Abuse Program (established for 1970-71); and those designed to meet high priority needs, e.g., Desegregation (established for 1971-72). The one year supplemental appropriation channel (supplementals may be renewed but only on an annual basis) allows experimentation with activities and techniques that may eventually be adopted in the system. The program structure must be dynamic, must facilitate change.

VII. PILOT ACTIVITIES AND PRODUCTS, 1969-70

Consistent with the strategies outlined in Section IV certain decisions were made with respect to piloting PPBES processes. These were (1) to obtain volunteers if possible to serve as pilots, (2) to pilot, in the main, in support programs, (3) to involve administrators prior to involving teachers instead of vice versa as is usually the case in major innovations and (4) to proceed on a system-wide basis and work "down" instead of starting at the grass roots and working "up."

The assistant superintendents for Physical Plant and Personnel volunteered as PPBES pilots with pilot activities and products to be undertaken with respect to the Personnel Services and Facilities Support Programs.

In each administrative office a person was designated to serve as liaison to the PPBES staff. These liaison personnel were provided special training in PPBES methodology by the project staff as well as through attendance at PPBES seminars conducted by government agencies. In effect these persons were "PPBES staff" members in the administrative departments. Their primary responsibility was to work with personnel in their departments using the PPBES project staff members as a resource.

Generally, in piloting activities and preparing demonstration products the following procedures were utilized.

— The PPBES staff designed the processes and the products.
— These processes and products were discussed with the liaison person in the appropriate department with necessary revisions being made.
— The project staff planned and conducted training sessions for personnel in the departments.

— The liaison person assumed the responsibility for seeing that the processes were carried out and the products prepared.
— The PPBES staff served as consultants to the pilots in an "on call" basis.
— The PPBES staff analyzed the products and suggested changes.
— The pilot departments considered those recommendations and incorporated those changes they felt to be desirable.

The major demonstration products resulting from pilot efforts were:

Personnel Division Program Memorandum, 1970-71[1]
Physical Plant Division Program Memorandum, 1970-71[1]
Personnel Division Program Report[2]
Physical Plant Division Program Report[2]
Exceptional Child Objectives/Indicators by Sub-program (Area of Exceptionality)[3]
Exploring the Application of Program Planning, Budgeting, Evaluating Methodology at the School Level: A Report on a Teacher Seminar[4]
Program Budget for Fiscal Year 1970-71[5]

Subsequently, in the design of system procedures, the knowledge gleaned from pilot efforts was used extensively by the PPBES staff.

VIII. OPERATIONAL ACTIVITIES AND PRODUCTS, 1970-71

The PPBES project staff and the existing budget section were amalgamated into a Department of Planning and Budgeting located within the Division of Finance. This department will be headed by a Director of Planning and Budgeting, a position which replaces the former position of Budget Director of Dade County Schools. One section in this department will assume the responsibility for maintaining and continuing the PPBES development begun through the efforts of the project staff. The formation and organization of this department was further evidence of the commitment to PPBES made by Dade County Schools.

The establishment of the Planning and Budgeting Calendar, which delineates the timetable for the preparation of the 1971-72 budget and planning documents and which replaced the budget calendar in the existing system, was a significant step toward full implementation of PPBES. The *Planning and Budgeting Manual,* which replaced the *Budget Manual* in the existing system, includes a comprehensive sec-

---

1Program plans for 1970-71; includes review of 1960-70 operations, 1970-71 plans, objectives, indicators and budget.
2Program summary for the period July 1, 1970-December 31, 1970, includes narrative summary and indicator data.
3Produced as a result of a one day seminar on PPBES conducted June 6, 1970, for Exceptional Child teachers and support personnel.
4Produced as a result of a one week seminar on PPBES conducted June 22-26, 1970, for selected teachers in Regular Programs.
5Produced using manual crosswalk procedures.

tion on planning guidelines and forms to provide assistance to operational personnel in planning and budgeting for fiscal year 1971-72. The objectives achieved as a result of the calendar and the manual were (1) the integration of planning and budgeting activities and (2) the implementation of program planning and budgeting at responsibility centers.

The project staff provided extensive assistance to personnel in support centers during the preparation of program plans and budget requests for 1971-72. Not only did this allow for smooth implementation but provided also the opportunities for valuable in-service training in an "on-site" manner. Documents* produced as a result of planning for 1971-72 include:

— *Budget Overview: Dade County Public Schools, 1971-72*

— *Program Memoranda: Regular, Special, and Support Programs 1971-72*

— *Program Plans: District and Division Programs 1971-72*

— *Program Plans: Capital Projects 1971-72*

— *Program Plans: Contracted Projects 1971-72*

IX. FUTURE PLANS

PPBES implementation in the preparation of the 1971-72 budget included program budgeting for all responsibility centers and program planning for support centers. Plans for 1971-72 include (1) the expansion and refinement of those procedures already implemented, (2) the expansion of the current accounting system to provide program expenditure data according to the same structure as the program budget, (3) expansion of the evaluation component initiated with the Program Reports referenced earlier, and (4) piloting of program planning practices at selected school centers.

A major problem in implementing PPBES in a large school district stems from the number of persons who are potential users of PPBES and who must eventually be trained in the methodology if the system is to be realized to its full potential. Although significant progress has been made in Dade County Schools in the area of in-service training for administrative personnel a substantial task in this area lies ahead.

It is imperative that school districts moving to install a PPBE System adopt a multi-year outlook with respect to development with the realization that proper utilization of such a system will take place several years after development is begun.

---

*Brief descriptions of these documents can be found on page 292; the two program memoranda documents planned were combined into a single document.

RATIONALE

This program structure is composed of four educational components — (1) instructional - general, (2) instructional - exceptional, (3) instructional - supplementary, and (4) support. The elements of the components are programs. The following rationale establishes the criteria for placing programs within the educational components.

I. Instructional - General

A program which —

A. Involves students for instructional purposes
B. Is designed for students who *are not* considered educationally exceptional
C. Does not exist mainly to support other programs.

II. Instructional - Exceptional

A program which —

A. Involves students for instructional purposes
B. Is designed for students who *are* considered educationally exceptional
C. Does not exist mainly to support other programs

III. Instructional - Supplementary

A program which —

A. Involves students for instructional purposes
B. Exists mainly to support programs classified under I and II
C. Cannot be classified under I or II

IV. Support

A program which —

A. Exists to support programs under I, II, and III
B. Cannot be classified under I, II, or III

PROGRAM STRUCTURE #1

INSTRUCTIONAL GENERAL	INSTRUCTIONAL EXCEPTIONAL	INSTRUCTIONAL SUPPLEMENTARY	SUPPORT
ART	COMPENSATORY	ART	ADMINISTRATIVE
BUSINESS	EMOTIONALLY	CO-CURRICULAR	Planning and Services
DRIVER TRAINING	DISTURBED	ACTIVITIES	EDUCATIONAL
ENGLISH (Language	HOMEBOUND/HOS-	COMMUNITY SERVICES	Planning and Services
Arts)	PITAL	CORRECTIVE READ-	FINANCIAL
FOREIGN LANGUAGE	LEARNING DISABIL-	ING	Planning and Services
HEALTH/SAFETY/	ITIES	GUIDANCE	OPERATIONS
PHYSICAL EDUCA-	MENTALLY HANDI-	ITV AND RADIO	Planning and Services
TION	CAPPED	LIBRARY/AV	PERSONNEL
HOME ECOMONICS	PHYSICALLY HANDI-	MUSIC	Planning and Services
INDUSTRIAL ARTS	CAPPED	PSYCHOLOGICAL	PLANT
INTERMEDIATE	SOCIALLY MALAD-	SERVICES	Planning and Services
KINDERGARTEN	JUSTED	READING	
MATHEMATICS		REMEDIAL READING	
MUSIC		SPEECH THERAPY	
NATURAL SCIENCES			
PRIMARY			
SOCIAL SCIENCES			
VOCATIONAL/			
TECHNICAL			

277

DADE COUNTY PUBLIC SCHOOLS PROGRAM STRUCTURE #2

I. THE BASIC LOGIC

The program structure includes categories of activities which reflect various levels of specificity. These categories, summarized in the chart below, are Program Area, Program, Sub-program, and Project.

PROGRAM AREA		
A grouping of programs which function to produce common major benefits structured by a defined planning viewpoint.		
PROGRAM A grouping of sub-programs which produce related benefits structured by a defined planning viewpoint.	PROGRAM	PROGRAM
Sub-program A set of interdependent activities which have been identified for planning, costing, and evaluating in terms of related objectives.	Sub-program Project Sub-program Sub-program	Sub-program
Project A set of interdependent activities which have been identified for planning, costing, and evaluating in terms of related objectives and which have been specially funded. If the objectives of the project are characteristic of more than one sub-program then the project is identified as a separate sub-program. If the objectives of the project are characteristic of only one sub-program, the project is identified within that sub-program.	Project	

II. APPLICATION OF BASIC LOGIC

A. This program structure is a benefit-oriented model of the school system, based on the current administrative and curricular organization.

PROGRAM AREA: INSTRUCTION

A grouping of programs of Dade County Public Schools which function to produce benefits consumed by the individual learner primarily through changes and development of learner concepts, skills, and attitudes consistent with the goals of the school system.

PROGRAM

A grouping of sub-programs which produce related benefits structured by the current types of instructional centers.

SUB-PROGRAM

A set of interdependent activities, which have been identified for planning, costing, and evaluating in terms of related objectives, yielding benefits directly or indirectly consumed by learners. These instructional sub-programs are classified into five categories:

Direct Learner Consumption

Category 1. Sub-programs whose activities provide instruction to learners not assigned to special target population sub-programs.

Category 2. Specifically identified sub-programs whose activities provide instruction to special target populations.

Category 3. Sub-programs whose activities provide varied services used primarily by learners.

Indirect Learner Consumption

Category 4. Sub-programs whose activities coordinate and improve the functioning of other instructional sub-programs at instructional centers.

Category 5. Sub-programs whose activities provide or maintain facilities necessary for the functioning of other instructional sub-programs at instructional centers.

PROGRAM AREA: ADMINISTRATION AND PLANNING

A grouping of programs of Dade County Public Schools which function to produce benefits primarily consumed by the school system as an institution through generating the necessary support to its instructional programs.

PROGRAM

A grouping of sub-programs which produce related benefits structured by current administrative divisions.

SUB-PROGRAM

A set of interdependent activities, which have been identified for planning, costing, and evaluating in terms of related objectives, yielding benefits consumed by the school system as an institution. These administration and planning sub-programs can be classified into three categories:

Category 1. Sub-programs whose activities coordinate and improve the functioning of other division sub-programs.

Category 2. Sub-programs whose activities yield system-wide benefits within the framework of an administrative division.

Category 3. Sub-programs whose activities provide or maintain facilities necessary for the functioning of other division sub-programs.

B. Activities (including first line supervision) that are instructional, consistent with the definition of the Instructional Program Area, are classified in appropriate sub-programs in the Instructional area, even though the responsibility for the planning and/or management of these activities may fall within the domain of a program in the Administration and Planning Program Area.

C. Administrative or supervisory activities that take place in a responsibility center where instructional programs are being conducted are classified as a sub-program within an instructional program.

280

DADE COUNTY PUBLIC SCHOOLS PROGRAM STRUCTURE #2

PROGRAM AREA: INSTRUCTION	
ELEMENTARY SCHOOL PROGRAM	MIDDLE/JUNIOR HIGH SCHOOL PROGRAM
Kindergarten Primary Intermediate Health/Safety/Physical Education Summer	Art Business Foreign Language Home Economics Health/Safety/Physical Education Industrial Arts Intermediate Language Arts Mathematics Music Science Social Studies Vocational Training for In-School Youth Summer
English as a Second Language Compensatory Corrective Reading Emotionally Disturbed Hearing Impaired Homebound/Hospital Learning Disabilities Spanish for Native Speakers Mentally Handicapped Physically Handicapped Remedial Reading Speech Therapy Socially Maladjusted Visually Handicapped	English as a Second Language Vocational Training for Disadvantaged Youth Compensatory Corrective Reading Emotionally Disturbed Hearing Impaired Homebound/Hospital Spanish for Native Speakers Mentally Handicapped Physically Handicapped Remedial Reading Speech Therapy Socially Maladjusted Visually Handicapped
Art Services Co-Curricular Services Community Services Library/AV Services Music Services Guidance/Counseling Services Psychological Services Visiting Teacher Services Media Services Transportation Services School Food Services	Co-Curricular Services Community Services Guidance/Counseling Services Library/AV Services Psychological Services Visiting Teacher Services Media Services Transportation Services School Food Services
Administration/Supervision	Administration/Supervision
Plant Support	Plant Support

PROGRAM AREA: INSTRUCTION	
SENIOR HIGH SCHOOL PROGRAM	ADULT PROGRAM
Art	Adult Elementary
Business	Adult Secondary
Driver Training	Employment Training-
Foreign Language	Apprenticeship
Health/Safety/Physical Education	Employment Training-
Home Economics	Disadvantaged
Industrial Arts	Employment Training-
Language Arts	Preparatory
Mathematics	Employment Training-
Music	Supplemental
Science	Employment Training-
Social Studies	Adult Preparatory
Vocational Training For In-School	General Adult Special Interest
Youth	Guidance Services
Summer	Library/AV Services
Compensatory	
Corrective Reading	
English as a Second Language	
Homebound/Hospital	
Mentally Handicapped	
Physically Handicapped	
Spanish for Native Speakers	
Speech Therapy	
Socially Maladjusted	
Visually Handicapped	
Vocational Training for	
Disadvantaged Youth	
Co-Curricular Services	
Community Services	
Guidance/Counseling Services	
Library/AV Services	
Psychological Services	
Visiting Teacher Services	
Media Services	
Transportation Services	
School Food Services	
Administration/Supervision	Administration/Supervision
Plant Support	Plant Support

DADE COUNTY PUBLIC SCHOOLS PROGRAM STRUCTURE #2
(Continued)

PROGRAM AREA: ADMINISTRATION AND PLANNING			
DISTRICT ADMIN./ SERVICES PROGRAM	VOCATIONAL/ TECHNICAL ADULT EDUCA-- TION SUPPORT- ING SERVICES PROGRAM	EDUCATIONAL PLANNING/ SERVICES PROGRAM	FINANCE PROGRAM
District-wide Management	Vocational, Tech- nical and Adult Central Program Planning, Manage- ment and Evalua- tion	Educational Planning Management	Financial Management
District-wide Supervision		Program Plan- ning & Develop- ment	Financial Planning and Budgeting
District-wide Staff/Program Development	Personnel Plan- ning and Services	Program Evalua- tion	Accounting
	Departmental Pro- gram Planning and Services	Staff Develop- ment	Auditing
	Vocational and Adult Staff and Instruction	Pupil Personnel Services	Internal Control
	Materials Devel- opment Services	Special Programs Planning and Administration	Payroll
	Finance and Accounting	Educational Specifications Planning	
	Purchasing and Inventory Control	Educational Media Services	
	Vocational, Tech- nical and Adult Pupil Personnel Services		
	Maintenance Plan- ning and Services		
	Operations Plan- ning and Services		
	Physical Plant Planning and Services		
	Transportation Support Services		
	Special Program Support Services		
Plant Support	Plant Support	Plant Support	Plant Support

283

PROGRAM AREA: ADMINISTRATION AND PLANNING			
PERSONNEL PROGRAM	PHYSICAL PLANT PROGRAM	SUPPORT SERVICES PROGRAM	SYSTEM AD-MINISTRATIVE SERVICES
Personnel Management	Plant Management	Support Services Management	System Management
Instructional Staffing	Maintenance Administration	School Food Administration	Administrative Services Management
Non-Instructional Staffing	Operations Administration	Insurance and Safety Administration	Administrative Research
Personnel Policy Development and Administrative Staffing	Plant Planning Security	Purchasing	Administrative Support Services
Personnel Operations and Records		Stores and Distribution	Central Data Processing
		Transportation Administration	Legal Services
			Policy Development
			Public Information
			School Activities
Plant Support	Plant Support	Plant Support	Plant Support

OVERVIEW OF DADE COUNTY PUBLIC SCHOOLS PROGRAM STRUCTURE
(Responsibility Center Dimension)

	Schools					District		System	
	Elementary Centers	Middle/Junior High Centers	Senior High Centers	Adult Centers	Special Centers	Instructional Centers	Support Centers	Instructional Centers	Support Centers
REGULAR PROGRAMS									
Kindergarten	X								
General Instruction	X	X	X						
Occupational Instruction		X	X	X		X			
Continuing Instruction				X		X			
Community Services								X	X
SPECIAL PROGRAMS									
Compensatory	X	X	X	X		X		X	X
Cuban Refugee		X	X	X	X				X
Drug Abuse		X	X					X	X
Exceptional Child	X	X	X		X		X		X
Reading Remediation	X			X					X
SUPPORT PROGRAMS									
Instructional Support	X	X	X	X		X	X		X
Auxiliary Services	X						X		X
Facilities Support	X	X	X		X		X		X
Administrative Support							X		X

IDENTIFICATION OF REGULAR PROGRAMS TO THE SUB-PROGRAM LEVEL *

	ELEMENTARY*	MIDDLE/JUNIOR HIGH*	SENIOR HIGH*	ADULT*
GENERAL INSTRUCTION*	Kindergarten Primary Intermediate Supplementary Services Co-curricular	Art Business Education Foreign Language Health Education Home Economics Industrial Arts Language Arts Mathematics Music Physical Education Science Social Studies Co-curricular	Art Business Education Foreign Language Health Education Home Economics Humanities Industrial Arts Language Arts Mathematics Music Physical Education Safety/Driver Education Science Social Studies Co-curricular	
OCCUPATIONAL INSTRUCTION*		Diversified Education Industrial Education	Agriculture Aviation Education Cooperative Business Education Distributive Education Diversified Education Health Related Technology Industrial Education Technical Education Vocational Office Education	Agriculture Education Business Education Distributive Education Vocational Home Economics Industrial Education Technical and Health Occupation Education
CONTINUING INSTRUCTION*				Fundamental/Literacy Education Languages Foreign Languages Mathematics Natural Sciences Social Studies Other General Education
COMMUNITY SERVICES	Inter-level/systemwide: community school activities			

*Denotes level at which controls will be incorporated into the BGT/FRS to support PPBES in startup phase.

IDENTIFICATION OF SPECIAL PROGRAMS TO THE SUB-PROGRAM LEVEL**

COMPENSATORY*

To be determined during the planning/budgeting cycle.

CUBAN REFUGEE*

English as a Second Language
Pupil Personnel Services
Instructional Development

DRUG ABUSE

To be determined during the planning/budgeting cycle.

EXCEPTIONAL CHILD*

Educably Mentally Retarded
Emotionally Disturbed
Gifted
Hearing Impaired
Homebound/Hospital
Learning Disabilities
Physically Handicapped
Speech Impaired
Socially Maladjusted
Trainable Mentally Retarded
Visually Handicapped
COPE Center
Pupil Personnel Services
Instructional Development

READING REMEDIATION*

Corrective Reading
Remedial Reading

*Denotes minimum plan/budget/control level.
**Support elements of these special programs which have been so earmarked are identified as sub-programs.

EDUCATIONAL MEDIA*

Media Administration
Instructional Radio/TV*
School Library/AV Services*
System Media Services

INSTRUCTIONAL ADMINISTRATION*

School Administration*
Community School Administration*

PUPIL PERSONNEL SERVICES*

Pupil Personnel Administration*
Guidance/Counseling Services*
Psychological Services*
Visiting Teacher Services*

INSTRUCTIONAL DEVELOPMENT

Program Planning*
Program Development*
Program Evaluation*
Staff Development*

*Denotes plan/budget/control level.

IDENTIFICATION OF THE AUXILIARY SERVICES PROGRAM TO THE ELEMENT LEVEL

SCHOOL FOOD*

School Food Services*
School Food Administration*

TRANSPORTATION*

Transportation Services*
Transportation Administration

IDENTIFICATION OF THE FACILITIES SUPPORT PROGRAM TO THE ELEMENT LEVEL

PLANT OPERATIONS*

Operations Services*
Operations Administration*

PLANT MAINTENANCE*

Maintenance Services*
Maintenance Administration*

PLANT CONSTRUCTION*

Plant Planning*
Capital Improvement*

PLANT SECURITY*

PLANT MANAGEMENT*

*Denotes minimum plan/budget/control level.

289

IDENTIFICATION OF THE ADMINISTRATIVE SUPPORT PROGRAM TO THE ELEMENT LEVEL

BUSINESS SERVICES*

Management*
Insurance/Safety Adminis-
    tration*
Purchasing*
Stores/Distribution*

FINANCIAL SERVICES*

Management*
Planning/Budgeting*
Accounting*
Auditing*
Internal Control*
Payroll

INFORMATION SERVICES*

Administrative Research*
Central Data Processing*
Duplicating/School Mail*
Public Information*

PERSONNEL SERVICES*

Management*
Instructional Staffing*
Non-Instructional Staffing*
Administrative Staffing/
    Staffing Control*
Personnel Records/
    Operations*

MANAGEMENT*

System Management*
District Management*
Instruction Management*
Legal Services*
Board Support*

* Denotes minimum plan/budget/control level.

290

The planning procedures and documentation established in this section in accordance with the PLANNING AND BUDGETING CALENDAR included in Section One are intended to accomplish the following major objectives:

(1) to integrate at the operational level program planning and budgeting processes

(2) to produce adequate documentation in support of the proposed budget.

Toward these ends the major thrust in the planning cycle will be the act of program planning at responsibility centers (support centers only for 1971-72). As a result, operational program plans will be produced at those centers. Additionally, two summary planning documents will be available for decision-makers during the planning cycle and subsequently published for general distribution; the cycle will culminate with the production of the official budget document of the school system. Brief descriptions of these operational and summary documents appear on page 292.

PLANNING DOCUMENTS

DOCUMENTS	DESCRIPTION
BUDGET OVERVEW: DADE COUNTY PUBLIC SCHOOLS 1971-72	The budget document. A document suitable for public district distribution which describes the types and quantity of revenues used in funding school system programs, analyzes significant changes in budgetary appropriations system-wide, and summarizes budgetary decisions by program, account, and responsibility center.
PROGRAM MEMORANDA: REGULAR, SPECIAL, AND INSTRUCTIONAL SUPPORT PROGRAMS 1971-72	A summary planning document suitable for public distribution which summarizes budgetary decisions by program, whether at school, district, or division level. Estimated program appropriations which are funded through Part IV will be included as well as appropriations funded by internal funds in the Occupational and Continuing Instruction programs.
PROGRAM MEMORANDA: GENERAL SUPPORT PROGRAMS 1971-72	A summary planning document suitable for public distribution which summarizes budgetary decisions by program (non-instructional) whether at school, district, or division level. Estimated program appropriations funded through Part IV will be included as well as internal funds supporting the School Food program. Proposed capital projects will be summarized within the Facilities Support section.
PROGRAM PLANS: DISTRICT AND DIVISION PROGRAMS 1971-72	An operational planning document for internal use developed at the support center level which identifies planned objectives, resources necessary to accomplish objectives, past year accomplishments and problems, plans to resolve problem areas, and needs for additional funds. In addition, each district/division will submit a summary statement describing significant achievements, both past and planned, for all centers summarized by type.
PROGRAM PLANS: CAPITAL PROJECTS 1971-72	An operational planning document for internal use which describes in detail facilities needs during the next year and over a multi-year period as well as each capital project currently underway.
PROGRAM PLANS: CONTRACTED PROJECTS 1971-72	An operational planning document for internal use which identifies the planned objectives for each probable and funded contracted project, resources necessary for those objectives, and the funding source.

Appendix D

CASE STUDIES PREPARED
BY THE
PILOT DISTRICTS

MONTGOMERY COUNTY

The budget preparation cycle in the Montgomery County Public Schools begins with community meetings in September on budget priorities as presented in the annual edition of the budget discussion guide titled, "Choices For Our Children." During early November the Board of Education holds open hearings during which indiviuals and representatives of P.T.A.s and other organizations present their opinions on budget priorities for the next fiscal year. While the Board of Education is receiving this testimony from the community, the negotiations process between the Board of Education and the Montgomery County Education Association commences in late October and continues through November and December.

The major avenues for community participation in planning educational programs are through the local P.T.A.s, the area advisory councils, civic associations, and the various advisory committees established by the school system. Student participation at the local school level is provided for through local student government associations and at the county level through the county-wide student government organizations that operate at both the junior and senior high school level.

In 1967, a Long-Range Planning Committee was established in the Montgomery County Public Schools to investigate the needs of students and the type of educational programs that would be required by 1980. The committee initially studied the general trends in population distribution, transportation, land use, occupations and employment, economic resources, communications, automation and the computer, morality and religion, political organizations, and medical science in order to determine the societal setting that students would encounter by 1980. The committee next considered the changes that would have to occur within the school system by 1980 and developed priorities for long-range planning in relation to the scope, program, and organization of education in Montgomery County. The committee finally considered the impact that changes in the societal setting and the scope, program, and organization of education would have in the areas of personnel, facilities, and materials.

Among the major recommendations made was one that called for the development of a "systems approach" in the school system in order to take advantage of modern technology. The committee envisioned an approach that would periodically sample the cognitive, affective, and psychomotor behavior of students, with these behaviors then being translated into goals of public education which would be adopted by the Board of Education. These goals, in turn, would then be translated into a variety of instructional programs by the professional staff.

Concurrently with the work of the Long-Range Planning Committee, members of the Board of Education and the professional staff became interested in the potential of the Planning, Programming, Budgeting System approach for making decisions concerning the allocation of resources. During the summer and fall of 1967, several seminars on PPBS were conducted for the members of the Board and selected professional personnel; and several staff members had an opportunity to visit other school systems then considering the development of PPB systems. The staff members participating in these activities were asked by the superintendent to give further study to the possibility of developing a PPB system for the school system. The preliminary investigation into the potential of PPBS and the impact of the recommendations contained in the report of the Long-Range Planning Committee resulted in the appointment in February, 1968, of an Operational Task Committee for Establishing a Planning, Programming, Budgeting System for the Montgomery County Public Schools. The committee submitted a detailed position paper on Planning, Programming, Budgeting System to the Board in June, 1968. The report was favorably received and the Task Committee was authorized to prepare a proposal for establishing a project on PPBS for inclusion in the FY-1970 budget.

The purpose of the PPBS Project established by the Montgomery County Public Schools was to begin the process of planning and budgeting within the existing organizational framework of the school system, including in-service and staff development requirements; to develop a comprehensive detailed plan for the long-range implementation of a PPB system; and to recommend such organizational changes as may be required to bring about a well coordinated PPB system within the Montgomery County Public Schools.

Between 1968 and 1970, additional objectives for the project were formulated. In FY-71, the Montgomery County Government began the implementation of a PPB system for the county that included the programs of all the agencies funded by the county. The development of the PPB system for the school system would have to be considered with the requirements of the county government's program.

As the project was implemented in early 1970, several concomitant objectives were soon identified. The Departments of Supervision and Curriculum Development and Pupil and Program Appraisal were interested in developing a systems approach to solving curriculum problems. The characteristics of the approach included: the ability to deal with complexity, to make available alternative strategies and solutions to anticipated problems, to evaluate proposed strategies, to operate efficiently as a total school system in solving problems, and to obtain accurate feedback on progress being achieved. The purpose of such a systems approach would be the improvement of the capability of the school system to make rational instructional decisions. This systems approach to instructional planning incorporated most of the aspects of a PPB system, and it was agreed that the development of the instructional systems design would parallel the development and implementation of the PPB system as a management system.

During this same period of time, a committee was studying the questions of quality assurance and accountability in the Montgomery County Public Schools. In its initial report to the Board of Education in April, 1969, the committee recommended that four promising parallel approaches be utilized to achieve quality assurance. The first approach called for a concerted effort toward development and installation of a powerful managerial systems approach at all levels of operation. This would include further support of the design, development, and installation of a PPB system together with accompanying training of all instructional leadership groups. The second approach called for the developing, field testing, funding, and installing of instructional support systems for local schools. The third approach required the development of improved linkage and communications capability between sub-systems within the Montgomery County Public Schools. The fourth approach called for the creation of a responsive emergency tactical capability for schools in trouble, including a team of trained personnel ready to take immediate action to assist the local school staff. As a follow up to this first report, the committee agreed to begin the development of a "Model for a Quality Assurance System" for the Montgomery County Public Schools. The requirements of the model that have been identified thus far will require an operational PPB system if they are to be realized. The achievement of accountability and the development of the quality assurance system that leads to it have become the second concomitant objective of the project.

While the objectives originally set for the project in 1968 still remain valid, in the intervening two years additional and concomitant objectives have been identified by the school system. Compatability with the requirements of the Montgomery County Government's PPB System and the school system reorganization plan had to be considered as did the common objectives identified as the system developed plans for a new approach to instructional planning, a quality assurance program, and a new organizational framework that would facilitate participation by many individuals and groups in real decision-making.

The Operational Task Committee for establishing a Planning, Programming, Budgeting System, following its formal report to the Board of Education in June, 1968, was authorized to prepare a detailed proposal for establishing a project on PPBS for inclusion in the *FY 1970 Operating Budget*. The committee identified the support and commitments required to implement a PPB system as follows: "The success and the quality of benefits will depend upon the supporting executive policy and the sincere efforts of school officials and administrators at all levels to insure its success. Certain commitments and involvements will be required:

1. Top officials and personnel at all levels as well as the public must participate and become informed regarding the PPBS concept.
2. A sincere desire by personnel at all levels to use PPBS for the good of the Montgomery County public school system is essential.
3. Common agreements regarding the visibility of goals, plans, programs, costs, and results, as well as the justification of expenditures and the on-going evaluation of goal achievement, are essentials.
4. Discipline and consistency with regard to program structure, timing of events, procedures, and formats for information and data must be practiced.
5. Commitment to the concept of developing individual program budget units at the local school level must be maintained.
6. Coordination is needed in developing program budget units by the central office departments.
7. A commitment to the use of feedback in decision-making for multi-year programs is essential.
8. Careful attention to the problem of analysis and consideration of the accuracy and effectiveness of the measure of quantity and quality must be pursued.
9. Sufficient lead time to establish a reservoir of data is essential.
10. Data processing capability is a basic requirement."

The Operational Task Committee further noted that the installation of such a system could be expected to arouse opposition; and in order to ease this lack of acceptance, it recommended that a well planned training and informational program be conducted to give personnel affected an opportunity to understand and to participate in its implementation.

The committee recommended that no new office or department be initially established to begin the development of a PPB System but that a project team be established for this purpose. The project coordinator with a staff of limited size would report to the superintendent through the deputy superintendent. The project team would provide assistance in developing and implementing the PPB System through the use of consultants and representatives from various departments who would remain in their present positions but serve as liaison personnel in planning and installing the system. The project coordinator and his staff and the various departmental liaison personnel would be responsible for training each unit involved in developing individual program budgets with the instruction to include the formulation of statements of measurable objectives; the development of alternative plans to carry out these objectives; the delineation of cost and noncost resources required as inputs; the preparation of assessment tasks for the stated objectives; and the evaluation of the findings in terms of goal attainment related to time, cost, and effectiveness. The implementation schedule as originally proposed by the committee was with the understanding that in the initial stages the PPB System would serve as a supplement to the current budget. The superintendent recommended and the Board of Education approved the inclusion of the funding necessary to establish the project in the *FY 1970 Operating Budget.* Appropriations were made to cover the salary of the coordinator, a secretary, and the half-time services of an assistant budget officer. Additional funds also were provided for professional part-time assistance to cover the cost of substitute coverage required for classroom teachers participating in PPBS project activities, consultant fees, staff development and travel, and supplies and materials. In December, 1969, a decision was made to transfer a senior high school principal to the coordinator's position at the beginning of the second semester in February, 1970. Prior to assuming this position, the project coordinator had an opportunity to attend the ASBO Regional Conference in Washington, D.C., and the N.A.S.E. Institute on PPBS.

The initial task undertaken by the project coordinator was the establishment of the advisory council for the project. In keeping with the recommendations originally made by the task committee, 23 members of the professional staff were asked to serve in this capacity, including a representative from each of the major departments within the central office and representative elementary and secondary school teachers and principals. The Montgomery County Education Association was invited to nominate two representatives to the advisory council, and the president of the association designated the director of employee relations for the association and a classroom teacher as the representatives. The steering committee met on three occasions with a group of consultants on PPBS.

In the period from June, 1968, to the implementation of the PPBS Project in February, 1970, the professional staff and the members of the Board of Education recognized that one of the essential steps in the process of implementing a PPBS was the need to re-examine the Goals of Education of the Montgomery County Public Schools. The superintendent proposed to the Board of Education in January, 1970, that a steering committee be appointed to undertake this task. The membership of the steering committee included the deputy superintendent of schools as chairman, the assistant superintendent for instructional and pupil services, the PPBS project coordinator, an area director, the vice president of the Montgomery County Region of Student Governments, the president of the Montgomery County Junior Council of Student Governments, the president of the Montgomery County Chamber of Commerce, and the president of the Montgomery County Council of P.T.A.s, the president of Montgomery County Education Association. The steering committee was charged with the responsibility for developing and implementing plans and procedures for reviewing the existing

12 Goals of Education and for developing new or revised goals which would then be recommended to the Board of Education for adoption.

As an initial activity, the members agreed to contact the representatives of some 250 school and community organizations to acquaint them with the assignment of the steering committee and to request their comments, suggestions, and criticisms regarding the existing Goals of Education. This preliminary survey was conducted during September and October, 1970; and at the same time, the steering committee developed a plan to create a 36-member advisory board that would provide assistance, direction, and feedback to the steering committee. The membership of this advisory board was chosen to be as broadly representative of the community and professional staff as possible.

During the same period of time that the system was studying the feasibility of developing a PPB System, plans were also underway to expand the system's capability to provide adequate data processing support for its management, administrative, and instructional division.

The members of the project team and the advisory council, as one of the outcomes of the orientation workshop in April, 1970, agreed that one of the high priority tasks to be considered was the development of a program structure that would accommodate the existing and future program of the Montgomery County Public Schools. During the orientation program, the members of the advisory council studied a number of program structures as proposed by the consultants; and they asked the members of the project team to follow up on this discussion and to prepare a tentative design for a program structure for the council's further consideration. During the summer of 1970, a teacher specialist was employed to assist the project staff in this undertaking. After a more detailed study of the several possible approaches, the project team prepared a tentative design that included separate program categories for preschool, elementary, junior, and senior high schools in the area of regular instruction. The teacher specialist reviewed this design with each member of the advisory council through a series of individual conferences. As a result of the criticisms raised in these interviews, the teacher specialist and the project team revised the original structure by eliminating the program categories based on age levels. The alternate proposed approach divided the entire area of instruction into two program areas — regular and supplementary. The specific programs under regular instruction were considered to be the usual academic disciplines as currently recognized in the system.

Throughout the time that the proposed program structure was under development, the project team and the staff were aware that the selection of any program structure by the school system also would require the development of crosswalk capabilities between the program categories included in the structure and the 18 functions required by the Maryland State Department fo Education in the conventional operating budget and that additional crosswalk capabilities also would be required between the school system's program structure and the program structure being utilized by the Montgomery County Government in the county-wide PPB System instituted in FY 1970. An additional requirement of the county government's PPB System was the annual preparation of six-year fiscal projections for all the public service programs supported in whole or in part by county tax revenues.

Prior to the time that the PPBS project became operational in February, 1970, other staff members were serving on a special committee at the request of the Board of Education to investigate the currently popular concepts of accountability, quality assurance, educational assessment audit, and performance contracting. In April, 1970, this committee prepared "A Position Paper on Quality Control in the Montgomery County Public Schools" for the Board of Education. As a result of the Board's discussion on this paper, the term "quality control" was changed to "quality assurance." The interest generated by this report led to a proposal to provide for the further study of these concepts during the July, 1970, summer workshop for administrative and supervisory personnel. Staff members were asked to continue their work and to prepare a tentative design that would relate the on-going and intended activities and commitments of the school system within the framework of a general accountability or a results-oriented decision-making system. The preliminary design for this general system was presented to the Board of Education on November 30, 1970.

Since the beginning of the PPBS project in the system, there has been continuous involvement on the part of the staffs from the Departments of Supervision and Curriculum Development and Pupil and Program Appraisal. The staffs of these departments and the members of the advisory council soon recognized that the process of redefining the Goals of Education would require an extended period of time and that much of the curriculum development work that had been previously done by the school system would still remain as valid instructional program under the new Goals of Education. Actually, since 1962, the primary approach to curriculum planning had been to relate the objectives of the various instructional programs (K through 12) to the existing Goals of Education and next relate the more specific course objectives to these broader program objectives. The various curriculum bulletins of the school system beginning with *Curriculum Design — The Institutional Level* and continuing down through the many course of study bulletins specify in considerable detail the expected outcomes for the learners. On the other hand, the approach utilized in pupil and program appraisal was not directly oriented to the particular objectives set forth for each program or course. The county-wide testing program traditionally utilized a series of intelligence and achievement tests at the third, fifth, seventh, ninth, and eleventh grade levels to assess pupil and program performance. More recently, the system had undertaken the development of its own achievement tests directly related to program and course objectives in the areas of elementary and junior high school mathematics, the seventh and eighth grade geography program, and the ninth and tenth grade U. S. history and government program.

The staffs of the Departments of Supervision and Curriculum Development and Pupil and Program appraisal agreed to inventory and evaluate the existing instructional program objectives and to determine the extent to which the achievement of these objectives could be assessed with existing evaluation techniques. They further agreed to inventory available evaluation instruments which, if utilized, could extend the range of objectives currently being assessed.

The Future of PPBS in Montgomery County

The task of developing a program structure for the Montgomery County Public Schools was completed during 1970. For FY 1972, the structure will be utilized to prepare a program budget in outline form, with the reading program and the instructional support programs in supervision and curriculum development, pupil and program appraisal, pupil services, and educational media and technology being developed in full detail. In 1970 a new position for a full-time reading program coordinator was created, and this coordinator will work with the PPBS Project Coordinator and the Budget Officer to prepare the detailed reading program budget. The personnel responsible for administering the support programs in the areas cited for detailed development will participate in a special workshop with consultant assistance in the spring of 1971 in order to prepare the objectives for their support programs and to identify the performance indicators for their programs. For FY 1972, the conventional operating and capital budgets will be maintained. The six-year fiscal projections required for the county government's PPB System will be based on the categories or functions included in the conventional operating budget.

For FY 1973, a detailed program budget will be prepared in parallel with the conventional operating and capital budegts, and for FY 1974, it is anticipated that the program budget would become fully operational. Crosswalking capabilities will be built into the financial subsystem that will allow for the conversion of the information contained in the program budget format into the formats required by the Maryland State Department of Education and the Montgomery County government's PPB System. The preparation of six-year fiscal projections on a program basis would also be initiated in the FY 1974 budget.

In summary, the experience of the Montgomery County Public Schools in attempting to develop and implement a PPBS management system clearly indicates that it requires a long-term commitment, an ability to modify the original objectives to meet new demands, and a willingness on the part of the executive staff and the Board of Education to provide the resources needed for additional staff, for consultant assistance, and for in-service training programs for large numbers of personnel. With this high level of commitment and substantial financial support, the task thus far has proved to be a difficult and complex one. Without this commitment and support, it would, no doubt, be an impossible one.

300

Finally, the best indication of the future status of the PPBS Project in Montgomery County is contained in a statement in the November 30, 1970, resolution of the Board of Education: "The coordinated and continuing development of these programs gives promise of making significant contributions to a quality educational program for the citizens of the community."

WESTPORT, THE GOAL-SETTING PERIOD

Goal-setting is a basic initial ingredient of any PPBS effort, but of course goal-setting existed and was practiced long before the advent of the application of the PPBS approach in education. Every school system has had a set of goals at some time and American secondary schools have ritually spruced up individual school goals for review by the visiting accreditation teams. In many school systems, these goal statements were earnestly generated and relentlessly pursued to judge their effectiveness. In some places, the goals were eyewash and bore little relevance to what actually went on.

Several years ago, the Westport Board of Education felt the need for a new statement of system-wide goals. The Board appointed a citizens committee to study the problem of school goals and to recommend goals to the Board. The Citizens Advisory Committee on School Goals, consisting exclusively of local citizens, functioned during school years 1967/68 and 1968/69, submitting its final report in May, 1969. During this same period two other citizens advisory committees were also operational — one on character education, another on a long-range school budget.

The Board set aside 1969/70 for a comprehensive review by the community and the teaching staff. This review identified some critical differences of ideology in the town. The original goals recommended by the committee were liberal in their orientation. Ian Wilson, the chairman of the goals committee, had led his group along individualistic, libertarian, international, intercultural pathways. Significant counter elements of the community expressed views supporting the *status quo,* nationalism, isolationism, regimentation, the 3-R's, and groupthink. The year-long review made for compromise on both sides.

Educational Goals for the Westport Schools

In order to achieve excellence in education, the Board of Education adopts the following goals to indicate the direction in which it wishes the schools to move in the decade ahead. It understands that they cannot be attained quickly or easily; some of them, indeed, can never be wholly attained, for they are dynamic rather than static in character. But these statements are designed to chart the future course of the Westport Schools, recognizing particularly that:

(a) The schools will have the individual as the focus of public education, and provide the opportunity for each individual to develop fully his potentialities and the skills essential to responsible participation in a complex society. These skills shall include a sound grounding in the basic intellectual skills and a capacity for critical thought and analysis — the requisites for effectiveness in work or further study.

(b) The schools transmit our American heritage and democratic traditions and laws, and their own philosophy and practices should reflect that heritage. It is the purpose of the schools to help the student develop as a responsible, self-disciplined citizen, with an understanding of United States historical development and the democratic process.

(c) Relevance — a relationship the student clearly perceives between schooling and life — is an essential condition to effectiveness in education, and

(d) The accelerated pace of change in our society will require continuing innovation and self-renewal of our school system, coupled with evaluation and accountability.

In pursuit of these goals, the schools shall seek to accomplish effectively and efficiently that which the community can afford to do. The goals shall be accomplished in a climate which enables the educational experience to proceed unimpeded and encourages self-realization and the free exchange of ideas.

The following sixteen goals were adopted by the Board in the fall of 1970:

Pupil Goals

Academic:

1. Students should acquire the intellectual skills basic to continuing self-development and further study.
2. Students should develop a capacity for critical thought, evaluation, and analysis.
3. Students should have opportunities to develop artistic and creative potentials and interests.
4. Students should have opportunities to develop physical fitness.

Interpersonal:

5. Students should learn to practice the principles and qualities of thought needed for democratic citizenship and responsible participation in a multi-racial, multi-cultural society.
6. Students should develop the perspectives, competence, and skills needed for living in a world of close, international interdependence.
7. Students should be helped to develop emotional maturity and sensitivity to the rights and feelings of others.
8. Within the limits imposed by students' educational progress and the schools' goals, students should have increasing responsibility for their own education so they become adults for whom learning is a natural part of life.

Personal:

9. Students should be helped to develop self-awareness and self-respect in order to permit their full development as individuals.

Program Goals

10. The instructional program of the Westport schools should be designed to meet the needs of the individual student and to enable him to make the most constructive use of his particular abilities.
11. Our schools should enhance the relevance and purpose of education through use of community resources and the active involvement of students in community life.

Organizational:

12. Our school system should conduct an effective program of evaluation and program development, designed to search out, select, and test the feasibility of achieving maximum education benefit for each student.
13. Recognizing that their primary obligation is to youngsters, our schools should become year-round educational centers for the whole community.
14. Our school system should develop its role in the regional educational community, consistent with adequate local control and responsibility.

Logistic:

15. Staff members should be encouraged and assisted in developing their skills, abilities, and unique talents within the framework of the systems goals, in order to develop and maintain a high quality of teaching performance.
16. The physical facilities of the school system should be maintained efficiently and updated on a planned basis to facilitate program development.

Board Objectives

Initial Efforts in Management by Objectives

A major development in PPBS was the introduction of annual Board of Education objectives. In response to the need for a logical and complete statement of the things the Board of Education wanted to accomplish during a given year, the administrative staff prepared for 1968/69 a list of Board Objectives. These objectives were grouped into nine major areas: instruction, program extensions, students, special services, community, administration, personnel, plant, and finance.

The first year the objectives were written by the Superintendent and approved by the Board. The only review was to take place when the objectives for the next succeeding year were to be presented.

303

The Superintendent prepared the objectives the second year with considerable input from his immediate staff. The objectives spelled out all that was considered important for 1969-70. Our hope was to overcome the problems of the past where directions were vaguely understood and informally agreed upon, where crash programs were the order of the day, and where there was a tendency to avoid by neglect those problems that were particularly difficult or painful.

That second year it was also decided to set up a system to make the accomplishment of objectives part of a complete framework. What were the step-by-step events needed to secure accomplishment of a given objective? When did certain tasks have to be done? Who had to be involved? What resources would have to be marshalled? How were we to close the gap between a statement of objectives and the actual attainment of those objectives? We needed a plain, simple programming tool.

We fell upon the event schedule and the planning calendar as appropriate tools to use in accomplishing Board objectives. The event schedule detailed all the major events required to reach an objective. A date was assigned for mandatory or desirable completion time. The events were numbered for ease in placement of events on the planning calendar. There is a compelling logic to the approach. The destination is laid out in detail, and the equipment and manpower requirements for the journey are specified. Real life, however, keeps raising its practical head.

Now in the third year of Board Objectives, the staff intends to continue its use of the event schedule technique and, if practical, will use the planning calendar as well. The incredible demands upon staff time continuously encroach upon our good resolve, however.

Westport is serious about its objectives. We get more done, more consistently, than before, even in a fairly unstable situation. The use of management by objectives in public education holds considerable promise for the future.

Instructional Objectives and Evaluation

The initial conceptualization of several important Westport activities predated the wide-spread awareness of PPBS as a management tool in education. Several of these activities were later identified as prime PPBS ingredients.

The appointment in July, 1968, of an assistant superintendent led to Westport's first formal move toward conscious introduction of PPBS. While a student in Harvard's Administrative Career Program, the new staff member had concentrated his studies in the area of systems analysis. He immediately saw the utility of a number of the activities conducted or planned in Westport in the absence of a unifying master plan, so he developed a master plan for introducing PPBS in a consistent manner.

Together with Westport's Director of Reading, the assistant superintendent devised the prototype of the program budget. They defined the program and subprogram, set down specific, measurable, performance objectives; identified the instruments to be used in evaluating the attainment of the objectives; and reported the results along with the expectations. Each subprogram had a facing page detailing the specific dollar cost of the subprogram.

But reading is only one program area and one which lends itself to quantification. What about the programs that are difficult to state in behavioral terms and even more difficult to measure? If appreciation is a valid objective in the fine arts and humanities, how does one go about measuring "appreciation?" In the preparation of instructional objectives, must one declare the instrument to be used to measure the attainment of the objective? One view in Westport was that the objectives should be developed in an ideal environment. That is, we would assume no constraints of time, staff, ability, or money and proceed to create objectives for each program assuming utopian conditions without worrying about the identification of assessment tools for the time being.

The opposing position was that the best approach would be the development of a complete inventory of nationally-normed tests in each program area. The availability of specific tests or test items would form the base for setting instructional objectives.

Our experience with most of the nationally-normed tests had been fairly negative to this point. The principal problem had been that Westport's curriculum does not follow national trends in most areas and the instruments do not test what we teach. This has not kept our children from running well ahead of national norms, but it introduces an overwhelming inconsistency of approach in that we would be teaching one thing and judging how well we were doing by testing something else.

Some of the problems that we were struggling with at that "early" point in time are now well on the road to solution, thanks to great effort in many other school systems.

The view that prevailed in Westport (directly in opposition to the writer's view) after confronting the problems for a considerable period was to seek to identify and make inventory of available test instruments and items to measure certain specific accomplishments.

During 1969/1970 we worked cooperatively with the Educational Testing Service to plan the best way of approaching the problem of generating a program-oriented source of tests and test items At the close of that year, the project was far from coming to a conclusion as to the viability of the proposed effort.

The future of instructional objectives in this country is very bright. Many school systems are introducing learning by objectives and the vigor of the Instructional Objectives Exchange is a clear indication that objectives will be with us for awhile

Some Cost Accounting Aspects

The Westport PPBS effort intentionally concentrated on planning and programming at the expense of budgeting. We felt as our leaders at ASBO's Research Corporation, that the management of educational resources was an approach far beyond just setting up a program accounting system. We still feel that way, but our most consistent successes have been in budgeting.

In the fall of 1969, we began developing a program structure into which all of our costs would fit. Our aim was to reflect what we do since our dollars, our people, and our time were all geared to present activity. For instance, one of the things we do is to provide for learning in mathematics. There is a guidance program. We clean schools, we provide utilities, we feed children. Our aim was not to re-structure the entire school system. We are not altogether unhappy with what we have, even though there have been criticisms of school systems that have converted to program budgeting without massive changes in substance and organization.

We wanted to answer several basic questions. From September to June what happens to a youngster in terms of learning? Can we tell in advance what ought to happen? Can we tell afterward what did happen? And how much did it cost? How long did it take? Could we spend less time in one area and more in another? Time allocation has a tremendous impact on dollar allocation, of course.

In order to approach these questions, we defined a framework which reflected our current activities. This permits us then to measure output in terms of these activities and permits precise dollar identification according to these outputs.

Having what appeared to be a workable budget format did not cause us to abandon the established budgets used successfully in the past. On the contrary, we prepared our budgets for 1970/71 as always and after they were in the hands of the Board and the public, we proceeded to do the whole thing over by program for practice. It was a good thing. We were beset with hundreds of questions of program assignment that could only be asked and answered by the process itself. We also had quite a time balancing to the "real" budget. We were working with a manual system and the amount of calculation time was very great, especially allocating elementary teachers against program and subprogram. We got the job done in three weeks.

For the 1971/72 budget, which was submitted to the Board and public in January, 1971, we converted to automation. Once the data were collected, reviewed, punched on cards, and corrected, all we had to do was to print out. What took days to calculate in 1970 took seconds to compute in 1971. We did not automate in 1970 because of the lack of programming lead time.

The Westport program budget permits dollar allocation to be viewed from several dimensions. First, we can print out a budget by standard federal account classification code. We need this budget to keep track of our money. We can print out by program and subprogram, identifying each item by standard federal account and verbal description. These printouts can be created by individual school as well.

Also, because this has proven useful over past years, the budget can show the reason for expenditures in the four major variable categories—costs of continuing commitments, costs due to students' distribution, costs due to negotiations, and costs due to program improvement.

The Westport budget solves the problem of "crosswalk" between a *Handbook II* system and a program system because it slices both ways. All budget items carry the standard code and a program code and can be extracted and assembled by either code. This can be done manually, without machine assistance.

MEMPHIS

The origin of program budgeting in Memphis may be traced from about 1951, when the growth of personnel accounting records exceeded the capacity of the conventional methods then in use. The machine accounting system consisting of key punch, card sort, and print out application of accounting procedures was augmented by information from a tub file system for all cafeteria warehouse operations in 1958. Greater use of machine operation was achieved when all testing was processed through the mark sense machine in 1959. By 1959 the system had outgrown the machine process, resulting in the installation of a 305 Ramac computer. But the 305 Ramac computer did not have sufficient capacity to handle the increasing workload; so another digital computer, an IBM 1401, was installed in 1962. In 1967 these computers were replaced by an IBM 360 computer, thus allowing the system to make better use of management information data.

Our present system now has about 1,000 digits of information on each of the 10,000 employees, including basic statistics, certification items, assignments, and student loads. Pupil data banks have about 5,000 digits of information, including basic statistics, attendance (which is a subsystem), grade reports, scheduling, and testing. Financial reporting has been provided by a coding system to generate information by funds, project, function object, school location, subject areas, and class periods. Facilities data information has been listed by buildings, classrooms, sites, and special area (size, equipment, etc.)

Thus the third generation computer has provided a data bank for a management information system that has staff, pupil, financial, and facility information available for reporting purposes.

Utilization of the latest management and reporting concepts led to an early interest in program budgeting and later to PPBS. Program cost analysis by school location as well as by individual instructional items as mathematics, science, or study hall have provided administrators with a variety of cost information on how the school dollar was spent.

This interest and experience of some ten years of computerized school accounting led to participation as pilot in the Research Corporation-Association of School Business Officials Planning-Programming-Budgeting Evaluation Systems Project. The objective for Memphis was crosswalking a program structure to the Memphis Budget pointing out ramifications of *Revised Handbook II.*

Project Objectives

Crosswalking Program Structure to Memphis Budget. Crosswalking a program structure to the Memphis budget and pointing out ramifications of *Revised Hankbook II* was the first objective of the Memphis pilot project. The relation of Educational Resources Management to *Revised Handbook II* was the second objective of the Memphis pilot project. The third objective was preparing the recommendations for codification that were generated from objective one and two.

Crosswalking a program structure to the Memphis budget was limited to an application of the process to one high school, one junior high school, and one elementary school. This application concerned itself with assignment of resources in terms of items that would remain constant. Such items included the number of staff assigned, space assignment, percent of time or man-time assignment and other percent of resources, rather than dollar assignments which would change with inflation and future operations.

The Crosswalk of the Memphis Budget Structure and the ERM Program Structure

Traditional Budget. In this section differences between the traditional budget and the program budget are compared. Throughout the section the term "Traditional Budget" is used to designate the function-object budget currently used by the majority of school districts.

Crosswalk Procedures. Although there are significant differences between the traditional budget and the program budget, it is generally possible to translate the data in the program budget into the traditional budget format, and conversely. The former translation — going from the program budget to the traditional budget format — is essential when planners are required to relate their plant to appropriation budgets or other funding documents not geared to the program structure. The latter translation — going from the traditional budget to the program budget — is desirable in the early stages of implementing a program budgeting system in order to provide an initial frame of reference and to clarify the relative quantitative importance of various programs and program elements.

Program-Sub-Program-Program Elements Defined. As a matter of definition, the term program is used in this report to describe the largest group of activities designed to achieve a specific objective. The term sub-program is used to mean the second level or second largest group of activities designed to achieve a specific objective. The term *program elements* is used to mean any of the specific activities in a given program. In this usage, for example, the term *program* is applied to the group of activities performed to teach fundamental skills or "Intellectual Skills Development" but not to those sub-groups of activities or sub programs, such as teaching language "Communication Skills" or teaching mathematics "Computational Skills." Examples of program elements in the ERM program structure are: reading, writing, mathematics, problem solving for elementary, and junior high. The high school programs include preparatory/post-secondary education and preparatory/post-secondary employment to be identified by terms such as *sub-programs* and *program elements* at the local school level.

Crosswalk Defined. The expression of the relationship between the ERM program structure and the traditional budget is referred to as a *crosswalk*. A crosswalk includes a tabular array, with the horizontal columns showing the traditional budget cost categories and the vertical rows showing the program budget cost categories. Underlying the crosswalk, of course, is a set of definitions and procedures for allocating the data in a cost category in one budget to a corresponding cost category in the other. The actual level of detail at which the crosswalk translation may be performed can vary greatly.

Individual School Budgets. The examples represent the budget of an individual school. The figures are based on an analysis of actual individual school budget data and the examples are reasonably typical of actual school experience. The program element analysis would vary among the 160 schools in Memphis since the district policy encourages innovation and experimentation. This factor of individuality creates different program elements at various locations of elementary, junior high, and high schools, so that no one school was representative of the total instructional offering in the system. Thus, the results obtained in these crosswalks were similar to the results that could be obtained for many schools, but would not be identical.

Cost Allocation by Programs and Sub-Programs. The crosswalk illustrates the ability of Memphis to allocate costs for salaries, supplies, and materials, and equipment by programs and sub-programs. The need to allocate costs at the program element is not considered practical for this project, but the present installation has the capability for program element accounting.

Steps in Crosswalk Preparation. For this project application it was necessary to have the curriculum department specialists define the program goals, objectives and/or intent as the first step in the preparation of the crosswalk. The second step was the identification of the resources by elementary, junior high and high school. These resources were the personnel, classrooms, materials, and supplies which were needed for each program. The third step was the allocation of resources by programs, sub-programs, and program elements. This writer found the curriculum specialists, super-

	STAFF				Pupils	Class Rooms	Equiv. Personnel	Materials
	Professional		Other					
	No.	%	No.	%				
Communication Skills	18	40			539	18	18	212.00
Computation Skills	18	20			539			84.16
Reasoning Skills	18	10			539			42.42
Culture	18	10			539			42.42
Behavioral Sciences	8	10			539			42.42
Life Sciences	18	5			539			21.20
Physical Sciences	*							
Physical, Emotional, Social	18	5			539			21.20
Student Activities	*							
Pupil Personnel Services	1	20			539			
The Arts	*							*
Languages								
Occupations	*							
Professions	*							
Practical Arts	*							
Mathematics	*							
Science								
English	*							
Speech	*							
Languages	*							
Social Studies								
Industrial Arts	*							
Business Education	*							
Superintendent								
Planning								
Program Coordination								
Program Operation		40			539	18		
Management Services		60			539	18	1	6.44
Library	1	80			539	Libr.	1	940.84
Audio-Visual	1	20			539			73.21
CAI								
Educational TV								
Operations			5	100	539	18		564.49
Maintenance			1	10				1265.68
Security								
Central Services								
Food			6	100	539	Cafe.		7692.83
Transportation								
Community Services								

ELEMENTARY SCHOOL

	STAFF				Pupils	Class Rooms	Equiv. Personnel	Materials
	Professional		Other					
	No.	%	No.	%				
Communication Skills	9	50			293	9	9	
Computation Skills	9	5			293			
Reasoning Skills	9	5			293			
Culture	9	10			293			
Behavioral Sciences	9	5			293			
Life Sciences	9	10			293			5.88
Physical Sciences	1	40			70			60.90
Physical, Emotional, Social	3	100			764		3	20.10
Student Activities	3	40			202			122.78
Pupil Personnel Services	1	100			764	1	1	5.00
The Arts	4	80			459	4	4	236.15
Languages								
Occupations								
Professions	*							*
Practical Arts	3	70			345	3	3	
Mathematics	1	40			64		1	
Science	2	80			205	2	2	
English	2	80			231	2	2	
Speech	*							*
Languages	1	40			34		1	
Social Studies	1	40			45		1	
Industrial Arts								
Business Education								
Superintendent								
Planning								
Program Coordination								
Program Operation	2	50			764		1	
Management Services	2	50	1	100	764		1	60.82
Library	1	80			764	Libr.	1	187.37
Audio-Visual	1	20			764	40		118.87
CAI								
Educational TV								625.00
Operations			7	100	764			1378.42
Maintenance								486.50
Security								
Central Services								
Food			9	100	764	Cafe.		571.04
Transportation								
Community Services								

JUNIOR HIGH SCHOOL

| | STAFF | | | | Pupils | Class Rooms | Equiv. Personnel | Materials |
| | Professional | | Other | | | | | |
	No.	%	No.	%				
Communication Skills								
Computation Skills	1	20			30			
Reasoning Skills	1	20			30			
Culture								
Behavioral Sciences								
Life Sciences								
Physical Sciences								
Physical, Emotional, Social	4	100			667		4	
Student Activities	10	80			583		10	2051.55
Pupil Personnel Services	4	100			1840		4	155.00
The Arts	2	100			372		2	677.60
Languages	NP							
Occupations	1	40			46			
Professions	1	100			120	1	1	
Practical Arts	5	100			677	5	5	942.84
Mathematics	7	100			894	7	7	
Science	6	100			194	6	6	
English	12	100			1815	12	12	
Speech	2	50			136	1	2	
Languages	5	100			430	5	5	
Social Studies	9	100			1086	9	9	88.00
Industrial Arts	1	100			104	1	1	225.02
Business Education	9	100			1231	9	9	27.72
Superintendent								
Planning								
Program Coordination								
Program Operation	3	40			1840			
Management Services	3	60			1840		3	
Library	2	90			1840	Libr.	2	1306.52
Audio-Visual	2	10			1840			322.39
CAI								
Educational TV								625.00
Operations			13	100	1840	53		1473.99
Maintenance								
Security								
Central Services								
Food			17	100	1840	Cafe.		27,685.11
Transportation								
Community Services								

SENIOR HIGH SCHOOL

vising staff, principals, and assistant principals very cooperative and helpful in the identification and verification of personnel, programs, sub-programs, and program elements in steps one, two and three.

Instructional Personnel Involvement Essential. This writer would recommend that any district planning to implement ERM should involve the instructional personnel at the very beginning of the planning. This will enable the instructional personnel to generate a clear set of instructional goals that would relate to the ERM structure. This writer found that the traditional budget structure and its programs (functions) provided no clear set of goals which could be identified within the ERM framework.

Summary Form Crosswalks Illustrate Basic Relationships. Although the crosswalks are in summary form, they can be used to illustrate some basic relationships between the traditional budget and the program structure. The procedure in using this example is to describe how the costs for each of the lines in the summary traditional budget have been allocated to each of the columns representing the programs. It should be emphasized, however, that the procedures illustrated in this example are only general guidelines for crosswalking between the traditional budget and the program budget. They are illustrations of the basic logic involved in performing such a crosswalk, and they should not be construed as the last word in relating traditional budget accounts to program budget categories.

All Costs Not Allocated. The program display used in the example is not exhaustive; therefore, all costs are not allocated nor do they appear. Further, the convention of not attempting to allocate indirect costs has gained acceptance among practitioners of program budgeting because it reduces the danger of unknowingly biasing costs of individual programs. Such biasing can occur because it is generally possible to conceive of more than one logical rule for allocation; and different rules can produce different results for identical circumstances. For example, for many indirect costs it might be equally logical to allocate either on the basis of the number of students or the number of square feet. Programs utilizing facilities on a high density basis will cost more using the first rule than they would using the second, even though the actual total costs involved do not change regardless of the rule used.

Differences In The Budgets

Crosswalk as a Communication Device. The crosswalk provides a useful communication device. It helps those familiar with the traditional budget understand the content of the various categories in the Educational Resource Management System. It helps those who decide to implement the ERM System develop a better understanding of current and past activities. However, many important differences between the ERM process and the traditional budgeting process are often obscured by the fact that crosswalk translations are possible. The existence of the crosswalk has been erroneously viewed as an indication that differences between program budgeting and traditional budgeting were simply differences in format.

ERM Differences Described. The major differences between the ERM program budget and the traditional budget can be described as follows: (1) content, (2) structure, and (3) time horizon.

Content. The differences in content between the two budgets are primarily differences in the completeness of description of the proposed plan. The complete program budget includes data on the objectives, the enrollment, the key design, and operational characteristic of each program and a full description of the resources required for the implementation of the budget plan.

Structure. There are two distinct types of differences in structure between the traditional budget and the ERM budget; differences in the presentation of various cost categories and differences in the way the costs in each category are related to the objectives and activities of the school district. The ERM budget structure is organized with reference to objectives, as embodied in the various program elements; while the traditional budget relates primarily to organizational units and functions.

Time Horizon. The third major difference between the ERM budget and the traditional budget is illustrated by the fact that the program budget shows the resource requirements for a longer period than the traditional budget. The traditional budget shows the financial impact for a single year; the ERM budget shows the financial impact over many years.

Difference in Approach to Planning. The difference between the program budget and the traditional budget are indicative of differences in approach to the task of planning. And, although it is possible to crosswalk between the two types of budgets, it is erroneous to conclude that the ERM budget is no more than a rearrangement of the traditional budget.

During 1971, Financial Accounting for State and Local School Districts (Handbook II) was revised. A draft of the revision presents a classification of expenditures indicative of a changing emphasis in financial accounting practices. The implied chart of accounts is compared with a program structure.

The relationship of the ERM System illustrative program structure to the chart of accounts for the revised Handbook II and to the Memphis City School budget structure is illustrated in Tables 1 and 2. Table 1 is at the level of detail used for naming a "program" (in the ERM System) or a "function" in the chart of accounts. Table 2 continues the detail at the sub-program and sub-function level.

If the program structure illustration portrayed in the ERM System is to prevail as a guide for the goal-objective-orientation in the development of the program structure, the justification for the revision of Handbook II is quite evident. The twelve classification dimensions for expenditures used in the revision more nearly support the structure found in the ERM System. The Memphis, twelve-dimension accounting system very closely follows the Handbook Chart. The transition from one system to the other does not appear to be difficult. The Memphis system should provide the capability for the adoption of the ERM System.

THE RELATIONSHIP OF ERM PROGRAM STRUCTURE
TO REVISED HANDBOOK II
TO MEMPHIS CITY SCHOOL BUDGET STRUCTURE BY SUB-PROGRAMS

EDUCATIONAL RESOURCES MANAGEMENT SYSTEM PROGRAM STRUCTURE	REVISED HANDBOOK II PROGRAM STRUCTURE	BOARD OF EDUCATION- MEMPHIS CITY SCHOOLS PROGRAM STRUCTURE
Sub-Programs	Level 5	Program (Functions)
°Communication Skills	°English Language Arts	°English Language Arts
°Computation Skills	°Mathematics	°Mathematics
°Reasoning Skills	°Mathematics	
Culture		
°Behavioral Sciences	°Social Sciences/Social Studies	°Social Studies
°Life Sciences	°Natural Sciences	°Science
°Physical Sciences	°Natural Sciences	
°Physical, Social and Emotional	°Differentialized Curriculum for Handicapped, Health, Safety, Physical Education, Recreation	°Physical Education-Health- Recreation °Driver Education-Safety
°Student Activities	°Co-Curricular Activities	°Student Activities
°Pupil Personnel Services	°Pupil Personnel Services	°Pupil Personnel Services
°The Arts	°Art-Music	°Art-Music
°Languages	°Foreign Languages	°Foreign Languages
°Occupations	°Technical Education °Trade and Industrial Occupation	°Vocational Education
°Professions	°Junior ROTC	°Junior ROTC
°Practical Arts	°Agriculture, Business	°Business
	°Distributive Education	°Distributive Education
	°Home Economics, Industrial Arts	°Home Economics, Industrial Arts
	°Office Occupations	°Office Occupations
°Superintendent	°Office of the Superintendent	°Office of the Superintendent
°Planning		°Research and Planning
°Program Coordination	°School Administration	°Curriculum Department — Supervisors and Directors
°Program Operation	°Instructional Administration	°Principals-Asst. Principals- Admin. Aides
°Management Services	°Fiscal Services, Staff Services	°Business Affairs, Personnel Services
°Library	°School Library and Audio Visual	°Library
°Audio Visual	°School Library and Audio Visual	°Audio Visual
°Computer-Assisted Instruction	°Computer-Assisted Instruction	°Computer-Assisted Instruction
°Educational Television	°Educational Television	°Educational Television
°Operation	°Operation and Maintenance of Plant	°Operation
°Maintenance	°Operation and Maintenance of Plant	°Maintenance
°Securities	°Operation and Maintenance of Plant	°Security Services
°Central Services	°General Services	°Central Services
°Food	°Food Services	°Food Services
°Transportation	°Pupil Transportation Service	°Non-Existent: Emergency Special Type Service

The staff at Memphis is of the opinion that if a school district is to adopt the ERM System the personnel of the district need to be aware that the ERM System will involve more work and the system cannot be implemented "overnight." The implementation of the ERM System will require a multi-dimensional accounting structure such as provided by the revised Handbook II and the large school systems will need a computer.

THE RELATIONSHIP OF ERM PROGRAM STRUCTURE
TO REVISED HANDBOOK II
TO MEMPHIS CITY SCHOOLS STRUCTURE BY PROGRAM

EDUCATIONAL RESOURCES MANAGEMENT SYSTEM PROGRAM STRUCTURE	REVISED HANDBOOK II PROGRAM STRUCTURE LEVEL 2	BOARD OF EDUCATION- MEMPHIS CITY SCHOOLS PROGRAM STRUCTURE
Programs	Program (Functions)	Program (Functions)
°Intellectual Skills Development °Understanding the Environment °Exploratory Studies °Preparatory Post-Secondary Education °Preparatory Post-Secondary Employment	°Instruction	°Instruction
°Personal Development °Management °Educational Media °Facilities °Pupil Services	°Supporting Services	°Administration °Operation of Plants °Maintenance of Plants °Fixed Charges °Debt Service °Capital Expenditures
°Community Services	°Community Services	°Community Services
NA	°Non-Programmed Costs	NA

The recommendations of the Memphis staff include a suggestion for *classification of expenditures* in the adoption of the classification of expenditures included in the revised Handbook II. The handbook provides a chart of accounts with an expanded code structure capable of providing ERM System accounting and reporting by programs, sub-programs and program elements. The pilot project application at Memphis is illustrated as:

PROGRAM CODE

Intellectual Skills Development

  Communication Skills

    Listening   151
    Oral   152
    Reading   153
    Writing   154
    English   155
    Additional Language   156
    Spelling   157
    Handwriting   158

In discussing how we could implement a systematic approach to decision-making, it became apparent that we were not ready to undertake all of the elements at one time. We felt that to be successful in implementing a complete ERM System, we needed first to acquaint our staff with some of the techniques of systematic planning.

In prior years, it had been the philosophy of the School District not to provide hot lunch programs in the elementary schools. Regular cafeterias were provided in the secondary schools. The elementary school buildings were strategically placed throughout the District, no elementary school pupil lived more than a very few blocks from school. The philosophy also was that the feeding of students was a parental rather than a school responsibility. Until recently, no State or Federal assistance was provided specifically to feed needy children. No planned facilities for a hot lunch program existed in any of the elementary school buildings.

During 1968 we experienced a substantial change in the nature of our School District with the annexation of the large area of territory on the north edge of our District. Overnight our District grew in size by one-third. In the annexed area there was no public transportation, and the location of the schools required the busing of students to and from school. Lunch programs existed in most of the annexed schools.

During this period, the problem of integration became a No. 1 issue in our District. The result was the development of a "Quality/Equality Program" which began the integration of our schools. This required a certain amount of busing and the need to provide lunchroom facilities for those children who were bused to other areas of the District. There also occurred a change in the attitude of the State and Federal governments with the appropriation of special funds designed exclusively to feed the needy youths of our nation. The need for a hot lunch program in our elementary schools became increasingly evident. The chief problem to be overcome was the fact that no facilities existed in any of the schools to provide the typical hot lunch program.

We were instructed by our Superintendent to find ways and means by which we could provide at least for the needy students in our District. We had a preliminary conference with the building principals to determine an expression of need and to review our philosophy and the feasibility of a comprehensive lunch program for the District. We met with varying opinions because of the different make-up of the various attendance areas.

We also had conferences with a local food purveyor who was very much interested in seeing a lunch program for the schools. We had visits from salesmen of a number of different firms and we listed a number of alternative systems which were available and which might be adapted to our situation. In order to get started, we initiated a pilot program at Irving School during the second semester of 1968-1969.

Irving School was selected because this was one of the predominately black neighborhoods. The system that we selected contemplated the preparation of food in a central kitchen, putting it into polyethylene bags, which were then put in freezers. The bags of food were to be delivered to the elementary school as needed, reconstituted in a hot water bath, and served at the school. Among the facilities required was a central kitchen, which included not only cooking equipment, but a filling machine to fill the bags and a sealing machine to seal them. Since we had no central kitchen available, we decided to use, on a temporary basis, a kitchen in a high school building which was also used to serve the students in that building. At Irving School, the equipment needed was a hot water bath. It was discovered that there was nothing on the market which would heat water in the quantity required fast enough to do a satisfactory job. Therefore, a method was improvised whereby the water could be heated to reconstitute the food in the frozen bags. The system also required a truck to deliver the food from the central kitchen to the local school. The food was served on disposable trays and with disposable utensels, so there was no dishwashing involved.

Irving School, which was located in a target (low-income) area, has an enrollment of approximately 600 pupils. We had about 90% participation in the program, partly because many of them received free lunches. Because of the high participation we felt that the program was serving the purpose for which it was intended. However, problems did arise that we had not foreseen. A most serious one was a new discipline problem because so many students that had formerly gone home for lunch, were now in the building and on the school grounds This .problem was particularly serious on inclement days when the students could not be outside. To alleviate the situation, the lunch period, previously a one-hour period, was reduced to one-half hour to get the children back into the classrooms as soon as possible. Among the other problems was the determination of eligibility for students to receive free or reduced price lunches without identifying them.

Beginning with the 1969-1970 school year, the pilot program was expanded to five schools. We did, however, change the method of feeding and serving the students. We still cooked the food in a central kitchen, which was now moved to a junior high school building in a kitchen that was also used to serve the students in that building. The food was cooked, then placed in bags and frozen as in the pilot program at Irving. However, we adopted the "China Foam" system, and instead of transporting the frozen bags to the elementary schools, they were heated in the central kitchen. The hot food was placed on China Foam trays with covers, which were in turn put in China Foam totes, and delivered to the schools ready to serve. This system facilitated the serving of the students in the elementary schools, because the China Foam trays were simply handed to students as they came through a line. As before, milk was delivered by the local distributor directly to the school building. This system of course, also required a truck to deliver the food from the central kitchen to the elementary school. This system worked very well, although there were times when the food was not as hot at serving time as is desirable.

Before the end of the 1969-1970 school year, the State Legislature passed a law which required all school districts in the State of Illinois to serve hot lunches to the needy children in their districts. This was to become effective in September, 1970. Because of the two pilot programs that had existed in our District during the past two years, we felt that we were now ready to embark upon a full-scale elementary lunch program. Our first thought was to expand the China Foam system, but this system required a central kitchen which we did not have. The kitchen facilities in the junior high school building simply were not adequate to provide a full-scale elementary lunch program throughout our District. So we had a local architect prepare a cost estimate for a central kitchen which would meet our needs.

When we discovered that the cost estimate was $750,000, which we did not have, we looked around for other possible systems. We did make the decision, however, to initiate a hot lunch program in September of 1970 which would serve *all* the pupils in the District.

We continued our conferences with local food purveyors, one of which was attended by a food expert from Caterpillar Tractor Company. We were surprised to learn that Caterpillar had abandoned its new, modern, up-to-date central kitchen, which served several of the manufacturing plants and the home office in Peoria, because they found that trucking expenses were prohibitive. They were using convenience foods almost entirely which were now on the market and which were delivered directly to the various plant locations. This information caused us to have a real second look at the propriety of building a central kitchen and were advised by local food purveyors that the trend definitely is toward industry furnishing packaged lunches for school children.

We made various trips to inspect different types of school lunch programs. These included a trip to the St. Louis public schools, a trip to the Mass Feeding Company Plant in Chicago, a trip to the Morton Frozen Food Company in New York, which company was experimenting with packaged foods for school students, and we continued our visits with other local food distributors.

After considering all of the alternative plans that we had seen, we invited proposals from several food companies, four of which seemed worthy of consideration. One system utilized the central kitchen concept. Convenience foods would be purchased and lunches would be assembled in the central kitchen. Convection ovens would be installed in each school to heat the food prior to serving. This system would have required a capital investment for equipment of about $123,000. The District would also furnish all delivery services, cold and dry storage, and would purchase and assemble the food packs, etc. We abandoned this concept because we had no money to provide a central kitchen. We also felt that the central kitchen concept for school districts is obsolete, in view of the fact that commercial food companies are expanding rapidly into school lunch programs.

A local vendor submitted a proposal using lunches already assembled, furnished by either Banquet, Pronto or Morton Frozen Food Company. Daily deliveries would be made by the vendor to each school. The vendor would furnish all equipment including convection ovens in each of the elementary schools at a cost figured separately from the food cost on a one, three, or five year basis, with the option to buy at the end of any of these periods. The cost per meal would not include bread, butter or milk which would be furnished by the District. The total capital investment in equipment, if purchased outright, would have been about $70,000.

Another local vendor submitted a proposal similar to the first, which also contemplated the vendor furnishing all equipment, supplies and food, but including bread and butter. This system also involved the use of convection ovens in each school where the food would be heated just prior to serving. The feature of this proposal was a separate cold-pack to include the bread, butter, utensils and a cold item, such as fruit, slaw, jello, etc.

The proposal received from Mass Feeding Corp. in Chicago, seemed to be the most appealing to us. Under this corporation's proposal, all food, supplies and equipment except bread, butter and milk would be furnished. Freezers would be installed in each elementary school to which weekly deliveries of food would be made. A convection oven would also be installed in each school. The food would be heated immediately prior to serving. The company offered either a one or a three year contract. This company buys prepared food and assembles it into individual trays in a factory located near Chicago. The use of this system would relieve the District from any capital investment in equipment or supplies, other than bread, butter and milk. The cost of the equipment is amortized over a period of years and this cost is included in the meal price quoted to the District. Since this system did not contemplate a central kitchen and required no capital investment in equipment, and since this appeared to us to be the modern trend in the serving of public school pupils, the decision was made to accept the proposal of this company on a three year contract. We asked that a clause be included in the contract which would provide its cancellation in the event the program did not prove satisfactory.

We also had meetings with the State Director of School Programs in Illinois to seek his counsel and approval of any system that we were contemplating, to assure our receiving State and Federal reimbursement. We were also working closely with him to determine how the District could take advantage of surplus food commodities in the lunch program selected. It is possible to utilize government surplus commodities in our system, especially butter, honey, fresh fruit, etc. (These are not items supplied by the contractor).

Before embarking on the program, we had a great deal of planning to do. We surveyed the facilities in every one of our 32 elementary schools to determine what space was available, what electrical wiring and gas lines were available. In many instances, the facilities dictated whether or not gas or electric ovens would be used. We also surveyed each school as to enrollment, expected participation, and the number of tables and benches that would be required. Gyms were to be used as serving areas. Some of the schools had no storage space to store tables and benches after the lunch period was over. In these instances the decision was made to use wall-hung tables that would fold into the frames provided on the walls. In other schools, because they were less expensive, we would use the free-standing, folding tables.

It was somewhat difficult to forecast participation in the program because economic conditions vary so widely from one attendance center to another. We had to provide for pupils bringing sack lunches to school if they did not participate in the hot lunch program. Another problem that immediately presented itself was garbage disposal. Since the program used disposable trays, utensils, etc., it did create a serious garbage disposal problem.*
A decision had to be made whether or not to continue the use of dumpsters or to go entirely to plastic bags which would be picked up by the local refuse company. This was an important decision to make because use of dumpsters would cost the District $18,000 more than just using plastic bags. The decision was made to try the system which uses only the plastic bags.

As in the pilot program at Irving School, discipline became a major problem. Where students had been going home to lunch in the past, now there were many students in the building and on the school grounds during the lunch period. The decision was made to go to half-hour lunch periods in all of our elementary schools to alleviate this problem. This, in turn, caused a change in bus schedules.

Prior to the initiation of the lunch program, it was necessary to employ lunchroom supervisors, lunchroom managers and clerks, and to indoctrinate the teachers into the new program. It was necessary to develop instruction and training programs regarding ordering, receiving and storing of food and the preparation of food for serving to the pupils. Also involved was the collection of money, preparing reports, setting salary rates, and working out the pupil traffic flow, so that there would be a minimum of congestion. It was necessary to determine the role of the principal, the teachers, and the custodians, in the implementation and operation of the program.

Budgeting problems also presented themselves. We found that we had not budgeted adequately for the electric wiring contracts and the like because the decision to enter into the full-scale lunch program was not made until after the budget was adopted. However, the Board of Education believed that the program was worthwhile. Therefore, we went ahead and incurred such expenses as were necessary to implement the program, hoping

---

*We have had some concern expressed about the waste products resulting from our lunch program. Plastic materials haven't been a problem, since the only product used that is plastic is the "silverware." The biggest culprit has been aluminum! The food is prepared and served in disposable aluminum foil trays. The aluminum could be re-cycled if we could afford the proper equipment. We do have one school equipped with a "washer-crusher" unit, but it required additional plumbing and the district simply doesn't have the funds to purchase and install these units." (We may *not* be able to ignore this problem indefinitely!)

that State and Federal reimbursement would cover the cost. Altogether, we employed 138 lunchroom supervisors, 33 lunchroom managers, 14 lunchroom helpers, and are using 32 students to help with the program.

Realizing that it would be impossible to start in all of the schools on the opening day of school, we decided to work into it gradually, selecting the impoverished area schools first. On the opening day of school, August 31, 1970, a hot, elementary lunch program was started in ten schools of the District. We then opened one, two or three schools each week thereafter, and finally, on November 16, every school in the District had a hot lunch program.

We find that participation ranges from 50% to 90% depending on the economic area in which the schools are located. The students seem to like the food and the system is working. However, we know that there are improvements which are necessary and we are now in the process of surveying the entire program to see where improvements can be made and where economics can be effected.

Considering the fact that the decision to implement a full-scale elementary hot lunch program in the Peoria Elementary Schools was not made until July of 1970, and by November 16, 1970, this goal was accomplished, it is obvious that a great deal of planning went into the effort. The pilot programs that we had used the two prior years were very beneficial in charting our course. We felt that many of the principles of PPBES were used in formulating and implementing this program. We defined our objectives, we listed alternatives and after reviewing them, decided on a plan and implemented it. After implementation we are reviewing it and evaluating it. We hope to continue the effort to work with ERM on many other projects in our School District.

CLARK COUNTY SCHOOL DISTRICT

The project objective for our District, as a pilot district was to establish a PPBE system for all the departments within the Business and Finance Division of the District.

The PPBS project was introduced to the Business Directors through staff and special project meetings. The initial starting point was an assessment of the functions and activities of each department. Terminology and format were developed as a team effort. Upon completion of the assessment, specific needs of the departments were identified. From these needs, objectives were suggested and developed. In a prior year, we had a rather bad experience when we developed objectives at top management level and then attempted to "sell" them to subordinates. It soon became apparent that we had to include the subordinates in the objective setting process. Subordinates had an opportunity to discuss objectives they felt were valid. All suggestions were recorded. The record was later reviewed with the section head, and objectives were selected. The next step was to determine the services (or activities) to be performed to accomplish the objective. It was necessary to define the resources — human, financial, and material — required to achieve the objective. Last, but far from least, was the evaluation or process by which the objectives of a program could be compared with the actual accomplishments.

In instances where the resources were either less or more than those needed to accomplish the objective, alternatives were suggested. There were cases where, with resources remaining the same and through the use of alternatives, slightly modified objectives were presented as choices for management.

The most difficult task was arriving at meaningful and specific objectives and then determining the means of evaluation. The easiest part of the task was the identification of resources and the listing of services.

Leadership for the project was furnished by the Associate Superintendent of Business and the Director of Financial Services, both of whom had been exposed to PPBS seminars and workshops in the past. No new staff was added for the project. Most of the work was accomplished during once-a-week, three-hour, night sessions over a period of several months. The actual writing of the programs was done by the individual Directors. The document was compiled by the Director of Financial Services.

Some of the benefits derived from the project as mentioned by the Directors are as follows:

"The assessment procedure provided me with a closer look at each of the Department's functions in relationship to priorities and available resources."

"The evaluation technique has placed more emphasis on meaningful reporting and accountability."

324

"The PPBS document serves as the basis for: future planning, ongoing departmental direction, and assessment of the application of resources to objectives in support of instruction."

"The striving to meet objectives has enabled us to recognize certain deficiencies in our processes and to know where to make corrective efforts."

"The working toward and reaching objectives gives people a feeling of accomplishment with a resultant improvement of morale."

The completion of the project with the resulting publication of our PPBS document for the Business Division has given us a direct and positive understanding as to what we are presently doing and what we are striving to accomplish within the near future.

The Associate Superintendent of Business is using the PPBS document as a management tool. Monthly meetings are held with the individual directors during which time their programs are reviewed and progress toward the attainment of their objectives is reported. All directors are involved in the development of reporting techniques which will clearly denote the measurement of attainment of their objectives. It is also visualized that these same reporting techniques will form the basis of a management information system for the Business Division and the District.

DEPARTMENT ___ Food Services

PROGRAM: Breakfast

Broad Objective

Make breakfast available in low economic area schools in accordance with legal requirements, District policy and administrative regulations.

Specific Objective

To serve a variety of nutritional breakfasts under optimum sanitary conditions, in six westside schools, to a minimum of 25% of the total ADA.

Services

Provide and coordinate a planned program of field technical supervision.
Develop breakfast menus.
Authorize the purchase of food and supplies.
Provide statistical data for proper control and operation of the program.

Evaluation

Maintain a sales record of 25% (or over) of total ADA.
Inspections to be made on same standard as Type "A" program.
Monthly menu to reflect breakfast changes.

Resources	1970-71			1971-72		1972-73	
	% of Time	Number of Persons	Cost	Number of Persons	Cost	Number of Persons	Cost
Director	2	1	$ 352	1	$ 389	1	$ 389
Assistant Director							
Food Supervisor	5	1	351	1	369	1	388
Food Service Account Clerk	5	1	384	1	403	1	387
Food Service Personnel	100	13	12,922	13	13,568	13	14,246
Purchases: Food & Supplies			17,853		18,567		19,310
Other Expenses			100		125		150
Budget Program Costs		16	$ 31,962	16	$ 33,402	17	$ 35,293
Equipment (Invested Cost)			1,500		1,500		1,500
Other Fund(s) Costs							
General Fund							
Cost of Needy Meals			1,200		1,300		1,400
Total Program Costs		16	$ 34,662	16	$ 36,202	17	$ 38,193
Expected Revenue — Food Sales & Federal Reimbursement			$ 26,000		$ 26,500		$ 27,000

DEPARTMENT   Accounting

PROGRAM: Accounts Payable — Evaluation of

Variables

The documents used in the evaluations are:
1. Form CC-4, Travel Claim
2. Form CC-34B, Special Purchase Authorization
3. Form CC-34A, Purchase Order either:
   A. Receiving department copy, or
   B. Accounting copy
4. Data Processing Department print-out entitled "Accounts Payable Paid Purchase Orders."

The variables relating to the CC-4's, Travel Claims, are:

Should the date be used that:
A. Represents the final day of travel.
B. The CC-4 was signed by the person doing the traveling.
C. The CC-4 was signed by the supervisor of the person doing the traveling.
D. The CC-4 was received in Accounts Payable.

The variables relating to the CC-34B's, Special Purchase Authorizations, are:

Should the date be used that:
A. The CC-34B was signed.
B. The CC-34B was received in Accounts Payable.

Experience has shown that considerable variation in elapsed time may occur between the date a CC-34B is written and the date it is received in Accounts Payable.

The Data Processing print-out groups the Purchase Orders, Special Purchase Authorizations and Travel Claims in consecutive numerical order within each group.

Objectives

The objective is to pay 95% of all bills within 30 days of receipt of goods or services. Ten percent of all documents are examined to determine if objectives are being met. It is assumed that the ten percent sample is representative of the whole 100%. The percentage of bills falling within the days of payment objective is considered to be the same as the like percentage in the test sample. The number of days of payment is defined as the elapsed days from, but not including, the date goods or services were received to, and including, the known date of mailing of the payment check. The receiving date used is:

1. For CC-4's — the date received in Accounts Payable.
2. For CC-34B's — the date written.
3. For CC-34A's — no choice available. See previous section.

Evaluation Design

The actual steps taken to collect the necessary data are outlined in this section.

1. Grouping — The CC-4's and CC-34B's are arranged numerically in separate groups. The receiving department copies and the accounting copies of the CC-34A's are comingled and grouped numerically. The documents for partial payments are grouped separately from the documents for statistical sampling method of random selection is used to determine which of the first ten documents is to be the initial document.

2. Recording — As each document selected is examined, the data is recorded on the Data Processing print-out. A reporting form is used to summarize the data the auditor has recorded on the print-out. The form reports the average days which elapse between receipt of goods or services to the date of mailing of checks for payment for each type of document. It also provides the percentage of documents paid within 30 days of receipt of goods or services. Specific documents can be identified for investigation; particularly those documents which reflect an unusual lapse of time between receipt of goods or services and the date payment checks are mailed. Of each group audited, the number of items falling within the objective area is divided by the total items examined. The quotient represents the percentage of items paid within 30 days. To determine the percentage of the total of all groups, the sum of all items falling within the objective area is divided by the sum of all items examined.

DEPARTMENT   Transportation

PROGRAM: Transportation for Support Services

Broad Objective

Provide various types of vehicles for District work crews and Administrative personnel.

Specific Objective

Provide vehicles and maintenance to serve the minimum needs of the District.
Maintain motor vehicles and implements for safe and economical operation.

This alternative provides for reduction in appropriations of $23,300 and a 5% reduction in the fleet.

Services

No vehicles will be available for replacement. As vehicles become unserviceable because of age or condition, they will be removed from active service.
Assignment of most vehicles to departments or motor pools instead of individuals.
Continue and enforce a preventive maintenance program including periodic recycling of vehicles at 4,000 mile intervals.
Take action to report and prevent abuse or misuse of equipment.
License all vehicles and provide guardianship for titles.
Set priorities on equipment retirement based upon age, mileage and condition.
Maintain at least one satellite service facility for rapid service and to assure economy.
Maintain day-to-day and historical records.

Evaluation

Maintain mechanical condition of equipment to provide accident free operation, resulting from mechanical causes, at 85% efficiency level and reported semi-annually.
Maintain vehicles at an operating cost not to exceed $.1250 per mile.
Maintain implements at $2,922 per month.

Resources	1970-71 % of Time	Number of Persons	Cost	1971-72 Number of Persons	Cost	1972-73 Number of Persons	Cost
Director	30	1	$ 5,549	1	$ 5,826	1	$ 6,117
Assistant Director	30	1	4,355	1	4,573	1	4,802
Garage Supervisor	30	1	3,719	1	3,905	1	4,100
Clerical	23	2	3,017	2	3,168	2	3,327
Mechanics	60	7	53,208	7	55,868	7	58,661
Supplies and Expenses			4,500		4,725		4,962
Fuel, Tires and Parts for Other Vehicles			70,200		73,710		77,395
Equipment – Shop			650		683		718
Budget Program Costs		12	$145,198	12	$152,458	12	$160,082
Equipment – Other Vehicles (Invested Cost)			350,000		350,000		350,000
Equipment – Shop (Invested Cost)			5,500		6,150		6,833
Total Program Costs		12	$500,698	12	$508,608	12	$516,915

CLARK COUNTY SCHOOL DISTRICT
Las Vegas, Nevada

DATE ___July, 1970___

DEPARTMENT ___Transportation___

PROGRAM: Transportation for Support Services

ALTERNATIVE

Broad Objective

Provide various types of vehicles for District work crews and Administrative personnel.

Specific Objective

Identify, specify and obtain type and quantity of equipment required to serve the needs of the entire District.

Maintain motor vehicles and implements for safe and economical operation.

This alternative requires an increase of $42,200 in the transportation budget.

It provides for replacing obsolete equipment of 1960 year model and older with new equipment to augment the military surplus equipment.

Services

Obtain military surplus motor vehicles and implements and prepare them for service.

Obtain replacement equipment for obsolete equipment.

Prepare specifications for all new motor vehicles and implements.

Continue and enforce a preventive maintenance program including periodic recycling of vehicles at 2,000 mile intervals.

Take action to report and prevent abuse or misuse of equipment.

License all vehicles and provide guardianship for titles.

Set priorities on equipment retirement and replacement based upon age, mileage and condition.

Maintain at least one satellite service facility for rapid service and to assure economy.

Maintain day-to-day and historical records.

Evaluation

Maintain mechanical condition of equipment to provide accident free operation, resulting from mechanical causes, at 95% efficiency level and reported semi-annually.

Maintain vehicles at an operating cost not to exceed 9¢ per mile.

Maintain implements at $2,797 per month.

Resources	% of Time	1970-71 Number of Persons	Cost	1971-72 Number of Persons	Cost	1972-73 Number of Persons	Cost
Director	30	1	$ 5,549	1	$ 5,826	1	$ 6,117
Assistant Director	30	1	4,355	1	4,573	1	4,802
Garage Supervisor	30	1	3,719	1	3,905	1	4,100
Clerical	23	2	3,017	2	3,168	2	3,327
Mechanics	60	7	53,208	7	55,868	9	71,136
Supplies and Expenses			10,200		10,710		11,246
Fuel, Tires and Parts for Other Vehicles			93,000		97,650		102,533
New and Replacement Other Vehicles			37,000		38,850		40,793
Equipment – Shop			650		683		718
Budget Program Costs		12	$210,698	12	$221,233	14	$244,772
Equipment – Other Vehicles (Invested Cost)			350,000		387,000		425,850
Equipment – Shop (Invested Cost)			5,500		6,150		6,833
Total Program Costs		12	$566,198	12	$614,383	14	$677,455

CLARK COUNTY SCHOOL DISTRICT
Las Vegas, Nevada

<u>EXHIBIT 8</u>

<u>DAILY ACTIVITY</u>
<u>REPORT</u>

SHIPPING SECTION

Date	Food Service	Manifesting	Stock Handling	Load - Unload	Delivering	Assist Others	Research - Post	Vendor Returns	Housekeeping	Other (explain)	REMARKS:
Kubic											
Sackett											
Snyder											
Hayes											
Moody											
Grimble											
Gilmore											
Abramo											
Cunningham											
TOTALS:											

<u>VENDOR RETURN ACTIVITY</u>

Cartons Prepared For Shipment: _____

Cartons Shipped Today: _____

EXCEPTIONS TODAY

Undelivered Shipments: _____

Missed Shipments: _____

STATISTICAL INFORMATION REPORT

	REQUISITIONS	CARTONS
Carry Over (from previous day)		
Received Today		
Sub-Total		
Released Today		
On Hand (end of the day)		

CGC _____ HGA _____ JTK _____ STAT CLERK _____

DATE POSTED _____

EXHIBIT 10

FILM DISTRIBUTION CENTER COUNT WORKSHEETS

1. Number of films to be delivered _____ D.P. count

2. Number of immediates _____ Count from list

3. Number unable to supply end of day _____ Count from list

4. Number of cancels _____ Count from notices

5. Number of films in inspection area at beginning of day _____ From previous day's end of day count

6. Number of films inspected

   Gene _____

   Dick _____

   Al _____

   M. _____

   X. _____

   TOTAL

7. Number of films in the inspection area at the end of day _____ Add lines 6 and 7 then subtract line 5.

8. Number of films returned _____

9. Number of films overdue _____ Count from overdue list

   A.M. _____

   P.M. _____

DATE _____

DOUGLAS COUNTY PUBLIC SCHOOL DISTRICT NO. RE 1(J)

Castle Rock, Colorado

ADMINISTRATORS' IN-SERVICE PROGRAM

The purpose of the Administrators' In-Service Program was to introduce the central administration personnel and the building principals to the concepts of a Planning-Programming-Budgeting System (PPBS). The Center for Advanced Study of Educational Administration (CASEA) model for PPBS was utilized as the primary document for the training sessions.

The Administrators' In-Service Program was originally scheduled for eight training sessions. These training sessions were to be held on an every-other-week basis, beginning in mid-January in the Douglas County School District Board Room. Unforeseen events and previous commitments reduced the number of instruction sessions to six. The instruction sessions were coordinated and directed by the Associate Director, Bureau of Educational Research, University of Denver. Graduate research assistants assisted with the presentations.

The instruction sessions were organized into four categories; (1) Orientation; (2) Behavioral Objectives; (3) Change Agent; and (4) PPBS Simulation. The Orientation instruction was scheduled for one session; the Behavioral Objectives instruction was scheduled for three sessions; the Change Agent instruction was scheduled for one and one-half sessions; and the PPBS Simulation instruction was scheduled for one and one-half sessions.

Orientation Session

The purpose of the orientation session was to specify the objectives of the In-Service Program and to present an overview of the CASEA model for a PPB System.

The director outlined the tasks that the Bureau of Educational Research desired to accomplish through the In-Service Program. The expected outputs for both the BER and the administrative personnel were discussed. A tentative schedule for the remaining instruction sessions was established.

The CASEA model of PPBS was explained to the administrators. Transparencies were used to aid in the discussion. The transparencies contained statements and diagrams which described the CASEA model. A list of books and materials relating to PPBS was distributed to the administrators. A question-and-answer session followed the presentation.

Behavioral Objectives Session

The purpose of the behavioral objectives sessions was to instruct the administrators in the development, writing, and critique of educational objectives in behavioral terms. One of the basic elements of a PPB System is the identification of the goals and objectives of the educational programs. With this concept in mind, the BER staff considered the area of behavioral objectives the most logical to start the instruction sessions.

Hand-out materials were prepared and distributed to the administrators. The hand-outs included models of behavioral objectives containing the different types of behavioral objectives and the elements which comprise an exemplary behavioral objective. A bibliography was prepared, and copies of books, manuals, and pamphlets pertaining to behavioral objectives were loaned to the administrators.

An evaluation instrument was administered at the end of the second training session. The results were tabulated and the items contained in the instrument were discussed during the third instruction session.

Change Agent Sessions

The purpose of the change agent sessions was to present the concepts of the administrator's role as the leader in bringing about educational changes within the district. The Havelock model of the diffusion process in bringing about change was used in the instruction.

The instruction was based upon the premise that a PPB System would be initiated in the district at some future date. The task of the administrators as agents of change would be to introduce the concepts of the PPB System to their staff and to assist in orienting their educational objectives to the system. A hand-out was prepared containing the six stages of the Havelock diffusion process. A discussion of the model and its relation to a PPB System was included in the session.

PPBS Sessions

The purpose of the PPBS sessions was to instruct the administrators in the processes required to implement a PPB System in the school district. The processes involved: (1) the identification of the existing programs; (2) the identification of the general aims or objectives of the programs; (3) the costs of the programs; and (4) the planning of new programs or alternative programs.

The CASEA model for a PPB System is flexible in organization so that the starting place for implementing is at the discretion of the school district officials. For the in-service program, a cost analysis of the elementary and secondary instructional programs was chosen as the first phase of implementation. The reasons for this choice were: (1) the instructional programs already in operation could be easily identified; (2) the cost factors were readily available; (3) the information collected could be stored and used as the base for a district data bank; and (4) a coding system could be developed.

Each building principal was given several Total Direct Cost Activity Matrix (TDCAM) charts. On these charts the principal could list each staff member (certified and non-certified) of his school, the monthly salary of each staff member and the time allocation devoted to each staff member's area of responsibility. TDCAM charts indicating costs for salaries and employee benefits, purchases and contracted services, materials and supplies, and capital expenditures were distributed also. The costs could be disaggregated over each instructional program for a given school building. By aggregating the cost figures for any particular instructional program, a profile of the expenditures for any instructional program in any school, and/or for the entire district could be obtained.

A TDCAM chart was developed for the district's transportation program. Other TDCAM charts were provided to the central administration personnel which could be used to further aggregate the data provided on the building principals' TDCAM charts to give a cost summary for the district's elementary, secondary and special education programs. A summary matrix chart for reporting cost data to the Board of Education was also provided.

Projected Budget Simulation

The purpose of the projected budget simulation was to provide the district with budget data projected over a five-year period. State support per student and district assessed valuation figures were projected, and through use of the University of Denver's computer, the district's budget for the next five years was simulated. The base-line data for the simulation was obtained from the district's 1970-71 budget document.

Summary and Recommendations

The Administrators' In-Service Program provided background information in four areas: (1) the processes involved in implementing a PPB System; (2) the processes involved in developing and evaluating behavioral objectives; (3) the processes involved in bringing about change with the administrator serving in the role of the change agent; and (4) the processes involved in the use of the computer to simulate budget projections. The In-Service sessions introduced the processes needed for implementing a PPB System and for evaluating the district's educational programs as specified in the *Program Planning, Budgeting. and Evaluating System (PPBES)* and the *Educational Accountability Act of 1971* recently enacted by the Colorado Legislature.

Since the Douglas County School District has a basic knowledge of the processes mentioned, the BER would recommend the following actions:

1. That the Douglas County School District continue with its long-range plan for the implementation of a PPB System.
2. That one school be selected for the implementation of a PPB System during the 1971-72 school year.
3. That a coding system for all financial accounts be implemented in accordance with the Colorado Department of Education guidelines.
4. That a district information data bank be implemented.
5. That the district develop and implement an in-service program for building staffs regarding the processes involved in PPBS and accountability.
6. That the Douglas County Board of Education consider the infusion of district funds to carry out the recommendations.

GLOSSARY

ACTIVITIES
Educational procedures designed to accomplish the specific goal or objective which has been established for a specific program.

ALTERNATIVES
Different courses of action or different approaches to accomplish goals and/or objectives. The word implies a comparison of two or more differing mixes of input for a proposed program plan or for a plan already in process.

ALLOCATION
Distribution of resources among individual programs as required to achieve stated goals and/or objectives.

ANALYSIS
Systematic separation of an activity, procedure, or organization into component parts for the purpose of determining how the necessary operations may be accomplished.

BASELINE CASE
A total multi-year program cost for continuing present commitments of resources.

BUDGET DOCUMENT
A written statement of an estimate or plan, describing expenditures or revenues for financing an organization's entire program for a specified time period, usually one year.

BUDGETING
The process which includes, in addition to final reconciliation of programs and available resources according to established priorities, the preparation of the budget document, the approval by a board of education, and the execution of the budgetary plans.

COST BENEFIT ANALYSIS
Systematic examination of determining the economic value of a specific program by establishing a ratio of costs to the results likely to be obtained. An analytical approach to solving problems of choice. Both costs and benefits are measured and analyzed in monetary terms.

COST EFFECTIVENESS ANALYSIS
Systematic examination of assessing feasible alternatives of a specific program by relating the cost of a particular alternative to the achievement of a goal and/or an objective. The purpose is to provide a means of comparing possible alternatives on a basis of least cost and greatest effectiveness.

337

COST, DIFFERENTIAL

Those costs which are different in the costs of two alternatives. In comparing the costs of alternative programs, only the costs which are different need to be considered.

COST, INCREMENTAL

The incremental cost is the cost of adding the next unit. The actions can be viewed as a series of alternatives which differ in quantity but not kind. Thus, the cost of adding one more student to a program, encompassing other students of similar kind, is the incremental or marginal cost. (Synonym: Marginal cost.)

COST, LIFE CYCLE

Costs associated with the project or program from its inception until its termination. Terminal dates may be arbitrarily set if the life cycle is in excess of the determined long-range planning structure. The three major life cost categories are: (1) Research and Development, (2) Investment Costs, and (3) Operating Costs.

COST, OPPORTUNITY

The value of a resource in its best alternative use. The alternative opportunity benefit that is sacrificed as the result of a decision.

COST, SUNK

The costs (usually for buildings and equipment) incurred in the past, which have been depleted or cannot be salvaged for use in future operations. These costs are not relevant to a current decision concerning the future; only the future costs are important.

CRITERIA

Statements of preferred outcomes that are used to test the relative degrees of desirability among alternatives; standards by which a course of action is evaluated. Statements of criteria include time, conditions, and specific results expected.

CROSSWALK

The expression of the relationship between the program structure and the appropriation/budget structure. It may be viewed as a table with the rows of the table listing the program categories and the columns showing the appropriations and budget activities.

EDUCATIONAL RESOURCES MANAGEMENT SYSTEM (ERMS)

The title of the conceptual schema which describes the application of the planning-programming-budgeting-evaluating system concept to education.

EFFECTIVENESS

The degree to which a given program achieves the stated objectives of the program. Ideally, it is measured in quantitative terms in relation to criteria.

338

EVALUATING

It is the process of assessing the attainment of objectives and the worth of programs.

GOAL

A broad statement of purpose to be achieved by society but to which the educational system will contribute by attaining related objectives.

INDICATOR (PERFORMANCE OR OUTPUT)

A measure of a characteristic of a performance or an output which can be tested. The measure may be an indirect observation which is assumed to be indicative of the desired characteristic.

INPUT

Resources employed to achieve objectives.

LINEAR PROGRAMMING

A mathematical technique for optimizing the overall allocation of resources to various activities where constraints are such that not all activities can be performed optimally. A requirement is that the relationship between the activities and the constraints and objectives be linear in a mathematical sense. The objective is to maximize or minimize some function. The decision problem is solved by finding the levels of the various activities that maximize or minimize the objective function while satisfying all constraints.

MANAGEMENT

A process to accomplish the achievement of predetermined objectives.

MATRIX

A rectangular array of mathematical quantities by rows and columns; used to facilitate the study of problems in which the relation between the contrasting terms is fundamental.

MODEL

An abstract representation of reality which describes, reflects, or simulates an actual system or situation.

MULTI-YEAR PROGRAM AND FINANCIAL PLAN

A plan which serves as a pattern for the future operation of the educational programs of the school district. The plan reflects the future implications of current decisions. (Synonym: program budget.)

OBJECTIVE

A statement of an outcome of a program which will contribute to the societal goal to which it is related.

OBJECTIVE, PERFORMANCE

A statement of educational outcome which includes descriptor phrases about expected terminal behavior, conditions, and criteria.

OBJECTIVE MEASURES

Evaluation data that have been determined by a quantitative observation of outputs in relation to objectives.

OPTIMIZATION

A mathematical procedure used to determine the best mix of inputs to meet an objective.

OUTCOME

The result obtained from the input of resources in the educational process in the form of growth of the learner, e.g., knowledge, skills, and attitudes. (Synonyms: Output, Product).

PLANNING

The process of guiding internal change so that the school adapts effectively to the dynamic society of which it is a part.

PPBS (See also PPBES and RADS)

Abbreviation for the planning-programming-budgeting system which is a conceptual approach to decision-making developed by RAND Corporation and installed in the Department of Defense in 1961. It is a structured procedure for determining policy in the allocation of resources for the accomplishment of priority programs; emphasizes long-range planning, analytic evaluative tools, economic rationality in the determination of programs and in the setting of goals and objectives.

PPBES (See also RADS)

Abbreviation for the planning-programming-budgeting-evaluating system.

PROGRAM

A series of interdependent, closely related services and/or activities progressing toward or contributing to a common objective or set of allied objectives.

PROGRAM BUDGET (See Multi-Year and Financial Plan)

PROGRAM BUDGETING: (NEW)

The preparation of a budget which emphasizes classifications by programs and reflects consideration of present and future costs of various programs designed to realize objectives. It does not necessarily stipulate the systematic analysis and multi-year perspective as presented in PPBS.

PROGRAM ELEMENT

Each part of the operating program identified by a discrete program classification. The purpose for identifying a program element is to facilitate the process of quantifying the several characteristics (properties) of the element.

PROGRAM PLAN

An instrument which describes the related components of each individual program included in the program structure.

PROGRAMMING

The process of developing program plans.

PROGRAM MEMORANDUM

An instrument for updating the program budget. The program memorandum includes information on a recommended change, the needs to which a program is addressed, the objectives of the program, the required resources, the expected effectiveness, and the target population.

PROGRAM STRUCTURE

An array for showing the priority for learning outcomes through the organization of program emphases; the format for the program budget.

RADS

Resource Allocation Decision System.

RESOURCES

Inputs available to the school system for use in attaining its objectives.

RESOURCES, HUMAN

An individual identified as a potential talent by reason of that person's knowledge or experience and who will help integrate his speciality with the accomplishment of an objective.

SUBJECTIVE MEASURES

Inpressionistic observations of the comparison of outputs with the criteria of related objectives for which those outputs were produced.

SUBOPTIMIZATION

Selection of the best alternative course of action which pertains to a subproblem, that is, to only part of the overall problem or objective. Usually necessary because alternatives at all the various levels of decision-making cannot be analyzed simultaneously before decisions must be made at some levels. Also referred to as any intermediate stage in a long-run goal attainment program.

SUBPROGRAM

A division of a program category. It combines activities on the basis of objectives within the broader objectives of the program category.

SUPPORT SERVICES

Those services which provide administrative, technical, and logistical support to facilitate and enhance learning objectives. Support services exist as adjuncts for the fulfillment of objectives.

SYSTEMS ANALYSIS

The analytical activity which allows for the organization and the examination of information on a regular basis so as to clarify objectives and the utility of different ways of achieving them. Analysis is used to identify controllable variables and noncontrollable environmental factors which affect the relationship of inputs and outputs.

SYSTEMS APPROACH

A rational approach for designing a system for attaining specific objectives.

SYSTEM, INFORMATION
The network of all communication methods within an organization.

SYSTEM, MANAGEMENT INFORMATION
A communications process in which data are recorded and processed for operational purposes.

Bibliography

Abt Associates, Inc. *Design for an Elementary and Secondary Education Cost-Effectiveness Model*. Williamsville: Western New York School Study Council, 1968.

Adams, Bert K. and others. *Principles of Public School Accounting*. U. S. Department of Education, State Educational Records and Reports Series, Handbook II-B. Washington, D.C.: Government Printing Office, 1967.

Administrative Leadership Service. *Systems Planning in Public Education*. Washington, D.C.: Educational Service Bureau, 1968.

Advisory Council of State Departments of Education. *Improving State Leadership in Education*. U. S. Office of Education. Washington, D.C.: Government Printing Office, 1966.

Advisory Council on State Departments of Education. *The State of State Departments of Education*. U. S. Office of Education. Washington, D.C.: Government Printing Office, 1969.

Alioto, R. F. and Jungherr, J. A. "Using PPBS to Overcome Taxpayers' Resistance." *Phi Delta Kappan*. November, 1969. p. 138-141.

American Association of School Administrators. *Imperatives in Education*. Washington, D.C.: The Association, 1966.

Anshen, Melvin. *The Program Budget in Operation (RM-4691-RC)*. Santa Monica, Calif.: RAND Corporation, 1965.

Association of School Business Officials. *Annual Volume of Proceedings, Addresses, and Research Papers*. Chicago: The Association, 1967-1970.

Association of School Business Officials. *School (K-12) Accounting; Junior and Community College Accounting: Principles and Procedures*. Chicago: Research Corporation, The Association, 1969.

Benson, Charles S. *The Economics of Public Education*. Boston: Houghton Mifflin, 1961.

Bliss, Sam W. *The Extent and Utilization of Management Information Systems and Planning Programming Budgeting Systems in State Educational Agencies*. Denver: Improving State Leadership in Education, 1971.

Burkhead, Jesse. *Input and Output in Large City High Schools*. Syracuse, N.Y.: Syracuse University Press, 1967.

California Association of Public School Business Officials, Southern Section School Budget Research Committee. *Program Budgeting in Public School Districts*. N. P.: The Association, 1967.

California Association of School Business Officials. *PPBS Workshop*. Sacramento: The Association, 1970.

California Teachers Association. *The Challenge of Planning-Programming-Budgeting-Systems*. Burlingame: The Association, 1969.

Campbell, Roald F.; Stroufe, Gerald E.; and Layton, Donald H. *Strengthening State Departments of Education*. Chicago: Midwest Administration Center, University of Chicago, 1967.

Carpenter, M. B. and Haggart, S. A. *Analysis of Educational Programs Within a Program Budgeting System (P-4195)*. Santa Monica, Calif.: RAND Corporation, 1969.

Carpenter, M. B. and Haggart, S. A. *Cost-Effectiveness for Educational Planning (P-4327)*. Santa Monica, Calif. RAND Corporation, 1970.

Carter, V. "PPBS in a Small School District: It Can be Done." *Journal of Secondary Education*. November, 1970. P. 313-19.

Carzo, Rocco, Jr. and Yanouzas, John R. *Formal Organization*. Homewood, Ill.: Dorsey Press, 1967.

Churchman, C. West. *The Systems Approach*. New York: Dell Publishing, 1968.

Clark, Jere W. and Clark, Juanita S., eds. *Systems Education Patterns on the Growing Boards for the Future*. Second Annual National Conference on General Systems Education, Cheshire, Conn., 1968.

Clark County School District. *Annual Budget Document*. Las Vegas: Board of Education, 1970.

Clark County School District. *Planning Programming Budgeting System for the Business and Finance Division*. Las Vegas: Board of Education, 1970.

Cohen, Burton J. *Cost-Effective Information Systems*. New York: American Management Association, 1971.

Colorado General Assembly, Committee on Public Education. *Committee Report to the Governor and to the Colorado General Assembly*. Denver: 1970.

Cook, Desmond L. *Program Evaluation and Review Technique; Applications in Education*. U. S. Office of Education, Cooperative Research Monograph No. 17. Washington, D.C.: Government Printing Office, 1966.

Coombs, Clyde H.; Dawes, Robyn M.; and Tversky, Amos. *Mathematical Psychology: An Elementary Introduction*. Englewood Cliffs, N.J.: Prentice-Hall, 1970.

Corrigan, Robert E. and Kaufman, Roger A. *Why System Engineering*. Palo Alto, Calif.: Fearon Publishers, 1965.

Coulson, John E. and Cogswell, John R. *Systems Analysis in Education*. Paper presented at the Conference on the Development and Use of Data Banks for Educational Research, Boston, December 4, 1964.

Council of Chief State School Officers. *State and Local Responsibilities for Education*. Washington, D.C.: The Council, 1968.

Dade County Public Schools. *Educational Program Planning for Fiscal Year 1969-70*. Miami: Board of Education, 1969.

Dade County Public Schools. *Program Budget for Fiscal Year 1970-1971*. Miami: Board of Education, 1970.

Davis, Joseph L., ed. *Educational Evaluation; Official Proceedings of a Conference*. Columbus: Ohio Department of Education, 1969.

DeYoung, Chris A. *Budgeting in Public Schools*. Chicago: John S. Swift Company, 1946.

Durstine, Richard M. and Howell, Robert A. *Toward PPBS: Program Budgeting in a Small School District*. Cambridge, Mass.: New England School Development Council, 1970.

Edding, Friedrich. *Methods of Analyzing Educational Outlay*. New York: UNESCO Publications Center, 1966.

Eidell, Terry L. and Klebe, John A. *Annotated Bibliography on the Evaluation of Educational Programs*. Eugene, Ore.: ERIC Clearinghouse on Educational Administration, 1968.

Eidell, Terry L. and Nagle, John M. *PPBS and Data-Based Educational Planning*. Eugene: Center for the Advanced Study of Educational Administration, University of Oregon, 1970.

Elam, Stanley and Swanson, Gordon I., eds. *Educational Planning in the United States*. Itasca, Ill.: F. E. Peacock Publishers, 1969.

Elementary Teacher Training Models: Nine Program Models. U. S. Office of Education, OE-58033. Washington, D.C.: Government Printing Office, 1969.

Elkins, Eugene R. *Program Budgeting: A Method for Improving Fiscal Management*. Morgantown: Bureau for Government Research, West Virginia University, 1955.

El Monte Union High School District. *Budget*. El Monte, Calif.: Board of Trustees, 1970.

344

Emery, James C. *Organizational Planning and Control Systems; Theory and Technology.* New York: Macmillan, 1969.

Engelhardt, N. L. and Engelhardt, Fred. *Public School Business Administration.* New York: Teachers College, Columbia University, 1927.

ERIC Clearinghouse on Educational Administration. *ERIC Abstracts: A Collection of ERIC Document Resumes on Program Budgeting and Cost Analysis.* Washington, D.C.: American Association of School Administrators, 1970.

Fantini, Mario and Weinstein, Gerald. *Making Urban Schools Work.* New York: Holt, Rinehart and Winston, 1968.

Feeney, George J. "A Basis for Strategic Decisions on Inventory Control Operations." *Management Science.* 1955. p. 69-82.

Fels Institute of Local and State Government. *General Design for an Education Planning-Programming-Budgeting System.* Philadelphia: University of Pennsylvania, 1968.

Firmin, Peter A. and others. *University Cost Structure and Behavior.* New Orleans: Tulane University, 1967.

Fisher, G. H. *Cost Considerations in Systems Analysis.* New York: American Elsevier Publishing, 1970.

Fisher, G. H. *The World of Program Budgeting (P-3361).* Santa Monica, Calif.: RAND Corporation. 1966.

Foster, Charles W., ed. *Report of the First National Conference on PPBES in Education.* Chicago: Research Corporation, Association of School Business Officials, 1969.

Fuller, Edgar and Pearson, Jim B. *Education in the States: Nationwide Development Since 1900.* Washington, D.C.: National Education Association, 1969.

Furse, Bernarr S. and Wright, Lyle O., eds. *Comprehensive Planning in State Education Agencies.* Salt Lake City: Utah State Board of Education, 1968.

Gardner, John W. *No Easy Victories.* New York: Harper and Row, 1969.

Gardner, John W. *Self-Renewal: The Individual and the Innovative Society.* New York: Harper and Row, 1964.

Gibbs, W. and others. "PPBS: What We've Learned in One Year." *Nation's Schools.* November, 1969. p. 43.

Gideon, Victor. *Transition Management.* Boston: Systems Development Corporation, 1970.

Glaspey, J. L. *Management by Objectives as Practiced by the Business Division of the Clark County School District.* Las Vegas: Board of Education, Clark County School District, 1967.

Goldman, Thomas A. *Cost-Effectiveness Analysis.* New York: Frederick A. Praeger, 1967.

Goodlad, John I. *Planning and Organizing for Teaching: Project on the Instructional Program for the Public Schools.* Washington, D.C.: National Education Association, 1963.

Green, Martin T. *Program Planning Budget System for the University School.* Tallahassee: Florida State University, 1970.

Hack, Walter G. and Woodward, Francis O. *Economic Dimensions of Public School Finance: Concepts and Cases.* New York: McGraw-Hill, 1971.

Haggart, S. A. and others. *Program Budgeting for School District Planning: Concepts and Applications (RM-6116-RC).* Santa Monica, Calif.: RAND Corporation, 1969.

Haggart, S. A. and Carpenter, M. B. *Program Budgeting as an Analytical Tool for School District Planning (P-4031).* Santa Monica, Calif.: RAND Corporation, 1969.

Harper, Ron and Wescott, J. Patrick. *Guidelines for the Implementation of Planning-Programming-Budgeting for School Systems.* Olympia: Washington State Department of Education, 1969.

Harris, Yeull Y. and Seibert, Ivan N. *The State Education Agency: A Guide for Recording and Reporting Information about State Education Agencies.* U. S. Office of Education, State Educational Records and Reports Series, Handbook VIII. Washington, D.C.: Government Printing Office, 1970. (Fourth draft preliminary).

Hartley, Harry, Jr. *Educational Planning-Programming-Budgeting: A Systems Approach.* Englewood Cliffs, N.J.: Prentice-Hall, 1968.

Hatry, Harry P. and Cotton, John F. *Program Planning for State, County, City.* Washington, D.C.: State-Local Finances Project, George Washington University, 1967.

Haveman, Robert and Margolis, Julius, eds. *Public Expenditures and Policy Analysis.* Chicago: Markham Publishing, 1970.

Helmer, Olaf. *Social Technology* (P-3063). Santa Monica, Calif.: RAND Corporation, 1965.

Hillier, Frederich S. and Lieberman, Gerald J. *Introduction to Operations Research.* San Francisco: Holden-Day, 1968.

Hills, R. Jean. *Toward a Science of Organization.* Eugene: Center for the Advanced Study of Educational Administration, University of Oregon, 1968.

Hinrichs, Harley H. and Taylor, Graeme M. *Program Budgeting and Benefit-Cost Analysis.* Pacific Palisades, Calif.: Goodyear, 1969. (Includes Extensive Bibliography.)

Hirsh, W. Z. *Intergrating View of Federal Program Budgeting (RM-4799-RC).* Santa Monica, Calif.: RAND Corporation, 1965.

Hirsh, W. Z. *Toward Federal Program Budgeting (P-3306).* Santa Monica, Calif.: RAND Corporation, 1966.

Hitch, Charles J. in "Analysis for Air Force Decisions," in E. S. Quade, ed. *Analysis for Military Decisions (R-387-PR)* Santa Monica, Calif.: RAND Corporation, 1964.

Hitch, Charles J. and McKean, Roland N. *The Economics of Defense in the Nuclear Age.* New York: Atheneum, 1964.

Hoag, Malcolm W. *An Introduction to Systems Analysis (RM-1978).* Santa Monica, Calif.: RAND Corporation, 1956.

James, H. Thomas; Thomas, J. Alan; and Dyck, Harold J. *Wealth, Expenditure and Decision-Making for Education.* Stanford, Calif.: Stanford University, 1963.

Jones, John W., ed. *Proceedings of the Educational Management Tools Training Program.* Carbondale: Southern Illinois University, 1970.

Joyce, Bruce R. *Alternative Models of Elementary Education.* Waltham, Mass.: Blaisdell Publishing, 1969.

Jungherr, J. A. *Can Small School Districts Use a Planning-Programming Budgeting System.* Paper Presented at 20th Annual Convention, New York State Association of School Business Officials, Grossinger, N.Y., May 21, 1968.

Kammerer, Gladys M. *Program Budgeting: An Aid to Understanding.* Gainesville: Public Administration Clearing Service, University of Florida, 1961.

Katzenbach, Edward L. *Planning Programming Budgeting Systems: PPBS and Education.* Cambridge, Mass.: New England School Development Council, 1968.

Kent, A. E. and Gibbs, W. F. "Why Skokie Switched to PPBS Grade Level Array." *Nation's Schools.* January, 1970. p. 44.

Kershaw, J. A. and McKean, R. N. *Systems Analysis and Education (RM-2473-FF).* Santa Monica, Calif.: RAND Corporation, 1959.

Kirst, Michael W., ed. *The Politics of Education at the Local, State and Federal Levels.* Berkeley, Calif.: McCutchan Publishing, 1970.

Kiser, Chester and Spengler, James R., eds. *Proceedings of the Workshop for School Business Officials.* Williamsville: Western New York School Study Council, 1968.

Knezevich, Stephen J. *Administration of Public Education,* 2d ed. New York: Harper and Row, 1969.

Knezevich, Stephen J., ed. *Administrative Technology and the School Executive.* Washington, D.C.: American Association of School Administrators, 1969.

Lichtenberger, Allan R. and Penrod, Richard J. *Staff Accounting for Local and State School Systems.* U. S. Office of Education, State Educational Records and Reports Series, Handbook IV. Washington, D.C.: Government Printing Office, 1965.

Lindman, Erick L., ed. *Approaches to Program Accounting for Public Schools.* Los Angeles: Center for the Study of Evaluation of Instructional Programs, University of California, 1968.

Lokken, Harry and Keenan, W. W. *A Year-Long Field Testing of the Program Budgeting and Accounting System Developed by the Mid-western States Educational Information Project to Lay the Foundation for Planning, Programming, Budgeting Systems in School Districts.* St. Paul: Minnesota State Department of Education, 1970.

Loughary, John W. *Man-Machine Systems in Education.* New York: Harper and Row, 1966.

Lyden, Fremont J. and Miller, Ernest G., eds. *Planning-Programming-Budgeting: A Systems Approach to Management.* Chicago: Markham Publishing, 1968.

McAbee, Harold V. *Planning-Programming-Budgeting Systems and State Educational Agency Administration.* Salem: Oregon State System of Higher Education, 1969.

McCullough, J. D. *Cost Analysis for Planning-Programming-Budgeting Cost-Benefit Studies (P-3479).* Santa Monica, Calif.: RAND Corporation, 1966.

McGivney, Joseph H. and Nelson, William C. *Program Planning, Budgeting Systems for Educators.* Columbus: Center for Vocational and Technical Education, Ohio State University, 1969.

McGowan, Wayne F. "How to Apply a Program-Planning-Budgeting System in Your State" in *Leadership for Education: Proceedings of the National Conference of State Legislators.* Washington, D.C.: National Committee for the Support of Public Education, 1966.

MacKeraghan, Lysle R. *Bibliography on a Planning-Programming-Budgeting System Model for Community Junior Colleges.* Gainesville: Florida Community Junior College Inter-Institutional Research Council, 1970.

MacNamara, James F. *A Mathematical Programming Model for the Efficient Allocation of Vocational Technical Education Funds.* Harrisburg: Pennsylvania Department of Education, 1970.

Malinski, J. F. "Minnesota Implements the Regional Concept in a State Committed to PPBS." *American Vocational Journal,* November, 1969. p. 36-38.

Midwestern States Educational Information Project. *MSEIP Documentation of Project Development and General System Design.* Des Moines: Iowa Department of Public Instruction, 1969.

Mitchell, Edward E. *What is PPBS?* Paper presented at New England Institute for School Business Officials, May 14-15, 1968.

Moll, Emmett, J. *Brochure of Instruction to Building Principals.* Milwaukee: Division of Planning and Long-Range Development, Milwaukee Public Schools, 1970.

Mood, Alexander M. and Powers, Richard. *Cost-Benefit Analysis of Education.* U. S. Office of Education, National Center for Educational Statistics, Washington, D.C.: Government Printing Office, 1967.

Morphet, Edgar L. and Jesser, David L., eds. *Cooperative Planning for Education in 1980.* New York: Citation Press, 1968.

Morphet, Edgar L. and Jesser, David L., eds. *Emerging Designs for Education; Program Organizations, Operation and Finance.* New York: Citation Press, 1968.

Morphet, Edgar L. and Jesesr, David L., eds. *Emerging State Responsibilities for Education.* Denver: Improving State Leadership in Education, 1970.

Morphet, Edgar L. and Jesser, David L., eds. *Planning for Effective Utilization of Technology in Education.* New York: Citation Press, 1969.

Morphet, Edgar L. and Jesser, David L., eds. *Preparing Educators to Meet Emerging Needs.* New York: Citation Press, 1969.

Morphet, Edgar L. and Ryan, Charles O., eds. *Implications for Education of Prospective Changes in Society.* New York: Citation Press, 1967.

Morphet, Edgar L. and Ryan, Charles O., eds. *Planning and Effecting Needed Changes in Education.* New York: Citation Press, 1967.

Morphet, Edgar L. and Ryan, Charles O., eds. *Prospective Changes in Society by 1980.* New York: Citation Press, 1967.

Mushkin, Selma J. and Willcox, Margorie. *An Operative PPB System: A Collaborative Undertaking in the States.* Washington, D.C.: State-Local Finances Project, George Washington University, 1969.

Novick, David. *Efficiency and Economy in Government Through New Budgeting and Accounting Procedures (R-254).* Santa Monica, Calif.: RAND Corporation, 1954.

Novick, David. *Origin and History of Program Budgeting (P-3427).* Santa Monica, Calif.: RAND Corporation, 1966.

Novick, David, ed. *Program Budgeting; Program Analysis and the Federal Budget.* Cambridge, Mass.: Harvard University Press, 1965.

Novick, David, ed. *Program Budgeting; Program Analysis and the Federal Budget.* 2d ed. New York: Holt, Rinehart and Winston, 1969.

Novick, David, ed. *Program Budgeting; Program Analysis and the Federal Budget.* Washington, D.C.: Government Printing Office, 1965.

Parsons, Talcott and Shils, Edward A., eds. *Toward a General Theory of Action.* New York: Harper and Row, 1951.

Partnership in School Finance: The Proceedings of the Ninth National Conference on School Finance. Washington, D.C.: Committee on Educational Finance, 1966.

Payne, David A. and McMorris, Robert F., eds. *Educational and Psychological Measurement.* Waltham, Mass.: Blaisdell Publishing, 1967.

Pearl River School District. *Proposed 1970-71 Educational Program and Fiscal Plan.* Pearl River, N.Y.: Board of Education, 1970.

Pearson, Jim B. and Fuller, Edgar. *Education in the States: Historical Development and Outlook.* Washington, D.C.: National Education Association, 1969.

Peat, Marwick, Mitchell and Company. *Conceptual Design for a Planning, Programming, Budgeting System for California School Districts.* Sacramento: California Department of Education, 1969.

Peat, Marwick, Mitchell and Company. *Financial Accounting.* U. S. Office of Education, State Educational Records and Reports Series, Handbook II, Revised. Washington, D.C.: Government Printing Office, 1970. (Draft).

Peat, Marwick, Mitchell and Company. *Planning, Programming, Budgeting System Manual for State of California School Districts.* Sacramento: California Department of Education, 1970.

Peck, Robert F. *Personalized Education.* Austin: Research and Development Center for Teacher Education, University of Texas, 1970.

Piele, Philip K. and Bunting, David G. *Program Budgeting and the School Administrator: A Review of Dissertations and Annotated Bibliography.* Eugene, Ore.: ERIC Clearinghouse of Educational Administration, 1969.

Putnam, John F. and Chismore, W. Dale. *Standard Terminology for Curriculum and Instruction in Local and State School Systems.* U. S. Office of Education, State Educational Records and Report Series, Handbook VI. Washington, D.C.: Government Printing Office, 1970.

Quade, E. S. *Systems Analysis Techniques for Planning-Programming-Budgeting (P-3322).* Santa Monica, Calif.: RAND Corporation, 1966.

Quade, E. S. and Boucher, W. I., eds. *Systems Analysis and Policy Planning: Applications in Defense (R-439-PR).* Santa Monica, Calif.: RAND Corporation, 1968.

Quattlebaum, Charles A. *Federal Educational Policies, Programs and Proposals.* U. S. 90th Congress, 2nd Session, House Committee on Education and Labor. Washington, D.C.: Government Printing Office, 1968. (3 volumes).

R. E. Corrigan Associates. *A System Approach for Education.* Anaheim, Calif.: R. E. Corrigan Associates, 1969.

Ramo, Simon. *Cure for Chaos.* New York: David McKay, 1969.

Reason, Paul L.; Foster, Emery M.; and Will, Robert F. *The Common Core of State Educational Information.* U. S. Office of Education, State Educational Records and Reports Series, Handbook I. Washington, D.C.: Government Printing Office, 1953.

Reason, Paul L. and White, Alpheus L. *Financial Accounting for Local and State School Systems; Standard Receipt and Expenditure Accounts.* U. S. Office of Education, State Educational Records and Reports Series, Handbook II. Washington, D.C.: Government Printing Office, 1957.

Robinson, C. L. and Barron, J. G. *Program-Based Resource Allocation Models at the University of Toronto.* Toronto: University of Toronto, 1968.

Scamman, James P., Jr. "Automated Budget Preparation Systems." *AEDS Monitor.* October, 1970. p. 11-15.

Scamman, James P., Jr. *Program Budgeting: Approaches and Problems.* Kenosha, Wisc.: Kenosha Unified School Board, 1970.

Schick, Allen. "Systems for Analysis: PPB and its Alternatives" in *The Analysis and Evaluation of Public Expenditures: The PPB System.* Washington, D.C.: Government Printing Office, 1969.

Scott, D. H. "How PPBS Is Being Used In California." *School Management.* February, 1971. p. 12-15.

Shaplin, Judson T. "Practice in Teaching." *Harvard Educational Review.* Winter, 1961. p. 437-51.

Shoreline School District. *Some Aspects of Planning Programming Budgeting Systems . . . for Washington State Association for Educational Data Systems Fall Workshop.* Seattle: Board of Education, 1970.

Siegel, S. A. "Method for Obtaining an Ordered Metric Scaling." *Psychometrika.* 1956. p. 21, 207-16.

Spencer, Ralph L. and Walters, Donald L., eds. *Systems Analysis Symposium Proceedings.* Philadelphia: Temple University, 1969.

Stanford Research Institute PPBS Staff. *Planning-Programming-Budgeting System in the New York City School System.* New York: Board of Education of the City of New York, 1967.

State-Local Finances Project, George Washington University. *Planning for Educational Development in a Planning, Programming, Budgeting System.* Washington, D.C.: Committee on Educational Finance, National Education Association, 1968.

State-Local Finances Project. *PPB Notes.* Washington. D.C.: George Washington University, 1967-68.

State-Local Finances Project. *What is PPBS?* Washington, D.C.: George Washington University, 1967.

State of New York Executive Department. *Guidelines for Planning-Programming-Budgeting.* Albany: The Department, 1968.

Temkin, Sanford. *A Comprehensive Theory of Cost-Effectiveness.* Philadelphia: Research for Better Schools, 1970.

Temkin, Sanford. *A Cost-Effective Evaluation Approach to Improving Resource Allocations for School Systems.* Philadelphia: Research for Better Schools, 1969.

Temkin, Sanford. *An Evaluation of Comprehensive Literature with an Annotated Bibliography.* Philadelphia: Research for Better Schools, 1970.

Terhune, George A. *Performance and Program Budgeting Practices in the United States and Canada.* Chicago Municipal Finance Officers Association, 1966.

Thomas, J. Alan. *The Productive School; A Systems Analysis Approach to Educational Administration.* New York: John Wiley and Sons, 1971.

Thurstone, L. L. *The Measurement of Values.* Chicago: The University of Chicago Press, 1959.

Trends in Financing Public Education: The Proceedings of the Eighth National Conference on School Finance. Washington, D.C.: Committee on Educational Finance, National Education Association, 1965.

Turnbull, Augustus B., III. *The PPB Systems Analyst: Skills and Training Requirements.* U. S. Civil Service Commission. Washington, D.C.: Government Printing Office, 1969.

Umans, Shelley. *The Management of Education; a Systematic Design for Educational Revolution.* Garden City, N.Y.: Doubleday, 1970.

Unified School District No. 259. *Handbook for Planning-Programming-Budgeting System.* Wichita, Kan.: Board of Education, 1969.

U. S. 89th Congress, 2nd Session, House Committee on Education and Labor. *Study of the United States Office of Education.* Washington, D.C.: Government Printing Office, 1967.

U. S. 90th Congress, 1st Session, Joint Economic Committee, Subcommittee on Economy in Government. *The Planning-Programming-Budgeting System: Progress and Potentials.* Washington, D.C.: Government Printing Office, 1967.

U. S. 90th Congress, 1st Session, Senate Committee on Government Operations, Subcommittee on Intergovernmental Relations. *Criteria for Evaluation in Planning State and Local Programs.* Washington, D.C.: Government Printing Office, 1967.

U. S. 90th Congress, 1st Session, Senate Committee on Government Operations, Subcommittee on National Security and International Operations. *Planning-Programming-Budgeting.* Washington, D.C.: Government Printing Office, 1967.

U. S. 91st Congress, 1st Session, Joint Economic Committee, Subcommittee on Economy in Government. *Analysis and Evaluation of Public Expenditures; the PPB System.* Washington, D.C.: Government Printing Office, 1969.

U. S. 91st Congress, 1st Session, Joint Economic Committee, Subcommittee on Economy in Government. *Innovations in Planning, Programming, and Budgeting in State and Local Governments.* Washington, D.C.: Government Printing Office, 1969.

U. S. General Accounting Office. *Glossary for Systems Analysis and Planning-Programming-Budgeting.* Washington, D.C.: Government Printing Office, 1969.

Usdan, Michael D.; Minar, David W.; and Hurwitz, Emanuel, Jr. *Education and State Politics; The Developing Relationship between Elementary-Secondary and Higher Education.* New York: Teachers College Press, 1969.

Western New York School Development Council. *An Operational Model for the Application of Planning-Programming-Budgeting Systems in Local School District.* Williamsville; The Council, 1969. (Pre-pilot test version.)

White, Alpheus L. *Local School Boards: Organization and Practices.* U. S. Office of Education, Bulletin 1962, No. 8. Washington, D.C.: Government Printing Office, 1962.

Wildavsky, Aaron. *The Politics of the Budgetary Process.* Boston: Little, Brown and Co., 1964.

Wildavsky, Aaron. "Rescuing Policy Analysis from PPB" in *The Analysis and Evaluation of Public Expenditures: The PPB System.* Washington, D.C.: United States Government Printing Office, 1969.

Williams, Harry. *Planning for Effective Resource Allocation in Universities.* Washington, D.C.: American Council on Education, 1966.

Winthrop Public Schools. *What Winthrop Faculty Should Know: Creating The Winthrop School Budget.* Winthrop, Mass.: Board of Education, 1969.

Womer, Frank B. *National Assessment Objectives.* Denver: Education Commission of the States, 1970.

York, Linda J., comp. *Coordinating Conference on Educational Planning and Management Systems: A Report of Outcomes.* Berkeley, Calif.: Far West Laboratory for Educational Research and Development, 1969.

DISSERTATIONS

Altergott, Bruce H. *Management by Objectives for the Public Schools.* (Doctoral dissertation, Indiana University) Ann Arbor, Mich.: University Microfilms, 1970. No. 71-11, 360.

Brown, Henry A. *A Time Network Analysis of Procedures Used in Selected Districts to Develop the School Budget and a Model Displaying the Interrelations of Those Procedures.* (Doctoral dissertation, Columbia University) Ann Arbor, Mich.: University Microfilms, 1970. No. 70-19, 681.

Dineen, David F. *A Conceptual Model of School System Evaluation.* (Doctoral dissertation, Boston University) Ann Arbor, Mich.: University Microfilms, 970. No. 70-22, 487.

Drehmel, Elwood W. *Cost and Budget Parameters in Higher Education.* (Doctoral dissertation, University of Minnesota) Ann Arbor, Mich.: University Microfilms, 1970. No. 70-27, 111.

Ewald, Albert A. *A Matrix Allocation Procedure for University Cost Accounting.* (Doctoral dissertation, Michigan State University) Ann Arbor, Mich.: University Microfilms, 1968. No. 69-11, 094.

Fisher, George W. *A Conceptual Framework for School System Planning.* (Doctoral dissertation, Ohio State University) Ann Arbor, Mich.: University Microfilms, 1969. No. 70-6772.

Fisher, Robert D. *An Investigation of the Structure and Potentialities of Management Information Systems in the Public Schools as They Relate to Educational Decision-Making and Reporting.* (Doctoral dissertation, Ohio State (University) Ann Arbor, Mich.: University Microfilms, 970. No. 71-7452.

FitzSimmons, Warren B. *A Model for a Public School Program Budget.* (Doctoral dissertation, Colorado State College) Ann Arbor, Mich.: University Microfilms, 1966. No. 67-1110.

Forbes, Roy H. *A Technique for Analyzing the Costs of an Educational Program Based on Behavorial Stated Instructional Objectives.* (Doctoral dissertation, University of Massachusetts) Ann Arbor, Mich.: University Microfilms, 1970. No. 71-9329.

Fox, Mark M. *A Program Classification for Colorado Public School Budget Reporting.* (Doctoral disserttaion, University of Northern Colorado) Ann Arbor, Mich.: University Microfilms, 1970. No. 71-4174.

Gott, John W. *A Study of Selected Factors Related to the Development and Dissemination of a Planning, Programming, Budegting, Evaluating System for Public Education.* (Doctoral dissertation, Washington State University) Ann Arbor, Mich.: University Microfilms, 1970. No. 71-4394.

Hagen, John W. *A Three Dimensional Program Budget Format for Public Schools.* (Doctoral dissertation, University of California) Ann Arbor, Mich.: University Microfilms, 1968. No. 68-11, 870.

Harper, Ronald R. *An Analysis of Planning and Evaluation Guidelines Relevant to a Planning- Programming-Budgeting System for First Class School Districts of the State of Washington.* (Doctoral dissertation, Washington State University) Ann Arbor, Mich.: University Microfilms, 1970. No. 70-16, 808.

Hill, LaMar L. and Mattox, Frank L. *Program Budgeting in Public School Districts.* (Doctoral dissertation, University of Southern California) Ann Arbor, Mich.: University Microfilms, 1967. No. 67-17, 687.

Holton, John B. *A Computer-Based Information System for Program Budgeting and Fiscal Management in Local Schools.* (Doctoral dissertation, Northwestern University) Ann Arbor, Mich.: University Microfilms, 1970. No. 71-10, 125.

Igoe, Joseph A. *The Development of Mathematical Models for the Allocation of School Funds in Relation to School Quality.* (Doctoral dissertation, State University of New York at Buffalo) Ann Arbor, Mich.: University Microfilms, 1968. No. 68-12, 450.

Jacobson, James A. *A Systems Analysis of Master Planning Public School Districts to Determine the Feasibility of Computer Utilization.* (Doctoral dissertation, Utah State University) Ann Arbor, Mich.: University Microfilms, 1969. No. 70-2438.

Jennings, Emery C. *Planning-Programming-Budgeting Systems: A Model for its Implementation in Comprehensive Community Colleges.* (Doctoral dissertation, University of Denver) Ann Arbor, Mich.: University Microfilms, 1969. No. 70-11, 925.

Jones, Russel A. *Guidelines for a Ten-Year Master Plan of Finance for Small Private Liberal Arts Colleges.* (Doctoral dissertation, Ohio State University) Ann Arbor, Mich.: University Microfilms, 1968. No. 69-4911.

Justus, John E. *Application of PERT to Educational Projects.* (Doctoral dissertation, University of Tennessee) Ann Arbor, Mich.: University Microfilms, 1967. No. 67-10, 738.

Levine, Donald M. *The Utility of PPBS for Urban School Systems.* Unpublished doctoral dissertation, Harvard University, 1971.

Levine, Jack B. *A University Planning and Budgeting System Incorporating a Microanalytical Model of the Institution.* (Doctoral dissertation, University of Toronto) Ottawa, Ontario: National Library of Canada, 1969.

Lipot, Charles A. *A Program Accounting Method to Support Program Budgeting for Public Schools: A Management Study.* (Doctoral dissertation, University of California, Los Angeles) Ann Arbor, Mich.: University Microfilms, 1970. No. 71-9392.

McCanna, Walter F. *College and University Planning, Programming, Budgeting: Criteria for the Definition of Programs and Program Elements.* (Doctoral dissertation, University of Wisconsin) Ann Arbor, Mich.: University Microfilms, 1969. No. 70-3611.

McGrew, William C. *Financial Reporting for School Districts in Oklahoma.* (Doctoral dissertation, University of Arkansas) Ann Arbor, Mich.: University Microfilms, 1967. No. 67-8702.

MacKeraghan, Lysle R. *A Conceptual Planning-Programming-Budgeting Model for a Community College.* (Doctoral dissertation, University of Florida) Ann Arbor, Mich.: University Microfilms, 1970. No. 71-12, 761.

Morris, Lee R. *Cost-Effectiveness: The Current State of the Art.* Unpublished Doctoral dissertation, Harvard University, 1967.

Raichle, Henry F. *A Cost-Utility Analysis of a Selected Post-Secondary Vocational-Technical Education Program.* (Doctoral dissertation, Florida State University) Ann Arbor, Mich.: University Microfilms, 1969. No. 70-16, 346.

Rarig, Emory, Jr. *AdministrativePractices in Institutional Long-Range Planning in Community and Junior Colleges.* (Doctoral dissertation, Columbia University) Ann Arbor, Mich.: University Microfilms, 1968. No. 69-8087.

Ristau, Robert A. *The Development of a Business Education Model for Methods and Procedures in a Planning, Programming, and Budgeting System (PPBS).* (Doctoral dissertation, University of Wisconsin) Ann Arbor, Mich.: University Microfilms, 1970. No. 70-24, 817.

Robertson, Lyle R. *A System for Determining Educational Program Costs: Application to Comprehensive Community College.* (Doctoral dissertation, Wayne State University) Ann Arbor, Mich.: University Microfilms, 1968. No. 69-6081.

Rogers, Edward de Lancy. *An Exploratory Study of the Development of a System of Program Accounting for Junior Colleges in California.* (Doctoral dissertation, University of California, Berkeley) Ann Arbor, Mich.: University Microfilms, 1968. No. 68-13, 877.

Rudiger, Charles W. *The Applicability of the Planning-Programming-Budgeting System to Local School Budgeting.* Unpublished doctoral dissertation, Harvard University, 1968.

Sabine, Creta D. *A Budget Form for Use in the Public Schools of Arizona.* (Doctoral dissertation, Arizona State University) Ann Arbor, Mich.: University Microfilms, 1968. No. 69-5718.

Sherwood, Robert P. *Cost Implications of Specific State Legislative Requirements: An Application of Program Budgeting to Selected California Unified School Districts.* (Doctoral dissertation, University of California) Ann Arbor, Mich.: University Microfilms, 1965. No. 66-3532.

Sims, Howard D. *The Design and Implementation Projections of a Management Information System for an Illinois Community College.* (Doctoral dissertation, Northern Illinois University) Ann Arbor, Mich.: University Microfilms, 1969. No. 70-3453.

Stearns, Gene F. *The Implications and Potentials of Program Budgeting for Public Schools.* (Doctoral dissertation, Ball State University) Ann Arbor, Mich.: University Microfilms, 1970. No. 70-18, 072.

Tope, Thomas, Jr. *Cost Analysis by Means of a Planning-Programming Budgeting System in a Public School.* (Doctoral dissertation, University of Houston) Ann Arbor, Mich.: University Microfilms, 1970. No. 70-23, 802.

Womack, Troy A. *An Analytical Model for Program Analysis of a Liberal Arts College.* (Doctoral dissertation, University of Houston) Ann Arbor, Mich.: University Microfilms, 1969. No. 70-4501.

Young, John R. *A PPBS Implementation Guide for Teachers Associations.* (Doctoral dissertation, University of Southern California) Ann Arbor, Mich.: University Microfilms, 1970. No. 70-25, 077.

Index

Accountability 71, 100

Acquisition cost categories 135

Administrative review 88

Agencies 44, 180, 181, 182, 194

Alternatives 65, 73, 82, 86, 108, 113, 118, 119, 129, 138, 208, 236,
    costing 112
    equal-cost 145
    equal-effectiveness 145
    ERM System 38

American Association of School Administrators 171, 195

American Federation of Teachers 195

Analysis 65, 74, 86, 87
    cost-benefit 212
    cost-effectiveness 83, 137, 209
    curve 232
    multiple criteria 214
    multi-year cost 110
    planning 144
    regression 117
    resource 107
       methodology 128, 129
       role 107, 207
       techniques 114
    sensitivity 119

Assessment, needs 166

Barro 208

Baseline case 110

Bibliography 343

Board, school 60, 85, 87, 88, 197, 198

Budgeting 77, 83, 91, 186
    definition 49
    procedures 51

Budget, program 92, 93, 108, 122, 199, 207

California Project 193

Carpenter 208, 212

Case, baseline 110

Categories, operational cost 132, 136

Carzo 41

Center for Advanced Study of Educational Administration (CASEA) 333

Cherry Creek, Colorado, School District 172

Churchman evaluating model 152
Cleveland, Ohio, "Yardstick Program" 155
Cogswell 150
Colorado Department of Education 154
Commensurability 213
Computer Assisted Instruction (CAI) 201
Computerization 149, 150
Conceptualization, ERM System 37
Constraints, cost 208, 209
Consultants 61, 172, 175, 176, 197
Control, inventory 233
Control, operational 88
Coombs 222
Cost 38, 39, 83, 110, 114, 131
    alternative programs 110
    concepts 108, 109
    constraints 208
Cost-effectiveness 137, 233
Cost, external 109, 110
Costs, proration 110
Costs, sunk 109
Costs, total 109
Coulson 150
Criteria 73, 79, 84, 144, 149, 153, 155, 209, 210, 238
Criterion 212
Critical Path Method (CPM) 201
Crosswalk 102, 108, 122
Curriculum development 165, 166, 171
    specialists 199
Cybernetics 149

Data 113, 239
    bank 156
    processing 118, 137
Dawes 222
Decision-making 44
Decision process 42
Decision theory 149
Denver, Colorado, School District 170
Denver, University 333
Designs, evaluating 150, 158
Development, curriculum 165, 166, 171
Discounting 111, 213
Douglas County School District, Colorado 333

Educational program 136
Educational Professional Development Act (EPDA) 204
Effectiveness 38, 73, 82, 141, 142, 143, 144, 208, 209, 225
ERM System, conceptualization 37, 71, 158
    decision-making 42
    rationale 37
Electronic Data Processing (EDP) 201
Equal-cost alternatives 145
Equal-effectiveness alternatives 145
Estimates 111
Evaluating 51, 52, 76, 77, 78, 86, 87, 147, 148, 149, 150, 153, 154, 187, 188, 202, 205
    designs, 150, 158
    functions 155
    procedures 52, 53
    responsibilities 158
External costs 109, 110
Evaluation
    ancillary 52
    measurement 152, 153
    multiple criterion 226
    plan 158, 160
Expenditure accounts 114
Expertise 193
Exploratory plan 77
Extended contracts 203

Federal agencies 61
Feedback 53, 205
Feeney 213, 233
Florida Commissioner of Education 155
Force, task 59, 60, 166, 167
Format, information 85
Folsom-Cordova Unified School District, California 167

Gardner 180
Gideon 189
Glossary 337
Goals 64, 71, 72, 74, 166, 195, 200, 208
Goldhammer 190
Goodlad 170, 171
Gott 193, 201
Governance of education 195
Group dynamics 201

Haggart 208, 212
Hartley 207
Hatry 212
Helmer 224
Hillier 237
Hitch 208, 209, 210, 212, 213, 215, 217

Implementation, program 87
Implications of ERM System 193
Independence 226
Indicators 209
    performance 226, 237
Individually Prescribed Instruction (IPI) 201
Information format 85
Information flow 41, 45
Information, program plan 48, 49
In-service education 171, 193, 194, 195, 203
Inputs 236
Interdependency 226, 227
Interdependencies, functional 236
Interfaces, state-local-federal 179
Interim plan 77
Inventory control 233
Inventory, resources 41, 92

James Elementary School, Kansas City, Missouri 172

Learner 68
Legislature, State 179, 180
Lieberman 237
Lindman 196
Long-range program plan 86

McKean 208, 209, 212, 213, 217
Management by objectives 197
Management Information System (MIS) 201
Matrix 93
Measure, single 139
Measurement 148, 152, 207, 238
Measures, performance 216, 220, 226
Memorandum, program 73, 99
Mesa, Arizona 172

Model 114, 149, 152, 172, 236, 237, 238
    Churchman 151
    Cost 114
    Resource/cost 118, 141
    Stufflebeam 151
Modeling 237
Monitoring System 161
Morris 208, 212, 236, 238

National Academy for School Executives 195
National Association of Elementary School Principals 195
National Defense Education Act 183
National Education Association 195
National School Boards Association 198
National Science Foundation 171
Needs 62
Needs assessment 166
New York State Department of Education 154
Northwest Regional Educational Lab 167
Novick, David 48

Objectives 38, 39, 64, 73, 75, 148, 153, 167, 168, 195, 197, 205, 207, 208, 210, 236
    performance 78, 81, 153, 167
Officials, school 59, 60, 76, 199
Operational control 88
Operational cost categories 134, 135, 136
Operational plan 77
Operational research 149
Outcomes 39, 44
Optimization 208, 232
Outputs 78, 236

Paraprofessionals 170
Pennsylvania Educational Quality Assessment 154
Performance objectives 78, 81, 153, 167
Performance measures 216, 220, 226
Personnel 149, 166, 199, 200
PERT 201
Plan, evaluation 156
Plan, exploratory 78
    interim 78
    operational 78
Planning 44, 45, 59, 113, 141, 197, 203, 237

Plan, program and financial 91
Plan, prototype 78
PPBES concept 193, 207
Priorities 66, 67, 170, 200
Problems 62, 141
Procedures, evaluative 155
Processes in an ERM system 37
    interrelationship 43
    schematic 41
Processing, data 118, 137
Products 39
Program 111, 128, 210, 231
Program and financial plan 123, 124, 125, 126
Program Budget 89, 108, 122, 128, 199, 207
Program, educational 136
Program memorandum 73, 99
Program plans 73, 75, 79, 80, 156
Programs 38, 111, 129, 135, 136, 140, 147
Program structure 69, 107, 119, 120
Programming 48, 73, 74, 183
    linear 149
    non-linear 149
"Program, Yardstick," Cleveland 155
Proposal writing 185
Proration costs 110
Prototype plan 77

Quade 207, 209, 212
Qualification 210, 224
Quantification 210, 223, 232, 238
Quattlebaum 180
Queuing theory 149

Rapp 212
Re-cycling 86
Relationships 117, 150
Reporting 71, 101
Requirements, resource 73, 82, 128, 208
Research, operational 149
Resource analysis 107, 195
Resource cost model 118, 141
Resources 37, 39, 62, 63, 73, 82, 107, 136, 138, 165
Resource file 155

Resource inventory 41, 92
Resource requirements 73, 82, 128, 208
Responsibilities 53
    budgeting 56
    evaluating 57
    planning 54
    programming 55
Review, administrative 88

San Diego County, California 170
Schick 207
Society 39
School board 59, 85, 87, 88, 197, 200, 202
School business officials 60, 76, 199
Sensitivity analysis 119
Set theory 149
Siegel 223
Simulation 149
Sowards 171
Specialists 149, 198
Staff 84, 85
    development 165
    involvement 166
State education agencies 61, 194, 198, 204
Structure cost element 114
Structure, program 69, 107, 108, 119, 120
Students 75
Studies, longitudinal 144
Studies, specific analytic 93, 99
Stufflebeam 151
Sub-optimization 220, 229
Sub-program 79
Sunk costs 109
Superintendents 60, 61, 85

Target groups 78, 80, 86, 202
Task force 59, 60, 166, 167
Teachers 85, 165, 166, 170, 171, 174, 201
Teacher negotiation 203
Team, programming 48
Thurstone 222
Total costs 109
Total Direct Cost Activity Matrix (TDCAM) 334

Trade-off 224
Tversky 222

United States Office of Education 181
University City, Mo. Schools 169
Unquantifiables 238
Unruh, Glenys 169

Value judgments 162
Vieland, Constance 175
Visibility, public 51

Western New York Title III Project 193
Wildavsky 207
Womer 153

Yanouzas 42